D0498400

POLICE STATE

POLICE STATE

HOW AMERICA'S COPS
GET AWAY WITH MURDER

GERRY SPENCE

ST. MARTIN'S PRESS 🐾 NEW YORK

www.stmartins.com

The Library of Congress Cataloging-in-Publication Data is available upon request.

ISBN 978-1-250-07345-7 (hardcover)
ISBN 978-1-4668-8520-2 (e-book)

Designed by Jonathan Bennett

Our books may be purchased in bulk for promotional, educational, or business use. Please contact your local bookseller or the Macmillan Corporate and Premium Sales Department at (800) 221-7945, extension 5442, or by e-mail at MacmillanSpecialMarkets @macmillan.com.

First Edition: September 2015

10 9 8 7 6 5 4 3 2 1

This book is dedicated to Edward Moriarity,
one of America's great trial lawyers,
a man of unfathomable courage,
and a loyal friend.

CONTENTS

LET'S BEGIN TOGETHER

I'm a trial lawyer. I make arguments. And I ask questions. I've defended the poor, the forgotten, the lost, and the damned for over sixty years in the courtrooms of America. Over my career I've shut out a haunting question I wasn't prepared to face: Are we safe from our own police? Have our police become killers on the loose who cover up their crimes—and too often there's no one to stop them?

Who could have stopped the long-standing police brutality in Baltimore that led to the death of Freddie Gray following his less-than-joyful joyride in a police van, hands cuffed behind him, and without the protection of a seat belt? The medical examiner found that Gray's "catastrophic injury"—his neck was snapped—happened when he was slammed into the back of the van's interior. The examiner reported that "a head injury Gray sustained matche[d] a bolt in the back of the van"—just another notorious "rough ride" awarded to citizens who dared be black and make eye contact with a cop.* Gray's case brought to the forefront other cases of broken necks, paralysis, and death and attempted cover-ups by the police in Baltimore. The brother of a man who died in police custody said he was so badly beaten they had to have a closed-casket funeral; the police medical examiner found he had died of a heart attack brought on by an underlying heart ailment and dehydration from the summer heat.†

In South Carolina, Walter Scott was stopped for a broken taillight, and

---

* Edgar Sandoval and Corky Siemasko, "Freddie Gray's Neck Was Snapped While He Was Riding in Baltimore Police Van," *New York Daily News,* April 30, 2015.
† For a discussion of the staggering spate of police killings in Baltimore, see Sheryl Gay Stolberg, "Baltimore's 'Broken Relationship' with Police," *The New York Times,* April 24, 2015. Baltimore police killed 127 people over the two decades ending in 2012, with multiple suits and settlements resulting from these killings and maimings.

when he ran he was shot multiple times in the back and killed. The killing cop tried to cover his crime with a phony story about Scott pulling a Taser. Who could have stopped that murder? And while we consider these questions we must remember that the police are our employees. *Ours.* How do we save ourselves from being brutalized and murdered by our own public servants?

Daily, across the land, we're deluged with shocking stories of the murder and maiming of our citizens by the police. Many of us no longer feel safe in our own homes, much less the public streets. One man told me that if he stood on the corner and screamed at the top of his voice about how he felt, no one would hear him—except, of course, the cop on the beat, who'd likely haul him off for disturbing the peace, and might kill him if he ran or resisted, or looked the cop in the eye. We instinctively take comfort in our sacred rights as Americans. But when faced with an arresting police officer with questionable sensitivity to human dignity, and a justice system that is too often overworked and undertrained, a system often diseased with prejudice and sold out to Power, we may discover that our constitutional rights could be as well chronicled by a ripped-out page from yesterday's newspaper blowing down the street.

We've been spoon-fed for decades on *Law & Order* and endless other cop shows assuring us that in America, whether we are rich or poor, powerless or otherwise, our police will protect us. We've been conditioned by the corporate media, the voice of Power, to believe that the police put their lives in danger to keep us safe, all of us, no matter our race, color, or creed. Sounds good. And it seems contrary to ordinary decency, even un-American, to ask the police to protect us and then point long, accusatory fingers at them and claim too many are sadistic killers at heart. Moreover, to question the very ones we must trust to keep us safe injects us with the invasive virus of foreboding, and we live with enough undeserved anxiety already.

When we hear someone breaking into our house, when we're assaulted by a brutalizing spouse, when a drunk or mentally disturbed member of our household is acting out, perhaps dangerously, we look to the police for protection. Many argue that the police may overstep lawful boundaries now and then, but the price we must pay for their protection is to make room for their occasional excesses. Besides, if they use unnecessary force it's usually against gangs, dope dealers, and other deserving criminals and not against good citizens such as us. But where do we find ourselves if we fear the police as much as we fear the wild-eyed crazies beating down our doors? In the end we find ourselves asking: What power do we possess to protect ourselves from criminal cops? And when the cops and prosecutors, and often the judges, are members of the same cabal of power, how can we hope to bring about meaningful reform? Are we shackled by our own powerlessness? Is our only remedy to quietly, subserviently trust the police and hope that the cops who arrive on the scene aren't suffering from an inborn or recently acquired but irresistible urge to maim and kill?

Even our vaunted United States Supreme Court has found ways to protect our "killing cops" and to thereby put us under the fully fledged threat of becoming citizens of a police state. The court recites how a citizen operating his car with only one headlight chose to speed away instead of exiting his car as demanded by the officer and how the police chased the car for more than five minutes at speeds in excess of 100 miles an hour.* Eventually the citizen was stopped, after which the police fired fifteen shots into the car, killing both the driver and his innocent passenger. The court held that such conduct did not violate the Fourth Amendment rights of the dead and that the police were protected by what the law calls "qualified immunity." What can we do? Perhaps we can do nothing more than shrug our shoulders and quietly recite one of those tired old saws: "The system isn't perfect, but it's the best damned system in the world—love it or leave it." Besides, if one of our unarmed kids runs from the police, he should be shot fifteen times and killed. And his date should be killed for dating a kid who would run from the police. Both had it coming, right?

As a trial lawyer, my day-to-day focus has been on protecting the rights of persons charged with crimes, men and women I'd learned to care for and who looked to me to fight for their freedom. I hadn't stepped back to examine the justice system across the land as a functional, operating organism. But one day, a startling insight slipped into a conscious moment. I realized I'd never represented a person charged with a crime in either a state or federal court, in which the police, including the FBI, hadn't themselves violated the law—and on more than one occasion, even committed the crime of murder. Could this possibly hint at what many Americans, even most Americans, face in our courtrooms today? Let me say this straight: I don't mean to suggest that every cop is a bully, a criminal, or a killer. I do mean

---

* *Plumhoff v. Rickard*, 134 S. Ct. 1156, 2014.

too many bullies and criminals and killers are cops. And most get away with it. And that bothersome question arises: What superior force is in place to stop them?

Several weeks ago I was speaking to a couple of hundred criminal defense attorneys, mostly public defenders. The average number of cases each of the lawyers had taken to trial or otherwise concluded was something in the neighborhood of fifty. I said to the group, "Please stand up if you can honestly represent to me that in *every one of your cases* the police or prosecutors have in some way violated the law." I couldn't believe what I saw. All but four stood up, men, women, older lawyers and young, all with sad, serious faces looking directly at me. I turned to the four who remained seated. "What about you?" I asked. "Why aren't you standing?"

The lawyer seated closest to me said, "Well, Mr. Spence, you said in *every* case the cops violated the law. I've had a couple where they didn't." The other three nodded their agreement.

My spontaneous inquiry to this gathering of criminal defense attorneys wouldn't excite most academicians, who are nourished by hard, rattling statistics. Still, simple arithmetic confirms that in more than a thousand criminal cases from across the nation, police or prosecutors or both had been observed violating the law. Let's ask another question: Do we expect police and prosecutors to charge themselves with their own crimes? And still another: Do we think the cops will become whistle-blowers on each other?

We're staring at something that's staring back, something that's inherently dangerous to a free society. I can no longer ignore what I've known all along—and have never wanted to admit: *Too many of America's police are potentially state-sanctioned killers* who know if they're called upon to answer for their crimes they'll likely be protected by prosecutors and judges. But police crime is not as easy to hide these days, with vast numbers of our population sporting cell phones with video cameras. And when shocking videos of police killings are publicly shared, the community can explode into reciprocal violence. Rage against excessive police force is becoming mainstream in America. Even the complacent middle class, which for decades has been lulled comfortably by the belief that police crime was isolated to the powerless poor and the voiceless minorities, is beginning to awaken. We remember it was a citizen's video of a white police officer shooting and killing an unarmed black man as he ran that sparked public fury in the Walter Scott case.

The police in many cities are transforming into paramilitary forces. In years just past, the Department of Homeland Security has doled out $35 billion to police across the land to purchase "weapons of war." And as the wars in Iraq and Afghanistan have simmered down, the Pentagon itself has dumped $4.2 billion in surplus weapons on America's police departments.* The militarization of America's police, granting them indomitable power over the people, brings on visions of a police state. We remember the German people who actively or passively supported the rise of the Third Reich. If we listen, do we hear the Führer's ghost laughing? If we listen, do we hear what history has tried to teach us? *When the police become the military, the people become the enemy.* Even the National Security Agency (NSA), "our international cop," has recently been caught illegally spying on us, reminiscent as it proves to be of Nazi Germany.

And now the F.B.I. admits that its elite forensic unit has given flawed testimony in hundreds of cases over two decades involving hair identification, including thirty-two defendants sentenced to death. Senator Richard Blumenthal (D-Conn.), a former prosecutor, said, "These findings are appalling and chilling in their indictment of our criminal justice system, not only for potentially innocent defendants who have been wrongly imprisoned and even executed, but for prosecutors who have relied on fabricated and false evidence despite their intentions to faithfully enforce the law." University of Virginia law professor Brandon L. Garrett said the results reveal a "mass disaster" inside the criminal justice system. And the *Washington Post* commented that the findings by the FBI so far "likely scratch the surface."†

Many speak for *Power*—the Power-owned media, the Power-owned politicians, even the Power-owned courts. Money and Power own America, but the people—who speaks for them? Has "Liberty and Justice for *all*" today become merely a meaningless slogan? And if so, do we cling to it at our peril?"

Erwin Chemerinsky, dean of the School of Law at the University of California, Irvine, writes in his timely and cogent article entitled "How the Supreme Court Protects Bad Cops":‡

> In recent years, the court has made it very difficult, and often impossible, to hold police officers and the governments that employ them accountable for civil rights violations. This undermines the ability to

---

* *The Week,* August 1, 2014.
† *The Washington Post,* April 18, 2015.
‡ *The New York Times,* August 26, 2014.

deter illegal police behavior and leaves victims without compensation. When the police kill or injure innocent people, the victims rarely have recourse.

How bad is it out there? Every day new revelations of outrageous police crimes erupt.* In Brooklyn a witness states under oath that a cop coached him to testify falsely, and some forty of the cop's cases are under review; in New Orleans a judge recently found that a black citizen spent more than forty years in prison (mostly in solitary confinement) under a conviction and sentence based on an unconstitutional indictment.† A peaceful march of thousands on Staten Island protested the police chokehold death of Eric Garner, a black man.‡ And even the UN's watchdog against racism urged the United States to halt the excessive use of force by police after Michael Brown, an unarmed black youth, was shot six times and killed by a white cop in Ferguson, Missouri.§

In this book, we'll look at some of my cases, everyday examples of how police have trampled the rights of American citizens, even executing them without trial. We'll return to the deadly siege and slaughter of innocent Americans at what has been candidly called "the massacre at Ruby Ridge." From Los Angeles to New York City, and day after day, as common as a summer cold, our attention is called to cases of police brutality and corruption throughout the country. Crowds of grieving citizens attend the funerals, parade in the streets, and write their senators and representatives. We call for investigations, and predictably the police are usually cleared.

Nothing changes.

The question is, why?

It starts with the social climate in which our police and prosecutors act—another way of saying it starts with us: with our cultural deference to and even adulation for the police, our fear that crime will spike if we limit them in any way, and perhaps our naïve assumption that most people in our system get what's coming to them even if they were innocent of the particular crime for which they're charged.

The police are the progeny of Power. Although cops are technically our

---

* For just a peek at the extent of the malady, see "Police, Prosecutorial and Judicial Misconduct," http://www.truthinjustice.org/p-pmisconduct.htm, where literally hundreds of cases are summarized: murder, police cover-ups, fraud, perjury, phony and false evidence, and multiple convictions of innocent citizens.
† *The New York Times*, October 2, 2013.
‡ *New York Daily News,* August 23, 2014.
§ *The New York Times*, November 25, 2014.

employees, they do not answer to the schoolteacher, the secretary, the lawyer, the doctor, the carpenter, nor to you or me. They do not answer to an American jury, for, except in rare cases, the police enjoy immunity from suit even for their intentional wrongs.* They answer to no one except to Power—to the politicians, and to themselves.

It's one thing to read cold statistics that suggest something's awry. But statistics provide us no real understanding of human pain and helplessness, and they do little to move us toward reform. Thankfully, most Americans haven't had an abundance of firsthand experience with overly aggressive police. Most of us have never been the victim of a police baton across the side of the head or a Glock 17 in the gut, or found our child dead in the street with six bullets through his body. Most of us have never faced the horror of pleading guilty to a crime we didn't commit to save ourselves from being convicted of a frightening list of added crimes we also didn't commit. In short, we cannot know the truth until we've lived in the skin of the people. Yet the business of the criminal law goes on every day in every community in the nation, and the dreaded shadows cast by brutal and corrupt police have too rarely been exposed to the sunlight.

Over the decades, yes, from the beginning, it's been a story often told but too rarely heard. Through a potpourri of whimpers, grievances, investigations, and even litigation we have, from time to time, protested the use of excessive force by the police. But today we have reluctantly begun to ask painful, fundamental questions: Do these recurring acts of excessive force signal something new? Are we headed into a budding police state? Some even ask themselves quietly: Have we already arrived? And when a citizen's camera phone tells its truth, and TVs blare the story and the people gather in the streets and confront the police, after a short while . . .

Nothing changes.

The question is, why?

We complain, and with justification, that the government sticks its nose into everybody's business. Shouldn't we expect government to at least take a passing glance at what's going on in its own house? Shouldn't we, who sermonize to the world about human rights, be concerned with how our own police treat our citizens, especially the poor and powerless, who, in the end, include most of us?

In 1994 Congress did take a look. Following the 101 California Street

---

* Chemerinsky, "How the Supreme Court Protects Bad Cops."

shooting in 1993 (eight persons were killed and six injured by an assailant with no known motive) and the siege at Waco earlier that same year (where more than eighty members of the Branch Davidian religious group were killed), Congress passed the Violent Crime Control and Law Enforcement Act. That legislation, among other provisions, requires the attorney general to collect data on the use of excessive force by the police and to publish an annual report on those statistics. But to this moment no accounting for the nation's seventeen thousand police departments exists.* After over two decades, *no data?* What's going on here? The stunning truth is that this law does not require any police agency anywhere in America to keep a record of any kind, much less provide information to the federal government. Moreover, Congress has consistently failed to fund it. As a consequence the Violent Crime Control and Law Enforcement Act was born dead. The *New York Times* reported: "For all the careful accounting, . . . there are two figures Americans don't have: the precise number of people killed by the police, and the number of times police use excessive force. In fact, to no one's surprise, *there are practically no statistics out there at all on the numbers the cops have killed*"(my emphasis).[†] That was in 2001. Today we are left still recognizing the shocking truth: There is no national database of police-involved killings.

Nothing changes.

Other competent sources provide us hints about the crisis: The National Registry of Exonerations, a joint project of the University of Michigan Law School and Northwestern University School of Law, tells us that from 1989 to mid-2014 the registry has recorded 1,587 exonerations, and it has been adding exonerations at about 200 a year.[‡] These law schools collected cases in which innocent men and women had been charged with crimes, sentenced to prison, and later had their convictions overturned because of perjured testimony, misleading forensic evidence, false accusations, false confessions, and false witness identification. One can only ponder that if our system has been forced to acknowledge fifteen hundred wrongful convictions since 1989, which number surely represents but a crumb in a trainload of crumbs, what numbing numbers we would face if we had an accurate count on *all* wrongful convictions.

---

* Ross Keith, "How Many Police Shootings Have There Been?" *International Business Times,* August 15, 2014.

† Fox Butterfield, "When the Police Shoot, Who's Counting?" *The New York Times,* April 29, 2001.

‡ National Registry of Exonerations, www.law.umich.edu/special/exoneration/Pages/about.aspx.

The *New York Times* recently focused on how our FBI was behaving. The *Times* obtained Bureau records through a Freedom of Information Act suit and reported that from 1993 to early 2011, FBI agents fatally shot about seventy "subjects" and wounded about eighty others—and every one of those killings was deemed *justified* according to interviews and internal FBI records.* Yes, the federal police will admit to some killings, but only when sued by a powerful newspaper, and according to their records, *all* of their killings have been justified. Are we comfortable with that representation?

Geoffrey Alpert, a professor of criminology and criminal justice at the University of South Carolina and a leading authority on police use of force, says that the lack of good data is "a national scandal."† The police belong to a culture separate from ours. Police departments are often like the gangs they encounter—both strive to keep their crimes secret. And we remember that current law aids the police in hiding any misconduct since they're not required by law to keep records that reveal it, even their killings.

For over twenty-seven thousand years, since the first cave paintings were discovered, and from Homer to the Bible, storytelling has been the chief means by which learning and history have been preserved. The power of story distinguishes us as a species. In these pages I will tell stories as I have experienced them, stories about real people who have suffered and died at the hands of Power. On the other hand, the media has taught us through story to embrace the police as our heroes. They are our heroes until we call on them, or perhaps, more worrisome, until they call on us.

It is not my mission to prove that law enforcement in this country is fundamentally corrupt. We are often served by careful, caring, devoted police officers. What I will show is that police brutality and killings are the product of the system, and until we enact fundamental change, the specter of an enslaving police state is clearly visible on the horizon.

In these pages we will examine why nothing changes, why too often the people have become the victims of crimes committed by the police, why legislation has been essentially useless, and, indeed, why gun-happy cops are endemic among our police. It will become clear that something is fundamentally wrong with the method by which our police are selected and thereafter trained.

---

* Charlie Savage and Michael S. Schmidt, "The FBI Deemed Agents Faultless in 150 Shootings," *The New York Times,* June 18, 2013.
† Quoted in Butterfield, "When the Police Shoot."

I have a corresponding duty to offer solutions. And I shall. I will outline how we must totally revamp the selection and training of our police and provide our citizens with a special agency designed to protect us from the wrongful and dangerous conduct of those we hire to protect us. As a society we're more comfortable with custom and precedent than with facing new and unfamiliar proposals. But let us be brave. Let us cast out what we know has not only failed us but has added substantially to the heavy inventory of crimes committed against us. Let us face the threat of an emerging police state and give new ideas a chance to raise their cautious heads and look around.

Nothing changes.

That dismal prophecy will prevail, as indeed it always has, and always will, unless we, the people, have the courage to take up this critical challenge and bring about a new police culture for the safety and well-being of we, the people, who still wait patiently to enjoy the promise of America:

Liberty and Justice for all.

A final note before we begin. Trial lawyers build their arguments from facts, but they also paint verbal pictures for the jury. From the dry details of the case they create scenes so the jurors who will decide the outcome can experience the accused in action and feel the full weight of Power as it descends on unsuspecting lives. So do I once more in the pages that follow.

I'm intimately familiar with the facts of these cases, but I also use literary license to breathe life into these accounts, to re-create the experiences as I have felt them deep to the bone. Except where explicitly noted, dialogue and quotations reflect the essence of the moment rather than being drawn verbatim from trial or interview transcripts or other sources.

CASE 1

MANDATE FOR MURDER

That day the FBI's hidden sharpshooter coolly displayed his skill. From over two hundred yards away he blew off half of the woman's face—shot her standing there in her doorway. Yes, she was armed—with her nursing child. Inside the shack, the Weavers' two young daughters saw their mother fall in a heap on the kitchen floor, blood and splattered flesh, the baby falling with her. Their fourteen-year-old brother, Sammy, still with a boy's high voice, had already been shot in the back, murdered by the marshals as he ran home.

The slaughter occurred in the back reaches of Idaho, a place called Ruby Ridge, where the Weavers had hammered together their scrap-lumber cabin in the woods, and where the family had retreated ten years earlier to prepare for the promised "Great Tribulation," as they called it.

I thought it ominous that twenty-one years after the national media had endlessly hashed over the Weaver case like bums at a garbage can, and at the precise moment I was inching toward my decision to write about the case, the FBI should renew its contact with Randy Weaver.

It was May 27, 2013. Randy had opened his mail to find an official-looking paper from the FBI that proved to be an inventory of the physical items the Bureau had seized at Ruby Ridge that had belonged to the Weavers—thirty-two supposed pieces of evidence that the Bureau had seized two decades earlier and had kept buried in the bottomless strata of its secret files. The FBI was finally ready to return what it had taken.

"What do you want of this *material* that we still possess?" In effect the Bureau was asking: *You want your boy's little vest that his mother made for him? Has a bullet hole through it.*

"Yes, I want the vest," Randy said.

You want your wife's fingertips? We cut her fingertips off, you know. We still have them. We can return them to you.

"Vicki's fingertips? You cut off her fingers?"

Yes, we can return them to you.

When Randy told me about the FBI's offer to send back his wife's severed fingertips, I decided I had to write about the Weaver case.

Nothing changes.

Before, during, and after the trial, and many an hour since, Randy and I talked and raged and wept together. Immediately following the August 1992 siege at Ruby Ridge, I traveled to the Weavers' pieced-together cabin in the woods. By then the army tanks had begun rumbling back down the mountain, and the noisy helicopters had flown off to chop away at other innocent air. The gawking surveillance cameras had been removed, and the troops, how many hundreds no one knows, had pulled up their tents and headed on to other bloody adventures that were aroused by the government's atrocities at Ruby Ridge, including the fifty-one-day siege at Waco, Texas, where on April 19, 1993, federal agents were responsible for the deaths of over eighty men, women, and children who clung to a religious cult known as the Branch Davidians. That holocaust was followed exactly two years later by the bombing of the Alfred P. Murrah Federal Building in Oklahoma City by a small group of survivalists, led by Timothy McVeigh, who were angered by what they saw as vicious government overreach at both Ruby Ridge and Waco. That bombing claimed 168 lives and injured more than 680 people.

But, as we shall see, *nothing changes.*

I defended Randy Weaver before an Idaho jury in the longest trial in the state's history, and the cold spoken words are recorded on thousands of pages of court records. I know and love the family, both the living and those murdered by our government and now in their graves. To accurately tell their story one must crawl into their hides and clutch their terrorized souls. And one must resurrect the dead. Such is the obligation of story. So I've come to tell the Weaver story. The siege at Ruby Ridge deserves to be told as story because it is the business of story to reveal the truth.

Before they'd come west to the mountains, Randy Weaver saw his life in Iowa as grasped by forces that wouldn't let loose. Randy didn't call it "forces." He called it "the will of God." You either believed it or you didn't, and if, as when he was a boy, you looked across a field of corn in the tassel with the early sun making the broad green leaves look gold and shimmery and you didn't believe in God, well, that was your business. "But a man's gotta listen," Randy said. "What the hell were we given two ears for if it wasn't to listen?" And Randy heard the Lord.

It hadn't been easy. He'd been listening every day since Vicki had her vision several years earlier. He listened with terrible concentration, with total faith, but for a long time he heard nothing. "You have to give Him a chance," Vicki said. One day when Randy was on his motorcycle speeding in and out of traffic, a most unlikely time for a conversation with the Lord, he heard it. Not a voice, not tongues—just heard it. Like a thought but not a thought. Like a feeling, but not.

"What did He say?" Vicki asked.

"He said the same thing He said to you. He said we're sinners and that the Great Tribulation is comin'. An' I heard it again when I was lookin' right at ya the other night."

"When the preacher was here, talkin'?"

"Yeah. But none of 'em ever read the Bible. That's why they don't know about anything 'cept the fuckin' money."

Nothing she could do about Randy's profanity. It was a part of him, and Vicki said you have to take people the way they are.

Vicki had fallen in love with this Randy Weaver, all cocky and profane and fresh from the army, his thin body muscled, this warrior who'd never gone to war but who'd volunteered for Nam, not one of those yellow-bellied whimpering protestors but a full-fledged volunteer who put in for the Special Forces, the Green Berets. He'd done jumps and had survival training, and he could make bombs out of practically nothing, and he was ready to lay it all down for his country. His face was tanned and smooth, and his blue eyes bright and brave as youth, and his black hair was clipped short, and he had a way of walking, a walk half a step short of a swagger, kinda bouncy, and to Vicki, he was beautiful.

But the army had sent Randy off to Fort fucking Bragg, North Carolina. "That's like using a well-greased M-16 to dig a shit hole," Randy said. Once he was part of an undercover drug bust at Fort Bragg, at least he got to do that much, but the captain in charge of the bust only turned in about half of the contraband that had been seized. "You don't bust them drug-dealin' bastards and then turn into one yourself," Randy said. He reported the captain to the company commander, who told Randy to mind his own goddamned business, and mind it good.

Vicki went to see Randy at Fort Bragg. They were engaged, and after he got out of the army, they married right away. Vicki vowed to raise her children in the way of the Lord, outside of the sin-infected public schools where children were exposed to drugs and sex and the false word. She'd raise them where no hippies and no perverts reading their obscene pornography could capture their innocent minds. And when the child was sucking at her breast she felt the tongue of God, and she knew what she must do because the world was boiling in sin. Jesus was about to return and the Great Tribulation would be upon them. The hordes would descend. It was prophesied by all who'd read the Bible.

"Anyone with five cents' worth of pig brains could see it," Randy said. He lit a cigarette with his Zippo and slammed it shut to emphasize the point. "Ever'body's gettin' divorced, and screwin' ever'body else's wife, and they're stealin' and cheatin.' Buncha the guys at the plant are stealin' tools and sellin' 'em on the outside. They're a crooked, loafin' lazy buncha low-lifers. All they do is hang around in the can readin' girly magazines and jackin' off. I'm sick of it."

"We have to leave," Vicki said.

"I'll get us a buncha guns," Randy said, "an' a shit-pot fulla ammo, and we'll sell the car and buy us a pickup truck, and rent a trailer, and we'll sell the house and get the hell outta here while the gettin's still good."

"Oh, my God," Vicki whispered as if the joy had all but choked her. And that's all she said.

Then Randy asked, "Where do you want to go, Mamma?"

She didn't speak for a long time. Then suddenly, "We have to go to the mountains. Matthew 24. 'Then let them which be in Judea flee into the mountains,' Jesus said."

The next morning Randy quit his job as mechanic foreman at the tractor plant even though he had ten years in. The boss said, "You're too fuckin' far out, and it ain't any of my business except when you stand there with a dozen of my men and keep 'em off the line while you're preaching your shit to 'em."

"I got a right to believe the way I believe," Randy said. "Free country."

"You can believe any bullshit you want. But you oughta learn to keep your bullshit to yerself," the boss said. "Good thing you're quittin'. Saved me the trouble of firing your ass for disturbance."

Next Randy went to the Bullet Hole, a pawnshop owned by his buddy Vaughn Truman.

"I'm leavin' this fuckin' hole, Vaughn," Randy said. "There's gonna come a big fuckin' tribulation, and when it comes I'm gonna be in the mountains with my family."

"You're kiddin'."

"I'll tell ya how much I'm kiddin'," Randy said. "How much ya want for that Ruger?" He was eying a Ruger pistol.

"What'll ya give me?"

"How about if I buy the Ruger and that Mini-14 over there?" The Mini-14 was a light semiautomatic rifle.

"That's a good Mini. Never been shot. Practically got the cosmoline in 'er yet."

"Maybe I'll buy two. Maybe three. And what are ya gettin' nowadays for a thousand rounds of ammo for the Mini?"

"Cheap. For you, a deal."

They talked like that for an hour, then two. "You got four thousand rounds at that price?"

"Must be a hell of a war a-comin'," Truman said.

"I can shoot up four thousand rounds in a afternoon. When it comes, it don't do no good to have shot three thousand rounds and then run out of ammo and have the bastards take yer ass out." Suddenly Randy put a hand on each of Truman's shoulders, and he looked Truman in the eyes like a father looks at his son. "Vaughn, I love you, and Jesus loves you. And ya better come with us. Better get the fuck outta here while the gettin's good."

After that Randy traded his equity in the boat and the motorcycle to Truman, which wasn't much, for three Mini-14s and the Ruger and four thousand rounds of ammo. There'd be no use for boats and motorcycles in the Matthew 24 mountains.

*T*he Weavers loaded up their '57 Dodge Power Wagon pickup with their essentials and said good-bye to their friends, some of whom wept, and then the family of five took off.

"This is one way, by God, for the family ta get close," Randy said, the five squeezed into the old pickup like sardines in a can. They were all smiles, their eyes set to the West. "So let's get goin'." Jesus, according to the Word, according to the prophecies, according to their own lucid revelations, was about to return, and He wouldn't wait on them or any-body else.

*T*en years after leaving the swarming evil of Iowa, there on the side of a mountain called Ruby Ridge they'd built their small cabin one board at a time, the lumber mostly scraps gathered at the mill. They cleared out their garden from the forest, dug their water well close to the creek so that the digging wasn't deep, and Vicki home-taught Sara and Sammy. They prayed for deliverance, prayed for guidance, for wisdom, and faithfully, patiently they prepared for the Great Tribulation.

And they waited.

In the same year a couple of Alcohol, Tobacco, and Firearms cops put their sights on Randy. He'd made a lot of noise. He'd been seen at some Aryan Nations get-togethers, a white supremacist Christian bunch that the FBI called a "terrorist threat." He, his wife, and those kids were obviously as poor as rats trapped in an empty garbage can. One day a couple of ATF operatives, with nothing more to do, approached Randy. They held them-selves out to be shady characters and asked him to cut the barrels off of two shotguns—offered him a couple of hundred dollars that the family sorely needed.

"They claim cutting this barrel off six inches is illegal. What's the harm?" Randy asked Vicki. "If I don't, somebody else will. Fuckin' water pump's down, and the kids need shoes."

Vicki said, "I'll pray on it."

"Well, ya better hurry up, because they said they was gonna get some-body else to cut the barrels." And that afternoon he took out his hacksaw and cut off the barrels of two 12-gauge Remington pumps, and the agents gave him the money.

Then the government agents, these officers of the Alcohol, Tobacco, and Firearms, a division of the United States Treasury, shed their cover. They had Randy Weaver like a mangy coyote in a trap. "They want me to go un-dercover for 'em," Randy said.

"We are servants of the Lord, not of men," Vicki said.

"They want me to lie to somebody else."

"You can't trap people with lies," Vicki said.

"If I don't they say they're gonna send me off."

"And what would happen to our home and to our kids?"

Then they prayed to Yahweh for guidance, prayed in the name of Yahweh so as not to take the Lord's name in vain. They prayed for wisdom and deliverance. They brought the family together and prayed with Sara and Sammy and with little Rachel. Randy also spoke of the trap to Kevin Harris, who, as a runaway teenager, had found a new family with Randy and Vicki and the kids, had helped build their shack, and over the years felt taken in, cherished, and adopted by them.

When the praying was over, Randy rose up and said he would not become the Judas goat who led the sheep to slaughter to save himself. And if he'd been wrong in cutting off the shotguns, which he would not concede, his wrong would not be made right by his lies against others.

"You can all go fuck yourselves" is how Randy put it to the agents of the United States government when they came back to see if he'd cooperate. "I ain't gonna snitch for you or nobody else."

The chief agent leaned his head out of his pickup truck and asked, "You sure of that?" and when Randy said he was sure, the government men turned to each other with sneers, and they drove off in their government pickup spraying gravel. Then the agent driving the truck leaned out of his window and yelled back, "See you in court, you stupid motherfucker."

One afternoon two months later, Vicki asked Randy to take her on a short ride—just to get out of the house. Pregnant with their fourth child and about to deliver, she knew she'd be cooped up soon enough with the new baby.

Randy, driving slowly and without fault, looked up ahead and saw an old pickup with a camper stalled at the bridge. A man was peering under the hood. Dressed in ragged clothes, a coat that looked like it had been dragged through a thrashing machine, and an old blue striped woolen stocking cap pushed back, he was shaking his head as if in the throes of consternation. Beside him stood a frail-looking woman in a coat too thin even for the thawing weather. She was holding on to herself, her arms tightly folded across her chest attempting to capture her escaping body heat. She was intently watching the man working under the hood, and when she heard the Weaver pickup approaching, she looked up but then looked back down again.

Randy, seeing the trouble, stopped his pickup. "I guess you better go see if you can help them," Vicki said. He got out and walked toward the stranded couple.

"What'sa matter there, folks? Got a little engine trouble?" Randy asked. The man looked up and nodded, and then, when Randy was about ten feet away, he wheeled suddenly out from under the hood with a 9 mm automatic in his hand. "Federal officers," he hollered. "Freeze." By this time the woman had her gun drawn, the one she'd been holding under her folded arms. She aimed her gun through the half-open window on Vicki's side of the car.

"Get out of the car," she ordered. "Federal officers." Vicki struggled to get her heavy body turned toward the door. "Hurry up," the female federal officer said.

"What's this all about?" Vicki asked, still struggling to get out.

"I'll ask the questions," said the woman with the gun.

The man with his 9 mm on Randy hollered, "Get on your belly, Weaver. You're under arrest."

"I ain't gonna get on my belly in this slush," Randy said.

Then from above the road came a heavy voice. "Get on your belly, Weaver, or I'll cut off your legs." A man was crouched on the overhanging cliff. He was wearing white camouflaged overwear with a white hood that blended in with the snow. He manned a machine gun sitting on a pivot. By this time three more fully armed agents had burst out of the back end of the pickup's camper.

One of the agents came up from behind Randy and pushed him down. The other agents were on top of him like a pack of mad dogs. They pushed his face into the slush and gravel, slapped cuffs on him, and dragged him to his feet, dripping. They patted him down and shoved him into the camper.

The woman with the gun told Vicki to get down on her belly.

"I am a citizen of the United States of America," Vicki said in a loud clear voice. "I have rights."

"You been harboring a fugitive," the woman with the gun said. "Get on your belly."

Vicki squatted slowly, attempting to comply. Then the woman pushed her over on her side into the mud and began to frisk her.

"I have not been harboring any criminals," Vicki said. "And you have no right to touch me there."

"I am not touching you, I am patting you down."

"You have no right to pat me there. I will report you to your supervisor."

"He's right over there, lady. Report away." She threw in a few extra pats for good measure and then put the cuffs on Vicki and ordered her to get up. With her hands cuffed behind her, Vicki struggled against the weight in her womb. She staggered, fell to a knee, then struggled again to right herself. The woman stood over her, her legs spread apart and her gun still out. She offered no hand. When Vicki had at last gained her feet, the woman glared at her, looked her up and down, saw her condition, saw the mud on her dress and on the side of her face where she'd lain on the ground, and shook her head as one who beheld a disgusting sight.

"You'd better repent," Vicki said. "You're serving the evil One World Government."

"You're one of those Aryan Nations crazies," the woman replied.

"That is another of your lies," Vicki said.

"Are you calling me a liar?" The woman started for Vicki, but Vicki did not turn her eyes away from the woman, and as she came close, threatening in the way she stamped down her feet and swung her shoulders, Vicki stood taller as if to meet the charge, her fists clenched inside the cuffs.

Stopping short, the woman said, "You aren't worth it."

"Take her cuffs off," the man said to the woman agent.

"What for?"

"We're not taking her in. Too damn much trouble. Want to deliver a kid up in the cell block? Hell of a mess."

"How would you know?" the woman asked. She removed the cuffs from Vicki. Then she gave Vicki one last slap on the rear and said, "Get the hell out of here, lady, if you don't want us to take you in for obstruction of justice."

"What justice?" Vicki said. "What are you going to do with my husband?"

"That's our business, lady," the chief officer said, and with that the officers slammed the hood of the truck shut, boarded the camper, and drove off through the wet January thaw with their prisoner. Vicki could hear the sound of the truck tires in the slush for a long time after it disappeared around the curve. When she could hear it no longer she crawled into the old family pickup. She didn't know how to drive a stick shift.

They put up their makeshift house in the woods to secure Randy's bond for his court appearance. Nobody would want that beaten-up, hacked-together shack, but it represented their total fortune.

Randy, charged with illegally sawing off those two shotguns, stood nervous and stiff before Magistrate Steven Ayers. Magistrate Ayers warned him that if he went to trial and lost he might lose his house as well. Later the magistrate admitted he'd misadvised Randy on the law. But at the time

Randy believed, "If I lose in court I get my ass thrown in the can forever and lose our house, too? That's all we got. And me and my four kids and Vicki'd be livin' under the fuckin' bridge." He couldn't afford a lawyer, and he wasn't about to go to trial before a bunch of pecker-bills who wanted to do him in and who'd throw his wife and kids to the dogs. They gave him the *wrong date* for his court appearance. So, of course, he didn't show and they had him on yet another charge—his failure to appear.

In the meantime the marshals held a big powwow—those government servants whose job is to keep citizens safe from vicious criminals. They formulated the best-laid plans that government minds could concoct on how to capture this vicious criminal who'd sawed off a couple of shotguns for a few desperate bucks. You can hear them. "And he's one dangerous motherfucker for sure. Remember, he was a former Green Beret. Could put a bullet right between the orbs from five hundred yards. And he's got all those guns and a truckload of ammo, and he taught the kids how to shoot, and the bunch of them are as crazy as a crowd of jazzed-up hop-heads."

Trapped in their little scrap-lumber shack, Randy and Vicki and the kids prayed on it some more. They came to a fairly reasonable conclusion: that if the ATF would set them up with a phony gun charge, make Randy a criminal, and then give him the wrong date to appear, thereby converting him into a fugitive from justice, the feds would end up taking their home, and they'd throw Randy in prison for the better part of his remaining life and leave his family fatherless and homeless. If they prayed long enough and hard enough, Yahweh would protect them. That was their best weapon—the intervention of Yahweh, who made it clear from above what was obvious from below: They had no choice but to stay put and fight off "the agents of the devil," as Vicki called them.

After Randy failed to appear in court, a gang of federal marshals dressed up in brand-new camouflage gear with their automatic rifles and night-spotting equipment began to secretly invade the Weaver property. Squatted in the woods, they began spying on the Weavers, "gathering data," as they liked to call it. They installed a TV spy camera up on the mountain behind the Weavers' cabin that monitored every move the family made. For months they sneaked and peeked around in the woods spying on this peaceful family.

Behind the house the Weavers had constructed a small "birthing shed," where Vicki had given birth to Elisheba, the Weavers' newest child. It had another purpose, too. According to the Weavers' interpretation of the Bible, during a woman's "blood time," she was to be separated from the family, which meant that she would stay in the birthing shed until her menses was completed. The marshals began keeping track of the days when Sara, the Weavers' teenage daughter, had her period. When they were ready and Sara's time came around again, they'd descend on the birthing shed and kidnap her, and when Randy tried to save his daughter, the marshals would capture him and take this vicious criminal into custody to be dealt with according to law.

In the meantime the feds needed to put the right slant on the case so the public would understand they were dealing with a dangerous criminal. So they conjured up a false history on Randy—even claimed he was a bank robber who was dragging a book full of prior convictions behind him. I mean, if all you've got to do is to capture a criminal whose worst crime is sawing off a couple of shotguns, well, you need a pretty good story behind it or you can't call out a bunch of armed marshals with bulletproof vests and helicopters for surveillance, and all those radios and listening devices and cameras that can, as they say, "catch a gnat farting from half a mile away." Accordingly the feds loaded the local and national media with demonizing stories about the Weavers so that if they killed him their actions would be fully supported by the public.

The feds also played up Weaver's association with the Aryan Nations, "a fascist bunch of racists." From their earliest reports on the case, the press would refer to Randy Weaver as a "*white supremacist* holed up in the mountains of Idaho." And with coaching from the marshals, the media remembered that the founder of the Aryan Nations, Robert Mathews, died in a shootout with federal agents in December 1984. Weaver was just another of that violent bunch of crazies. So the clear message was "Get ready for the killing."

Then one day when the wind happened to be just right, the Weavers' dog Striker, an old yellow Lab who'd beat you to death with his wagging tail, smelled the marshals and began raising all kinds of commotion. It sounded as if the hounds of hell had come face-to-face with the devil himself. Given the volume of the dog's barking, the Weavers thought it was probably a bear. Kevin Harris, along with the Weavers' only son,

Sammy, a fourteen-year-old who still spoke in a boy's high voice and didn't weigh more than eighty pounds, if that, decided to investigate what was going on down below the house.

"Striker's gonna get us a bear!" were the words from Sammy's excited lips, and the two boys took out after old Striker. Of course, the boys grabbed their rifles. Randy took the higher road in case the bear headed in that direction.

The marshals later claimed they were afraid of this waggly-tailed old dog. When he got to where they were hiding and he was about to flush them out, they shot him on the spot. You could hear him yelp as a bullet from one of their automatic rifles passed through his body, and then you could hear his slow, dying whine into the bright morning sun.

Little Sam heard the shots and saw old Striker fall. Who would shoot an old yellow dog? His dog. He hollered into the woods, "You sons of bitches, you shot my dog!" The sound of such bristling words from the soft lips of a child was startling. Then, standing in the open and in full view of the hidden marshals, the boy fired his rifle in the direction of the marshal's shot.

Randy heard the shots from the upper end of the forest. "Come on home, Sam," Randy shouted.

"I'm comin', Dad." Those were Sammy's last words.

The marshals, still hidden in the forest, opened fire on the boy as he ran toward home. First they shot his arm—shot it all but off so that it was dangling by the hide. Then they shot the boy in the back. Kevin Harris turned toward the place in the forest where he'd heard the marshals' shots come from and fired in that direction, once. Then he, too, turned and ran toward the house.

*T*he marshals still hid in the dense pines, their bodies wedged prone against the boulders for protection, their faces smudged the color of dirty grass, their eyes, also unblinking, staring up the road. Staring. Their mouths clamped against words. A marshal in a new camouflage uniform looked for a long time at the body lying in front of him. Marshal Bill Degan was his name. He brushed at the air to keep the flies from the eyes of the dead man, open and unblinking. Then his hand returned quickly to his automatic weapon, and he stared back up the road, waiting.

When the marshals heard the people coming to reclaim their dead, they remained silent as the grasses. Then the marshals saw the three walking slowly down a road of two tracks through the summer brome, a tall, younger man on one track, a woman on the other, and following behind the woman an older man, smaller than the first and no taller than the woman. The smaller man, without hat or weapon, wore old coveralls, faded army green. His hair, graying around the ears, was clipped short. In the low evening sun the shadows of the people were long as trees, long, slow-moving shadows that lumbered downward toward the hiding men. In the evening sun the faces of the three were flaming and their eyes were the eyes of agony staring down the road.

The woman, in a once-white cotton dress, the skirt reaching to her ankles, moved with a grace not witnessed in the men, a smoothness in her steps so that her head did not bob up and down with each step like the heads of tired horses in their traces. The younger man stopped, and the others stopped with him. He looked down, and the others, in silence, gathered around where he looked, and it was then that the terrible wailing began, the sound of the woman's voice first, the sound of the people wailing in terrible agony banishing the silence.

The woman fell to her knees, and the smaller man behind her fell to his, and the sounds of their suffering joined into a single wavering cry that stretched out into long thin threads of sound. Then the younger man walked on down the road to where the old yellow dog lay. He slipped his foot under the dog and turned the dog over, but the animal was already stiffening. Then the younger man turned slowly and trudged back up the hill to the source of the wailing. It had stopped. Then it burst into short sobs and billowed into high shrill peaks, sounds rising, quivering, and dying like ancient sounds.

The woman and the smaller man lifted the boy's body, the man at the head, the woman with her arms under the knees. They lifted the body face-upward, and the evening sun shone on the boy's body. The right arm fell halfway down and stopped in midair as if to make a point. The left arm hung from a patch of loose skin and swayed back and forth as the body was raised, and the arm twisted like the pendulum of a tired clock with the small boy's fingers extended, beckoning the people home.

The smaller man, the father, started back up the road. He walked backward so that the mother following and holding the legs of her child could walk forward. The man and the woman facing each other did not look at each other, the woman guiding them like a tiller on a small boat. Once the father stumbled and fell, and the body fell with him, part of the body on top of the father, but the mother held on, and the head of the boy moved stiffly, but the mother did not drop her son. The father, refusing the help of the larger, younger man, struggled to his feet and walked on backward still bearing his son, the red sun fierce on the father's wet face.

Sara, their daughter, saw them coming and ran out of the house and down to the porch to meet them. When she saw what her parents were carrying she stopped, afraid to come closer. Afraid of the dead. Afraid to look at the face of her brother, younger by two years, the brother who had laughed when she was frightened in the forest, and who promised more than once he would take care of her, forever, and who now had broken his promise.

"Open the door to the birthing shed," Randy Weaver said, his panting voice speaking to no one. Sara stood as if she did not hear her father. Then she suddenly ran to the birthing shed and unlatched the wooden knob at the top of the door and flung the door open. She held the door open, and her father backed in with Sammy, head first, and they lifted the child onto the bed, the left arm still twisting in perpetual protest. Kevin Harris picked up the arm and laid it across the boy's chest, and after that Sara, who had not looked Sammy in the face, ran to the house, wild-eyed and without weeping.

The mother untied her dead boy's shoes. Sammy was a growing boy; they'd bought his shoes a size too large, and they slipped easily from his stiffening feet. Then the mother and father removed their son's other clothing, and Vicki brought in a pail of water with soap from the kitchen, and they bathed the child's hairless body for the burial, and they dried the body with a clean towel. When they turned the body over they saw the entry wound in the back, a bullet hole the size of a pencil, neat and round and glistening red. The mother, with lips as tight as silence, touched lightly at the edge of the wound like one confirming what the eyes had seen.

"I seen it," Kevin Harris said. "That's when I shot the bastard that shot Sammy."

Suddenly, without warning, Randy dropped the bloody cloth he'd been using to bathe Sammy's wounds and ran from the birthing shed. Vicki saw him run toward the house, and when he came out he had a Mini-14 rifle in one hand and clips of ammunition in the other. He had an automatic pistol on his hip. And she knew. For when they have killed the only son they have murdered the line, cut the unbroken line that reached back to savage stone beginnings. She knew that a man cannot bear such killing. Killing begets killing.

Vicki ran in those long graceful steps to cut off his path, and when they were face-to-face, he stopped.

"Where are you going?" She stood larger than herself in front of him.

"Don't be in my way, woman," he said. The sadness was gone from his face.

"They will only kill you. That will do us no good." He tried to push past her, but she stepped quickly in his way again. "If they kill you we'll all die here. And our children will die here." She put a hand on each of his cheeks. She felt the roughness of his whiskers on her palms. She pushed his face up so that his eyes had to see her. His eyes were killing eyes. "Our children will die here with me," she said.

"Get out of my way," he said.

"Then you have to shoot me first," she said, still holding his face. He tried to escape by pulling free, but she was quicker than he, and in front of him again. "You have to shoot me first," she said again. He tried once more, but again she was in front of him. He struck out in her direction with the barrel of the gun, though not to hit her. "Let me be," he said. "I have to go. It's my place to go."

"It is not a matter to argue about," she said. He had seen this in her eyes before. The implacable. One cannot argue with the storm. Then he lifted his rifle to the sky and emptied it. Twenty shots, the small caliber with its high eerie cry exploding in far places, wounding the atmosphere. His cry of agony grew louder, higher than the shots from the gun, his cry of one mortally injured. He filled the rifle with another clip and again emptied its twenty shots. And all the while she stood back and watched and let the man empty himself.

And when all of the ammunition he had brought from the cabin had been fired, he pulled out his pistol and shot it in the air until it, too, was empty. He pulled the empty trigger, once, twice, again and again, and then he fell to the ground. And he wept and he did not rise up off of the ground until it was dark. Then he walked like the dead to the cabin.

The marshals had interpreted Randy's firing to mean that a horde of his followers had engaged in the battle. The marshals called for help. At half past one in the morning the rescuers arrived at Ruby Ridge—the sheriff's men, highway patrolmen, town constables, and volunteer firemen who, being of that kind, had volunteered themselves into the sheriff's posse. They had volunteered to kill. In the dark of night, seventy-three men without discipline or order crept and stumbled into each other hugging their weapons close to their chests, their fingers ready.

The hiding marshals heard them coming and hollered, "Who goes?" Then one of the rescuers answered, "Hey, man, it's us," and the forest suddenly came alive with men expelling their breath and shouting in loud words so long held back.

"How many in that Weaver outfit are there?"

"Don't know how many. Fire comin' from every direction."

Another said, "Musta shot a thousand rounds into us."

"More'n that, maybe."

"You musta heard it. Everybody heard it."

"They were layin' for us. They got Bill here. Shot through the heart."

"They knew we were comin'."

"Chased us down with dogs."

"Ambushed us. Some of them Aryan Nations crazies—Weaver the worst."

"Fuckin' crazies. Had it out with them kind before up north."

"Seen one, ya seen 'em all. Vicious sons-a-bitches, I'll tell ya that much."

"Thought you guys'd never get here. Where ya been?"

"We gotta get Bill outta here."

"Where they at now?"

"We haven't heard anything from 'em since about sundown. Then we heard a lot of screamin' and a lot of shootin'. Sprayed the place with lead."

"I don't know where all their reinforcements come from."

Then a couple of rescuers with flashlights searched the forest for small dead standing trees, pulled two of them over, trimmed them with a hatchet, and made an Indian travois, a frame of two long poles inserted through the arms of the coat of the dead marshal. They proceeded to drag him down the mountain, the rickety thing making scraping sounds against the rocks and the timber along with the panting of the men with death at their heels. Music for the dead.

By the time they arrived at the staging area, the sun was up, and armored personnel carriers had taken over the scene like bullies on the playground. Tents had been pitched, maybe fifteen, maybe twenty. Hundreds of cars were parked helter-skelter. National Guardsmen in full combat uniform, helmets and all, milled among the cars and pickup trucks and campers. Some were serving fresh-baked flapjacks and bacon from the tailgates of their trucks. When the rescuers pulling the travois came by, the Guardsmen opened the way and peered curiously at the dead man. Then, after the dead had passed, they went on eating. And laughing.

The television crews had also arrived. They jockeyed for position like horses out of the gate. Violence, blood, and death. We are addicted to blood and violence. When the rescuers dragged the travois by, the cameramen zoomed in on the dead man's eyes, the cornea beginning to dry up, looking rough and dull, and his mouth hung open like the mouth of an old man sleeping. And the living, knowing they were on camera, smiled, and one man waved. And the millions on television were sold pizza, beer, and cars—fast, pretty cars.

The TV man shoved the microphone in the face of Senior Deputy U.S. Marshal David Hunt. "What happened?" he asked.

"We were ambushed by a bunch of those Aryan Nations individuals. We were hit. They trailed us with dogs. They were shootin' at us out of a pickup truck. I don't know how many. They killed Deputy Marshal Bill Degan there. One of the best. I'd like to be on record for that. Member of the Special Forces. Seen a lotta combat. Knew what he was doin'. But they got him."

"How many of you were there?"

"We were outnumbered. Just the six of us. I don't know how many there was shootin' at us. Roderick called on the radio for help. The three of us came runnin' down as fast as we could. Ran through a rain of fire like you couldn't believe. Twigs snappin'. Dust flyin'. Shots hittin' all around us. Musta shot a thousand rounds at us. When we got close, Roderick yelled out to us. And we dove in beside 'em. We had a medic with us. The medic said Bill was already bled out. Didn't even try to give him CPR. I've already called Washington for 'em to bring in the Hostage Rescue Team."

"Sounds like a war."

"Big-time," said Senior Deputy U.S. Marshal Hunt, and he nodded his head with a sharp little nod and thereafter gave the TV man the long, deep look of a man confirming the truth.

*T*hrough the torment of shock, grief, anger, and fear the Weavers hadn't slept that night—none of them. The small brown mutt the kids called Buddy jumped up on Sammy's bed, and they heard his whining through the thin walls. Nor did the chicken, Roger, sleep. Rachel named her chicken for Roger Rooster. They'd eaten all the other fryers out of the hatch except Roger. She'd protected Roger from the ax. But Roger had grown up to be a hen. The child held on to the chicken all night, squashed it to her until the chicken's feathers were wet, and smelled.

Night was the worst. One cannot see things clearly in the mind at night. It takes the eye of day to see what's in the mind. Randy saw the blood of his son on his hands. There was no water in the house for washing. They'd snuffed the kerosene lamps so that they wouldn't be silhouetted against the door. Then Randy and Kevin went to the spring for water, but even at the spring Randy didn't wash away the blood of his son.

Randy, grown calm and silent as empty rifles, made fifteen trips to the spring below the house, taking Kevin with him. Kevin could carry more. They ran out of pails, and the men filled empty gasoline cans, empty milk cartons, empty honey cans, and bowls and cups and empty fruit jars. They filled flower vases, the pots and kettles and the washbasin, but not for washing—for drinking. Six people drink a lot of water. They secured waxed paper over the top of the containers and tied the paper around with old store string, some with yarn, to keep out the dust and the flies, for in the morning the feds would surely cut off the spring.

Randy, too numb to weep further, had duties to the living. He began readying the guns. He hung their Remington 12-gauge with the short legal barrel on the west wall of boards, three shells in the magazine, the magazine legal. He hung the 12-gauge next to Vicki's black Sunday hat, next to the camouflage jacket Sammy wore in the fall, hunting deer with Randy. He hung a single-shot 12-gauge on the wall around the corner, eye level, where it would be in easy reach. Then he stacked twenty boxes of shotgun shells on the floor, Federal brand, double-aught buck. Good for deer, but also capable of punching fifteen holes through a man at ten feet. Shoot a man with double-aught buck at close range and the argument's over.

"Are they gonna kill us, too?" Rachel asked her mother in her small voice. The chicken clutched at her chest looked out with one wild eye, the other smothered against the child.

"No," her mother said. "Yahweh will protect us."

"Why didn't Yahweh protect Sammy?" Rachel asked.

The mother didn't answer.

Randy laid an AK-47 on the red sofa and set a case of ammunition beside it, and he laid a semiautomatic pistol there as well. The weapons were laid where the children could reach them, for the children, trained to survive the invading hordes that would descend during the Great Tribulation, knew how to fire all of the guns.

On the far wall, which was no wall but bare studs filled with bats of insulation and covered with plastic sheets, Vicki hung two bundles of candles—one red, one blue. She placed a box of kitchen matches beside the candleholder on the shelf, next to five boxes of .357 Magnum pistol ammunition: Western brand, hollow points, semijacketed. Kill a man easy.

"Y'all 'member how to use the gas masks?" Randy asked the room. No answer. Five black rubber World War II surplus gas masks gaped down like foolish black skulls. A year ago Randy had hung them on the wall, also low enough for the children to reach. "I asked, do y'all 'member how to use the gas masks?"

"Are they gonna gas us?" Rachel asked.

"If they try, I'll kill ever' one of the sons-a-bitches," Randy said.

"Why did they kill Sammy?" Rachel asked. "He never did anything to them." She began to cry again. Sara came to her and put her arm around child and chicken.

"It just happened," Sara said.

"Why?"

"I don't know."

"This was Sammy's Mini," Randy said, but he fought against the weeping.

Vicki handed him a cup of coffee. "I'll get your milk."

He looked at her, and he saw in her what he had always seen in her, and when she handed him the cup he let his finger touch her hand, the finger with the blood of his son, dark and dry. "This'll keep me awake," he said in small protest.

"You aren't gonna sleep tonight," she said. Her voice was soft like her eyes. "Nobody is gonna sleep."

"We could pray," Rachel said.

"Yes," her mother said. "We can pray." The baby had begun to cry again and she patted its back, but it did no good. "My milk is gone," she said.

"Pray," Rachel said. "Please, Mamma, you know how to pray best."

The mother sat down on a case of vegetarian beans and put her arm around the child.

"Go bring Sara here," her mother said. "Gather up your father, and Kevin, too." The baby was still crying.

"Come on, Sara. Mamma is gonna pray," Rachel said.

Then Sara took her father by the hand and gave a little nod to Kevin that he should come, and she led her father to the box where the mother sat jiggling the crying child. Vicki looked past her grief for the dead into the waiting faces of the living, and she reached out her hand, the baby in her other, and Rachel grasped the hand, and Sara took hold of the other arm of her little sister, the arm holding the chicken, and Randy took the other hand of Sara, and, with Kevin, the family made a small tight circle. But the circle was never closed, for Vicki held on to the baby with the last closing hand, and Kevin did not take hold of the arm of another man's woman.

Then Vicki began to pray through the wailing child. "Oh, Yahweh, bless those who attack us, and who would do all nature of evil to us," she began in a voice made high to transcend the crying baby. "Oh, Yahweh, hear my prayers for my children, for they are Thy children. Oh, Yahweh, do not forsake Thy children. This I beseech Thee, Yahweh, do not turn Thine ear from them, for they are afraid." Then she put her hand on Rachel's head. "And bless this child. Take her fear from her. Save these, Thy children. And Kevin, too. Amen."

The baby stopped crying for a moment.

"You didn't pray for yourself," Sara said. "You should pray for yourself," but Vicki, without answering, walked into the kitchen patting the baby.

Randy pulled the first aid kit from under the bed. "Here's the first aid kit," he said, giving it a shove with his foot. On the far wall of the bedroom was pinned with ordinary straight pins a WEAVER FOR SHERIFF bumper sticker. If he'd won the election this never would have happened.

"We won't need the first aid kit," Sara said, looking at Rachel. "Mamma prayed."

"Just the same, here it is," Randy said.

In the kitchen the mother was silent, the fog of grief upon her, her fear for the living transcending. "Colic," Vicki said. "Sara, bring me the baby's bottle with some warm water. And the baby aspirin."

Suddenly Kevin was in the room. "The baby knows I killed a man. And the baby don't want me in this house. I am poisonin' the house. Babies know."

"Babies know nothin'," Vicki said. "Babies have the colic."

"If I hadn'ta shot him he woulda shot me. He already shot Sammy. Them feds had already shot ol' Striker. They was layin' for us. They was hid in the woods waitin' for us."

"You did right," Vicki said, picking up the baby, her voice breaking with her patting of the child.

"I seen 'em shootin' at Sammy. I mean, he didn't do nothin' 'cept put a round into where they was hidin' after they shot ol' Striker, an' Sammy was runnin' home."

"You did right," Vicki said again. "Nobody blames you. Yahweh knows what was in your heart."

Then Kevin and Randy walked down to the spring for more water.

When they returned with the last of the water, Randy held his pack of cigarettes out to Kevin, and after he took one, and Randy took one and lit the cigarettes with his World War II Zippo, and after he'd blown out the smoke he looked at Kevin and stayed silent. Kevin knew he was supposed to wait for Randy to speak. Randy took another drag. Then he gave a small kick at a blue-green plastic suitcase that had held Kevin's few things when he'd come to the family.

"Better get yer stuff together, Kevin," Randy said.

"I ain't goin' no place," Kevin said. "Vicki says all that's wrong with the baby is colic."

"In the mornin' it'll be too late."

Then Kevin said the words again. "I ain't goin' no place. An' ya need me. 'Member how I shot that gopher at a hundred yards and ya said I couldn't hit it?" He took another drag. "Bible says a man's got a right to defend himself."

"Better git," Randy said.

"I done what I had ta do yesterday. Sammy woulda done the same fer me. And if the little bastard was here he wouldn't want me ta take off runnin'. Sammy knows." He took another drag and blew smoke. "I spec' he's watchin' right now, an' ol' Sammy says for me to stay and help his ol' man and his mamma, and that's what I intend ta do, with all due respec'." The tears came to Randy's eyes. "An' don't be cryin' about it. There ain't no more ta talk about."

"You ain't thinkin' right," Randy said.

"I beg ta differ with ya, with all due respec'," Kevin said. "Them feds has got listenin' equipment, and they're probably listenin' ta everything we're sayin' right now."

"Well, if that is the case, let me say somethin' they can hear," Randy said. "Fuck you, you dirty rotten cowardly chickenshits. Fuck you!"

"Hush. I can't get the baby to sleep," Vicki said.

"Better get some clothes," Randy said to Vicki.

"We are not going anyplace," Vicki said. "This is where Sammy is. This is our home. And we're stayin' put. It's the Great Tribulation," Vicki said. "It is descending upon us. This is the place Yahweh sent us."

Then he walked up close to his wife, held her with his eyes, only his eyes, and spoke so that the children could not hear, but so she could hear above the crying of the child. "Mamma. They are going to kill us all."

There was a long silence as they looked at each other. They searched with their looks, the husband searching the wife, and the wife the husband. Finally Vicki said, "If they kill us all, it is the will of Yahweh."

The husband turned from the wife. He looked once more at the blood on his hands. He started to speak to his wife, but held back his words.

"We gotta take it as it comes," Vicki said. "Rachel, honey," she hollered over the top of the baby's head, "why don't you feed your chicken? She's hungry. She hasn't had a thing to eat or drink all day. You could feed her some Quaker Oats."

"She isn't hungry," Rachel said.

"Maybe you're hungry," Vicki said. "I could fix you a bowl of your favorite Campbell's chicken soup and a peanut butter sandwich."

"I'm not hungry," Rachel said.

Then Vicki began to sing to the baby in her arms, the baby sobbing in little jerky sobs.

They'd prepared themselves, a little at a time as they got the money. They knew that to survive the Great Tribulation required more than weapons to stave off the invaders who would, as was clearly predicted in the Word, descend upon them as mobs to rob and pillage and rape. They needed a massive store of food.

Randy had worked odd jobs, as had Kevin. They logged in the winter with horses and built fence for neighbors. They took jobs at the sawmill. They lived sparingly, and they lived off the land. Their garden produced bountifully—spinach, lettuce and chard, radishes, parsnips, turnips and beets. They grew cauliflower and broccoli, cucumbers and squash, and pumpkin plants crept along the garden's edge, and after the first frost the pumpkins were like great orange eggs dropped from some primordial beast, and the kids carved them into jack-o'-lanterns, after which the fearsome things were converted to pumpkin pie.

The garden produced tomatoes. Bushels of tomatoes. Vicki canned them ripe. She canned them green. She made relish. She made ketchup. She made juice when the profusion of tomatoes exceeded her ability to can them. It was Sara's garden, watered from their well, pumped by the power created from a small surplus generator for which Randy had traded a World War I Enfield .30-06 rifle. It was Vicki's canning that saved the money, and Randy's hunting that brought in the venison. And the children wore hand-me-downs without shame, for the children were not exposed to public school and taunting children who made fun of old clothes.

As they had scraped the money together, they bought flour by the hundred-pound sack, and against the west wall of the living room they stored cartons of canned goods bearing the Independent Grocers Alliance (IGA) label. Sometimes they got together with neighbors, and Vicki covered the boxes with her mother's old linen tablecloths and thought it all looked nice. Over time they'd bought cases of quick oats and several cans of Maxwell House coffee in the blue gallon tins. Coffee costs a lot. At the time of the Great Tribulation they'd have to do without the coffee.

When Vicki tried to think, all she could see was the body of her son. She saw the lines of small frail ribs sticking through the translucent skin. She saw the arm, as if it had been sliced deep and horribly with a knife so that the ruby red muscle in the forearm bulged out. She saw the flesh was dry, the bone sharp and white. She saw the boy's face, the eyes that did not see her, the mouth without the ready smile, the terrible look of death on the small boy's blameless face. Mothers die with their dead children.

The baby began to cry harder. On the pine dresser behind a vase of red dried flowers sat their squatty kerosene lamp, the one she lit every night as she prepared for bed and then blew out before she climbed into the covers. To light the fire and to blow it out—that was a ritual, like priests have rituals. Rituals were forbidden by the Word, but this one secret ritual surely would be forgiven, for it made her feel secure, as if what she did she had always done, and what she always did she would always do. But she could not do the ritual tonight. She could not sleep. What she saw through the eye of the mind would not let her sleep. And the wailing of the child was a blessing, for the demands of the living kept her from embracing the dead.

Randy said, "Give her some of that powdered milk. Maybe she'll quit crying."

"I already tried. She won't take it," Vicki said.

Randy said, "Mamma, maybe if ya got some rest and ate a little somethin' yer milk will come back."

Sara took the child from her mother. "You go to bed, Mamma. I'll bring you some tea and a peanut butter sandwich."

"I can't sleep. Not with Sammy layin' out there in the shed," Vicki said.

"Ya gotta sleep, Mamma. The baby will get sick," Sara said.

"Ya gotta sleep, Mamma," Randy said. "Me and Kevin will go out in the kitchen." He motioned Kevin toward the kitchen table. They sat for a long time in silence. Randy opened a new pack of cigarettes, offered one to Kevin, lit them with his Zippo, and blew out the smoke.

"Ya wanna know what Sammy's last words were?" Kevin spoke in his high, kindly way so that his words were still touched with respect.

"I guess I do."

"I heard ya callin' him," Kevin said. "An' Sammy's last words was, 'I'm comin', Dad.' An' then Sammy turns around and starts runnin' home and the bastards opened fire on him."

"I heard his last words, then," Randy said. "And I heard the shootin' an' I couldn't get him ta answer, so I shoots my 12-gauge into the air a coupla times tryin' ta get him ta answer or ta come home or ta get his attention or somethin'."

"It was too late," Kevin said. "I heard a little kinda cry, a kinda whimper outta Sammy, and I seen his arm a-flyin' an' he dropped his gun, and then they hit him again and I seen him fall. He was runnin' home."

Silence except for the crying of the baby.

Then Randy saw Rachel had come into the kitchen. He saw the horror on the child's face. "We shouldn't be talkin' about this in front of the kids," he said.

"They gonna shoot us, Daddy?" Rachel asked.

"They ain't gonna shoot nobody," Randy said. "Now you go upstairs an' go ta bed."

"I ain't goin' ta bed," Rachel said in a distant voice. "I ain't goin' up there alone. I want Sammy," and she began to cry. Randy walked over to her and picked the child up. He carried her back to the table, where Kevin still sat, and he held her close to him.

"We're gonna be OK," the father said. "Let's go play a game."

"I don't want to play a game," Rachel said.

He carried the child over to the bookcase where the games were stored along with the children's home study books about geography and history and English and a McGuffey Reader, all of which were taught to the children by Vicki. The bookcase sheltered a set of old Compton's encyclopedias, the King James version of the Holy Bible, a set of World Books, *The Late Great Planet Earth*, *How to Stay Alive in the Woods*, and the visionary book *Atlas Shrugged*. The games were stacked on top of the bookcase, Scrabble, Rummikub, Last Word, and several others.

"Pick a game," Randy said.

"I don't want to play if Sammy isn't here," Rachel said. "Will I see Sammy in heaven?"

"Yes," Randy said.

"When?"

"Someday, child. Someday. Pick a story. I'll read to you." The child began to cry. "I want Mamma," she said, and she ran from her father's arms into the bedroom, where Vicki lay with her eyes open staring at the ceiling, the peanut butter sandwich and tea sitting on the dresser undisturbed.

"Come get in bed with me."

Vicki put her hand on the child's head and, still staring at the ceiling, pressed the child's head to her.

"Are they going to kill us, Mamma?"

"Remember, honey," the mother said, still pressing the child to her, "Mamma prayed," and after that she pressed the child close to her for a long time.

They waited all night for the feds to attack—to burn them out, to gas them. Maybe to throw grenades through the windows or plow the house over with their army tanks. Randy nailed the front door closed. He nailed blankets over the windows. But no one slept. Nor did the baby ever sleep.

In the full, clear light of day, the end would come.

*V*icki Weaver, eyes strained and weary, saw the light leaking around the edges of the blankets that covered the windows. The day had come, and she felt relief. Better to look in the face of the enemy than stare at the ghouls of night. Like one bearing heavy burdens, she shuffled slowly to the kitchen in her gay pink slippers to fire up the stove for coffee. Sara was already up. She stood peering through the small hole in the blanket that covered the front window. "I don't see anybody out there," Sara said.

"They'll be coming," her mother said. She poked at the coals with a piece of kindling, once, then again, and when the coals flared back she tossed in the kindling. "They aren't gonna show themselves to us."

Randy next entered the kitchen. "They're hidin' out there like bloodsuckin' ticks. You makin' the coffee, Mamma?"

"I'm makin' it."

"The cowardly bastards won't show themselves." He was smoking still. Smoked all night. "Gonna pick us off from ambush."

Vicki lifted the claw hammer from the kitchen table and began to pull the nails that held the blanket.

"Don't be takin' that blanket down," Randy said. "They'll shoot us right through the fuckin' window."

"We gotta have light to think," Vicki said. She tacked the blanket back and loosened the upper half to let the north light flood into the room. Then she did the same at the west window, and the window on the east. Ah, the blessed light of the east! She breathed in the light. The flat light cut through the smoke of fire and cigarettes.

She poured the coffee, stirred in the powdered milk for Randy's, pulled the sugar bowl down from the shelf, and, knowing the exact quantity of sugar, stirred in two teaspoonfuls and handed the cup to her man. She did the same for Kevin, who'd been sitting quietly in the dark corner.

"You gotta come out of there and get into the light," she said to Kevin. "An' kinda stoop down in front of the windows when you walk by. You're taller." He took the coffee. Then the mother opened the firebox to the stove and picked up another stick of kindling.

"Careful, Mamma, we only got a little wood left," Sara said. "The wood's out on the porch."

"I know," the mother said. "But a person's gotta have coffee to clear the mind. We haven't slept. And we need to think."

"I'll go out and get some wood," Sara said, heading for the door.

"I nailed the door shut," Randy said.

"You can unnail it, Papa. They aren't gonna kill me. I never shot anybody."

"Neither did old Striker. Neither did Sammy."

"We gotta go out there sometime, Papa. Sammy's out there."

"I ain't forgot about him," Randy said, his eyes tearing up again. "How we gonna get Sammy buried, is what I been thinkin'."

"They know we gotta come out," Sara said.

"I'll go out and get the wood," Kevin said with his soft words. "An' I'll go dig the hole for Sammy, an' if they shoot, I don't give a damn."

"Nobody's goin' no place," Randy said.

"Did you hear those planes over us all night?" Kevin asked.

"Yeah. They were flyin' around and around," Vicki said. "I couldn't sleep."

"Takin' night pictures of us," Randy said. "We used to do it in the service."

"I hope things looked nice," Vicki said. Then she pulled the curtains on the door window aside and quickly peered out.

"We need to go, Papa." It was Sara. "If we go out now we can get it all done before they decide what to do. Remember how you used to say that government men drink coffee till ten, think what they are gonna do till eleven, get their stuff together, and then go have lunch. Remember? We could go now while they're still thinkin'."

"I ain't gonna let ya. I lost one kid already."

"Somebody has to. They aren't gonna shoot a girl."

"Don't count on it."

"I'm goin' out. Just out on the porch."

"I don't like it."

"I am." She picked up the hammer and started for the door. She pulled at the nails until Randy took the hammer. He heaved up on the hammer handle and down again until the nails pulled free.

Sara walked up and down the porch, strutting some as if to show no fear, her feet making noise on the plywood floor. She looked around. "They must be moving an army in," Sara said. "You can hear the trucks."

"Probably tanks," Randy said.

"Would they bring tanks in against just us?" Sara asked.

"Ever see the gov'ment do anything that made sense?" Randy said. "The way you figger the gov'ment is figger what you wouldn't do and that's what the gov'ment'll do—ever' time."

Sara went out for another load of wood. Off in the distance the helicopters hacked at the air, circling, but not coming close. Sara stood, watching. She hauled in another load of firewood.

"Just as well get it while the gettin's good," Randy said.

She brought in two more loads of wood and stacked it up against the east wall.

"Nobody's out there," Sara said.

"It isn't nine o'clock yet," Randy said. "Besides, it's beginnin' ta rain."

Kevin started out the door. "I gotta go," he said.

"I wouldn't go out there without my rifle," Randy said.

Kevin picked up his .30-06 and headed for the door.

"I'll go with you," Randy said. "I gotta go, too." He grabbed his Mini-14, and the two ran out into the rain. Vicki stood at the door watching, the baby in her arms.

"I gotta go," Rachel said. She nodded toward the outhouse.

"I'll go with you," Sara said.

"Take your rifles, then," Vicki said. "Maybe they won't shoot so fast if you're armed." And Sara and Rachel grabbed their rifles, then ran in the rain to the outhouse.

When they came back, the mother was sitting on the couch looking out into the gray day, her eyes quiet, but the tears welling up and slipping down at the corners. Thank Yahweh the baby, exhausted, was finally sleeping. Kevin sat alone.

Then Randy said, "I gotta go feed the chickens. Just 'cause the fuckin' feds are out there is no sign the chickens gotta starve." Sara said she would go with him, and as she walked out the door she picked up the egg basket with the red-and-white-checked towel in the bottom, and they grabbed their rifles and they fed the chickens and gathered the eggs. Randy shut the chicken house window against the rain, and then they ran back into the house.

The day crept by like a tired old man. They heard the grunting and groaning of the gathering army below, the trucks, and occasionally, with the air currents right, the sound of men's voices coming up clear in waves and then disappearing as soon. The people in the cabin talked in low gray tones that matched the sound of the rain on the roof, and they talked in short sentences, and they did not talk about burying Sammy anymore, but it was on their minds, that and the war that was about to come.

Toward evening Buddy, the little brown cur, began to fuss. "They're here," Randy said, and they all grabbed their rifles. Randy ran out the door.

"What the fuck's the matter?" Randy asked the dog. Buddy was straining at his rope and yapping, his head pointing below to the road.

"Come back in," Vicki said, standing at the door, now nursing the baby. Randy ran to the rock. Sara followed, and then Kevin.

"Get your asses behind the rock," Randy said, and then he moved, a little at a time, around the big rock the size of a small school bus. He was peering in the direction where the dog had been pointing, the dog still yap-yapping away. It had stopped raining.

Then suddenly Randy started for the birthing shed, at a fast walk first, then at a run, and Sara and Kevin, seeing him go, followed after him. When he got to the birthing shed he reached up with his right arm to turn the latch at the top of the door, and it was then that the shot broke the air.

The high crack.

The whine.

Randy half fell, crouched down. Sara was there by then.

"I been hit," Randy said. "The motherfuckers hit me."

"Where? Where, Papa?"

"In the arm," he said, still holding his rifle in the other hand.

Vicki opened the door, the baby in her arms, the door wide open, her standing there as plain as day behind the open door screaming, "What happened?"

"I been hit," Randy hollered back.

"Come on, Papa," Sara said, lifting at him, pulling him, and then pushing him in front of her. "We gotta get to the house."

Randy, dazed, staggered forward, moving toward the house, partly running, with Sara pushing, pushing at his back, running and crying, "Come on, Papa. We gotta get to the house." And she cried, "If you want to murder my Papa, you have to murder me, too. Come on, Papa, come on."

Kevin was behind, Sara shielding the bleeding body of her father. As she ran, she knew she would be shot. They couldn't miss her. The next shot would be for her, shot through the back like Sammy.

And when they got to the door, Vicki was holding it wide open, Elisheba, the baby, in her arms, and the mother screaming, "Hurry, hurry!" and the father staggering toward the house with Sara pushing and Kevin behind.

"Hurry, hurry! Hurry before they kill you," the mother cried.

And as the three got to the porch, the mother, armed with the baby, was holding the door open.

"I'm hit, Mamma," Randy cried.

"Get in here!" she shouted.

The three reached the door about the same time, Sara still pushing Randy through the door held open by the mother, and Sara diving into the house behind her father, Kevin on her heels. Then the second shot.

And the splintering of glass.

Sara felt sharp fragments cutting at her cheek, and her left ear was ringing, and she knew she'd been hit.

The FBI sniper, a marksman trained to kill, Lon Horiuchi was his name, had put his bullet into Vicki Weaver. Blew the whole side of her face off. She fell, the baby clutched to her, and after she fell, Randy, already wounded, was somehow able to pry the baby from her hands, and then Randy and Sara dragged Vicki's body over to the side of the kitchen, her blood flooding the kitchen floor. The same bullet that hit Vicki pierced Kevin's chest. He had passed through the door just behind Vicki as the sniper's second shot reached them.

"Jesus, God," Randy cried. "Jesus, God!" He stood staring at his wife, her face gone.

Sara found a blanket and laid it gently over her mother. Then Sara led Randy to a chair, and he sat bereft of words, bereft of thought. Filled with the agony of blood and death.

In the horrors of the night that followed, only Sara seemed alive—the others dead. Dead in horror. Dead in mortal pain. The child Rachel dead, too frightened to speak. And the baby?

In the night Kevin came to life, screaming, begging to be relieved of the pain, for Randy to kill him.

"Shoot me, for Christ's sake, Randy. I can't take 'er no longer."

Randy didn't answer.

"I'm beggin' ya, Randy. I'd do the same fer you. Shoot me." The high-pitched screaming came from lips robbed of faint smiles, lips twisted in agony.

Sara had tried to stuff gauze from the first aid kit into their wounds. But there wasn't enough gauze, and it didn't stop the bleeding. The pain was too great, and she didn't know what to do or how. She brought them water. Kevin couldn't drink. Randy took a silent sip. She poured peroxide on their open wounds and applied cayenne pepper and goldenseal to fight the infection as she'd learned from her mother. Then Sara tried to feed Elisheba. The baby was weak, and Sara was afraid she would die.

What would it be like for a child to exist, to continue breathing, alive and awake for seven days under that roof with the mother lying dead on the kitchen floor in the heat of summer?

The mother rotting.

Day on day the mother rotting.

Day on day the father moaning from his wounds and their friend begging for death.

The feds had crawled under the house and attached devices to listen to the horror they'd authored. They knew their sniper, Horiuchi, had killed the mother and perhaps had fatally wounded the men. The FBI kept the family awake with screaming noisemakers, the noise like sirens from hell, attacking, shattering sounds, yapping noises like crazed giant hounds—noises beyond the experience of man, sounds that stabbed at the ears and rattled sanity. Then came an evil voice wounding the wounded and laughing at the children. "Did you sleep well last night, Vicki?" the voice asked.

The FBI listened with its listening devices and heard the high, broken sobs of the children, the baby's wailing, and at last their silence.

The FBI listened to the feeble moaning of Randy, the crying to Yahweh to save them, and to deliver them into the peace of death.

The FBI taunted the living with its high evil voice from the loudspeaker: "Show us the baby, Vicki."

The FBI covered the house with flashing spotlights at night so the children and the wounded and dying could not sleep. And when the sun rose the voice asked, "What did you have for breakfast, Vicki?"

Such were the government servants of the people, servants in the pay of the people, servants who were sworn to uphold the Constitution and to keep the people safe—the people's protectors.

As we shall see, the authorization to torture and to kill came from the highest authority of law enforcement in the United States. The headman knew there had been no warrant for Vicki's arrest. Not one of the hundreds of United States officers who invaded Ruby Ridge held a warrant to arrest anyone. They had no warrant to arrest little Sam. But they were resourceful. They did what they could without warrants. They killed, and when they could not kill they wounded. And after they wounded they taunted the wounded.

The feds created their own rules under which they could kill—something they called "the Rules of Engagement." The police, including the FBI, are permitted to kill only in self-defense. But the FBI manufactured its own law *in the middle of the crisis.* The first draft said that any adult with a weapon *could* be the subject of deadly force. But the final version included the words "can and *should* be the subject of deadly force." Its new rule of engagement, without notification to those that were to be killed, was *to kill any armed person.*

Kill them.

The feds knew the Weavers always carried their weapons to protect themselves. The feds knew the Weavers were not told that the rule of law no longer protected them, that the rule of self-defense had been discarded, and that if they came out of their own house with any weapon, the hidden snipers, waiting in exquisite excitement, would kill them.

The FBI's new rule was a mandate for murder.

The snipers had spent years perfecting their sweet expertise at killing. Would not all that time be wasted if after years of dreaming, when the "subject" is clean in the crosshairs and the finger is touching an eager trigger, one could only turn away? Such dreams shrivel up in old men who sit on the front porch and rock and remember the days when they could have killed. But at Ruby Ridge their dreams were not wasted.

The new rule was *Kill any armed person,* and Vicki was armed, remember, armed with a baby. It is merely how one interprets the rule.

Unless rescued, Randy and Kevin would soon die from their wounds. The children would be orphaned. In a way, the feds had killed the children with deep, invisible wounds—the unspeakable sight and sound and smell of decay and death that would be forever imprinted on the psyches of the innocent.

Then the FBI sent out a robot, something like a little tank with a 12-gauge shotgun attached to it, sent it up to the front porch, and they broadcast endless entreaties on their loudspeakers trying to entice Randy out of the house so the snipers could finally kill him.

None of the feds, none at the pinnacle of the FBI, not even the director himself, asked the simple question: Under the law, what is first degree murder? It is defined as a malicious, premeditated, intentional killing. If the same act were committed by any other person, such killing would necessitate the citizen's arrest, trial for murder, and, after due process of law, incarceration for life in prison or, more likely, death by lethal injection—strapped to the gurney to face the insertion of the needles of death.

*C*olonel Bo Gritz telephoned me the following day, a Saturday. I was at home. Gritz was a massively decorated Vietnam War hero then running for president. The colonel had offered his services to talk Randy down from Ruby Ridge. Gritz was known to share many of Randy Weaver's beliefs, and he and Randy were fellow servicemen. Surely Randy would trust Bo Gritz.

With consent from the feds, Jackie Brown, a longtime trusted friend of the Weavers, was the first from the outside to enter the cabin. She entered alone. She checked on the wounded. Kevin was weak. High pulse rate. Fever. The wound hole in his arm was large and gaping and ugly. Randy was feeble but coherent.*

The following day Gritz went up to talk Randy down, Jackie Brown with him. The first order of business was to remove Vicki's body from the cabin.

Jackie said, "Randy cradled his wife's head and upper body in his arms while Bo supported her lower body. Together they tenderly tucked her into the blue body bag Gritz had brought along."

"I love you, honey," Randy said. "You'll be all right now. Look, Bo. Look what they did to my wife. She had such a beautiful face."

"I know, brother. We'll see that justice is done." Bo's voice was quietly reassuring as he pulled the flap over Vicki and zipped the bag shut. It was Jackie who cleaned up the blood and gore on the kitchen floor.

The next day, the eleventh in the standoff, Randy still wouldn't come down. He said the girls wanted to stay. But Kevin was not doing well, and might die if he wasn't evacuated. So Randy was reconsidering.

When Gritz phoned me, I knew only what I'd read of the Weaver case in the paper. "The area is sealed off," the colonel told me. "About five hundred militarized police are up there. The FBI is in charge. They have their hostage and barrier teams surrounding the cabin. The Idaho State Police are up there, along with the county police, the Bureau of Alcohol, Tobacco, and Firearms people, and the U.S. Marshals Service."

"Are any of Randy's supporters around?" I asked.

"There's an assembly of two hundred or more at a roadblock that's been put up at Deep Creek—about four miles from the Weaver place. Been a vigil there since last Saturday." Then he added, "They had a big funeral in Quincy, Mass., for Marshal Degan—they say seven thousand people attended. He was supposed to be the most decorated marshal in the history of the service."

"Who killed Degan?" I asked.

"The Bureau is claiming that Degan was killed by Sammy. That he cried out, 'You shot my dog,' and then fired his .30-06 rifle and killed Degan. They'll claim they shot the boy in self-defense."

---

* A remarkable account of the Weaver surrender as well as an insightful and caring description of this historical saga can be found in the hard-to-come-by and singularly worthy work *The First Canary* by Tony D. and Jackie J. Brown (Colburn, ID: Big Pine Publishing, 2000). I have relied on this book (especially pages 105 and 113) for details in the following scene. This account is drawn from that as well as from my interviews with many of the participants, government documents, and court records.

I was trying to put the scene together. A bunch of marshals hidden in the woods shooting a kid in "self-defense"?

"But about five days ago the U.S. attorney, Maurice Ellsworth, said they have this young man, Kevin Harris, charged with shooting Marshal Degan and also shooting Sammy," the colonel said. "That's the way the U.S. attorney has it stacked up now."

"Why in hell would Kevin Harris kill Sammy?" I asked.

"I don't think he did, sir," Gritz replied and said nothing more.

"Weaver will be charged with murder," I said. "I predict it. And how does Randy know of me?"

"I raised your name to him because Paul Harvey on his news program said twice for two days running that he personally would hire the best lawyer in the country. And so when I was talking with Randy about two hours ago I told him maybe we could get Gerry Spence. I learned that Randy had previously talked about you to some folks—referenced work you did in the Karen Silkwood case." That was a suit I'd brought against the Kerr-McGee Corporation for Karen's death; the movie *Silkwood*, starring Meryl Streep and Cher, was made about it.

"Randy will have a long, terrible row to hoe," I said. "He'll have a hell of a time getting a fair trial anywhere. From what I read, the FBI is already demonizing him—making him out to be a monster—so that a jury soaked up with all the feds' propaganda won't take long to convict him."

Gritz nodded. The colonel's voice was strong and calm. "They're trying to connect him to the Aryan Nations, but he never belonged to that bunch." Then Gritz said, "I asked Glenn, the FBI chief, if there was either a search warrant or an arrest warrant for Randy. I asked, 'Was there anything that would allow camouflaged federal officers to come on Randy's land, to shoot their dog, much less Sammy?' The blank look on their faces told me what I needed to know."

"What do you want of me?" I asked.

"I'd like to tell Randy that you'll be his lawyer, and if he'll come down from the mountain with his daughters he'll have your voice in his defense."

Finally I said, "Well, you heard quite a silence from me. I don't think I've ever been asked to take a case without first having met my client."

"We have to get him down before any more damage occurs. To use an old hackneyed phrase, it's pretty hard to think about draining the swamp when you're up to your ass in alligators."

"You can tell him that if he'll come down I'll meet with him. They'll put him in a jail someplace," I said.

"I really appreciate that. I believe he would consider it an arrow in his quiver."

"Is there anything more you want me to do at the moment?" I asked.

"Don't know. A five-minute trip to the top of the hill took me two hours. There were so many military and police vehicles around that just getting through them became the most onerous task of the day. I'm already late. I probably won't get down until dark."

The good colonel must have misunderstood me. I found out later that he told Randy that I had *agreed* to represent him if he'd come down. I'd never agreed to represent anyone from afar. In a way, the attorney-client relationship is like a marriage. You try to understand each other, to care about each other, and you end up living in the same house together—the courthouse. If you can't lay it all down for the honest issues in the case, the jury will sense it. If I try to convey to the jury that I care about my client, but in that private place where my feelings are sheltered I don't truly care, the jury will know it. You can't ask a jury to care if you don't care.

Based on Bo Gritz's assurance to Randy that I had *agreed* to represent him, Randy surrendered. Ambulances hauled away Randy and Kevin and what remained of Randy's family. They locked Randy and Kevin in jail, wounds and all, offering only the most minimal care—just enough to keep them alive for trial.

Single-handedly, Gritz and Jackie Brown had done what an entire army of cops and soldiers and seven days of merciless torture couldn't do. Gritz had approached the crisis not with power and terror but with caring. Power never learns. Bo Gritz had always been a hero. I suspect he was born one. He continued to be one the day he brought Randy Weaver and his dying family down from Ruby Ridge.

*M*y son Kent, one of my partners, and I met Randy in his Boise, Idaho, jail cell on the evening of his surrender. His eyes had no light in them. He was unshaven and dirty, clothed in yellow prison coveralls, and he was cold. His feet were clad in rubber prison sandals. In the stark setting of the prison conference room he seemed diminutive and fragile. He'd spent eleven days and nights in a standoff against the government and he had lost. His wife was dead. His son was dead. His friend was near death. He had lost his freedom. He had lost it all. And now he stood face-to-face with two strangers who towered over him and whose words were not words of comfort.

"My name is Gerry Spence," I began. "I'm the lawyer you've been told about. Before we begin to talk, I want you to understand that I do not share any of your political or religious beliefs. My daughter is married to a Jew. Many of my dearest friends are Jews. My sister is married to a black man. She has adopted a black child. I deplore what the Nazis stand for. If I defend you I will not defend your political beliefs or your religious beliefs, but your right as an American citizen to a fair trial."

His quiet answer was "That's all I ask."

Once again I was about to challenge the United States government with its unfathomable power—its armies, its weaponry, its lawyers and judges, and the media it manipulates so that the people's minds are set against one of their own. Yes, I was afraid. But I'd learned that fear is my friend. It has always readied me for the fight.

We were preparing our defense of Randy Weaver. The feds had their man, feeble, without family or friends, a man benumbed in grief and imprisoned in a foreign city. How was such bravery kept alive? His feeling center must be jammed. His beating heart must be near paralyzed.

"Tell me where your strength comes from," I asked Randy days later. He was thin like a Bataan death marcher, his once-dark hair graying on the edges. He held on to the bars to steady himself. His fingers were little more than bone.

"I want to live," he said in a flat voice; his eyes said otherwise. "I got kids who need me."

The federal government proceeded as I predicted: They charged Randy with the murder of Marshal Degan, along with nine other felonies that included—aiding and abetting murder, conspiracy to murder, assault, and, of course, the always included obstruction of justice. Obstruction of justice is a charge that comes like putting a period at the end of a sentence, and often carries the most severe punishment. The government's strategy was not artful—something like fishing with ten fishhooks hoping to catch a fish with one, any one. (We safeguard our fish by making multiple hooks unlawful, but no such protection is granted mere human beings.) And if the accused pleads not guilty, the jury will catch him with something. They almost always do.

A defense attorney can defend one charge after another, and at last the jury concludes the defendant must be guilty of *something*. Somebody has to pay. It's the cops' word against that guilty-looking defendant sitting over there with two marshals behind him to make sure he doesn't break loose in the courtroom and kill somebody else. That tells you about all you need to know, doesn't it?

By April 13, 1993, a jury had been selected to try Randy Weaver and Kevin Harris in the federal district court in Boise, Idaho, before Judge Edward Lodge. David Nevin, already a great trial lawyer and later to become nationally celebrated for his many courtroom victories, represented Kevin Harris. I led our team for Randy Weaver, one buttressed by Chuck Peterson, a young lawyer from Boise who'd volunteered to help, along with his partner, Gary Gilman. Ellie Matthews, a veteran trial lawyer, provided his solid services, and my son Kent was there with his insights and support as well. These were the unsung heroes in the case. Not one lawyer received a penny for his services, nor did any expect to. We were rewarded with the opportunity to take on a system that itself had gone criminal. We became the prosecutors of cops as well as of prosecutors. Assistant U.S. Attorney Ron Howen was in charge of the government's case. He was a big, square-jawed, stern, emotionally immobile fellow who, in or out of court, smiled so rarely that if he ever broke into one, it would scare the children. He was as tough and intransigent as an oak tree stump.

Yes, the government could have prevented that shameful massacre at Ruby Ridge. David Hunt of the Idaho marshals had learned that the Weavers' vow to fight to the end was the product of Magistrate Ayers's erroneous statement that if Randy were convicted, the Weaver family could lose their home. Marshal Hunt—give him credit—wrote Prosecutor Howen and suggested the prosecutor could probably end the standoff by assuring Randy that if he surrendered, his home would remain secure.

But Power does not bargain with the powerless.

Prosecutor Howen wrote back that the areas of negotiation "are the type of matters properly addressed in exchange for guilty pleas, but not Weaver's *mere surrender*" (my emphasis).

*A*t trial Howen began those weary, predictable government tactics: Make the jury fear and hate the Weavers by associating them with that dangerous cult the Aryan Nations. The Weavers had never been members of the Aryan Nations. Yes, they had attended some of their events, but in the end had rejected their doctrines. Still, the government lost no opportunity to broadcast its toxic propaganda—that the Weavers embraced religious beliefs that would be offensive to most of the jurors who'd be trying Randy Weaver. Never mind our constitutional right to freedom of religion. That right is mostly extended to those whose religion is substantially the same as mainstream America's. Hanging out in a minority religion in America has been dangerous from the beginning. Ask the Indians.

Howen subpoenaed one of Randy Weaver's skinhead friends, William Grider, whose son also wore his head shaved. He asked Grider how Randy wore his hair. The clear implication of Howen's questions was that Randy was a skinhead and probably had a swastika tattooed on his rear. Howen was forcing me to object, causing the jury to wonder if I was hiding the ugly truth about my client. Over our objections, Howen was able to remind the jury that the Aryan Nations hated blacks and Jews, and that Randy once wore an Aryan Nations belt buckle. Howen's subliminal argument came down to this: Since we are afraid of skinheads, and since Randy once shaved his head, and possessed an Aryan Nations belt buckle, we must find this dangerous individual guilty of murder. No further proof of Randy's guilt would really be necessary.

Howen subpoenaed other witnesses who told the jury about the Weavers' belief that the world would soon end—Armageddon—and how they'd armed themselves to fight off the hordes who would descend upon them. Without saying it in so many words, Howen portrayed the Weavers as fearsome individuals on the fringe who were itching to kill. Howen asked for the death penalty.

Howen called witness after witness, and their testimony dragged on for over three months. Often their testimony was so irrelevant that we had to be careful on cross-examination not to give Howen's case credibility by overreacting to it. It's a prosecutor's standard strategy—if you have a weak case, put on endless witnesses, creating the impression you've proved your case beyond a reasonable doubt. The juror thinks, "The prosecutor never left a stone unturned."

And the juror also thinks, "That Spence fellow is in there accusing that good judge and the prosecutors of violating the rules. They're just trying to do their jobs. And remember, Spence's client was a 'Jew hater' and a 'nigger hater,' and we have enough of those types in this country. And they're dangerous. Probably killed the marshal. Maybe the Harris kid did kill Sammy."

Howen's attempt to hang Randy Weaver on whatever Randy's beliefs were did prove one thing—that the government had no case. You don't get the death penalty in this country for what you believe, no matter how repugnant your beliefs are. Not yet. But Howen had to face what took place at the Y intersection in the trails where the old dog, Striker, and little Sammy were killed. A case can sometimes be won in a few questions when the tainted core of the prosecution is exposed: They killed a kid's dog. Then they killed the kid.

I was cross-examining Deputy Marshal Larry Cooper.

> SPENCE: "Now the dog's big crime was that he was following you, isn't that true?"
>
> HOWEN: "Objection."
>
> JUDGE: "Sustained."
>
> SPENCE: "Did the dog do anything that was illegal?"
>
> HOWEN: "Objection."
>
> SPENCE: "Let me put it to you this way: As a member of the Special Operations Group, had you, in your training, been taught that because you had automatic weapons and you were wearing camouflage gear, you had the right to kill somebody's dog?"
>
> COOPER: "No, sir. That has never been taught to me."
>
> SPENCE: "Do you know of anyone in the history of the world that Striker ever bit?"
>
> COOPER: "No."

Remember, Randy was still near the house when Sammy was shot. Yet Randy was charged as a conspirator in the killing of Degan. And as the facts were beginning to show, the only conspiracy was the feds'—to charge and prosecute Randy and Kevin for crimes the feds themselves had committed. A memo written by FBI Deputy Assistant Director Danny Coulson on the fourth day of the siege made this all too clear:

OPR 004477 SOMETHING TO CONSIDER:

1. Charge against Weaver is Bull Shit.
2. No one saw Weaver do any shooting.
3. Vicki has no charges against her.
4. Weaver's defense. He ran down the hill to see what the dog was barking at.

[Coulson got that wrong. Randy never left the area of the house.]

> Some guys in camys shot his dog. Started shooting at him. Killed his son.
> Harris did the shooting. He [Weaver] is in a pretty strong legal position.

The trial would put on display the remarkable creativity of the government in attempting to tie Randy to Degan's death. The FBI produced a bullet it claimed killed Degan and came from Randy's rifle.

Let's set the scene: When the shooting occurred at the Y, Randy was at the house. Between the Weaver house and the place at the Y where the bullet was supposedly found stood a quarter mile of solid forest. You couldn't throw a rock three feet through it. Yet this bullet was supposedly found lying on top of a fallen leaf on the edge of the road at the Y. Not a scratch on the bullet. And to have been Degan's murder bullet, it would have had to pass through his bone and flesh without a scratch and without leaving a trace of blood.

I called it "the magic bullet." I thought that the FBI would be ashamed to resurrect another magic bullet like the one found on Governor Connally's gurney after supposedly passing through both President Kennedy and the governor without a scratch. Before the trial was over, we were able to show that the magic bullet hadn't come from Randy's gun at all. It came from a .223 that belonged to Sara, a rifle the FBI had confiscated in its investigation. And Sara never left the house at any time relevant to Degan's death. Far be it from me to suggest the unpatriotic thought that the FBI would manufacture evidence.

Under cross-examination, the FBI agent who claimed he discovered the bullet at the Y said he just happened to come onto it. He had, he said, picked it up and put it in his pocket, and sometime later put it down again at a place he thought was near where he found it so that the government photographer could take a photo of it lying there. But Howen had offered the photo as the genuine thing.

Nearing the end of the trial and during a recess, my son Kent was inspecting the backpack Degan had been wearing when he was shot. Kent discovered a second bullet hole that had not been mentioned by the government experts. The shot appeared to have come from *behind* Degan at an angle but traveled clear through the side of the pack without hitting Degan. The looming question: Who had shot at Degan from behind?

We remember the marshals were equipped with automatic weapons so that several rounds could be fired in a split second. That meant that the fatal round and the round that Kent discovered in Degan's pack might have come from the same rifle. Did Kevin Harris miss Degan altogether? Had Degan been killed by the hysterical fire of one of his own men?

At last Howen called the FBI sniper, Lon Horiuchi, to the stand. He was escorted down the hall to the courtroom by a platoon of surly, scowling, fully armed members of the sniper team, the FBI's professional killers. At that moment I happened to be coming up the same hallway. When we met, that gang of toughs occupied the entire width of the hall, and when I tried to pass by I was shoved to the wall. It was an unsettling experience— one would think that in a federal courthouse one would be as safe as in a mother's arms. Yet they could have decommissioned me in one of their esoteric ways and provided eyewitnesses from their gang to say they were only protecting themselves.

On the stand Horiuchi glared out at me. I asked the court to require him to disarm before I began my questioning. He immediately admitted to having held his crosshairs on Randy's spine as Randy reached up to unlatch the door of the birthing shed where Sammy's body lay. Just at the moment Horiuchi pulled the trigger, Randy moved, and the bullet entered his back and came out his armpit.

I handed Horiuchi his rifle with its scope and heavy barrel, the one that Howen had shown the jury.

> SPENCE: "This is the gun you shot Mrs. Weaver with, Mr. Weaver with, and Mr. Harris with, isn't it?"
>
> HORIUCHI: "Yes, sir, it is." His voice was like a single note played from the middle range of a flute, a chilling sound that never varied.
>
> SPENCE: "You intended to kill both [Kevin and Randy], didn't you?"
>
> HORIUCHI: "Sir, if they came out all at one time, we were intending to take them all out at one time, versus waiting for one individual to come out and take him piecemeal. Our normal procedures are whenever you have more than one subject, you try to take them out one at a time."
>
> SPENCE: "You saw somebody you identified as Kevin Harris?"
>
> HORIUCHI: "Yes, sir."
>
> SPENCE: "You see him in the courtroom?"
>
> HORIUCHI: "Yes, sir, I do."
>
> SPENCE (POINTING TO KEVIN HARRIS): "That's the man you were intending to kill, isn't it?"

HORIUCHI: "Yes, sir." The politest of killers.

SPENCE: "You wanted to kill him, didn't you?"

HORIUCHI: "Yes, sir."

SPENCE: "Just before you shot the second time, you knew the door was open, didn't you?"

HORIUCHI: "At that time, yes, sir."

SPENCE: "Didn't you know that there was the possibility of someone being behind the door?"

HORIUCHI: "There may have been, yes, sir."

SPENCE: "You heard a woman screaming after your second shot?" That would have been Sara Weaver.

HORIUCHI: "Yes, sir, I did."

SPENCE: "That screaming went on for thirty seconds?"

HORIUCHI: "About thirty seconds, yes, sir."

SPENCE: "I want us to just take thirty seconds now and hear in our mind's ear the screaming."

I said nothing and looked up at the clock on the courtroom wall. The jurors, one and all, were glued to the clock as it ticked off thirty seconds. In the silence, the silent screaming was deafening and thirty seconds became an eternity.

Horiuchi denied he ever saw Vicki Weaver. The FBI claimed that the curtains at the cabin door were closed, and therefore Horiuchi didn't see Vicki standing there with her baby in her arms.

As the old saw goes, "The truth will out." The FBI, committed to the lie whenever useful, had simply lied again. It had willfully violated the court's order to provide us all *exculpatory evidence* in the case (meaning evidence that tended to exonerate the accused). The FBI had intentionally withheld a pivotal drawing made by Horiuchi that had been in the possession of the agency from the beginning, one that showed exactly what Horiuchi saw when he shot and killed Vicki Weaver.

The drawing showed a window with *no* curtains. In the lower right-hand corner were the tops of two heads—Sara and Randy, who had dived into the house just ahead of Kevin. Horiuchi intended to kill Kevin by shooting him in the back as he ran for the house, and he had to know that someone was standing at the door, holding it open. This killer had the eyes of a hawk. Through his high-powered scope he could have seen the pores on his victim's face. Yet he claimed he couldn't see Vicki with her baby.

Howen, a hardened career prosecutor, had been exposed to such FBI tactics in the past. Finally even he could stomach no more. His investigating team, led by the FBI, was concealing and perhaps manufacturing evidence, and after months of this, near the end of the trial he confessed to Judge Lodge that the FBI had withheld this crucial evidence by having sent it to him Fourth Class Mail from Washington, D.C., just slightly faster than by Pony Express on a crippled horse.

Judge Lodge, as serene and emotionally expressive as mashed potatoes, came unglued. Yet what could he do? He couldn't dump the whole Bureau in jail. Horiuchi wasn't in charge of producing the evidence. Howen had done his honorable duty by disclosing the Bureau's tactics. Finally the judge ordered that the Bureau pay us one day's fees for our trouble. Of course, we were working without fee. And thereafter the government never offered to deliver a government check to us, again thumbing its bureaucratic nose at the judiciary, and at us. Some federal judge out in Idaho was not going to order the mighty Bureau to do anything. Nevertheless, the judge's order served to make a powerful statement. A respected federal judge had officially found that the FBI would cheat to win a case. We'd known that all along. Judge Lodge made it official.

Judge Lodge further officially found: "The actions of the government, acting through the FBI, evidence a callous disregard for the rights of the defendants and the interests of justice. Its behavior served to obstruct the administration of justice." If you or I obstruct justice, we have committed a felony that could land us in the penitentiary for years. The FBI responded with little more than a yawn.

Howen rested the government's case; that is to say, he couldn't dig up one more witness or one more exhibit. We moved for an acquittal on the grounds the government had failed to prove its charges. It's a motion defendants must lodge to preserve their record for an appeal, and it always includes the defense's futile hope that the judge will throw out at least a few of the many charges that make up the prosecution's habitual overcharging.

Howen was beginning his argument to Judge Lodge opposing our motion to dismiss the case when he suddenly stopped short. He began shuffling through his notes like a child lost in the woods who couldn't find his map. We waited. He kept shuffling. He stared out at the judge for a very long time. Finally in a wavering voice he said, "I'm sorry, Judge. I can't go on." He sat down. Marshals and FBI agents hurried to his side, and the judge called a recess.

Howen never returned for the rest of the trial. He left the case in the hands of his assistant, Kim Lindquist, a man who was younger and proved to be even more aggressive than Howen, a prosecutor perhaps better able to deal with the government's misconduct.

We offered no witnesses and rested our case. That meant we wouldn't call Randy to testify. Why? If he took the witness stand, he'd be cross-examined, maybe for days, by Lindquist. A contest between Randy Weaver and Prosecutor Lindquist would be like Randy trying to survive in the ring with a professional wrestler, one who'd slam Randy down flat to the floor and beat him to a bloody pulp. I try to keep my clients from wrestling with prosecutors. I'll do my client's fighting. It's not that the accused lies. It's that the prosecutor, in a reasonably skilled cross-examination, can make nearly any accused look guilty.

In Lindquist's final argument to the jury, he set his theme. As he saw it, this was a case in which two people decided to defy the law and to violently resist arrest, all the while trumpeting their religious belief of hatred. He wrote the word HATRED in large red letters on the courtroom chart. Lindquist argued that the Weavers had intentionally brought on this confrontation with the government because they believed that otherwise Armageddon would not come to pass. No evidence supporting that statement ever appeared in the case.

David Nevin made a careful but powerful argument for Kevin Harris. He took more than two hours to examine the facts, one at a time, and to uncover in clear language the falsehoods that made up the government's case. Nevin closed with one of George Washington's arguments: "Government is not reason. It is force. Like fire, it's a dangerous servant of a fearful master."

I could feel my own fear preparing me for my final argument. What if I got lost in the tangle of facts we'd heard over three months of trial? What if I was too old, too tired, too shattered after months of war to convince the jury? I'd argued the case on the outskirts of sleep all night. What if I failed this poor man? What if his wife and son died for naught, and they hauled Randy off to prison to rot for the rest of his life in some vile concrete hole? Who would raise his kids? I thought of little Rachel. I thought of Elisheba, who was cradled in her mother's arms when her mother died.

I spoke to twelve folks whom I'd come to know although we'd never exchanged the first word. I told the jury the truth. "Since my argument starts with me, I ought to tell you how I feel," I said. "I feel afraid. I feel inadequate. I wish I were a better lawyer than I am right now."

I turned to the man on the far left of the front row. He often smiled at me. I needed a friendly smile. I said, "May we all agree that government agents are bound by the law the same as we? They're bound by the same morals and by the same justice and decency as we? May we agree that government agents can't lie and say it's all right because they're officers? And they can't come into court and play hide-and-seek with the facts and say that's all right because they're federal employees.

"And they can't persecute people and they can't entrap people, and they can't state the wrong law, and they can't use their huge forces and their power simply because they are federal officers. And they can't turn what began as a piddly two-bit case, one they manufactured themselves, into a major case in which they expended millions of taxpayers' dollars because they are federal officers.

"And they can't attack us simply because of our religious or our political beliefs. And they can't come into Idaho from Washington, D.C., and claim that Idaho law is null and void, like Mr. Rogers, the head of the task force, did, and say 'I am the law,' simply because they're federal officers.

"We have three people dead—Sammy Weaver shot in the back, a little boy whose voice hadn't even changed, and Mr. Lindquist says nothing about it. Killing him was like putting on your pants in the morning. Nobody seems concerned that Sammy Weaver was shot in the back and murdered. No investigation. Nobody charged. What's going on here?

"We have Vicki Weaver shot in the head. Nobody seems to care. Killing is like putting on your shirt in the morning. No investigation. Nobody's charged. Nobody seems to care. Now, what is this all about?

"We have Kevin Harris shot. We have Randy Weaver shot. What is happening?

"And so if you are the federal government, what do you do? Do you come up to His Honor and say, 'Judge, we're sorry, we killed Vicki Weaver, and we shouldn't have,' and do you go over to the judge again and say, 'We're sorry, we killed Sammy, shot him in the back, and we shouldn't have'? What do you do?

"Well, instead, you charge Randy Weaver with everything you can imagine. And then you send the FBI out, and you do what psychologists call *demonize* him, to make the people of the state of Idaho hate Randy Weaver, to despise him because of his religious beliefs or his political positions. If you can demonize him in the press so when the jury is brought together every one of the jurors has read something about him and distrusts and hates him because he's been called a Nazi and a member of the Aryan Nations and a far right kook and cultist, if you can charge him with the murder of a federal officer and charge him with all of those other charges and counts, then maybe you, the government, won't have to answer why Sammy Weaver was shot dead in the back and his mother shot dead in the face.

"Now, you saw that happen in the courtroom not more than a few hours ago. You saw Mr. Lindquist put up a chart. By the way, Mr. Lindquist, I understand you don't have the chart anymore, is that right?" (During the recess I had asked Lindquist for the chart, and he said he no longer had it.)

Lindquist replied, "I have it."

"May I have it, please?" I asked him.

"I'm going to use it when I rebut this, as you well know."

"I have a right to see the chart, and I would like to have you bring it up here so that I can answer it."

Judge Lodge settled the matter. "The chart should be produced, but you shouldn't write on it. It is Mr. Lindquist's product."

Lindquist produced the chart, the one that had HATRED written across it in large red letters.

As I argued I pointed at the chart. "What is the relevance of whether somebody has an Aryan Nations belt buckle? What is the relevance about a child whose head is shaved, Mr. Grider's little boy? These are people who said Mr. Weaver was their friend. Mr. Weaver wore an Aryan Nations belt buckle and his head was shaved? You met the little boy when he stood up here, and I said to Mr. Grider, 'Is this your son?' And he said, 'Yes.' And I said, 'Are you proud of him?' And he said, 'You bet I am.'

"What is the relevance, ladies and gentlemen, of hauling in the ammunition, piles of it, but they don't bring in the honey and the wheat and the canned goods and the supplies and the clothing? I mean, what's the relevance of telling about the firearms when they are all legal, all fourteen of them? I bet there are people on this jury who own fourteen guns, or who have in their past. I'd hate to have the ATF come look in all my closets. But if they hauled them out in the courtroom and laid them out here, it might make you distrust me.

"What's the relevance of talking about the Weavers' position that the government is satanic, but in the next breath admitting that it's all right to believe whatever you believe? A lot of people think the government is satanic. As Mr. Nevin said, George Washington thought the government was satanic.

"What's the purpose of talking about their religious beliefs? Why? Randy isn't the sweetest-looking guy I've ever seen—excuse me, Randy—but I've seen more innocent-looking fellows, but he is entitled to his beliefs."

I turned to one of the most attentive women jurors in the back row. "Suppose the government brought in all your kitchen knives and laid them down, paring knife, cleaver, butcher knife, other knives, all across the floor. Some your kids gave you, some are dull and you can't use, some you use every day. And then they began to tell the world about your witchery, your crazy beliefs. Don't hold her beliefs against her—you mustn't do that—but we want to tell you about them anyway. You heard me object, and I pounded the table about it, and they continued to say, we will tie it in, it's 'inextricably entwined.' You heard that until you must have come home and said to your spouse, 'Darling, you and I are inextricably entwined.'" Some jurors laughed.

"They put an evil twist on everything—there wasn't a thing that Randy Weaver did that was decent and right, not *one* thing. And when they opened their case they began by telling you about all of the people in the Aryan Nations that he knew. No evidence came in on that, but they told you about it.

"They showed you Mrs. Weaver's little letters, which I thought were pretty gutsy. And I wish I had known her. If she were standing here today I would put my arms around her, and I would tell her how much I loved her. I think that this world could use more people who are no longer afraid of the government.

"So, ladies and gentlemen, the theme in this case is to make Randy Weaver into an ugly, hateful, spiteful person so that they can cover the murder of a little boy shot in the back, and the murder of a woman shot in the head. That is the theme.

"Now, somebody has to say no to this. I can't do it. The only thing I can do is ask you to do it. You have more power than His Honor, and I don't know many people who've got more power than His Honor. You've got a lot more power than Mr. Lindquist and Mr. Howen. You've got a lot more power than the Federal Bureau of Investigation and the ATF. You've got more power than the marshals. You've got more power than anybody *because you can say no.*

"And not only that, but *every one of you* has that power, *each* of you *individually,* because the verdict has to be unanimous. So any one of you can say no and that is the end of the government's case. When you heard Mr. Nevin talk about George Washington and his desire to set up a federal government so you wouldn't have to be afraid of it, that's why our founders gave you that power, and that's why you are so special.

"Now, after you kill a little boy at the Y, how do you arrange to cover this up? You would do just what they did. You would tell the Hostage Rescue Team half a story. Do you remember I asked Mr. Rogers on cross-examination, 'Were you told about the Weavers being an Aryan Nations white supremacist cult?' 'Yes.' 'And that they killed a U.S. Marshal?' 'Yes.' 'And that they fired indiscriminately?' 'Yes.' 'And they were heavily armed?' 'Yes.' 'And highly dangerous?' 'Yes.'

"And they said the place was full of—you remember—booby traps. There weren't any booby traps, and the marshals knew it—kids and dogs must have been very smart kids and dogs to live there day in and day out without setting off some alleged booby trap. Please!

"But the Hostage Rescue Team was told that the house was armed with booby traps. We saw the marshals' surveillance tapes taken before the marshals shot the dog—hours of tapes showing little kids flying around on their bicycles and the old dog wagging his tail, and the people walking and living all over that little place up there, and yet the Hostage Rescue Team was told there were booby traps.

"The Hostage Rescue Team was getting excited, because they finally had a war. They could bring in their helicopters and their snipers, and they could have themselves a big war up in northern Idaho. In August. Get out of hot Washington, D.C.

"They were told that this man was a Green Beret and he had explosives training, and that his wife, Vicki Weaver, was crazy, and would kill her children—do you remember that? Likely the word was that Randy Weaver wouldn't surrender as long as Vicki Weaver was in control.

"So did they tell the Hostage Rescue Team the truth? Did they say, 'These marshals shot the dog and then they shot the boy in the back'? Degan was shot by somebody, and we're not sure who shot Degan. Kevin and Sammy were just walking down the trail. They weren't wanted for anything. They committed no crime. They'd done nothing. The marshals were hiding, and the marshals were in camouflage. Did they say that? No. They said the marshals were 'ambushed' by Randy Weaver and Kevin

Harris. They didn't say that Randy Weaver wasn't even around where the shooting took place.

"The Hostage Rescue Team? Who were *hostages* up there, after all? That's what they call themselves, the Hostage Rescue Team, which are nice words for 'trained, expert killers.'

"What Mr. Rogers told you—that federal law supersedes state law, that federal law sits on top of state law—is wrong and he knows it." I read to the jury the court's Instruction 40: *Federal law as governs the conduct of federal officers, so far as the law of self-defense is concerned, does not supersede the law of the State of Idaho.*

"We proved that the feds lie. Nothing new. The only thing new was that they were caught. What makes government lies so detestable is that these liars are *our* servants, *our* employees. They work for us. But they lie *against* us."

I looked over at Lindquist. He was faking utter boredom, his eyes closed, his head leaning heavily on his hand, his elbow propped against the tabletop. I walked over to his table, clapped my hands loudly at his face, and shouted, "Wake up!"

He jumped.

Some jurors laughed.

"It wasn't Horiuchi who should be charged with murder, but those at the highest echelons of government who were so arrogant that they claimed their power nullified state law, those who brought on the killing of Sammy and Vicki, and the wounding of Kevin and Randy. The big shots were the true killers. But what they received for their killing were fat government pensions.

"Have you ever tried to defend yourself when you're not guilty? The more you defend, the worse you look. But I can defend Randy because we have cross-examined fifty-six witnesses, and after fifty-six of their witnesses testified we haven't called a single witness, because the evidence is that this is a man who has been the victim of a frame-up and whose wife and child were murdered. And I say he has been hurt enough and smeared enough and I don't want him to suffer any more of it!

"And what did Judge Lodge say? 'A defendant has the right to remain silent and never has to prove innocence.' Now, isn't that a blessing that in our country we don't have to prove our innocence? How could we ever prove our innocence? In Nazi Germany you had to prove your innocence.

Nobody would listen to you. Here, if a defendant does not testify, his silence can't be held against him.

"Ladies and gentlemen of the jury, this is a murder case. But the people who committed the murder have not been charged. The people who committed the murder are not here in court.

"Now something horrid is happening here. What is happening in America when the government points not at criminals who are joined in conspiracies like dope dealers, and bankers who join in behind-the-scenes conspiracies and cheat old ladies out of their savings, but the government points its accusing finger at our *families*? The new low in American jurisprudence is to attack the American family and to charge that the American family can now be guilty of a conspiracy because they are a *family*.

"The indictment here alleges that Randy and Vicki, including some 'other members of the Weaver family,' were in on the conspiracy. Does the little child Rachel enter the conspiracy? They saw her coming out with her gun. I suppose Rachel, now as she tries to protect her daddy, is a conspirator. All those people are now guilty of a conspiracy to kill Degan? So, be careful, because if you have a family you could be guilty of a conspiracy. Big Brother will be listening!

"One other thing that I can't let go unsaid—the business of calling this little house a *compound*. Now, is that a compound up there? Roderick fights to the end to call it a compound. Cooper, too. The FBI people want to call it a compound. Why? Because if you kill them in the compound it's all right, but if you kill them in their little house it might not be all right. Those are the kinds of demonizing uses of language we've encountered.

"The government had even charged Randy with shooting at a helicopter that had Geraldo Rivera in it. They talked big about it but called no witnesses to prove it. The judge dismissed that count. The government, trying to make sure it would get Randy for something, even charged him with being a fugitive from justice who was in possession of weapons. They hauled out all of those guns to shock you. But Randy wasn't a fugitive. The judge dismissed that, too."

I told the jurors that Randy would go to prison for the rest of his life if it would bring back little Sammy and Vicki. "But hasn't he been punished enough? Doesn't this terror, this horror, have to end sometime? Shouldn't you have the courage to stand up and say no?"

And with that I left Randy's case in the hands of those twelve good citizens.

The government always gets the last word in a criminal case. When I sat down I would be silenced forever before this jury. Lindquist struggled with the facts, and I thought him best in the last minutes of his argument. Here is what he said:

"The statement was made that Randall Weaver would go to the penitentiary for life to get his boy back and his wife back. Well, I will tell you there is a wife and two boys who would give most anything they have to get their dad back." He was, of course, referring to the Degan family.

*T*he jury marched wearily out to deliberate. The lives of the Weavers had once been in the hands of government agents. Now those who had survived would be in the hands of twelve jurors who had never met Vicki or Sammy or, before this trial, Kevin and Randy. The system had been sorely tested over months. Would the system work to acquit the innocent?

The jury deliberated for twenty-three days. Jurors got sick. Jurors argued and fought. They formed alliances on certain issues and subgroups on others. Some couldn't sleep. Some slept during deliberations. They weren't allowed any outside contacts. Their newspapers were censored for any stories about the case. One woman was about to have a baby.

The juror who'd been smiling at me all along and who I thought believed I was on the right side of the case turned out to be the foreman. Later I discovered how wrong I could be in judging members of my species. He wanted both Kevin and Randy convicted and was smiling about it. After about two weeks of being sequestered with eleven others, he claimed he was sick. The judge called up one of the alternate jurors, and, of course, the jurors had to start their deliberations all over again.

I can't imagine what Randy Weaver and Sara and little Rachel went through, waiting for the jury's verdict. Randy was in jail, alone, and the torture of waiting, of seeing his family taken from him, of realizing he might spend the rest of his days in prison, was a horror that must have clung to his belly like an eternal, unbearable cramp.

The jury's twenty-three-day-long deliberations were the longest I'd ever heard of. How did we survive the wait? We visited our clients in jail. We could give them little solace and no answers as to why the jury was out so long. We tried to prepare them for the worst. If they were convicted we would appeal, of course.

To stay sane we took trips into the backcountry of Idaho. Gary Gilman—a fine photographer—and I took many photographs. The team ate together and spent long evenings together. We talked and tried to laugh away our fears. We held each other up emotionally. Yet to this day we've never had the first understanding of the pain our clients endured during the wait. At last, on July 8, 1993, the jury returned its verdict. They acquitted Kevin Harris of all wrongdoing, and he walked out of the courtroom free, holding on to his great and faithful lawyer, David Nevin.

The jury acquitted Randy Weaver of all charges except his failure to appear on the charge of sawing off that shotgun. After four years of sneaking, peeking, lying—after all their killing and wounding, and the expenditure of millions of dollars—the government had only been able to convict Randy Weaver of failing to appear in court.

Randy Weaver's trial gave America the opportunity to see the criminal justice system as it was then and, in all relevant ways, as it is today, and that painful gift will give him entry into whatever pearly gates may exist. I can see him one day up there pounding away, smoking and hollering to be let in.

"Open up the fucking door," I can hear him hollering. He is who he is. He is real. He has courage. Perhaps too much. But he is a true American hero.

After the verdict, Howen came alive again. He wanted Randy sent off for three more years in prison for his failure to appear on the gun charge. I responded, "The only evidence the court needs to consider is that this family needs their daddy." I asked the judge to give Randy credit for the fourteen months he'd already served in jail after he came down from Ruby Ridge and until the jury's verdict. The judge gave him four months more, then released him to go home to reconstruct his life and to care for his children.

The Justice Department called for an investigation, summoned a lot of witnesses, and then blamed Howen for "faulty judgment and overzealousness." There was a congressional investigation as well. You can predict that not one person in authority, not one member of Congress—*not one*—ever suggested that criminal charges should be filed against those who killed Sammy and lied about it. Nor did those at the highest echelons of the FBI—those who nullified the law and turned Horiuchi loose on Randy, Kevin, and finally Vicki—breathe a word of condemnation against their own killer. Power, then and now, dictates the law, not the people.

We sued the government for the death of Sammy and Vicki. But Power didn't want the additional publicity that such a suit would reveal to America. The government offered the surviving children $1 million each, $3 million in all, and Randy $100,000. Randy and the family didn't want to reenter that hellish landscape for another protracted trial. The family took the offer.

*S*o what is there to say about the case?

It exposed the rotten underbelly of Power. It demonstrated the massive bravery that ordinary citizens can possess against the gigantic muscle of government. It identified a caring and courageous member of the judiciary—Judge Lodge—and equally courageous jurors who made the system work despite its frailties. It revealed trial lawyers at their best, who, no matter the cost, were willing to fight for justice until they dropped. And it provided the faint hope that occasionally justice prevails in America, the whole truth being that it fails most of our citizens most of the time.

It proved a truth that persists to this moment: that too many police will kill at will—even a child running home, even a mother armed only with her nursing babe. And it proved that Power will attempt to cover its own crimes.

No one was ever convicted for the murders at Ruby Ridge. That massacre proved that the Constitution can be set aside by Power at its whim, that the FBI could, and did, change the law as if it, not the people, created the laws of the land. If the United States, through its agencies, can garner sharpshooters, armies of hundreds, tanks, helicopters, and the forces to support them, and if they can change the law so that killing our citizens is foreordained when their opponents are but two wounded, dying men, three little girls, and their mother dead on the kitchen floor, their small brother dead in the shack behind the house—what more need be revealed of the crushing, mindless forces of Power?

Should we provide a name for such Power? Are we on the outer edges of the cliff looking down into the depths of a totalitarian state from which there is no return?

America does not provide enough well-trained lawyers to ensure that most accuseds will be afforded the kind of trial that Randy and Kevin were provided. A senseless murder of a small boy and his mother by their own government attracted a dedicated team of pro bono lawyers who laid it all down for the poor, the lost, the innocent, and the damned. The killing of our families by trigger-happy government agents is too high a price for a citizen's chance at justice.

I praise those who praise America. They embrace the hope of our forefathers. As the old refrain goes, "Hope springs eternal." Without hope, and the courage to fight for our dreams of freedom, we will have fallen over the precipice. We cannot limit justice to only those cases in which the entry fee is the murder of our families. The Weaver case demanded change. It demanded that we remain vigilant and dedicated to restoring America to the land of the free and the home of the brave.

But nothing has changed.

THE SECRET LIES OF THE FBI

Brandon Mayfield was a lawyer just getting by. He looked like a forlorn professor with his beard and glasses, and he wasn't the kind who sprayed large quantities of charisma around. He worked in his smallish rented law office west of downtown Portland, Oregon. Mona, his wife, was born in Egypt—that turned out to be her greatest sin—but she had an open, winning personality and acted as his secretary. The two of them likely would have toiled in obscurity helping immigrants and the poor if not for a series of events that began across the globe in Madrid, Spain, on March 11, 2004.

That morning a group of terrorists, now thought to be related to Al Qaeda, set off a series of coordinated bombings on the Madrid commuter train system that killed 191 people outright and wounded 1,800 others. The Internet images that made their way around the world were of bloody, mutilated body after body laid next to one another in a straight line that stretched for nearly two city blocks, each waiting its turn to be identified, tagged, and hauled away.

A wounded mother, half naked and too shocked to weep, holding her dead baby in her arms, the tiny corpse emptying its blood on the pavement . . . the screams of the injured, the moans of the dying, the hollering of ambulance drivers, the police shouting orders, and sirens crying . . . the crazy cacophony of chaos and death—the doors of hell had been blown wide open. Brandon Mayfield, along with millions of others, read about the bombing in the morning paper. "Horrible. What's happening in this world?" he thought. Then he poured himself another cup of coffee.

The Spanish police lifted fingerprints from a blue plastic bag that had once contained the detonators for the bomb, and they promptly submitted digital photographs of the fingerprints to Interpol, an organization of police from 190 countries that cooperate in solving international crime. When the Latent Print Unit of the FBI received the print from Interpol, an agent turned to the FBI's Integrated Automated Fingerprint Identification System (IAFIS) for help. The FBI claims its computer stores the largest biometric database in the world and houses the fingerprints and criminal histories of more than 70 million subjects in its criminal master file, along with more than 34 million prints of civilians. Included in its criminal database are fingerprints "from 73,000 known and suspected terrorists."* The FBI's computer automatically performs searches for the print in question by optically scanning the submitted print and comparing it with those in its files. This computer has eyes.

The FBI gave the Spanish fingerprint an unpretentious name—"Latent Fingerprint #17" (LFP 17 for short)—and on March 15, 2004, the FBI's computer dutifully listed twenty candidates as possible matches. Brandon Mayfield was on the computer's list—ranked the fourth most likely to match the print on the blue plastic bag. The computer also told the FBI that Brandon was thirty-eight years old, a former U.S. Army officer with an honorable discharge, and a practicing Oregon lawyer, and that he had never been convicted of any crime and had not been outside the United States since 1993, when he, his wife, and three children visited Mansoura, Egypt, Mona's place of origin.

One thing we know, and we know it because we've been taught it since we were old enough to watch cop movies on TV: The agents of the FBI are honorable, supercompetent men who keep us safe, and no loyal American would doubt a fingerprint identification made by the FBI. I was taught that in law school, and I took careful notes: "If an FBI expert testifies that the fingerprint on the murder weapon belongs to your client, well, it belongs to your client. Period." It hurts me to now report that our belief in the infallibility of the FBI's fingerprint experts has been little more than a cultural lie.

Once the fingerprint computer identifies an initial list of subjects, human eyes take over for a closer evaluation. Agent Alfred, a senior fingerprint examiner, concluded that Brandon's *left* index fingerprint matched LFP 17, the fingerprint on the blue plastic bag. That erroneous identification was confirmed when the FBI, following its protocol, submitted the print for

---

* From the IAFIS page at www.fbi.gov/about-us/cjis/fingerprints-biometrics/iafis/iafis.

verification to Mr. Smart, a so-called independent fingerprint examiner. Mr. Smart had once been an employee of the FBI, but for reasons not clear on the record, he'd left the Bureau and was thereafter hired on a contract basis to do fingerprint examinations. During his term as an FBI employee, Smart had been reprimanded on at least three occasions concerning his work in fingerprint identification.

When a tragedy of errors gets rolling, its momentum is hard to stop. Had the FBI given even a passing, competent squint to the photo furnished by the Spanish police, it would have been obvious from the relative position of all the prints on the blue plastic bag that LFP 17 could *not* have come from Mr. Mayfield's left index finger. Moreover, there were but a few points of similarity between 17 and Mayfield's print—not enough for any qualified agent to declare a match, not to mention the important dissimilarities such as interruptions in what the experts call the "ridge flow." That's how an innocent American citizen can one day wake up facing the death penalty as a mass murderer. And *what's* your lawyer going to say when the FBI expert slowly turns his sad smile on the jurors and tells them that the fingerprint belongs to you?

External factors were also in play. Not only was Mona born Muslim, she had convinced her Baptist husband to convert to Islam—by 2004 a virtual crime in itself in the eyes of many Americans. What's more, the FBI was still feeling the lash of its 9/11 failures. Solving the Madrid bombing in record time could restore the FBI's tarnished luster in the eyes of the public and loosen Congress's purse strings for the Bureau.

On March 20, 2004, the FBI issued its formal report proclaiming to the world that print 17 belonged to Brandon Mayfield. That splendid bit of FBI science transformed a loyal American, husband and father and ethical lawyer with a spotless record, into a member of an international conspiracy that was responsible for the mass murders in Madrid.

But the Spanish police provided their report to the FBI. They advised the Bureau that they'd compared print LFP 17 to Brandon's, and their conclusion was *no match*. How dare a cluster of cops from a minor member of the European Union like Spain contest the match made by the FBI, the world's ultimate authority on fingerprint identification? In fact, a unit supervisor chief in the Latent Print Unit of the FBI, Stephen Meagher, once testified that in the entire history of fingerprint examination the FBI had never made a misidentification in a court case. He said *never*.

Still, the Spanish no-match report caused serious reverberations at the

FBI. A "false positive" fingerprint identification could result in the revocation of the professional licenses held by the erring FBI examiners and could even lead to a revocation of the American Society of Crime Laboratory Directors certification of the FBI itself. And this Mayfield mess could bring on a congressional investigation that might fracture the FBI's credibility worldwide.

Worse still, in the two years before the Madrid bombings, lawyers had mounted challenges in several federal courts claiming that fingerprint examination as a science did not meet the evidentiary standards required by the United States Supreme Court in a case referred to as *Daubert*. The very reputation of fingerprint analysis itself was at stake. The FBI couldn't risk public embarrassment, and despite having been officially told by the Spanish that 17 was not a match to Brandon Mayfield, the FBI continued to insist its Mayfield print match was correct.

Am I saying the FBI was willing to convert an innocent American citizen into an international terrorist, and subject him to the ultimate penalty—*death*—in order to save the jobs of its agents and the reputation of the Bureau itself? Given the right circumstances, might our revered G-men end up sending one of us, an innocent American citizen, to the death house? On April 21, 2004, to shore up this bureaucratic crime, the FBI sent its agents to Madrid to meet with their Spanish counterparts—their mission, to convince the Spanish that the FBI's match was correct. But the Spanish remained steadfast: 17 and Brandon's print were *not a match*, they insisted.

After its erroneous fingerprint match, the FBI made application to a *secret* court created by Congress, the Foreign Intelligence Surveillance Court (FISC). That *secret* court authorized the FBI to place electronic listening devices ("bugs") in the intimate rooms of the Mayfield family home, *and* to make covert "sneak and peek" searches of their house. Soon FBI agents were following the Mayfields and putting their modest home under surveillance. The agents discovered when the kids would be in school and Brandon and Mona off to work at Brandon's law office. Then the agents surreptitiously entered the Mayfield house—in broad daylight. Some of the best lock-pickers in the business are respected members of the FBI. The irony here is that the FBI was about to terrorize innocent American citizens in its proclaimed "war against terror."

History now permits us to watch these G-men at work. See them in the Mayfield home, sneaking, searching, snooping—into the family's private drawers and closets. See them handling the family's most personal posses-sions, copying the kids' computers and hard drives and taking DNA sam-ples from the butts of Mona's Camel cigarettes.

Watch them as they install those tiny microphones under the bed and under the breakfast table and affix taps on their phones. Yes, I hear those who are unwashed in the troubled waters of our times innocently saying, "What's the big deal? I have nothing to hide." Personally, I have everything to hide in the privacy of my home. Animals from rabbits to bears, and birds from wrens to eagles, have nothing to hide. But their hole, their den, their nest, is their private, infinitesimal part of the universe that belongs only to them. Put your hand under an old hen who's sitting on her eggs and see what happens to your hand.

It wasn't long before the Mayfields began to feel something was awry. When they came home, they found their door locks locked in the oppo-site order—the upper lock was now open and the lower lock locked. Then one day the electric clock was half an hour slow. Someone must have turned off the electricity so the house alarms would be disconnected. Nothing seemed to be missing, but Shane, then fourteen, had been reading *1984* and was beginning to believe they'd entered the nightmare world of George Orwell. He shouldn't believe everything he reads, his father advised. They'd committed no crime, except, of course, they did go to the mosque, but they were protected by the Constitution. Mona couldn't sleep. Brandon tried to set her mind at rest. They were blessed in America by the protection of our Constitution.

The Mayfield family began criticizing themselves for their unwarranted paranoia. Just the same, they double-locked their doors at night and found themselves whispering at the dinner table. They wouldn't say anything over the phone, not even the grocery list. They lay at night with their eyes staring at the ceiling, wondering. Worrying. Listening for the smallest of strange sounds.

Then that old, comforting refrain would return. "Forget it. *We have nothing to hide.* There's nothing and nobody out there trying to get us. The demons are only in our minds." But no sooner did they vow to relax than their fear, as pervasive as their breathing, returned. "This constant fear thing is a sure sign of mental illness," Brandon said. "We have to stop this."

A few days later Shane was home with the flu. He heard noises. He looked out the window and saw a man trying to break into the house. Terrorized, he called his mother, but before she arrived the FBI's lookout parked across the street saw her coming, and the agent left before she got there. Brandon and Mona wondered if Shane wasn't suffering from some kind of hallucination attributable to the fever of his flu. Besides, Shane had been reading that chilling Orwell stuff.

During the same time, the FBI secretly entered Brandon's law office, rifled through his confidential client files, installed electronic listening devices, and wiretapped his phone—the once-sacred attorney-client privilege having been cast aside as collateral damage in our supposed "war against terror."

But the European media was about to expose the FBI's botched Mayfield investigation. The Bureau also learned that the *Los Angeles Times* was ready to come out with its story discrediting the FBI's match. The Bureau had to act fast, and it concocted misleading and false affidavits in order to justify the arrest of Brandon as a "material witness." An FBI investigator submitted an affidavit to a sitting federal judge in Portland. This affidavit reiterated that the three previous fingerprint experts considered 17 a *"100% positive identification"* of Brandon Mayfield. No mention was made of the fact that the Spanish National Police didn't agree and had so reported to the FBI. Instead, the affidavit claimed that the Spanish National Police "felt satisfied with the FBI laboratory's identification."

These sworn statements from the FBI also focused on Brandon's association with fellow Muslims—as we all know, an activity fully protected under the Constitution. In support of search and arrest warrants, the agent included in his affidavit that Brandon advertised his legal services in a directory from Jerusalem Enterprises, known as the "Muslim Yellow Pages." A cursory look at the website of the "Muslim Yellow Pages" would reveal that major American car rental agencies such as Avis, motel chains such as Best Western, and airlines such as United also advertised on this site. In their searches of the Mayfield residence, the agents had even seized one of the children's homework for Spanish class, which the FBI offered as proof of Mayfield's connection to Spain.

On May 6, 2004, Brandon Mayfield was arrested as a "material witness" and hauled off to the Multnomah County Detention Center, a euphemism for jail. There he found himself imprisoned with the usual collection of drunks, dope dealers, felons, and crazies. It was as if he'd stepped into the pages of Kafka's *The Trial,* having awakened to discover that he'd been charged with a crime he did not commit, the nature of which was never revealed to him, and that some impersonal, unidentified authority had taken control of his life.

Mona remembers, "I was about to prepare my husband's lunch when two FBI agents knocked on our door. I was vacuuming. I thought it was the mailman." She said the agents sat her down at her dining room table and began ransacking her house. "I left everything as they left it. I didn't have the strength to clean up the mess."

On May 20, Brandon was still in prison garb staring out from behind bars, still caged with the desperate and degenerate, a man dazed and confused by a nightmare from which he could not awaken.

He was a mass murderer?

The presiding judge in Portland's federal court thought something must be seriously awry. Mayfield, a solid, ethical member of the Oregon bar, had traveled to Spain and was somehow involved in an international conspiracy to kill innocent Spanish people? The judge needed convincing before he would issue a warrant for Brandon's arrest.

No problem. The FBI brought in one of its noted fingerprint experts, who proceeded to show the judge the comparisons and assured him there was a solid match. Having no expertise of his own, the judge, like jurors in untold thousands of cases over scores of years, had to accept the word of that institution's expert. The judge reluctantly issued the warrant.

Brandon Mayfield was as good as dead. By trial time the jury would have been soaked in a downpour of media concerning the Madrid bombing. The stories would spare no words describing the blood and horror, and how Brandon, with his Muslim connections, had been irrefutably connected to this mass murder when the FBI identified his fingerprint on the blue plastic bag. He would be given a media nickname, something like "the Muslim Bomber." Would the government really need a trial?

The FBI's fingerprint expert would take the stand. Jurors know the FBI never errs in fingerprint identification. The testifying agent's manners are impeccable. Of course, he's been chosen by the FBI to testify in this case because, over the years, he's become such a powerful presence on the witness stand that the government always wins in his cases. Occasionally he smiles that trademark small sad smile at one of the women—one of the motherly type.

"Yes," he says as a plain matter of fact, "this print belongs to Brandon Mayfield."

"Will you identify Mr. Mayfield for the jury, please?" the assistant U.S. attorney asks.

"Yes, of course," and the FBI expert points at Brandon. "He's there at counsel table, the gentleman with the beard and glasses who is sitting next to his lawyer." The jurors turn and stare at Brandon to see what his reaction will be. Brandon stares back at the FBI man. What else can he do? If he jumps up and hollers, "You're lying," the judge will throw him in jail for contempt. If he says nothing, the jury wonders how he can be so cool, so unmoved by the agent's damning testimony. If he silently shakes his head in denial, well, that's what every guilty man would do.

Soon the FBI expert puts up those huge enlargements of Brandon's print alongside print 17, and with a pointer he shows the jury the ridges and the valleys and the jumps and the gaps, and after he's finished there's little doubt in anyone's mind that that print belongs to that man sitting over there staring at the jury.

"Mean-looking bastard," the reporter from the *L.A. Times* whispers to his counterpart from the *San Francisco Chronicle*.

"Yeah. Those Muslims are like that."

Brandon can't afford the price of a famous defense attorney. Their home is mortgaged. He no longer has any income from his little law office. He's worse than broke. His family needs every penny he can beg or borrow to live on. The public defender is his only hope. And the public defender is no match for the assistant U.S. attorney who's been specially selected for this once-in-a-lifetime international case. Of course, Brandon's public defender will put on a fingerprint expert of his own, but his expert will be a retired police officer from somewhere who got his own training from the FBI and whose testimony can't stand up to the impeccable competence of the government's expert witness.

At last the jury is shown photos of the twisted, bloody body parts and the stacks of the dead from the bombing. The photos are in color and so graphic the jurors almost retch. The jurors look over at Brandon. He is stoic as usual. His face reveals nothing. Then the jury hears about his connection to certain Muslims. He once represented a convicted Muslim terrorist. He's advertised in Muslim publications. He goes to the mosque and is a recent convert. He is obviously part of that dangerous worldwide hate group.

When Brandon takes the stand to testify he's still his stoic, unemotional self. As human and loving as Brandon is, he's laced with fear as he sits up there on the witness stand trying to defend himself. He denies any connection to the bombing. He only represented the convicted Muslim terrorist in a child custody case, and that was before he knew anything about his client's connection to Al Qaeda. He was never in Madrid or anywhere else except home when this all occurred.

The government prosecutor pounds him mercilessly on cross-examination.

"Where were you on the day of the bombing?" the prosecutor demands.

"I don't keep track of my days. I had no need to."

"You're claiming you don't know?"

"I was at home as usual. I was at my office, I was . . ."

"I suppose your wife and kids will testify to that," the prosecutor says, "and you want us to believe them."

"Yes."

"I suppose that one of your Muslim clients can tell us where you were on that day?"

The prosecutor extends a long knowing look to the jurors. The more Brandon protests the charges, the deeper he sinks into the morass from which he is trying to extricate himself. It's like someone being thrown into quicksand and trying to struggle his way out.

And what if Brandon doesn't take the stand? Then the jurors will later argue that if they'd been charged with such a heinous crime they sure as hell would have taken the stand. They would have *nothing to hide,* and they'd fight to tell the jury and the world the whole truth. They'd never hide behind the Fifth Amendment, not for a damned minute! "But this Mayfield—you saw him. He just sat there staring out at everyone."

And don't forget. We are engaged in a "war on terror." Good Americans called to jury duty will do their job and vote to convict the accused if there is any reasonable evidence to support such a verdict. They know going in that the prosecutors wouldn't bring the case if the case weren't just. And the defense attorney? Their kind defend the Manson types and try to make them look like Mother Teresa's baby brother. Good Americans have to protect their families and their neighbors from these terrorists. If jurors won't protect themselves, and the rest of us, who will? And thank God for the selfless service the FBI provides America. God bless the FBI.

Later, I asked Brandon why he hadn't produced the records in his office that would prove where he was when the bombing took place. His answer echoed what I've heard time and again from those feeling the full weight of Power's bootheel. "True, I hadn't been out of the country since 1993," Brandon said. "But why would they listen to me? I was the terrorist. And I was terrorized. I couldn't believe this was happening in America. My public defender was afraid they were going to send me to Guantánamo, and I was more worried about Mona and the kids than anything. What would happen to them? And they were rifling through my confidential client files. No lawyer can permit that. Yet I couldn't stop them."

Mona was afraid not only for Brandon but for herself and her family. They weren't safe, even behind the locked doors of their home. And they didn't have a husband and father to protect them. All she could tell her children was that it would all work out, their daddy didn't do anything wrong, there'd been a terrible mistake. But she knew that the real mistake was that they were Muslims. And she knew that the ringing guarantee in the Constitution that Americans are free to worship as they please had crumbled around them. Nothing in the Constitution would save her husband. Or her. Or their children.

Then the Spanish police—not the FBI, not the Department of Justice, not our courts or judges or jurors, not even our sacred Constitution—saved Brandon Mayfield. On May 19, 2004, the Spanish National Police advised the world that they had matched the fingerprint on the blue plastic bag to an Algerian, Ouhnane Daoud. Like the proverbial culprit caught with his hand in the cookie jar, the FBI quietly, in a soft international mumble, admitted that its fingerprint identification of Brandon Mayfield was in error, and, incredibly, the FBI then stated that LFP 17 was "of no value for identification purposes."

No value?

No value.

And Brandon was released.

How had Brandon's false arrest affected the Mayfield children? Shane, fourteen, the Mayfields' oldest, had been waiting for his mom to pick him up after school. He remembers his mother coming toward him with tears in her eyes, a sight he'd rarely seen. "Your dad's been arrested by the FBI," she said.

At first Shane didn't believe it, but his mom kept crying as they drove to Sharia's school to pick her up. Shane went in to get her and shared the news: "Dad's been arrested by the FBI." At first Sharia thought it was a joke, but when she saw the truth in Shane's eyes she, too, started crying.

When they got home the doors to the house were wide open, swinging in the wind. The first thing Shane saw was sticky notes with foreign handwriting on them—one on the exhaust fan in the kitchen and one in each of the other rooms in the house, labeling each room. The place looked as if a cyclone had hit it. They found the cats locked in the closet.

"My life had been so normal," Shane said. "I couldn't believe it could get so weird, so fast." He went up to his room. He'd saved his old homework and shoved all the papers in a cabinet underneath the TV—a stack of papers seven or eight inches high. Now his homework was thrown across the floor. On the other side of the room, his soccer shoes and his shin guards were on the floor where they'd been dumped out of his soccer bag. The cops had even taken his computers and hard drives.

Later that evening Shane looked through the blinds of his room and saw the lights and the television trucks. The phones were ringing, and his mom was outside, trying to talk to the press. That weekend his friend Abdul called and said, "It's a good thing you didn't come to school on Friday because things got really hot about what happened." Shane said he was afraid to go back to class. "Who out there was going to believe that my dad was innocent and not a terrorist?" He remembered a visual from one of the television stations that had MADRID BOMBING in red blood dripping down a yellow screen.

A few days later, when Shane returned to school, he worried that someone would beat him up and that his grades would be affected. His Spanish teacher asked for his homework, and he said, "I don't have it, it's been confiscated." The whole class was staring at him. Shane thought, "Everybody who ever liked me is thinking, 'Man, that guy's related to a terrorist.'"

In his literature class the kids started asking him questions. The teacher just listened and looked on. It embarrassed and scared him. The more he tried to argue that his father was innocent, and presumed so under the Constitution, the more kids argued against it. The FBI wouldn't arrest an innocent person. How do you argue against that?

Shane told me that suddenly he found himself the man of the house, and he didn't know how to comfort his mother and the two younger kids. His mom was brave, but the family was panicked. What if they killed their father? What if they had to move out of their house? What if they didn't have enough money to eat? If they could take his dad, who was innocent, they could take his mom, too, Shane thought. Both his dad and mom were Muslims. Maybe the FBI would kill them all. He remembered going to their law office with his mother and seeing a footprint on the tabletop. He'd looked at the place where the phone lines were and saw duct tape around the wires.

The worst was when he visited his father in jail. "I was sitting in a room with a lot of people I didn't normally sit with. It felt creepy. They gave us an alias. Then a police officer would call us in. When it was our time to go it was like, 'Mr. Taylor's visitors'—and, oh, yeah, that's us, the Taylors." The family was led to the far end of the visiting booth, where they could see his father, in chains, standing behind the door. Then the guards led his father in on the other side of the bulletproof glass that separated them, and Shane thought, "I'll never be able to touch him again. He's going to prison for life. And they'll probably kill him."

When he saw his father, he said to himself, "Suck it up, Shane. Dad can't see you like this." Shortly the guard came in and said, "Time's up." Shane put his fist up to the window and his father put his fist up to the window.

Shane was in math class when he got a phone call at the principal's office from his mother. The good news: His father was out of jail and was home. He said, "I was so happy, but when I got home Dad still had that really concentrated look on his face because he was under house arrest."

"What's going to happen, Dad?" Shane asked.

"They are going to put me on trial. But don't worry. The jury will find me innocent."

*B*randon contacted me through a mutual friend, Michele Longo Eder, one of America's great women lawyers. He wanted me to represent him against the U.S. government for the devastation he and his family suffered at its hands—the hands of their own government. I invited him to come to Wyoming to tell me his story, and he did, this serious-looking young lawyer with the hurt in his eyes and the weight of the world sitting on his slumped shoulders.

As I listened to Brandon I began to wonder: How could any person fully recover from such a lethal attack? He'd been falsely accused by his own government of unimaginable crimes he did not commit and threatened with death for their commission. He'd been helpless to prove his innocence and was teetering on the edge of both emotional and actual extinction at the hands of the FBI, an institution created to protect him and his family that had betrayed them instead.

Michele Longo Eder and I decided to bring in a leading Oregon lawyer who knew what to do in cases in which critical, abstruse issues of law were embedded, a man who could find his way around the Oregon court system like a hound dog at home, Elden Rosenthal. We three filed suit for the Mayfield family members against the individual FBI agents as well as the U.S. attorney general, John Ashcroft. Why didn't we sue the FBI? Under law, we citizens are not permitted to sue our government. The only recourse is to sue the individuals our government employs and hope the federal judge will allow the case to go to a jury.

Our team wanted simple justice for an innocent father and for the pain his innocent family had suffered. But Brandon wanted his and the family's suffering to stand for something more than money damages. He wanted the so-called Patriot Act to be declared unconstitutional since it permits the government to accomplish its clandestine invasions into our private lives without first demonstrating that *probable cause* exists that the subject of such secret surveillance has committed a crime. Probable cause has always been the bedrock of our protection against a police state in America.

On April 7, 2005, Dan Eggen of the *Washington Post* wrote:

> The Justice Department is acknowledging for the first time that the FBI used a secret search warrant to copy and seize material—including DNA samples—from the home of Brandon Mayfield, a Portland, Ore., man who was wrongly arrested and jailed last year in connection with the March 2004 train bombings in Madrid.
>
> In statements and testimony this week, Attorney General Alberto R. Gonzales . . . said that some of the special powers used to spy on Mayfield were strengthened by the USA Patriot Act. . . . The department acknowledged that during clandestine searches of his home the FBI made copies of computer drives and documents, and that "ten DNA samples were taken and preserved on cotton swabs and six cigarette butts were seized for DNA analysis." Authorities took approximately 355 digital photographs. . . .
>
> [Mayfield was also] "the target of electronic surveillance and other physical searches authorized pursuant to FISA"—the Foreign Intelligence Surveillance Act, which governs such warrants and was expanded under the Patriot law.
>
> [Representative John] Conyers wrote to Inspector General Glenn A. Fine yesterday that "it is a frightening prospect that an innocent person can have his home secretly searched, his DNA secretly taken and stored

and his computer files raided by the federal government. Now the Bush administration apparently believes that Mr. Mayfield is not even entitled to know the extent to which his privacy has been invaded."

Our team's Michele Longo Eder was a natural-born ferret and, more than Rosenthal or I, was responsible for the facts we gathered. I remember finding her on her hands and knees facing a mammoth pile of articles spread out on the floor of her office. She missed nothing printed or hinted. She attended a national investigators' conference where the supervisor of the FBI's fingerprint experts was giving a seminar at which he made excuses for the Bureau's wrongful identification of Brandon's fingerprint. Michele was our mole, all right. And daily she was reporting to me.

During the discovery phase in our lawsuit, the government was ordered to furnish us all relevant evidence, which included an e-mail from an unidentified FBI operative dated May 5, 2004, a time *before* the FBI was exposed by the Spanish for its false identification of Brandon's print. The operative wrote:

> There is a man living in the Portland area who has been tied to the Madrid bombing by a fingerprint at the scene. His name is Brandon Mayfield, Muslim convert and attorney. [Note "Muslim convert" comes *before* "attorney."]
>
> Earlier this week, an *LA Times* reporter in the Paris Bureau called the Legat* in Spain, Ed Sanchez, to ask about information the reporter had heard that there was an American tied to the Madrid bombings. At that time, we don't think he had the name or location or the fact that the evidence is a fingerprint.
>
> The problem is there is not enough other evidence to arrest him [Mayfield] on a criminal charge. There is a plan to arrest him as a material witness if and when he gets outed by the media.
>
> Neither the National Press Office nor the Portland Division has received any media calls as of this morning. If you receive a call from the *Times* we would ask whether or not publication is imminent. *The powers that be are trying to hold off as long as possible on any arrest, but they want to make sure an arrest happens before anything hits the media* (my emphasis).

---

* A legat, or legal attaché, is an FBI liaison with a foreign law enforcement or security service.

To complicate things, the Legat just notified Portland that he *and it had the details about the evidence that it said it planned to publish soon* (my emphasis). Thanks for your help.

[Signature blacked out.]

The FBI had just barely beaten the press. Brandon was arrested the next day before anything hit the papers.

*T*he judiciary itself was about to become involved. Yes, *the judges.* Federal judges hang out in high, rare ether free of contamination and are said to be as meticulously honest as nuns at a card game. Even their thoughts are sanitized. In Oregon the selection of a federal judge to try a newly filed case is made randomly by the court clerk's computer. We were fortunate in the Mayfield case. We drew a respected judge, one we had confidence in, Judge Ann Aiken.

But suddenly Judge Aiken was taken off the case by order of the chief judge. A short time later Elden Rosenthal, by mere chance, met Judge Aiken at a joint meeting of the bar and bench. During polite conversation he told her he was sorry she was disqualified to sit on our case. Elden thought perhaps she'd somehow been personally connected to a lawyer or a party in the case—something like that. To his surprise she told Elden she'd been quite willing to sit on the case, but she'd been removed by the chief judge without any reason offered. She said this was happening frequently to her and another woman judge.

Some of the senior federal judges in the district had apparently decided to secretly circumvent the random selection of the computer, leaving us lawyers who practiced before them believing that the random selection of judges was at work as usual.

The chief judge, who'd been calling these behind-the-scenes shots, assigned our case to another senior judge in the circuit; let's call him Judge Smith. Judge Smith (whom I had never met) apparently was not overly delighted to see Gerry Spence come tramping into Oregon's federal court system. He told a group of lawyers and judges at a judicial function that Gerry Spence would never be able to get away with the antics and tactics he pulled on Judge Haas in the Sandy Jones murder case, a trial that ended with her acquittal on all charges. Smith had never been in a courtroom with me.

Judge Harl Haas, who sat on the Sandy Jones case, happened to be present when Judge Smith made those public remarks. Judge Haas was offended and immediately advised me of Smith's prejudicial remarks. The above mentioned court rule providing for the random assignment of cases to judges protects both judges and litigants from any suggestion of impropriety. Now, what happens if the chief judge violates that rule with no given reason except that he has the power to do so? The indiscriminate use of such power can lead to abuse. Already two women judges in the circuit were complaining. Moreover, the assignment of a case to a judge who had an advertised adverse attitude toward one of the attorneys, namely me, could dilute one's confidence that an impartial judge was overseeing the trial. That's why the computer did the selection in the first place.

Why did those I perceived as the "good old boys" on the circuit want Judge Aiken off our case? Maybe, in fact, no one wanted her off. But this was a case that would challenge the Patriot Act and would make national news and the law journals. Maybe Judge Smith lobbied the chief judge to give him the case. Maybe not. In any event, for some undisclosed reason he got the case that the computer had assigned to Judge Aiken.

Lawyers have an obligation to protect the judiciary from undue criticism, but that duty does not silence a lawyer when he faces an opposite responsibility. We couldn't take a chance on Judge Smith. Brandon's case was a watershed case that could change the course of the law. We immediately filed a motion that set forth a summary of the facts just stated and demanded the case be returned to Judge Aiken, the lawfully selected judge in our case. Absent such relief we sought the appointment by the Ninth Circuit Court of Appeals of an out-of-district judge to supervise discovery and to hear our motion.

As fast as one could blink a judicial eye, the case was summarily reassigned to Judge Aiken by the chief judge—one of the more timely decisions I've experienced in a federal court. I suppose the chief judge and Judge Smith weren't particularly breathless to have us put them on the witness stand and ask simple questions like "How did Judge Smith get this case when it had been regularly assigned to Judge Aiken? For what reason was this change of judge decided? Name all the judges who took part in this decision. Why was Judge Smith selected? Had he requested the case at any time either before or after its assignment to Judge Aiken? Did you advise Judge Aiken as to why she was removed from the case? By the way, in passing, how often has this sort of thing happened in this jurisdiction before with female judges in the district? And for what reason? And finally, as a judge, what discipline would you suggest against judges who violate their own rules in such a case as this?"

We were now suing agents of the FBI for having violated the Mayfield family's civil rights. In such cases you usually enter the gates of doom and fight your way across its entire landscape, including years of struggle through endless government tactics, before you can even get to a jury. Many times the courts throw these cases out for reasons excavated from a universe of legalese. But one day the government suddenly wanted to settle our case before we'd gotten much more than started.

"No, we shouldn't settle," Brandon insisted. "This case is more important to America than to us. That so-called Patriot Act lets them break into our homes without a showing of probable cause. That's police state stuff. We're not going to let them buy us off with a settlement. We need the money. But we'll get by somehow." Mona agreed.

But the government was persistent. Through its assistant U.S. attorneys the government said, "So you want to test the constitutionality of the Patriot Act? All right. We'll settle all your damage claims if we can reach an agreeable amount, and you can still contest the constitutionality of the Patriot Act."

"It's because the FBI doesn't want all of their illegal sneaks and peeks made public in a public trial," Rosenthal said. "They like their secret courts. That's why they want to settle." I thought that more important to the FBI was its reputation of infallibility in the supposed science of fingerprint identification. Our case could forever scar that reputation. Yet the government was making a no-lose offer to the Mayfields.

I said, "But if we don't take their offer, and Judge Aiken overrules all of the government's motions and forces the government to trial, the government will appeal her ruling to the Ninth Circuit. That'll take a year. Maybe two. Then if the Ninth Circuit says we can have a trial, we have to get a trial date, which could take a year. Then we have to try the case and win it. And if we win it, the government can appeal that, too. The case could go on for years. Brandon needs money now. This case has ruined his practice. Who'd hire a lawyer who's been in jail as a suspect in a mass murder case? People who are looking for a lawyer don't want to hire one with that kind of baggage."

"And the Ninth Circuit can throw the case out for any reason they can drum up," Michele said, "or for no real reason at all. Then Brandon and

Mona will have lost their chance for what might have been a decent settlement."

"They're buying us off," Brandon said. "The people ought to know what the FBI did to us. The people need to know that it can happen to them."

But Brandon and Mona couldn't make an intelligent decision until they knew what kind of money the government was actually offering. And what were the chances of getting a decision from Judge Aiken that the Patriot Act was unconstitutional? After weeks of negotiations the government finally offered $2 million to Brandon and his family—*and* the government would destroy its documents relating to its electronic surveillance and return all seized physical materials to the Mayfields, and our right to contest the Patriot Act would be fully preserved. Before we agreed, I insisted on one additional demand: The government must publicly apologize to the Mayfields for its wrongful conduct.

The government agreed.

The case was settled.

I was stunned.

The infallible FBI admitted it had been wrong and would apologize. I thought that was pretty good going—the *first* apology from the United States I'd ever heard of, and the only one I've heard of since. For Brandon and Mona, money would not heal wounds to the soul. But money is the only poultice a money system provides. Nothing salves such wounds. Yes, time fades the scars, but the scars are permanent.

We said to the press, "The Patriot Act is decidedly not patriotic, for it is the first step by the Bush Administration to weaken our sacred civil rights to be secure in our homes."

Then one day we found ourselves once more in front of Judge Ann Aiken arguing the constitutionality of the Patriot Act, as was our right under our settlement agreement with the government. I argued to the judge in the same way I would argue to jurors. It's the only way I know how to argue. Yes, I hear it frequently from judges who admonish me, "We are not jurors, Mr. Spence. We are *judges*."

The problem is that more than a few judges think that when they are anointed and ascend to that seat on high, some unidentified power causes their humanness to disappear and replaces it with a brand of lofty judicial insight that one can experience only if one's posterior is affixed to the judge's chair. Once in an empty courtroom I slipped up to the judge's chair and sat down, firmly, and waited and waited. I never felt a bit smarter. Perhaps it was because I hadn't donned the black robe.

I began my argument to Judge Aiken. "This day will enjoy a unique history in this court. We speak as patriots against an act which asserts by its title that if we are not willing to give up our sacred constitutional rights we are *not* patriots." Judge Aiken looked bored. I hoped it was her defensive look—she was a judge, remember, not a juror.

I let the full power of my voice come rolling out, and I spoke the truth. "I recall as a boy when we were attacked by the Japanese, and every American made grave sacrifices. Women went to work in the war plants and built ships and planes. We planted Victory Gardens. Gasoline and other essentials were rationed. And a draft of every fit male, not a volunteer army, took our young men into harm's way, and thousands willingly and bravely gave their lives in combat for our freedom.

"Today, in a so-called war against an amorphous enemy called 'terror,' the principal sacrifice we have been asked to give at the altar of fear is our constitutional rights. There has been no showing we are any safer, indeed, that we are as safe today as we were before we delivered, on a platter of fear, our blessed rights to the FBI and the Department of Justice by means of this fraudulently named legislation called 'the Patriot Act.'"

I spoke the underlying truth. "In many respects the people are left in the most fearsome of all conditions—they are left against an enemy they cannot see. Indeed, who would tell them that the enemy *might be their own government*? The so-called Patriot Act is a law that was born of Power, and embraced by a frightened people under the empty promise that they would be safe if they gave up their freedom.

"One day the truth of all of this came to rest in a case we are here to discuss, the case of the Brandon Mayfield family." I gave Brandon's history, the farm boy honorably discharged from the army after serving his country, his marriage to a Muslim, to Mona. "That marriage was his only connection to a foreign power."

I told how the FBI, without a traditional warrant, broke into the Mayfield home like common thieves—sneaking and peeking and pilfering—and how the FBI destroyed the security of that home, planted secret microphones, tapped their phones, and confiscated their computers, even the children's.

I went on to say, "The fruits of this despotic, secret invasion of the privacy of this family were spread over countless government agencies across this land and abroad. In our FOIA [Freedom of Information Act] request the government admitted as recently as August 8, 2007, that they have 14,754 pages that are floating around in an uncontrolled no-man's-land of federal agencies, and the government, although it took this material illegally, says it won't destroy this material—that it won't even try to do so."

The government argued that the Mayfields had no standing to bring the case because they hadn't been damaged. And if they'd been damaged, the government had paid for it—the $2 million it paid the Mayfields. Was there other damage? I asked. "What about those 14,754 pages of personal, private information concerning this innocent family that festers in the government's files? Is that damage?

"'Just trust us,' the government says.

"We learned, according to a report from the Justice Department's inspector general, that from 2003 to 2005 the FBI issued over 143,000 requests for searches through those so-called national security letters. The report also found that the Bureau has often used the letters improperly, often illegally.

"We have learned that the Department of Justice, through Alberto Gonzales, even came to the hospital bed of then–Attorney General Ashcroft, who was feeble and barely able to speak—their attempt to get him to sign off on a noncertified Domestic Surveillance Program authorizing spying on American citizens, which included allowing the government to engage in warrantless wiretapping. To his credit the AG refused.

"This is America!

"It is *probable cause* that protects us under the Constitution. Mere suspicion can never be the standard. Never.

"The requirement of *probable cause* is a perfect balance between liberty on the one hand and security on the other. To do away with *probable cause* is to deliver the justice system to an uncontrolled government that has proven itself over and over to be untrustworthy in safeguarding the rights of American citizens.

"Judge Victor Marrero of the federal district court in Manhattan recently wrote that he feared these intrusions into the role of the judiciary that would be 'the legislative equivalent of breaking and entering, with an ominous free pass to the hijacking of constitutional values.'

"We are seeking a declaration that the Patriot Act violates the Fourth Amendment. Indeed, the breaking and entering mentioned by Judge Marrero occurred in fact to the Brandon Mayfield family, and the government was given an ominous free pass to the hijacking of our constitutional values. What happened to Brandon can happen to any of us.

"Under our Constitution only the judiciary can approve such intrusions. But the Patriot Act takes this prerogative from the judiciary and reduces its role to that of a mere clerk. Judge Marrero wrote: 'Congress and the executive must abide by the rule of law in times of domestic tranquility and of national crisis, in war and in peace. . . . Too often memory is short. The pages of this nation's jurisprudence cry out with compelling instances illustrating that when the judiciary lowers its guard on the Constitution, it opens the door to far-reaching invasions of liberty.' "

I turned to one of our great freedom fighters. "Martin Luther King Jr. reminds us: 'A time comes when silence is betrayal. I could never again raise my voice against the violence of the oppressed . . . without having first spoken clearly to the greatest purveyor of violence in the world today—my own government.'

"I ask this court not to be afraid to say it. Let Freedom Ring!"

Judge Aiken seemed unimpressed. But judges never applaud—not even for Darrow or Jesus, and I did not approach either.

Elden Rosenthal, our legal guru, argued with energy and intelligence all the impenetrable polemics about standing and jurisdiction and other such judicial vagaries. Judge Aiken was leaning forward, listening and taking notes and asking questions, and I thought, "Thank God for brains like Elden Rosenthal's." We were as different as fried chicken and chicken cacciatore. He not only understood the niceties of the law but was masterful in delivering solid, compelling legal arguments that would whet the appetite of the most jurisprudential gourmet. He ended with this jewel once voiced in Parliament in 1763:

"The poorest man may, in his cottage, bid defiance to all the forces of the crown. It may be frail. Its roof may shake. The wind may blow through it. The storm may enter. The rain may enter. But the King of England cannot enter. All his forces dare not cross the threshold of the ruined tenement."

Some months later, Judge Aiken's opinion came floating down from on high. It was built one brick at a time so that the appeals court could never blow it down. She wrote, "At issue here are two fundamental concerns: the safety of our nation and the constitutional rights of citizens. With the passage of the Patriot Act, these concerns are now placed in conflict." Yes, she said it exactly.

She went on to write strong, agile, liberating words. "Now, for the first time in our nation's history, the government can conduct surveillance to gather evidence for use in a criminal case without a traditional warrant, as long as it also has a significant interest in the targeted person for foreign intelligence purposes." That meant the feds could break into your home *at will*.

She wrote more. "Since the adoption of the Bill of Rights in 1791, the government has been prohibited from gathering evidence for use in a prosecution against an American citizen in a courtroom unless the government could prove the existence of probable cause that a crime has been committed."

Finally she said, "Our Founding Fathers anticipated this very conflict as evidenced by the discussion in the Federalist Papers. Their concern regarding unrestrained government resulted in the separation of powers, checks and balances, and ultimately, the Bill of Rights. . . . The Fourth Amendment has served this Nation well for 220 years. . . .

"Moreover, the constitutionally required interplay between executive action, judicial decision, and congressional enactment has been eliminated by the FISA [Foreign Intelligence Surveillance Act]. . . . These constitutional balances effectively curtail overzealous executive, or judicial activity regardless of the catalyst for overzealousness. The Constitution contains bedrock that the framers believed essential. Those principles should not be easily altered by the expediencies of the moment."

The judge was simply saying this: Because we think we've got a problem on our hands, say, with a few international killers who fly airplanes into our skyscrapers, we ought not throw the Constitution down the drain as if the damn thing is in the way of our safety. Besides, remember: *We have nothing to hide.*

Judge Aiken took on the government single-handedly. She wrote, "The defendant here is asking this court, in essence, to amend the Bill of Rights, by giving it an interpretation that would deprive it of any real meaning. This court declines to do so.

"For over 200 years, this nation has adhered to the rule of law—with unparalleled success. A shift to a nation based on extra-constitutional authority is prohibited, as well as ill advised. . . . Therefore, I conclude that 50 U.S.C. §§ 1804 and 1823, as amended by the Patriot Act, are unconstitutional because they violate the Fourth Amendment of the United States Constitution. Plaintiffs' Amended Complaint for declaratory relief is granted."

We won!

Michele Longo Eder wrote me, "When I heard the news I was in Anchorage. I stood outside the federal courthouse there in front of their great big American flag and sang 'My Country 'Tis of Thee,' 'America the Beautiful,' and 'The Star-Spangled Banner' at the top of my lungs."

The question remained, would any song save Judge Aiken's brave opinion from the Ninth Circuit Court of Appeals? On February 5, 2009, Elden Rosenthal argued our case, America's case, soundly and persuasively before the Ninth. Ten months later, the court delivered its judgment.

Consider this bit of irony: *Our* government was *our opponent*.

Who is *our* government?

We, the people, of course.

Has *our* government been seized by a power that no longer answers to the people?

By reputation the Ninth Circuit Court of Appeals is a reasonably friendly, liberal court. The government argued that we had no standing and that Judge Aiken was without jurisdiction. The government made the anemic argument that the Mayfields were not damaged by the government's failure to destroy the 14,754 pages that remained in the uncontrolled no-man's-land of federal agencies, and therefore Judge Aiken had no jurisdiction. The Ninth did not contradict Judge Aiken's brick-built opinion. It simply trotted around the end.

I've struggled through the opinion numerous times and still do not understand its reasoning. But here is what the judges did say in December of 2009: "We agree that Mayfield suffers an actual, ongoing injury, but do not agree that a declaratory judgment [which was the kind of case the government and we stipulated we would bring] would likely redress that injury. We therefore reverse the judgment of the district court with regard to standing.

"We also vacate the district court's judgment on the merits and do not address the question of whether the challenged provisions of FISA, as amended by the Patriot Act, are unconstitutional." In other words, the judges *didn't disagree* with Judge Aiken or us. They just said, in effect, so you were injured. So what? You didn't show that your case before Judge Aiken would give you any relief—something like that. The chirping chickadees at my bird feeder made more sense.

But perhaps we should give the Ninth Circuit Court a break. Perhaps they are wiser than we think. Perhaps they were saying, "Yes, the Patriot Act may be unconstitutional. But if we go down that street the government will take the case to the U.S. Supreme Court, and a majority of that court does not appear to cherish people's rights very much." Perhaps the Ninth was saying, "Let's be patient. Let's wait until a more people-oriented Supreme Court comes into being."

Elden Rosenthal was exactly right in his statement to the media: "The court ducked the issue by ruling on a technical basis having to do with standing. We strongly disagree with the appeal court's decision. The law is not always just, the courts are not always right. What is right here is that American citizens are entitled to protection from an oppressive government. What is wrong here is that that right was not provided."

Nevertheless, we appealed to the U.S. Supreme Court, but on November 10, 2010, that court said, in effect, "Go away, little folks." The judges denied certiorari. Those fancy legal words mean the high court judges refused to open the court's doors to us.

So, in the meantime, if you hear a noise downstairs at Christmas time, it may not be Santa stuffing your stockings. It may be your own government sneaking and peeking *without a search warrant based on probable cause* to see if they can make a case against you, an American citizen.

After it was all over, I asked Mona, "How did all that horror affect your kids?"

"They've had their trouble," she said. "It changed them in ways. They lost their innocence. They don't talk about it. It's too frightening."

"And Mona, how about you?" I asked.

"I try not to think about it either. But it makes me distrust everyone. I never used to be like that."

"And Brandon?"

"He won't say how he's suffered. Like servicemen who've been in the war." She lit a Camel and blew out the smoke. "The police in Spain saved us from our own government," she said. "If it hadn't been for the Spanish police Brandon would be long dead, and Lord knows what would have happened to us."

"We need a lot of luck in this life," I said.

"Praise Allah," she said. Her voice sounded happy. I thought at her core she was a happy woman.

CASE 3

KILL HIM—DON'T TOUCH HIM

*I*f ever there was a case that should be my last, this was it. The cops killed an innocent, unarmed, naked, perhaps dying young man who needed their help, not a dozen officers' bullets through his body. The cops claimed they were afraid. So if a cop feels fear he has the right to kill us rather than help? It was my son Kent's case; he was a skilled trial lawyer, and I thought this could be a father and son seeking justice in a case in which the police had committed murder—because they could.

It was September 8, 2005, in Clackamas County, Oregon. Fouad Kaady was in his twenty-seventh year. In ways he was still little more than a boy, with dark, soft eyes that denied a single hostile gene, and his smile was set on a hair trigger. But that day wasn't his day. His car ran out of gas. He'd borrowed his parents' car along with a five-gallon can, filled the can with gas, and was on his way to rescue his car when things suddenly went wrong. Somehow the car he was driving caught fire and exploded into a consuming inferno—and Fouad, trapped inside, was burning alive. He lost control and smashed the car into other vehicles parked alongside the road. His burned flesh hung from his body like meat on a spit, and he was seen running crazily through the woods, naked. Soon a dozen or more cops responded to calls that reported the accident.

A veteran deputy sheriff from Clackamas County, David Willard, and a police officer of more recent tenure from the City of Sandy, William Bergin, discovered Fouad. Somehow he'd traveled through the thick woods and across an open field. The cops found him sitting on the pavement's edge of a nearby road. He was, according to the cops' statement, in critical shape. His skin was peeling off; he was covered with blood, catatonic, and unresponsive. Months later Fouad's parents called our office for help. My son Kent, who was an expert in civil rights cases, had responded.

We had a copy of the police reports that introduced us to the two officers involved, including photos of both. Their interviews, conducted by someone in their department, were provided to us as well as to the media. I'll allow the two police officers to take up the story from here as revealed in the interviews conducted by a fellow officer. As we all know, if ten people see the same incident they'll provide ten differing accounts. It's worth noting that while Willard and Bergin were supposedly questioned separately, their answers were nearly identical.*

First, Deputy Willard. His photo revealed a man with an extraordinarily high forehead, one you might see on a Harvard professor. He stood about five-ten, wore glasses, and had a thick mustache that turned up slightly on the ends like Groucho Marx's. He sported a full head of short black hair. I judged him to be in his late forties. Here's what the supplied record revealed.

> DEPUTY SHERIFF WILLARD: The man we were directing our
> attention at was completely nude, sitting about a foot off of the shoulder
> Indian style, kinda bent down with his hands in front of him like this
> (indicating his hands at his lap).

The younger cop, Officer Bergin, offered his story. About the same height as Willard, he wore glasses on a round baby face with prominent ears and the closely cropped haircut standard among cops. His appearance offered no hint of any hidden personality demerits.

> OFFICER BERGIN: This male subject was sitting on the ground, in
> what we called in elementary school (chuckle) "Indian style." He had his
> hands tucked between his legs.
> WILLARD: His head was down as if he was in a prayer kind of mode.
> Every portion of his body had some blood on it. He appeared to be
> burned, the upper portion of his body from his waist up.
> BERGIN: As soon as we pulled up I could see his skin was brown and
> it was peeled back all over his entire body.

---

* The statements of Willard and Bergin have been edited to eliminate redundancies.

WILLARD: He had small lacerations, little cuts and things all over him, and he appeared to have dirt and leaves and other things on him.

BERGIN: His skin was charred.

WILLARD: The first thing that struck me was that this man was seriously injured. I could see his burns from clear back at the car. He is not looking up at us. He is not doing anything. I tell Bergin, "I don't see a weapon, do you?" And Bergin said, "No."

I told him, "I'm going to transition to nonlethal [meaning putting aside his firearms], and I am going to take my taser out."

BERGIN: I gave him the command to show me his hands, and he showed me his hands right away.

WILLARD: And I started to approach him telling him to get on his stomach. I had my taser on the guy.

I later asked my grandson Cade, then age ten, "What do you think police officers should do when they come onto an unarmed person who's badly burned and covered with blood and sitting peacefully on the ground?"

"Call for an ambulance. They got *radios,* Grandpa." He acted like I should have known.

"An ambulance was already there, waiting for the police to finish whatever they were doing," I said. "Should the police make him lie on the hot pavement on his burned stomach?"

He looked like he was about to cry. He didn't answer.

WILLARD: As I'm getting up to him, and see the burns and am sorta accessing him physically, my concern is two things: One, I decide I am not going to let this man leave here, because we have heard some pretty bizarre things, and secondly, and almost as important, I am going to get this man medical help. He needs help right now. But I need to make sure we're safe. So I tell him to turn around and lay down on his stomach on the pavement. I had dealt with burn victims before.

BERGIN: He was saying, "OK," but then he wouldn't get on the ground.

WILLARD: He looked up at me and he says, "No."

BERGIN: We told him to move to the grass and get on his stomach because there were concerns about the asphalt and the heat, 'cause it was a hot day. And he wouldn't comply with that.

WILLARD: And I says, "You gotta do this. I need you to lie down." And he says, "No," again.

BERGIN: I told him to get on his stomach or he would be tased.

WILLARD: I repeated that several times. And again, he just sort of leaned forward and ignored me.

BERGIN: We wanted him to lay on his stomach so we could get him in restraints [handcuffs].

WILLARD: I said, "Look over there. See the grass?" And he says, "Yes." And I says, "Carefully go over there and lay down on the grass." It was cooler and I thought he might accept that. And he said, "OK." And I said, "Are you going to do that?" And he just sat there. I don't think there was any response at that point. At that point I was about to deploy the taser. And the Sandy officer [Bergin] deployed his taser. The Sandy officer got behind him and had his full back. From training, that is actually the best shot. It will affect more of the muscle tissues.

One may believe that Tasers are a humanitarian compromise weapon. They allow the cops to immobilize a man without killing him. Unfortunately, it's not that simple. Between 1999 and 2005, the American Civil Liberties Union reports, at least 148 people died in the United States and Canada from being shocked by cops with Tasers.

BERGIN: At this point I walked behind Deputy Willard to the rear of the subject to get a better shot with my taser. I had put my firearm away [holstered it], turned my taser on, and got behind him and told him again to lay on his stomach or he'd be tasered. He appeared to be catatonic, and I got a good shot with the taser. Both prongs went into his back.

WILLARD: He had loose, hanging, burned flesh, at least a couple of layers down.

BERGIN: When I tased him he flopped backwards on the ground. And from his behavior after I tased him, and the ineffectiveness of the taser, I even made the comment to Deputy Willard, "I don't wanna get hands on this guy." I just knew if we were to get hands on with him in a physical fight there would be no stopping him. He woulda not felt any pain.

WILLARD: The first time I tased him he fell back, flat out, proned out on his back on the ground. He was shaking a little, which is fairly typical of someone who is taking an electrical shock. When that five-second shot was done I said to him, "You need to do what we ask you to do. We need you to go over and lay down on that grass, and if you don't do what we ask you to do you are going to get tased again." And it was right around that time, and I am still looking at him assessing him—and I am thinking I don't want this guy even near me. And if he complies, what am I gonna do? We'll wait until other officers get here before we do anything.

WILLARD: Somebody needs to glove up before they touch this man. He's got blood literally from head to toe and multiple lacerations and cuts and dirt. And I didn't want to touch this man. I really felt there was a real risk to my safety and the officer who was there if we weren't protected before we came into physical contact with this man.

BERGIN: We again told him to roll on his stomach or he would be tased. The prongs from my taser were still in him. So I did another pull of the trigger with the taser, and I noticed that one of the barbs was a good hit, the other was in him, and he was getting the shock from my taser, but it wasn't really stuck and it hung on him. At this point he was laughing and giggling while I was tasing him the second time.

WILLARD: He started to get on his left side and was looking at me. And that was the first time he was also growling at me. It was a sort of a low level growl, and I remember him showing his teeth because on one side the blood was running down and it looked sort of bizarre with his growling and his teeth out. He started to go up on his side towards me, and the Sandy police officer hit him with the taser again. This time he fell back on his back and it appeared to me that the taser was still being deployed when he started sitting up. While we are tasing him he comes forward, and you can see him still getting shocked. He is getting the electrical current and he gets up.

WILLARD: And the Sandy police officer hit the taser again. My gosh. He is being tased and he is still getting up. He reached back and knocked one barb off because I remember watching that drop to the ground. Then he took off running away from us.

WILLARD: I started to go after him, to get close enough so that the taser would continue to be effective. He turned and faced us.

BERGIN: He started growling again.

WILLARD: And I went for another reload. And almost at the same time he turned around and he started screaming, "I'm gonna kill you,

I'm gonna kill you," and running right toward me. His saying that was a little weird and extremely frightening because of the blood and the strength he had displayed.

As I read this police report I began to imagine how I'd present these facts to a trial jury. Wasn't this exactly what the cops wanted Fouad to do—to charge them? The cops didn't want to *touch* him. Was their best tactic to torment him to the point that they could kill him? Witnesses up the road both saw and heard what was going on, and not one heard Fouad say, "I'm going to kill you."

Elaine Thornlimb, a forty-six-year-old school librarian who lived nearby, offered her own perspective. She followed Fouad for about a half mile north on 362nd. At one point, he waved and smiled at her. She said that Kaady's hair was matted and bloody and that skin was hanging from his arms. She followed him slowly in her car. He jumped onto the roof of Thornlimb's Ford Explorer and down again. Thornlimb told the grand jury that when Fouad sat down in the road she told 911 dispatchers that he appeared to have given up. "I felt all along that the officers were there to help him," she said. "When they shot him, I drove home and sobbed for hours." One witness said he heard Fouad say to the officers, "Please don't." I felt sick. I didn't want to admit that what I was reading in the transcript represented acceptable human conduct.

Under the law, before you can kill in self-defense you must *retreat to the wall*, the legal jargon meaning you must retreat to the point where retreat can no longer save you from your attacker. Only then can you kill in self-defense. That law applies to the police.

The cops admitted Fouad got up and ran away, but they next claimed he turned back, charged Willard, and screamed he was going to kill him. Willard claimed he retreated and was "extremely" frightened for his own safety.

BERGIN: At this point I saw Deputy Willard retreat.

WILLARD: I started to run around the rear of the police car and looked back and he was gaining on me. He was about three or four feet behind me.

BERGIN: And at the same time he was still growling like a wild animal.

WILLARD: And still screaming, "I'm gonna kill you, I'm gonna kill you," and making this kinda clawlike motions with his hands and intermittently growling. I ran around the rear of the police car. That was when I decided this man needed to be stopped. I couldn't leave him . . . and I was scared.

BERGIN: And he ran between us, and I had concerns that he'd be charging at Deputy Willard and might get at Deputy Willard's shotgun, and I also saw that Deputy Willard had a weapon in his hands that he could get at and use on either Deputy Willard or me.

WILLARD: I tossed my taser on the trunk of the police car.

BERGIN: I can't get my taser into my holster, and I tossed it up on the windshield of the car.

WILLARD: And I transitioned to [got out] my handgun.

BERGIN: Deputy Willard was at the rear of my patrol vehicle. The subject was still growling like a wild animal and jumped up on the hood or the roof of my car still charging toward Deputy Willard and screaming, "I'm going to kill you," and screaming like an animal.

WILLARD: I came up on him and remember taking a look across my front sight right at him, and I remember clearly yelling two things: "I'm the police and you need to get down." And I'm sure this is all just a matter of a few seconds. But it seemed like a long time. The Sandy police officer had come around to that side of the car, too, and was right next to me.

I wasn't consciously aware of what he [Bergin] was doing, but I was on him [Fouad]. I think I yelled, "Shoot." I might not have. I might have just been thinking it. But in any case, when it appeared he was going to leap off the car at me, I fired.

BERGIN: I fired several shots at him.

WILLARD: And I know I fired two very quick successive rounds. He stepped back on the car and stopped jumping, and then it appeared he was going to come toward us, but down toward the trunk. I fired one more round.

BERGIN: Until he was down.

WILLARD: And almost simultaneously with firing that last round his right foot slipped on the rear window of the car, and he fell on his back on the right against the lower right rear window, and then hit the car and slid off the car headfirst. I remember hearing his head hit the ground.

UNIDENTIFIED VOICE: What was the subject's reaction when he was shot?

WILLARD: I guess "shocked" would be the best way to describe his reaction.

UNIDENTIFIED VOICE: While you were looking down your sight with your gun pointed at him, what were you thinking?

WILLARD: I was thinking, I don't want this man touching me. I don't want him getting on me.

UNIDENTIFIED VOICE: You mentioned that you had concerns about this man making contact with you. What were those concerns and risks?

WILLARD: In my training as a police officer I had a number of classes regarding blood-borne pathogens and hazards, and my concerns were hepatitis. This man was bleeding as if he was on some form of drugs. I know through my training that hepatitis is fairly common among IV drug users.

My first and foremost concern was hepatitis, and secondly for the AIDS virus being transmitted through blood. And with the volume of blood he had on him, even with standard precautions, gloves and mask, it would have been very possible to get blood in my eyes or in my mouth or I actually could have an open wound at the tip of one of my fingers at the time that I was concerned about.

Of course, the best way to prevent Willard from having to touch Fouad was to kill him. Willard was telling us about IV drug users. What evidence did he have that Fouad Kaady was an IV drug user? The toxicologist reported that Fouad was not under the influence of any drugs. Moreover, this young man had no criminal record. As those in the police business would have to admit, "He was clean."

As would be expected, the prosecutor called a grand jury, and that body, led by the prosecutor, found that the police were justified in shooting Fouad Kaady to death. Some argue, especially the police, that we have to make room for the dangers police face daily in their work. Well, all right, let's assume you are a cop in the Fouad Kaady case. Your job is simple to define—to protect the people, not to kill them. Fouad Kaady happens to be a citizen and is entitled to your protection. As a matter of fact, technically he's your employer.

You find him naked, unarmed, and his burned flesh is hanging from his body. He's sitting quietly on the pavement. He refuses to lay his burned flesh down on the pavement or the grass. But you are a cop. People, even if they are crazed with pain, better do what you say or else. You now decide not to call the ambulance folks who are waiting but to show this naked man, who may be dying of his wounds, who's boss. When he fails to submit to your commands you decide to tase him—to further injure him. You continue to tase him. And for what? So you can handcuff him?

Now you claim that from the tasing itself you've created a monster, this naked, unarmed, perhaps mortally wounded citizen. How do you protect yourself from this monster? You can't walk away? You can't get in the police car? You can't give the situation a little time? You can't call in the ambulance people? You only have one way, right? You must kill him.

What do we learn from this story? The case teaches: Never bleed in front of the police, and if we're injured we better not ask the police for help. They would rather kill us than touch us. If what the police did here was acceptable police conduct, would any of us ever be safe from the very people we hire to keep us safe?

The grand jury's finding did not prevent us from filing a civil rights suit against the cops for the Kaadys' loss of their son. As we know, grand juries are often but tools by which prosecutors gather the evidence they seek to discover or preserve—in this case evidence to clear their cops. We filed our case for the Kaady family. The police's insurance companies stepped up to defend them, and their lawyers had learned what I've preached for years: You can never successfully defend a case. You can only attack, and for the insurance companies that meant attacking the dead, namely Fouad Kaady.

In preparing their defense, the insurance investigators claimed they talked to Fouad's girlfriend, who supposedly said he wasn't himself that day. The investigators claimed they had a witness who would testify he put eight cigarettes in his mouth at one time and lit them all and then drove over the curb of the parking lot of the store where he'd bought the cigarettes. The witness claimed he dumped out a lot of change on the counter, more than the price of a pack and left the excess with the clerk. So Fouad was obviously mentally deranged, and dangerous. The case never went to trial and was settled before I had the opportunity to talk to this supposed witness. But our investigation didn't discover a single witness in the world who would claim that Fouad had been suffering from any kind of mental aberration before or on the day of his death.

Then the insurance lawyers were ready to introduce their newest invention—that Fouad suffered from "excited delirium," a gimmicky piece of purported science lately used by the police around the country to excuse their killings.

Persons supposedly suffering from "excited delirium" were said to be very strong, irrational, impervious to pain, and therefore dangerous. But Eric Balaban of the American Civil Liberties Union pointed out in 2007 that "excited delirium" has *not* been recognized by the American Medical Association or the American Psychological Association (still true in 2015), and he says that "the diagnosis serves as a means of whitewashing what may be excessive use of force by officers during an arrest."* Nowhere in the *Diagnostic and Statistical Manual of Mental Disorders* can such a diagnosis be found, which to me is another way of saying that credible authority will not create an excuse for police murders where none exists.

Police psychologist Mike Webster testified in 2007 at a British Columbia inquiry into Taser deaths that there is a link between the excess use of Tasers and this defense. Indeed, in his testimony, Webster went on to say that he believed police have been "brainwashed" by TASER International (the manufacturer) to justify "ridiculously inappropriate" use of the electronic weapon. Webster called "excited delirium" a "dubious disorder" used by TASER International in its training of police.† Am I hearing correctly: The proper police response to citizens who are wild with pain is to shoot them in the back with those Taser darts and jolt them with 50,000 volts, yes, 50,000? That should calm them right down.

When we eventually got to trial I thought we should ask a jury: "What about receiving multiple blasts of 50,000 volts into one's hide that has already been roasted away in a fire? Is it all right for the cops to then shoot the victim with their Tasers? Naturally, the victim goes crazy from shock and pain. Have the cops by their own actions earned the right to kill the citizen because he might present some kind of speculated threat to them, something with a scientific sounding name called '*excited delirium*'?"

Now, coincidentally, hear how Bergin had described Fouad in the police reports: "I had, uh, you know, I *knew* that he had a very bad mental health problem or he was *definitely* under the influence of drugs or a combination of both" (my emphasis).

Kent was all over that. "How could Bergin claim to know that Fouad

---

* Laura Sullivan, "Death by Excited Delirium: Diagnosis or Coverup?" NPR, February 26, 2007.
† "Police Are 'Brainwashed' by Taser Maker," *Vancouver Sun*, May 14, 2008.

had a 'very bad mental health problem'? Bergin had never met or seen Fouad before; much less did he know anything about any supposed mental health problems."

Every legal pretrial motion the insurance companies dumped on overworked judges ensured delay and earned their lawyers thousands in fees. Pretrial they continued to claim that Fouad was under the influence of drugs or was otherwise mentally disturbed or psychotic. They argued that the cops had immunity, meaning they couldn't be sued since they were government employees who had acted reasonably and without malice. They asked the judge to throw the case out without a jury trial.

I wasn't afraid of the standard "immunity defense" that people's lawyers nearly always face in every case they bring against the police. The law protects cops by holding they are not liable in damages for their killing even if they were negligent. Under the law, we were required to make even greater proof than negligence to earn our right to a jury trial. We had to prove that the police were *grossly* negligent or "willful and wanton." I believed if we couldn't make such a showing in Fouad's case the police could always get away with needless killings of our citizens. But beyond this high legal bar was the even higher bar of the likely years of delay before the judge would set our case for trial.

Unavoidable delay comes about like this: The insurance company lawyers make their argument to the trial judge that the cops are immune from suit. It sometimes takes a year or more in a busy court to get the judge's ruling on that. If the judge holds against the cops, the insurance company lawyers can then make what's called an interlocutory appeal to the circuit court (an appeal before the jury has even heard the case), which usually results in another couple of years of waiting. If we get a favorable decision from the circuit court, the case will eventually be set for trial. More time. If we win with a jury at trial, the insurance company lawyers can appeal again. On and on. And we could lose the case anywhere along the way. So delay and the uncertainty of how judges will rule, not a lack of proof in our case, were the danger, as they are in all such cases.

For insurance companies it's cheaper to pay big fees to their lawyers than to let a jury cast its collective eye on such a case as this. Delay wears down even the hardiest people with the best resources. For the poor, delay is often impossible to weather. They need money for funeral bills and lost wages, and they grow poorer and more desperate with every passing day, and finally they lose confidence in their lawyers because they can't understand such delays, and they agree to settle for a pittance. And their lawyers may have thousands of hours in unpaid labor and more thousands in expenses during all of those years. The insurance companies take the spilled red blood of the victims, watch it dry and crumble over time, and finally turn to the green of the money they've saved by delay.

But for some unexplainable reason the county, on behalf of Willard, failed to raise the immunity defense. Only the city's insurance company on behalf of Bergin had raised the defense. As is sometimes my way, I lost my patience. I said, "Let Bergin out of the case. That'll save us years of delay, and we'll collect every penny of damages due the Kaadys from Willard's insurance. Under the law we can recover only *one* total sum for Fouad's death anyway." Besides, I was getting older. It was becoming more difficult for me to endure long days in long trials, and I wanted to try this case before the last of me was used up.

Kent was adamant that we should hold further negotiations with Bergin's insurance company. "Calm the lion" was his mantra. I was the lion. "Let's see if we can get some money out of Bergin's insurance company before we get all huffy and turn his insurance company loose."

In May of 2009, Kent settled the case against the city and Bergin for $1 million, while I'd been willing to dismiss Bergin and go for the whole load against the county and Willard. Thanks to Kent, we provided the Kaadys with immediate, sure funds, and we still had our case against Willard.

I began in earnest to prepare for that trial.

*I*n preparing for the Kaady trial, I'd been filling an old brain with new facts. Kent and I had both worked those long, focused hours that consumed days and nights. I read the depositions that Kent and others had taken of the witnesses. Mountains of work lay ahead, and as the trial date loomed I was deep into the preparation of my cross-examination of the insurance companies' experts and the arguments I'd make to the jury.

The one thought that kept my belly tight and ready for the fight: If we can't turn to our police to help an unarmed, perhaps mortally injured citizen, if they would rather kill a citizen than touch him, then the police are killers on the loose.

Shortly before trial the company that insured Willard offered us another million to settle. Should we agree to settle the whole case for what would total $2 million? I'd proclaimed this was a case we should never settle. It was my habit to fight, not settle. But how did I know I could win yet again?

Most often the odds in my cases were against winning, and I was eighty-one. Even old champions in the ring eventually had to give up. I wasn't ready. Stepping out of the ring had something to do with dying.

How could one love such a fight? You walk into a courtroom and face judges who've been appointed by Power. You face prosecutors who unlawfully hide the evidence, and who knowingly haul lying witnesses into court, especially snitches who buy their way out of prison with their lies. Because Power owns the media, year after year it dumps on us endless propaganda that undermines our belief that we are all presumed innocent as guaranteed by the Constitution. That's just fancy lawyer talk. Continuous cop shows and movies portray criminal defense lawyers as greedy, soulless shysters, and in the minds of the American public that sacred rule of law has been changed. Today the accused is presumed *guilty*. He'd better prove his innocence or he'll be convicted.

The Constitution? What about the Kaadys? Should we ask them to endure a renewal of their pain in a long trial? Day after day the lawyers would examine every drop of blood shed by their son, his inconceivable pain from the cops' Tasers, and they'd hear every shot that had been fired into his burned, naked body. Then they'd hear the insurance companies' experts take an oath that Fouad was suffering that phony invention they liked to call "excited delirium."

If you loved the mother, even a little, would you put her through all of that for money? Mothers suffer most. For a moment become the mother. Your son has been ruthlessly killed by the cops. The prosecutors have already convinced a grand jury that the cops were guilty of no crime, that the killing of your son was justified. The only justice left is a civil suit for money—dead money for a dead child.

The mother asks, "How can I take money for my child?" That's also the cruel argument insurance company lawyers like to make to the jury: "She wants to get rich from her dead child!"

Moreover, the law takes every means possible to keep jurors from knowing that the cop himself doesn't pay the jury's verdict but, instead, an insurance company does. Jurors think a greedy mother is trying to squeeze $20 million from some poor cop who, like them, works for a living and has no assets except, maybe, his mortgaged home. That's the justice game being played in *every* court in America *every* day.

Courts do not tell juries the truth, nor does the law allow anyone else during the trial to tell juries the truth—that neither the cop nor the city nor the county will pay the jury's verdict. The insurance company will. If I were to tell the jury that truth I would be held in contempt, possibly thrown in jail and my case dismissed. The law protects the insurance company. The law does not serve the Kaadys unless it is cornered and forced to.

Still in the role of the mother: She asks, "If I spend the money for myself, it's my child's life I'm spending. If I go out to dinner, what am I eating? If I take a vacation, am I trying to have a good time from the mangled flesh of my son?"

At last perhaps the mother says, "If my son had lived, he'd want me to have the money. And if need be, he'd have taken care of me in my old age." The mother is entitled to justice. But money is all the justice there is. Yet not a penny of it would come from the cops who killed her son; it would all come from one of the most powerful of all power entities in the world—the insurance company.

Kent argued that collecting a total of $2 million for the Kaady family was an incredible settlement. That settlement would be larger than any collected verdict in Oregon's history for a similar case. He argued I ought not interject my crusading instincts ahead of our clients' needs. The Kaadys had suffered enough even if they had agreed to take the painful journey into a long and torturous trial.

"Besides, Dad," Kent said, "if the verdict gets out of hand and the jury awards millions more than what the company is offering, the company will appeal, and that could take another couple of years and maybe a new trial. You could extend the Kaadys' pain indefinitely. I say it's better for everyone to put the case to rest and give the Kaadys a chance to reconstruct their lives." And, yes, maybe I wouldn't live to see the end of the battle I had demanded.

A man has finally grown up when he can listen to his son.

Although that good family agreed to the settlement, they, too, will never recover. Money does not buy justice. Nor does it buy peace, nor does it erase horror. I love Mrs. Kaady. She is a dear, dear woman and a devoted mother, and I shall always admire her.

Both Kent and I and the Kaadys take some comfort when we're told years later that the case continues to influence law enforcement training, such as when the *Oregonian* reported, "Clackamas County sheriff's deputies use the scenario [of the Kaady case] as part of their Crisis Intervention Training Program, which deals with how to respond to highly agitated subjects—

mentally ill or not."* Perhaps Fouad's death will save other lives at the hands of cops who kill because they can or because they do not want to even touch the injured.

Bergin resigned from the Sandy police force in October 2008. He pled guilty to unrelated charges in other cases that constituted official misconduct. Last I heard, Willard was still a cop in Clackamas County.

I couldn't get Mrs. Kaady out of my mind. A mother who loses a child is a wounded woman. We hear her laugh again, and see her go about her business of surviving, but she has been wounded and the scars go deep. I am grateful for mothers out there like Mrs. Kaady who have the strength to go on and to live full, useful lives, and who can continue to love. Such is my definition of a hero.

And I thought of men who need to kill the children of mothers. The black and white winter birds were at my feeder. They do not kill each other. And I thought that perhaps the world should be ruled by small black and white winter birds and, yes, by mothers.

* March 15, 2010.

CASE 4

KILL THE RENEGADE

John Singer grew up in Nazi Germany. His father, an ardent Nazi, shipped him off to a Hitler youth camp. But his mother didn't share her husband's affinity for the Führer. They would battle for their child's mind and soul in a struggle that would culminate after the war when his mother escaped to America with John. She settled in Salt Lake City, where she and her child joined her "brothers and sisters" in the Mormon Church. John Singer vowed he would never subject his own children to an educational environment that was contrary to his religious beliefs, as he and his mother had suffered in Germany.

John married Vickie in 1965. They had seven children and were described by neighbors as a close, loving, and unpretentious family living in the rolling hills in Marion, Utah. They had a small farm, and John worked as a TV repairman. They were devoted to their beliefs, were self-sufficient, and wanted to raise their children safe from what they viewed as the evil influence of the public schools. The Singers felt driven to follow the admonition of the scriptures that placed a nondelegable duty on them to educate their children and "to walk upright before the Lord." But here in this celebrated haven of ultimate refuge, men in power wanted to force their children into the public school in nearby Kamas and were dictating how their children would be educated. Singer thought that was prohibited by the scriptures. He saw history repeating itself—the state, as in Nazi Germany, dictating what his children would be taught.

The official Mormon Church, considering the players, could only pretend that this tragic story was immune from the church's influence. Val Edrington, the superintendent of the local schools, was a Mormon. Robert Adkins, the Summit County prosecutor, was a Mormon, as were the juvenile court judge, Charles Bradford, and the state superintendent of schools, Dr. Walter Talbot, as well as the governor, Scott Matheson. Even the United States District Court judge, David Winder, admitted he had grown up as a practicing Mormon.

I saw John Singer as a man stretched between two prongs of fear—fear of men in power and fear of the Lord. He could turn to no one for assistance. He remembered Joseph Smith and many other Mormons who'd been murdered as their earthly reward for their faith, and Christ hanging from the cross, a renegade in the eyes of the Romans. Yes, John Singer was a renegade. He'd also refused to "sustain the presidency," which is church language meaning he would not agree that the church president alone received the word of God and was therefore empowered to speak for him, to interpret the word of God for him, and to even think for him. Mormons must "sustain the presidency" or face excommunication. Singer's refusal created a dangerous breach between him and Utah's power structure, which, in significant ways, was synonymous with the Mormon Church, officially known as the Church of Jesus Christ of Latter-day Saints (LDS).

The Singers believed their children were being exposed to dope, disease, and decadence. And the last straw that finally triggered their decision was a child's reader containing the pictures of George Washington and Martin Luther King "side by side as equals and great men," as Vickie put it in her journal. John Singer didn't believe textbooks should promote a mixing of races.* On March 29, 1973, he and Vickie took their three oldest children out of the public school and attempted to begin their own program of homeschooling.

Val Edrington, the superintendent of South Summit School District, wrote to State Superintendent of Public Instruction Dr. Walter D. Talbot seeking guidance: What power did he possess to regulate the Singers' homeschooling of their children? In a letter dated May 9, 1973, Talbot responded that under Utah's compulsory attendance law, the parents didn't

---

* The material facts that follow were first reported from the affidavits of participants, the testimony of witnesses in the many juvenile court proceedings, the motions and arguments of lawyers in the cases, and even the lengthy journal of Vickie Singer, after which these facts were gathered into court documents before Federal District Judge David Winder, and thereafter gleaned and interpreted by that judge and set forth in his opinion in *Singer v. Wadman*, 595 F. Supp. 188 (1982). Our office spent over two years gathering evidence in this case. My then-partner Bob Schuster led the team that took the deposition testimony of seventy-eight witnesses, which added up to thousands of pages.

have to be certified as teachers, but their teaching had to meet minimum requirements. Yes, but minimum requirements dictated by whom?

Edrington wrote the Singers informing them that the local board would send someone to evaluate their schooling methods. If the board was satisfied that its teaching requirements were being met, it would issue a certificate of exemption, and if not, the board would be forced to report the parents to juvenile court. The message was clear: You better teach your kids the way we want them taught or you'll face the judge.

Singer's response to Edrington was tinctured with his childhood experiences under Hitler. He wrote to Edrington:

> My God has let me know by His scriptures and by His Holy Spirit that I am not required according to His Laws, to bow under laws which trample upon my liberties by which my God has made me a free man. . . .
>
> My God is more powerful than you and your illegal laws, and only slaves will bow under those conditions; therefore, all I can say is go to Hell you and your kind for such unrighteous demands.

Edrington turned once more to Dr. Talbot, the state school superintendent, who in turn consulted with the Utah attorney general. Talbot then wrote Edrington: "The District would not be discharging its responsibility if it did not do as the law requires and report this matter formally to the juvenile court in your area." So Power's ducks were all lined up against this one Utah citizen and his family, whose only opposing power was whatever divine benevolence drifted down from on high.

By October 18, 1973, the case was festering in the Juvenile Court for Summit County. On the information of Val Edrington the Singers were charged as criminals for neglecting their three oldest children in that they had refused to comply with the Utah compulsory attendance law. The Singers were summoned to appear in juvenile court on December 10, and when they failed to appear, a warrant for their arrest was issued.

At this point one is put to wondering about Power's concern for the Singer children. If the Singers were hauled off to jail, would Edrington see to their feeding and shelter? When the sheriff came to arrest John, he asked him to go with him peacefully, but John refused. "Well then," the sheriff said, "the judge will probably send about ten guys after you and break the door down to get you."

John replied, "If that's the case there will be bloodshed."

On January 10, 1974, John Singer was arrested while he was making a television repair call. The charge was child neglect. He offered no resistance, spent the night in jail, and was released the next day after agreeing to appear at a designated time. In their attempt to appease the authorities, the Singers filed with the school board an outline of what they'd be teaching their kids. And the case against him was postponed.

Next Edrington demanded that the Singer children be tested. Still attempting to appease the school authorities, the Singers allowed their children to be given the school's standard achievement test. Their scores were lower than the group average in the equivalent grade. The school board let matters ride along until Edrington got into the act again the following year. He wanted up-to-date testing of the children. This time the Singers refused.

Edrington reported the Singers to State Superintendent Talbot, who passed the well-worn buck to the juvenile court again. This brought Summit County Attorney Robert Adkins into Judge Bradford's juvenile court. Adkins, ex parte, discussed the Singer problem with Judge Bradford. ("Ex parte" is a legal term meaning that Adkins talked to the judge without the Singers being present. This is not permitted in most courts in this country.) To his credit, Judge Bradford told Prosecutor Adkins he thought that parents should be permitted "substantial discretion in the matter of the education of their children." Adkins reported back to District Superintendent Edrington that in view of Judge Bradford's attitude, it would be difficult to put pressure on the Singers.

Edrington would not retreat. On November 29, 1976, he reported to Dr. Talbot that the juvenile court was "failing to act." Talbot said he would follow up but suggested that Edrington "keep it low key." Talbot then contacted Attorney General Robert B. Hansen, and Hansen, ex parte, talked with Judge Bradford. And if that wasn't enough pressure on the judge, a probation officer from the juvenile court told him that he'd heard that Talbot had complained about the judge to the governor. All of this pressuring of the judge, this "back-dooring" behind the backs of the Singers, was a violation of proper court proceedings.

Now enters the ghoul named Politics. Dr. Talbot happened to sit on the Juvenile Court Commission that screened candidates for the juvenile court judgeship, and Judge Bradford's term was about to expire. Judge Bradford was soon to learn that he was not one of the three judges recommended to the governor for reappointment. But Judge Bradford also discovered that one of the three who had been selected for his job was a partner of one of the juvenile court commissioners who would be voting on the matter. This wouldn't pass the smell test from fifty miles off. When this good-old-boy move was discovered and exposed by Judge Bradford, Talbot had no choice but to have the commission reconvene, and this time Judge Bradford's name got on the list.

Following the suggestion of Superintendent Edrington, the members of the school board then voted to bring John Singer before them once more. Their message to Singer was the same: We have the power over you and your children. So show us why we shouldn't revoke your exemption that permits you to homeschool your kids.

Singer appeared in his best pair of jeans and a clean, pressed shirt. He stood alone before the school board without a lawyer. His face was deeply burned from the sun, and his voice was marked with an obvious German accent acquired from his early years in Nazi Germany. He pled his case into the faces of strangers. Singer told the school board that his family was holding school 180 days a year, the same number required in the public schools, and was covering the same subjects. However, he told the school board he would not allow the board to monitor his children's schoolwork or further test his children.

On March 11, 1977, the school board notified the Singers it had withdrawn the certificate of exemption that had allowed them to teach their children at home because of their refusal to allow testing of the children. The board gave the Singers until March 18 to send their children back to the public schools, failing which the Singers would be reported to the juvenile court.

On May 3, John and Vickie Singer were charged with the crimes of contributing to the delinquency and neglect of Heidi Singer, Suzanne Singer, Charlotte Singer, Joseph Singer, and Timothy Singer by failing to send those children to the public school.

On June 7, a preliminary hearing was held before Judge Bradford. The Singers were present. They had no funds to pay a private lawyer and refused the services of a court-appointed attorney. Vickie Singer said she remembered talking in a "personal manner" with Judge Bradford, explaining to him that they believed "what was happening was unconstitutional." She said the judge actually agreed with them.

Now real trouble was about to begin. On August 3, Judge Bradford appointed a guardian ad litem for the Singer children. The word "guard-ian" sounded to John as if the court had taken away his children. In fact, the judge was appointing someone with legal standing to represent the interests of the children during the trial.

In a letter to Judge Bradford dated August 7, Singer, suffering from his mistaken belief that his children had been taken from him, wrote as follows:

> Dear Mr. Bradford!
> I have received your orders by which you appointed Robert
> F. Orton as guardian for my children.
> My reply!
> You, Mr. Bradford, by making a court order of this nature are, according to the laws of the land, a lawbreaker, & to pursue this matter further against me & my family makes you also the law-breaker in the eyes of Allmighty God. I have lost all confidence in you as an officer of Justice & as a man of God. God's remedy of restoring confidence, is, that the transgressor repents.

Singer warned that if Robert Orton came to his home as the guardian of his children he would "personally . . . throw him out." He went on to write:

> You have placed us in a very peculiar situation, namely, either to transgress the laws of my God & obey men's corrupt laws, or obey my God's laws & defy men's corrupt laws. I, fearing God more than men, have chosen the latter.

The matter was set for hearing on August 23, 1977, before Judge L. Kent Bachman, who had suddenly replaced Judge Bradford just a week before. How or why the change of judge came about remains a secret on the rec-ord. At the juvenile court hearing, Singer reported the number of hours the children were being homeschooled. He identified their textbooks and described the little schoolhouse that he and the family had built, in which their teaching took place. Yes, a schoolhouse built by the hands of the Singers and their children—an exemplary part of a child's education, one might argue.

The record does not reveal Singer's struggle at cross-examining Val

Edrington, and others. His efforts were likely lacking. Lawyers spend years learning the art, and many never learn it. But when Singer testified, he told the judge that God had given him the responsibility to rear his children, and that he'd done so according to his beliefs. He insisted that he was a responsible parent and denied he'd been negligent.

One of the reasons Singer had been cited was that he wasn't teaching a full five and a half hours a day. But Singer felt he was being punished for his efficiency—two and a half hours a day of focused learning was, in his view, equal to the education children were getting in the longer public school day due to the "goof off" periods between lessons, as he referred to recesses and in-class exercises when real teaching was not performed.

When it came time to rule, Judge Bachman found that there had been a "neglectful situation" in the Singers' failing to teach their children the basics of education, but the record was silent as to what the exact failures were. So the judge decided to have Dr. Victor Cline, a psychologist from the University of Utah, deal with the matter. In the meantime the Singers were committed to the county jail for a period of sixty days and ordered to pay a fine of $299, to be suspended upon compliance with the court's orders. No official seemed to care who was going to feed, provide for, and protect the children during that sixty days. By letter the Singers declined to meet with Dr. Cline and tried to explain with "all due respect" that they would be judged by God, not by the psychologist.

On August 29, 1977, the Singers filed their notice of appeal, but their appeal was dismissed when the Singers "failed to perfect it," which simply meant that they didn't use proper legal language in the time required by law. On September 13, the Singers were ordered to appear before Judge Bachman to explain why they'd failed to comply with the court's order to meet with Dr. Cline for testing. Worn down, they finally consented to Dr. Cline's evaluation of the children and met with him on September 15 at the university, and again on September 27 at the Singer home in Marion. Then the psychologist sought to test both John and Vickie. The Singers concluded that the power structure was preparing to declare them both unfit to teach their own children. Both John and Vickie Singer refused to permit the psychologist to test them.

It was around this time that the Singers learned there might be a different way to achieve their goal of homeschooling their children. They were contacted by Tom and Mary Bergman of Porterville, Utah, who had incorporated a private school, though, in fact, they were teaching their own children. Presumably this tactic had allowed them to homeschool their children without government interference, since the public school board seemed reluctant to exercise its power over privately incorporated schools. The Bergmans shared a copy of a letter they'd received from Dr. Talbot stating that private schools were not subject to state regulation. Sometime in October of 1977, the Singers filed articles of incorporation for a private school called High Uintahs Academy, Inc.

But on November 1, the judge found that the Singers had failed to submit to an evaluation by Dr. Cline, and again ordered the Singers to pay a fine of $299 and sentenced each to sixty days in the Summit County jail. After praying about the matter, the Singers decided to allow Dr. Cline to test them. On November 15, Dr. Cline's report on the Singers was reviewed by the judge. The contents of the report do not appear in the record, but something was clearly worrying Judge Bachman. He told the Singers that if he allowed them to continue their home teaching, and if they wouldn't "bend," he ran the risk of losing his job. Losing his job? Who exactly was in charge here—the juvenile court judge or some outside political power threatening the judiciary? From our earliest times in grade school we learned that in America our judges are independent from all the other branches of government.

Singer reported to Judge Bachman that he'd given up his job repairing televisions in order to teach full-time in their private school. Finally the judge vacated the jail sentences and fines he'd previously imposed, noting that he would give thought to the information contained in Dr. Cline's report. On December 4, John Singer wrote a letter to Judge Bachman, the prosecutor, Terry Christiansen, and the guardian ad litem, Robert Orton. The letter was written on the stationery of the Singers' newly incorporated school, High Uintahs Academy, Inc. After reviewing their history with the school board, John concluded his letter:

> My family and myself have been smitten more than three times since
> these troubles have begun; and we have not reviled against you people,
> nor did we seek revenge, but we were always in hopes that you people's
> hearts would be softened and show fairness to our beliefs and freedoms.
> But now, since this has not been the case, and the threat that my
> children would be taken out of our home still exists, *I now warn you in
> the name of Jesus Christ, my Lord, to cease your mischief against my
> family and myself.* This letter is also my *second* Standard of Peace that

I raise to this court, and all others concerned. Hoping you people will repent, is my deepest desire.

On December 15, the Singers sent another letter to Judge Bachman in which they respectfully declined to appear at the upcoming trial accusing them of criminal child neglect. That trial had now been reset for December 16. The Singers wrote in part:

> According to the Supreme Law of the Land and of God, the jurisdiction over my children is strictly vouched safe in my hands. Also, we are incorporated legally, by the State of Utah, as a private home school.

In response, Judge Bachman issued a bench warrant for John and Vickie's arrest, and the trial was again continued until January 3, 1978. The following day, John Singer sent an additional letter to the judge that in part stated:

> I have tried to raise the standard of peace twice before. Your decision to have me arrested is an indication that you have ignored my attempts to live at peace in this community. Therefore, in accordance with the law of God I am raising the third standard of peace and implore you in the name of the living God, the God of Abraham, of Isaac and of Jacob to dismiss all charges against me and my family.

Sympathetic members of the Singers' community had learned of the struggle the Singers were facing. Indeed, a significant population of "fundamental Mormons" (those who embraced polygamy), along with other friends and concerned citizens, were aroused at the continued abuse the Singer family was suffering at the hands of the school district and protested to the school board. As a consequence Edrington decided to "set the record straight," and on December 22, 1978, he came out with a detailed press release that outlined the extraordinary patience, tolerance, and consideration the school district had given the Singers, who, on the other hand, were unyielding and had refused to conform to reasonable requirements necessary for the well-being of their children.

Remembering what John Singer had earlier told the sheriff who threatened to arrest him—that if his arrest were attempted there would be "bloodshed"—one might surmise that Edrington's press release was intended to prepare concerned citizens to see the conflict from the standpoint of Edrington and the school district if bloodshed did in fact occur.

The Singers failed to appear for the January 3 hearing. Dr. Cline was at the hearing and testified that he'd seen the Singers on four occasions, that the children had been deprived of intellectual stimulation, and that the test differentials between the parents and the children were "shocking." Even though Vickie Singer was a "marvelous mother and woman as far as the emotional life of the children was concerned," she was "in no way competent or prepared, really, to teach these children."

Cline further testified that the Singer children tested in the bottom 8 percent of their peers, while the Singer parents tested in the top 20 percent of theirs. One wonders if Dr. Cline took into account that one child was mentally disadvantaged from birth.

Dr. Cline recommended that the Singers and the school district "negotiate" to accommodate the personal and private values of the family, while affording the children a "remedial educational experience" by having properly trained teachers come into the home. If things continued unchanged, he worried, the Singer children would suffer some "very negative, very very major adjustment problems, both vocationally as well as socially, in their later adolescent and adult lives." At the same time, he noted that in his view "yanking" the children away from their parents and putting them in another environment would not serve their interests.

Judge Bachman took Cline's recommendation. He ordered that the Singer children have daily tutoring under the direction and at the expense of the South Summit School District, specifying that the "interests, feelings, and beliefs of John and Vickie Singer . . . be taken into consideration in the type of materials used so that they are not personally offensive," and that the parents be allowed to assist in preparing the plan for the education of their children. He further ordered that the tutoring of the Singer children be monitored through testing by Dr. Cline every two months, and that Dr. Cline work with the parents and children "to bring the children to a level where they will not fall within the status of being intellectually deprived" until August 1, 1978, "at which time a hearing shall be held to examine the progress of the children and determine whether the children are prepared to return to private or public school."

The court also ordered that John and Vickie Singer "permit and allow Dr. Victor Cline . . . and school personnel into their home to teach and test their children and to cooperate fully with said persons." They would be held in contempt of court if they refused.

On January 30, 1978, the final approved plan for the tutoring of the children was mailed to the Singers by registered mail. The Singers did not respond.

On February 21, Edrington met with the Citizen's Group, a small, attentive, but vociferous group that had been previously formed to provide community input concerning school district issues. Over time their interest had expanded to include the Singer case. When a member of the group stated to Edrington that he felt the Singer issue should not be pursued, Edrington responded that he intended to press the matter to "the very ultimate."

"To the ultimate?"

People at the meeting objected. Certainly the matter should not be pushed to the point that John Singer would be killed. (A curious irony was at work here: In an earlier time John Singer had saved Edrington's son from drowning in a nearby reservoir.)

On March 1, members of the South Summit School District Board of Education met with Judge John Farr Larson, who had replaced Judge Bachman on the case. Again, why Judge Bachman was replaced is not revealed in the record. There is also no record that the Singers had been invited to the meeting. This was another of those ex parte get-togethers that are prohibited in the law. Judge Larson promised he would take action on the Singer case and "not allow the court to be backed into a corner by what has taken place in the past." Judge Larson issued an order for the Singers and their children to appear in court on March 14, 1978, to show cause why the Singer children should not be placed in custody of the state for the Singers' failure to comply with prior court orders and why John and Vickie should not be held in contempt.

Was it in the best interests of children to be ripped from the love and protection of their parents and put in the foster care of utter strangers? I wondered what I might do in the face of such threats if I were poor, without a lawyer, without a legal education, and otherwise powerless. Sheriff Ron Robinson later testified that when he served the order on the Singers, John said he'd never let anyone onto his property to enforce it.

The Singers appeared in court as ordered. Judge Larson found both John and Vickie in contempt and imposed a thirty-day jail sentence and a $200 fine, but stayed the fine and sentence for seven days to allow the Singers a chance to appeal. Judge Larson said, "The olive branch is still out. But this court cannot tolerate just a complete ignoring of the system." Vickie recorded the following in her journal:

> After analyzing our situation and praying, John experienced a marvel-ous feeling and everything was made plain. If we appealed this case to the Supreme Court it would make *null* and *void all* that we'd done in the way of setting God's laws in motion, by sending the three Standards of Peace and having performed the ordinance of the washing of our feet. We both saw the clearness of the way—that we should *not* appeal the case, and it became plain that the "olive branch" that the Judge said was still out towards us, was another subtleness of Satan.

But on March 20, one day before the stay of sentence was to expire, an unsigned notice of appeal was filed with the court. The Singers had not filed it. When they heard of it Vickie wrote, "We really felt that perhaps Satan was trying to pull trickery on us to 'thwart' the purposes of the Lord, which an appeal would do." Since this was not their appeal but one filed by an impostor, the appeal was never perfected.

When news of the supposed appeal first came to the courthouse, Terry Christiansen, the prosecuting attorney, yelled from the basement, "I've got good news—the Singers have appealed to the Utah Supreme Court!" Shortly after, Sheriff Robinson went to the Singer home and told them of Christiansen's reaction and encouraged them to appeal. Obviously the power people wanted the matter lifted from their hands and dumped in the lap of the Utah Supreme Court. Judge Larson was even willing to provide a transcript of the record free of charge and an attorney if the Singers would only appeal. *Appeal!* Perhaps the power people were experiencing doubts about the legality of their action.

Sheriff Robinson failed in his efforts to have the Singers appeal. Power seemed trapped by its own power, leaving the judge no alternative but to back off, admit defeat, and leave the Singers be. But Power does not surrender to the powerless. The judge directed Sheriff Robinson to take John and Vickie Singer into custody under the judge's thirty-day jail sentence. But again the court continued the matter to July 7, 1978, for further review.

In the meantime the public was becoming even more concerned.

Some contacted their local representative, who in turn contacted the sheriff. Judge Larson, too, was called by caring citizens. Again the sheriff approached John Singer and asked him to appeal, but the Singers, nailed to their belief that an appeal would void their work with the Lord, refused. Then the national press got interested in the story. Their publications began supplying Utah with an abundance of adverse publicity.

Governor Matheson, embarrassed, agreed that the actions of the officers had been excessive and promised that from that point on he himself would personally approve all arrest plans. The legality of his proclamation is not clear.

Reporters from a Salt Lake City television station were interviewing Dr. Cline. Speaking with all due professorial authority, he stated that because of their isolation on the family farm the children were *"brain damaged"*!

Stop!

If one hears a respected expert from the University of Utah state on TV that parents are brain-damaging their seven children, might not one agree that those kids should immediately be taken from their brain-damaging parents?

Sheriff Robinson, unarmed, again went to see John and asked him to surrender peacefully. John refused.

Judge Larson gave the Singers yet another week to comply, but remarked from the bench, "Compulsory attendance law is the law of this state. . . . It's not the court's desire to remove these children from their home unless they are denied the required minimal educational opportunities, which I believe can be afforded them without interfering with the parents' teaching their moral and religious matters. . . . I would hope that the parents will take this opportunity now to seek an appropriate solution to this important matter."

Robert Orton, the guardian ad litem for the children, wrote asking the Singers to meet with him to resolve the issues. Vickie's journal reveals the Singers' response:

> They *must* think we're stupid—to trust such a trick—we know that we would be arrested right on the spot! Besides, we have literally washed our feet of them and we have nothing more to say to them. As far as we're concerned, that court doesn't exist.

Then State Representative Samuel Taylor and two other legislators visited the Singer farm with the Bergmans, the family who, as we remember, had incorporated their own private school without any objection or intrusion by the school board. The Bergmans offered to assist in any way to "appease the courts." And again Judge Larson stayed the proceedings.

But do we understand? From the Singers' point of view, the judge had decreed that their children be taken from them and placed into the hands of strangers if the Singers did not submit to his orders. They believed the government was filled with tricksters. The Singers had made their commitment to God. God stood in the way. Their very souls were at stake. John Singer was a fugitive. What escape was there? We recall: Randy Weaver at Ruby Ridge had faced this same impasse.

Was the solution to kill the father of the children? Was the solution to thereafter take the children from the surviving mother? Was that in the best interests of the children? The Bergmans recommended that the charges be dismissed, that the Singers be left alone.

On July 3, 1978, another hearing was held, at which time Robert Orton asked the judge to vacate the order placing the children in the custody of the Division of Family Services and to grant probation to John and Vickie Singer, and a qualified homeschool person testified she'd visited the Singers' school facilities and would assist in the Singers' program. Thoughtful people were telling Power to surrender. But Judge Larson believed he had a duty to sustain the compulsory attendance law unless it was declared unconstitutional, and no constitutional issues had been raised in the case. The judge said he would give the Singers an opportunity to raise them. Finally he vacated the order granting custody of the children to the state. But in the same paper he ordered the arrest of John Singer, and to ameliorate the likelihood of violence he provided in his order:

> The sheriff shall, in his sole discretion, employ such means and take such time as are reasonably calculated to avoid the infliction of bodily harm on any person.

The judge wanted the Singers to keep their kids, but he ordered the arrest of their father?

Representative Taylor and the Bergmans again visited the Singers in a futile attempt to get them to "bend a little." On July 4, Representative Taylor wrote them a letter stating that the judge had given them "98%" of what they wanted and asking, "What will you do about the other 2%?" Again, this effort proved futile.

The judge stated that the action against the Singers could not be dismissed since there were children who had been "duly adjudicated as neglected and their parents duly convicted of a criminal offense," which was another way of saying that Power can never surrender. At the same time, the Singers were still trapped between man and God.

On July 12, Judge Larson wrote Governor Matheson a three-page letter to "inform and update" him on the Singer matter. Why did a judge feel it necessary to appease the governor? The judge's conclusion: "I cannot in good conscience excuse [Singer] from complying with the law of this State because of his threats of violence nor his claimed communications from God."

On July 17, 1978, John Singer, without a marriage license, married himself to a second wife, Shirley Black. At the time John performed this marriage, Shirley Black was legally married to Dean Black. Did this polygamous marriage in a state framed, founded, and historically fed on polygamy provide the last straw?

Sheriff Robinson now asked the judge to amend his earlier order requiring the cops to avoid violence. He argued that he could not predict what Singer would do, and therefore he could not arrest Singer under the terms of the judge's order. Judge Larson amended his order, opening the door to killing. Looking back, we remember that the original charge against John Singer—a failure to send his kids to the public school—was a misdemeanor, something slightly more serious than parking in a no-parking zone.

Randy Weaver at Ruby Ridge would have understood: His failure to appear in court as ordered led to the killing of a dog, to the killing of his son, and to multiple deaths and horror. Ah, *Power!*

The sheriff wanted more help. He commandeered more officers from the Narcotics and Liquor Law Enforcement Division with Governor Matheson's approval. After Judge Larson heard of Singer's illegal marriage, he ordered the children back into the custody of the Division of Family Services and ordered that Vickie be arrested for their neglect. *Polygamy* was the Singers' latest crime committed against Mormon Power, which to this day knowingly tolerates nearby polygamist settlements. Power now jammed the door wide open for a killing.

Arrest the Singers and put their kids in the hands of the state?
John Singer would die to prevent that.

Robert Wadman, the director of the Narcotics and Liquor Law Enforcement Division, Larry Lunnen, the Utah commissioner of public
safety, and Highway Patrol Superintendent Robert J. Reid put their minds
together: How could they arrest John Singer? These agencies, with scores
of armed men, now directed their focus on this one "renegade Mormon"
who simply wanted to educate his own children (and shelter a second wife).

Aware of the challenge a cornered Singer presented, the lawmen held at
least three meetings to plan the arrest. They first considered masquerad-
ing as hunters in the area, and when Singer left to retrieve his mail from
his postal box some distance from the house they'd arrest him. This plan
was rejected. Hunters would be armed, and if Singer suspected they were
cops he would likely arm himself. They wanted no confrontation with an
armed John Singer.

Next they considered posing as religious people sympathetic to polygamy, but this plan was rejected because the law enforcement officers were
not sufficiently knowledgeable regarding religion to pull off that ruse. For
similar reasons they shot down a plan to pose as sympathetic attorneys
who wanted to help.

The arrest plan on which they finally settled was for the cops to pose as
news reporters. Wadman and two of his agents went to the Singer farm,
and Wadman identified himself as a journalist and offered to pay John for
his story. Two other officers posed as his camera crew. As they shook hands
with Singer, they planned to advise him they were officers and place him
under arrest. But as Wadman later testified in his deposition, Singer didn't
go easily.

A. We were wrestling trying to put handcuffs on. . . .

Q. What prevented you from getting Mr. Singer subdued?

A. He was just too strong for me. . . .

Q. Do you know of anybody who showed him a badge?

A. Bill Riggs [one of the other cops] did. At one point Singer pulled
out a gun.

Q. How could the officer show him a badge when you were engaged in
the struggle?

A. It was afterwards when he [Singer] was waving the gun around.

Q. Did anybody show him a badge before?

A. No, sir, not that I seen. . . .

Q. As a matter of fact, as he was struggling with you it would have been as reasonable for him to believe that you were lying to him about being police officers as well as lying to him about being newspapermen, isn't that right?

A. I guess.

Vickie's journal provided a decidedly different story:

> John had gone out to meet the press and was shaking their hands, when they all started to grab him and started lifting him into their van. John began kicking and struggling, as the men held his hands behind his back.
>
> I ran out and grabbed the man who was on John's back and was ready to smash him hard in the face, when he pulled back with a startled, scared, look on his face, and said, "No! Don't!" I said, "I'll knock your teeth out!" I didn't have to strike him because he let go.

As I read her account, I was shocked to see that sweet, humble, retiring woman in such a ferocious frenzy. She reminded me of the hummingbird that will attack even a man if you invade its nest. She went on in her journal:

> Just before that time, John had gotten his hands loose somehow and was able to get his gun out of his pocket. . . . The kids started to pound on the cops.
>
> Right away the men said, "We'll leave!" They looked *really* scared. They were white and sickly looking. . . . They left in a cloud of dust! . . . They did not identify themselves at the first as they said they did in the newspaper.

Governor Matheson didn't remember giving the OK for this group to arrest John, and said he was opposed to their ploy. Nonetheless, the next move of the police was to obtain a felony warrant against Singer for his "assault on police officers."

On October 30, 1978, Judge Larson submitted a new order stating that because his previous arrest orders on both John and Vickie Singer had not been executed, he was ordering the sheriff of Summit County to arrest the

Singers "upon penalty of contempt." In layman's language that meant, "Arrest the Singers, Mr. Sheriff, or I will throw you, badge and all, in jail." The Utah lawmen next had the Singer situation reviewed by a number of law enforcement agencies, including the FBI, the Los Angeles Police Department, the National Guard, the Salt Lake County Sheriff's Office, and the police departments of Provo, Ogden, and Salt Lake City, Utah. Surely all of these experts could come up with a reasonable plan to arrest the Singers, who were peacefully staying home, trying to educate their kids, and keeping themselves safe from invading cops.

The record reported that among the plans these lawmen considered was shutting off the power and water, and putting tranquilizing drugs in the water supply, but these were deemed too dangerous to the children. They ultimately decided to carry out a twenty-four-hour surveillance of the Singer place by disguising themselves as vacationing skiers. They carried on this surveillance for eighteen days.

Governor Matheson was asked by Harald Singer, John's brother, to pardon John and to let the whole thing just go away. Matheson said he couldn't, because the power to grant a pardon was vested in the Board of Pardons, not the governor.

By January 15, 1979, the Singer farm was in full winter regalia. The snow was deep. Three snowmobiles with two officers each, all with bulletproof vests, and fully coordinated by radio, would descend on Singer when he left his house to get his mail. Two more snowmobiles, two officers on each, would cut off his retreat. At the time, some lawmen called the plan "stupid" and "dangerous." At about 12:15 P.M., John Singer walked down the snow-covered lane to the family mailbox. Suddenly six officers on three snowmobiles roared full speed toward him, brandishing shotguns. Neither the officers nor their snowmobiles bore any police markings.

Singer, alarmed by this charge by armed strangers, drew his pistol in an attempt to frighten them off, but he didn't shoot. Instead, he turned and ran toward his house. But he never made it—he was shot with multiple rounds of buckshot in the back. Officers on the shooting team would later admit that under this arrest plan the killing of John Singer was foreordained, a conclusion confirmed by the later deposition testimony of preeminent police experts.

The officers would dispute the claim that they weren't wearing police identification jackets and that only one shot from a shotgun was fired. They admit that Officer Lewis Jolley was about twenty feet from Singer when he was shot. Jolley says he saw Singer squint his eye as if aiming at him. John fell facedown in the snow.

The officers later claimed that they hollered they were police, but Jolley, closest to Singer, heard no such thing. An officer turned John over where he lay in the snow, bleeding but still alive.

Charlotte Singer was in the house watching through binoculars just before her father was shot. She said, "I seen his mouth go open and blood come out." Then she saw him fall. I wondered if the power people thought a child seeing her father killed was an appropriate part of the child's education?

Vickie had been teaching when Charlotte screamed. She grabbed her .22 rifle, and Singer's second wife, Shirley Black, found a pistol, and little Heidi took her bow and arrow. That meager contingent would face ten fully armed lawmen with enough shotguns, buckshot, pistols, and ammo to blow away half of the county. Heidi heard *two* shots. One of Shirley's children heard two shots. Both Joseph and Benjamin Singer, eight and six years old respectively, testified at their depositions that they also heard two shots.

Officer Ron Gunderson told Officer Jolley that he, Gunderson, had also fired, but he changed his story at his deposition. But on the day of the shooting another officer reported, "Gunderson thought he had shot. He said that he was squeezing the bastard [the gun] so hard he had to have shot."

After John Singer fell, the cops, without determining if first aid was called for, loaded him into the front seat of a pickup truck. Vickie Singer testified that when the truck left, it turned away from, not toward, the hospital. Given the fact that his death was predictable, it is noted that no medical personnel were included among the platoon of officers who took part in his arrest. The trip to the hospital required half an hour. It was no surprise: *The subject was DOA.*

Vickie was hauled off to jail. The record is silent on how she learned of her husband's death. Her children were taken from her and lodged in a "Salt Lake detention center," harmless sounding words for jail. Good education for kids, right?

In such a notorious case one would expect an exceedingly careful investigation. The state medical examiner, J. Wallace Graham, recovered only two of the shotgun pellets in the body of Mr. Singer and two others from Mr. Singer's clothing. He gave the four pellets to a Summit County deputy, who recalled at his deposition that he had signed a receipt for the pellets but could not specifically remember ever receiving them. Late in September of 1980, it was discovered that the pellets from Singer's body as well as his shirt were missing. Tests for gunpowder residue on the hands of the cops were not made. Neither the officers' guns nor their ammunition was ever collected. Meaningful diagrams and photographs, standard in police investigation, were never made. No better cover-up of a crime can be imagined than no investigation at all.

One would expect the state to charge forward with all information necessary for a full and fair review of the incident. The state contended publicly that John Singer was shot only once when the autopsy photos showed a spray of projectiles across his back. And the eminent pathologist Dr. Werner Spitz testified at his deposition that Mr. Singer was shot multiple times.

The same concerned citizens' group asked the attorney general to submit a list of more than twenty questions to a grand jury, but they were ignored. The FBI investigated, but the results have never been published. The county attorney's office did its investigation, but those results remain unpublished, too. Preparing to defend possible lawsuits, the Utah attorney general's office also investigated. The Summit County attorney then issued a statement that he found no grounds to file any criminal actions against any of the officers. As we recall, the case against Horiuchi in the Weaver case was also finally dismissed, and no officer was ever charged with the killing of Little Sammy and his mother.

Yet another hearing was held in Judge Larson's court on January 19, 1979. Vickie was released after four days in jail, but the children were kept in "protective custody." Protection from a mother's care and comfort after having witnessed the killing of their father?

A local printer called me and put me in touch with Vickie. When we talked on the phone, the sound of her voice and her straight, clear, simple plea for justice moved me. But if we were to represent her I needed help. I'd been appointed the special prosecutor in a criminal case I would soon file against Mark Hopkinson, the evil, psychopathic killer of at least five Wyoming citizens. That trial began on September 3, 1979, and was followed by my defense of the Rock Springs sheriff and fast gun Ed Cantrell, who was charged with murder and whose trial began on November 12, 1979, and continued to the end of that month.

I asked my partner Bob Schuster to investigate, and after his initial fact gathering he recommended that we file suit on behalf of Vickie and her children for the death of their husband and father, and that we take the necessary depositions to support a case Schuster believed was waiting to be fully unearthed, one that would show that John Singer had been wrongfully killed.

We brought suit in the U.S. District Court for the District of Utah in Salt Lake City against Robert Wadman, the director of the Division of Narcotics and Liquor Law Enforcement, and Val Edrington, the county superintendent of schools. We sued Governor Matheson, Sheriff Robinson, the county attorney, and a bunch of deputies and secondary participants in this story. In fact, we sued about everyone in sight, and some who were hiding. Our sixty-five-page complaint named them all.

Our case was about the violation of John Singer's right to life. The surviving Singers claimed they were deprived of other constitutionally protected rights—to due process of law, to be free from "a systematic scheme of harassment and intimidation by law enforcement officers," to be free from unlawful assaults, to be free from malicious prosecution, and to be free from discrimination because of their religious beliefs. We sued the defendants for their negligence, gross and otherwise, along with other causes of action.

In December of 1982, my assistant, Rosemary McIntosh, and I drove up to Mrs. Singer's home near Marion, Utah, in the mountains. It was a farm with outbuildings; the house was a rugged wooden structure with faded greenish paint. Vickie Singer met us at the door and invited us in. She was plain, yet in plain ways beautiful. She wore no makeup. Her blond hair fell in a single long braid down her back. She was obviously missing some teeth, and she was dressed in a simple cotton dress that extended to her ankles. Yet if I were to pick one word to describe her it would still be "beautiful."

This was a widow with seven children. Her husband had been killed and the surrounding facts covered up. She was calm, quiet, and sweet in a naïve and simple way. I thought her ability to forgive, perhaps even to love, was somehow in control. We met only her younger girls. Presumably the boys were working. The girls, too, wore long skirts.

The kitchen was large with a woodstove. Tomatoes were lined up on the windowsill to ripen. A large eating table sat in the middle of the room. Mrs. Singer and I adjourned to the living room, a small, worn, but cozy place where we could be alone so that whatever she told me would be protected by the attorney-client privilege. That privilege would be lost if a person not her attorney were present during the conversation.

After we left I asked Rosemary, a good judge of character, what she thought of Vickie Singer. She said, "I like her a lot. She was open and quietly committed. Yet she seemed gentle. Her beliefs were a little outside the norm. But she had a good sense of humor and laughed easily." I agreed.

By the time the federal district court judge, David Winder, found time for our case, some twenty-odd motions were pending before his court, including motions to throw the case out brought by all of the officials we'd sued.

Approximately a thousand pages of legal memoranda had been filed in the case. We'd taken the pretrial testimony of seventy-two potential witnesses—depositions, as they're called—that included thousands of pages of their transcribed testimony. Judge Winder endured nearly two full days of oral arguments from the litigants, including us. The issue: Had we made enough of a case to present to a jury?

Judge Winder labored over his opinion, one that took on the proportions of a book, perhaps the longest in Utah's judicial history. Ironically it took him 218 pages to conclude that we had no legal claim of merit, that there was nothing for the jury to decide, and he dismissed our case, depriving Vickie Singer and the Singer children the right to a jury trial—or any trial, for that matter. "Get out of here. Go home" was the effect of the judge's message to Vickie and her kids.

Judge Winder related most of the facts I've recited here, but he also faced testimony by leading experts who stated that the cops' arrest plan, as well as the execution of that plan, violated basic police protocol, and that both the planning and its execution—yes, the official conduct of the police themselves—were grossly negligent and in violation of standard law enforcement procedures. Despite this testimony in the record before him, Judge Winder tossed our case into the judicial garbage pit.

We'd asked Winder to disqualify himself from hearing the Singer case and appoint a judge from outside the district, someone free of local political and religious influence. Winder was a friendly man with a sparkling reputation. But cases exist that the best of judges cannot try, for despite their occasional suggestion to the contrary, judges are people, often good people, and it is hard for good people to be disloyal to their friends and those who have befriended them. And it's hard for a good person to ignore the culture, teaching, and beliefs of the community in which he was born and reared, in this case the Mormon establishment. It is the obligation of such a judge to disqualify himself if any of the foregoing might influence his decision. What am I talking about here?

Glenn Hanni became the spokesperson for most of the defendants we'd sued, including Governor Scott Matheson, County Attorney Adkins, Attorney General Robert Hansen, and Deputy County Attorney Terry Christiansen, who, along with Judge Winder, were all fellows of the Utah Bar. Hanni and Judge Winder were close friends and had practiced law together for eleven years. And who originally appointed Judge Winder to the bench? Governor Matheson had elevated him to the state court bench in 1975, before Winder became a federal judge. What rights would we expect a powerless widow of a dead "Mormon renegade" and her childen to have against such a cadre of power?

Further, Judge Winder had been reared in a Mormon family, though in response to our motion to disqualify him he assured us he was no longer a *practicing* Mormon. Undoubtedly most of his friends and associates were practicing Mormons, and their continued approval of the judge's decisions would likely be important to him.

Vickie Singer herself was so concerned about the judge's ability to impartially hear her case that during our arguments before Judge Winder she asked to address him personally. I shall never forget hearing her trembling words in open court to a powerful federal judge in his black robe peering down at her. She could have just come in from the garden. She was wearing her usual cotton dress that came to her ankles without frills or flowers. Her shoes were low heeled and round toed and scuffed from long use. She held on to her calloused, cracked hands as she spoke, and wore a small sad smile on her face. Her eyes were gentle and her voice soft with quavers that fell off at the ends of her phrases.

As she spoke, the judge leaned forward to hear her, her words plain and clear as the song of a distant prairie bird. She took the judge in with kindness but never took her eyes from him. Here is what she said:

> I humbly and respectfully approach you, and I want to tell you that this is not strategy. I'm a very deep-feeling individual, as was my husband. We have had a very hard time of it because we are in the minority. Very much so. Our sacred beliefs have been defiled and trampled upon by those who do not understand, by those who may be, perhaps, in the

lower realm of progress. Not that I am boasting that I am in a higher realm, but I have seen that those who are on the opposing side cannot and do not rightfully consider our deep and sacred and holy beliefs. . . .

And I truly believe that you are an honorable person. I have talked with a friend of yours who went to school with you and he said, "I'm really glad that you have him for a judge." . . . I am very worried, and I am worried for you. . . .

I am worried for me. Because I have to be heard as I am and I haven't had that chance. My husband never had that chance because he was looked upon as a renegade, as a stubborn and rebellious person. Not one of you in here knew my husband, and I feel badly. And I'm afraid because of the atmosphere and the things that were said the other day that no one will be able to know my husband. . . .

And you have to believe me that I am telling you truth, and I humbly tell you that you are in a very peculiar situation and very hard situation. And I'm afraid that if you continue to carry forth with this case you will have to put everything on the line to be able to be just. And I know you want to be just. I feel that in you. I'm afraid that you can't be just unless you are willing to pay the price that I have paid and that my husband paid.

But her simple, eloquent plea did not move Judge Winder. Later, some of the judge's personal feelings escaped into his opinion. For instance, when we complained that those we sued had attempted to manipulate the judges and the press, for which there was ample evidence in the record, Judge Winder wrote:

> Only disciples of Jacob and Wilhelm Grimm [of Grimms' fairy tales] could accept as reasonable the inferences which plaintiffs' counsel *seeks to foist* on this court (my emphasis).

To his credit, the judge wrote, "I know the heat is on me." Respecting his ability to impartially judge, he wrote, "I didn't say I can do it. I am going to try to do it." A judge who isn't sure he can be impartial ought not *try*. Why would a fair judge require John Singer's heirs to take the risk that he couldn't be impartial? And if he couldn't be impartial, how would he know it? Our self-judgments are usually the most myopic and most prejudiced.

Judge Winder should have taken himself off the case.

If one reads his opinion, which carries on with the committed endurance of a long-distance runner, one comes across jewels like "There are no objective facts in the record from which it can be inferred that the defendants manipulated witnesses to present false and misleading information to the juvenile courts in order to obtain their objectives." But I ask, how many ex parte conversations, meetings, and the like were held in the absence of the Singers? The inferences of impropriety were scattered over the entire record like dust in a desert dust storm that a jury trial would have uncovered.

The judge wrote, "Without attempting to become embroiled in a debate as to the propriety or impropriety of these alleged contacts, the court states only that this objective evidence does not give rise to an inference that the defendants conspired to commit a lawful act by an unlawful means." That simply means, "Those ex parte carryings-on in the juvenile court may have been improper, but I, the judge, am not going to look, and a jury isn't either."

Judge Winder passed the ever-ready buck. He found that "it was for the [juvenile] court to determine the constitutionality of the school law that forced citizens into public schools when their religion was in conflict with the same." *The juvenile court?* Too bad, he said in effect—you may have been prosecuted under an invalid law. Who knows? (And who cares?) And pray tell, why were those judges taken off the juvenile court and replaced by other judges from time to time like flat tires on a jalopy? No one knows to this day.

How does a decent judge who says he is no longer a practicing member of the church perform the necessary surgery on his subconscious mind and extract the influence of the very culture he was born in, grew up in, and lives in every day of his life? We asked too much of the man. He asked too much of himself. I think he knew it.

We appealed to the circuit court, first charging that Judge Winder should have disqualified himself. Among other rulings, the appeals court wrote that Judge Winder's former partnership with a lawyer for one of the defendants did not require his disqualification, and the court held that "the various remarks made by the district judge [Judge Winder] during the course of the proceedings do not, as counsel suggests, substantiate the claim of bias or prejudice. On the contrary, in our view, the district judge exhibited commendable patience and restraint throughout this admittedly and understandably emotional affair."

The court continued in its opinion, "Applying the definition of a civil conspiracy to the instant case, the record indicates beyond any doubt that though the defendants, or some of them, were acting in concert, they were not committing an unlawful act." I suppose that the repeated ex parte meetings with the various judges, and the application of Governor Matheson's influence on juvenile court judges, were not unlawful. "On the contrary," the appeals court ruled, "the defendants were committing a lawful act, enforcing the Utah Compulsory Attendance laws and arresting a person for whom there were outstanding arrest warrants."

What about shooting John Singer in the back as he was running home? Here's what the court wrote: "With respect to the claim for relief alleging excessive force, the depositional testimony shows that Singer, who on prior occasions had stated that he would resist arrest and that any attempt to arrest would involve 'blood shed,' resisted arrest on this occasion by pulling a gun from his belt and pointing it at the law enforcement officers. In such circumstances, the deputies did not have to wait for Singer to fire first; they had a right to shoot to kill." I wondered what the appeals court judges might have concluded had they joined the pathologist in digging out the shotgun pellets that had been sprayed across the back of the running John Singer. Is the new rule of law that if you run, you are resisting arrest and the cops can shoot you in the back?

The appeals court said the court did not want to repeat the facts contained in a 218-page opinion. I don't blame them. As my old grandfather used to say, "Enough is enough, and too much is aplenty." Lost in this storm of judicial rhetoric was the original issue: *the welfare of the children.* One wonders if the judges felt comfortable in deciding that the children's interests were protected by multiple slugs in their father's back, compounded by the loss of their right to a jury trial for his death. Judge Winder's decision, as confirmed by the court of appeals, stopped any further exposure of the embarrassing facts in this case and, as we shall see, led to the killing of yet another American citizen.

We, of course, appealed to the U.S. Supreme Court, but, as expected, certiorari was denied—cold, hard, dead words, which, when John Singer's penniless heirs knocked at that great court's door and pled for admittance, simply meant, "Keep out. We have important cases to decide (when we get around to it)."

John Singer was buried in the Marion, Utah, cemetery on January 22, 1979.

I wish I could say that this was the end of it. But I have said more than once: One can suffer all nature of physical injury and survive; one can never bear the supreme injury of being deprived of justice. The pain is too deep and too real, too disabling and too lasting. As time passed, the need for retribution became an irresistible compulsion to the Singer family. Such is the resulting disease of injustice.

John Singer became a messiah to his surviving family. We must believe in messiahs. They connect us to hope. Even in our short lives we have witnessed budding messiahs, and seen them deified. Mother Teresa and Martin Luther King Jr. come easily to mind. And Gandhi.

After nine years, starved of justice, and facing the rejection and disdain of the Mormon establishment, Addam Swapp, who had married two of John Singer's daughters, Charlotte and Heidi, came to a belief that questioned sound minds—that the destruction of a Mormon symbol, namely one of its churches, would so please their messiah, John Singer, that he would reappear. Swapp, his two wives, and their six children, along with Vickie and her family, lived on the same two and a half acres near Marion where John Singer had lived and died.

On January 16, 1988, two days before the ninth anniversary of John Singer's death, and to fulfill his revelation, Addam Swapp broke into the Kamas LDS Stake Center, the local Mormon church. He lugged in fifty pounds of dynamite, along with a booster of ammonium nitrate intended to double the charge, and detonated it at three in the morning as the family watched. The blast rocked the neighborhood and was said to cause $1.5 million in damage. Stuck in the ground at the scene the authorities found a spear with nine feathers standing for the nine years that had passed since John Singer had been murdered.

The Summit County sheriff's office immediately requested help from the Utah Department of Public Safety, and because explosives had been used, the department called in the ATF and FBI. Within twenty-four hours, an army of more than a hundred law enforcement officers surrounded the premises, along with a canine corps of attack dogs. Because of the six children who huddled in the house, all under the age of six, the authorities were instructed not to fire their weapons. Their tactic was to capture the leader of the clan, Addam Swapp, on the assumption that thereafter the rest would surrender.

In an attempt to exhaust and demoralize the Singer clan in their standoff, the attackers day and night barraged the house with flashing floodlights and blaring sirens, which made sleep impossible. The government attackers next shot out the house's power transformers to deprive the family of electricity. The main water line to the house was severed so that the occupants had no water or sewer facilities. A public address system was installed that emitted high-pitched electronic static, intended to force into submission people whose mental stability was already in question.

Inside, the Singer family prayed to God and to his son, and to John Singer. They prayed for salvation, for guidance, for deliverance, and for peace and, yes, they prayed that their attackers would be forgiven. After more than a week of torture, the Singers still refused to surrender. Their revelation was that an armed confrontation was necessary to bring the resurrection of John Singer, and that was worth dying for.

In the meantime, as many as fifty Utah citizens descended on Governor Norman Bangerter's mansion to demand a peaceful conclusion to the standoff. The governor sent a letter to the Singers asking them to surrender. But in a seven-page responding letter Swapp wrote, among other things:

> We are independent and separate from your wicked society of ever changing laws and dark councils. . . . Those who would come against this my people, will I verily cause to be destroyed.

Vickie Singer joined in the correspondence, writing a nine-page letter that said, in part:

> I am John Singer's faithful wife. Prophet of God [Christ] was persecuted and martyred because he would not compromise the truths of Heaven. . . . [The authorities] will not take our children for they are a heritage of the Lord and they are the children of Zion, the covenant children of the Lord. . . . We will not compromise our stand. . . . The matter of the bombing of the church was of God making bare His arm through his servant, Addam Swapp. . . . Church, state and nation will be brought up to a standing like a wild colt to a snubbing post.

On January 28, 1988, the police commissioned something they called a "flashbang," essentially a blinding, deafening explosion. When Swapp left the house at six in the morning and began to tear down a loudspeaker, the flashbang was ignited, intended to put Swapp out of commission. Immediately following the flashbang a police dog handler released his dog to attack Swapp, but the dog was as startled by the explosion as was Swapp and ran from the scene without attacking. Swapp fired at the dog and missed.

The feds then decided they would turn two trained dogs loose on Addam and Jonathan Swapp, his brother, when they next left the house to feed the animals and milk the goats in the early morning. After they finished the chores and started back to the house, a couple of cops, who'd been hiding along the windowless side of the building, jumped out and loosed the dogs. But before the dogs could reach Addam and Jonathan, three shots were fired from the house. One shot killed one of the dog handlers, an officer named Fred House from the Utah Department of Corrections. Both dogs were uninjured.

Swapp put his rifle to the ready, but before he fired he, too, was hit; a bullet went through his wrist, traveled into his chest, and lodged in his back. He managed to run to the house for cover. Meanwhile, more shots were fired from the house, with one hitting FBI agent Don Roberts, who was saved by his bulletproof vest. Then Swapp came running out of the house waving a bloody white towel and surrendered, and with his surrender came the surrender of the entire family and the end of a thirteen-day siege.

Addam Swapp, John Timothy Singer, Jonathan Swapp, and Vickie Singer finally were brought to trial in the state court of Summit County, where they were charged with murder along with many lesser charges. These nine years after the killing of John Singer, our firm was no longer representing the Singers. The cases against the Swapps and the Singers were defended by court-appointed lawyers.

In the state court criminal cases, Addam Swapp and John Timothy Singer were convicted of manslaughter for the death of Fred House. Jonathan was convicted of misdemeanor negligent homicide; it was his bullet that had hit House. Vickie, who hadn't fired a weapon and had nothing whatsoever to do with building a bomb, was found not guilty of any state crimes. That she should escape punishment was unacceptable to Power. So the feds came with a new eight-count indictment that recharged the same four with various other crimes—from building, possessing, and using bombs to resisting and assaulting the FBI, attempting to kill FBI officers, and possession of a sawed-off shotgun.

Addam Swapp was the only defendant at the federal trial who testified. He said that he never aimed at or tried to shoot any of the law enforcement officials, although he had plenty of chances, and that he knew the siege had to be over after he'd been shot. He said that when he saw the bomb explode it looked as if many evil spirits were rising above the church. He said God told him to stand and fight like a man. He admitted he owned a sawed-off shotgun.

On May 9, 1988, the jury returned its verdicts in the federal court, finding Addam guilty of seven of the eight counts, Vickie guilty of five, and Jonathan and John Timothy each guilty of three. U.S. District Chief Judge Bruce Jenkins gave Addam Swapp a fifteen-year prison sentence, plus five years probation. He sentenced Vickie Singer to five years in prison and five years probation. Jonathan Swapp and John Timothy Singer were each sentenced to ten years in prison and five years probation for attacking federal officers and using guns in the siege and shootout.

Vickie Singer, in her quiet way, said she didn't believe justice was done, but she thanked God that court-ordered tests proved she was not mentally ill. "I just ask you to please release me so I can go home and take care of my family," she said, weeping, to Judge Jenkins.

The children! We remember that this tragedy began when the forces of Power were exercised over a simple matter: John Singer wanted to home-school his children, something that across America is common today. But Power is merely power. It is not wise. It does not love those over whom it exercises its supremacy. Power loves only power.

A few years earlier, when John Timothy Singer was seventeen, a tree fell on him and paralyzed him, confining him permanently to a wheelchair. He'd been taken from public school at age five and educated by his mother and father. John Timothy had no education or experience in the criminal law. He was terrorized when he was arrested by the feds, and he didn't understand his Miranda rights that protected him from saying anything to the authorities.

John Timothy, in his wheelchair, told the police that he hadn't surrendered earlier because he felt doing so would mean he didn't believe in the Lord. In pure innocence he made statements to the authorities on his way to jail that incriminated him as well as other members of his family. He said he fired shots at the dogs. He did not aim his gun because he didn't need to. The Lord would guide his bullets. Later the FBI claimed it had been a bullet from John Timothy's gun that hit and killed Fred House.

Although this young man talked to the officers on his way to jail, the officers, of course, claimed that they'd fully advised him of his Miranda rights to remain silent. At the police station they had him sign a waiver of his rights.

Michael DeCaria, a psychologist, testified that he had examined John Timothy and concluded that he was very susceptible to coercion, that he was unable to make decisions based on a rational intellect, that he was unable to exercise his own free will, and that he would have been unable to make a knowing and intelligent waiver of his constitutional rights. Nevertheless, surprising no one, the trial judge let John Timothy's confession go to the jury, and the court of appeals agreed, with an accompanying judicial yawn.

The federal trial judge thought that Addam Swapp should only be sentenced to count one, and not count two of the complaint since both counts relied on the same facts. But the appeals court disagreed, and Swapp was sentenced to fifteen years in federal prison for the bombing and to an *additional* five years for using explosives in the bombing. I have never understood how one could be guilty of bombing without explosives having been used. Might that teach one not to appeal? Swapp was sent to a federal prison in Indiana, and after spending more than twenty years in prison he was recently released on parole.

John Timothy Singer and Jonathan Swapp both served ten years in the federal pen and were released. Vickie Singer served three and a half years and finally came home to her family.

As in the Weaver case, again the haughtiness of Power and the stubborn belief of citizens in their constitutional rights brought on death. The triggering acts were simple: in the Weaver case, the killing of their dog; in the Singer case, parents who wanted to homeschool their own children. Both the Weaver and Singer families claimed to be following the revelations of God. Both believed that God and the Constitution would protect them. Both families were mistaken in both instances. None of the foregoing purports to approach the unfathomable grief and loss suffered by the families of the slain on both sides. No one won. Only dead Power prevailed.

Years later I got a letter from Vickie. I value it more than any fee I might have received. She wrote:

> [I remember] the magnificent performance and tremendous sacrifice
> that you gave in behalf of my husband's wrongful death. It shall never

be forgotten. The powers that be wouldn't have otherwise been exposed at that time. I am not a vindictive person, God knows, but the truth shall be known, believe me. Your monumental work was not in vain. You shall yet witness the fruits thereof. May you be blessed beyond words.

Bob Schuster, my partner, spent massive portions of his life attempting to force the justice system to open its doors and give her and her children a fair trial for their damages brought on by the death of John Singer. But not even the United States Supreme Court had the inclination to hear the plea of this saintly woman for justice.

Let us ask simple questions:

Why was this family deprived of any justice? *Any.*

Should a federal appeals court permit a federal trial judge to sit on a case against the Mormon power structure when that judge, from his earliest days, had been affixed to that same Mormon power structure like an apple to an apple tree and suffered his own doubts about his ability to be impartial?

Is it acceptable in America for our courts to turn their judicial backs on the surviving family of an American citizen whose underlying crime was simply his refusal to give his children over to others to educate in ways he believed would damage their souls and his?

Is it acceptable in Utah, or anywhere in America, for officers to shoot a fleeing citizen in the back who was running home to escape arrest?

Is it acceptable that the killing of an American citizen by the police should be covered up by the deliberate failure of the police to preserve the evidence, so that a competent investigation could never be made?

Deprive a human being of justice and the human will die for it. Ask the martyrs of history. The refusal of justice plants a cancer in the soul. The refusal of the justice system to give the Singers the opportunity to have their case heard by a jury, a celebrated American right, caused the cancer to grow and to finally detonate nine years after John Singer's murder with the church bombing by Addam Swapp.

I think of Vicki Weaver, the mother. I think of Vickie Singer, also the mother. Both were powerless and poor. Both were simple, gentle, loving women. One was killed by a sniper's bullet. The other has died endless deaths over the murder of her husband, her long years of imprisonment, and the imprisonment of her children. Both mothers were martyrs for religious beliefs not embraced by Power. Both were the victims of Power. And both glowed in that certain light of the saints. But Power has little ability to understand mothers, because Power, in the end, is ignorant of the nascent goodness of the human species, especially its mothers.

CASE 5

SMASH THE STEEL BUTTERFLY

After the verdict, no one wanted to touch her story, not my literary agent at the time, not my former editors or publisher—no one. Gaggling reporters proved more interested in Imelda Marcos's several thousand pairs of shoes than in the criminal conspiracy with which she'd been charged.

I never met Ferdinand Marcos. What I knew of him I was told by Power's propaganda machine, the media, that conditions the way we see things—most of us. I do not contend that Marcos was a virtuous man. I do not deny that he was a tyrant and a crook. I do not know. I do not claim that his wife, Imelda, was but an innocent wife. I do not know. Let me be clear: The mission of this story is not to pass judgment on the Marcoses. I left that to a New York jury. The mission of this story is simple: to tell what I experienced in the defense of Imelda Marcos. That is a true story.

The story will provide its own facts, many of which have never found their way to a public page. It is a story that reveals an unapologetic, unabashed police state, one that was in full, shameless bloom, in which some of the criminals lounged in the White House, and their crimes extended across the globe to the Philippines. This is a story that has never been told because Power would not permit its telling.

For two decades Ferdinand Marcos had ruled the Philippines as its virtual dictator. He was not without opposition. In 1983 Benigno Aquino, the popular opposition leader, had been assassinated. Marcos, denying involvement and expressing appropriate shock, promised to bring those responsible to justice. He appointed a commission to investigate. But asking Power to investigate itself is like asking the Mafia to cough up facts to send its membership to prison.

This case will introduce us to a truth that lingers in the hazy, duplici-
tous rule book of international law: that our basic ideals—truth telling,
loyalty, compassion, even our adherence to the criminal law—can be cast
aside as rubbish in the wind, as irrelevant and even foolish, when Power's
interests are at stake. This case will force us to ask uncomfortable questions: Who were the criminals here—the Marcoses or the various func-
tionaries in our own government, beginning with our then-president?

In 1984, when debating Walter Mondale for the presidency, Ronald
Reagan said, "I know there are things there in the Philippines that do not
look good to us from the standpoint of democratic rights. But . . . I think
that we're better off . . . trying to retain our friendship and help them right
the wrongs we see rather than throwing them to the wolves and then facing a Communist power in the Pacific." Reagan understood geography—
the close proximity of Communist China and North Vietnam to the
Philippines. American bases in the Philippines were at stake. That exigency
opened the door for a new set of rules involving the Marcoses, even their
kidnapping and prosecution.

Day by day the Marcos abscess on the Philippine body politic had
continued to fester. Ferdinand's downfall seemed imminent. At the urg-
ing of the United States that Marcos solidify his power, he called for a snap
election, and who might one predict would be his opponent? Why, to be
sure, Corazon Aquino, the widow of Marcos's assassinated challenger,
Benigno Aquino.

Marcos claimed he won the election by at least a million votes, but massive crowds took to the streets and charged the houses of government in a
movement called the People Power Revolution. The United States, conclud-
ing a change of power was inevitable, urged Marcos to vacate the premises.

The Marcoses and the Reagans were more than diplomatic compatriots
who sipped tea and dipped tarts. They'd become close friends, and Reagan made promises to Marcos. If Marcos would relinquish power to Corazon Aquino, the United States would airlift Marcos and his family to
the safety of their home in the northern reaches of the Philippines. To seal
the deal Reagan sent Senator Paul Laxalt to Manila. Marcos wanted assurance that he and his family would be "spared vindictiveness and revenge."
Such assurances fell from Laxalt's lips like bubbles from a seltzer bottle.

On February 20, 1986, relying on these promises from their longtime
friend Ronald Reagan, the Marcoses gathered up their most vital posses-

sions and boarded the plane supplied by the United States. But instead of landing at home in Ilocos Norte, the Marcoses found themselves in Honolulu, U.S.A., kidnapped and captives of the United States government.

Why the double-cross? Of course, we never heard the dialogue between the new takeover regime of Corazon Aquino, President Reagan, and his loyal attendants: If one had been privy to the conversation one could have heard the Aquinos shouting from Manila across the 8,400-some miles to Washington. "So, Mr. U.S. of A., you want your military bases over here? Let us tell you the price: We want the Marcoses out of here. We do not want them ever again on Philippine soil, not even in a Philippine prison. Dump them into one of your own prisons." But how could our government prosecute the Marcoses in the United States for alleged crimes committed in the Philippines?

Now enters a hungry-eyed politician by the name of Rudy Giuliani. He'd gotten himself appointed to the U.S. attorney's job for the Southern District of New York. Giuliani had been suffering surging urgings for the mayor's job of that great city. We cannot assume there'd been no get-togethers between Giuliani and the powers that be in Washington, D.C. In support of the Grand Old Party, Rudy got right to work and called a grand jury to indict, in *New York, U.S.A,* America's newest Filipino guests living in *Hawaii* for alleged crimes committed in the *Philippines.* That sets any functional legal mind to spinning. A Harvard law professor could have a marvelous time untangling all of the possible ins-and-outs of that twisted jurisdictional scenario.

We remember the old axiom, "A grand jury will indict a ham sandwich." And presto! Giuliani's grand jury returned indictments against both Ferdinand and Imelda for RICO crimes (the Racketeer Influenced and Corrupt Organizations Act) stemming from the purchase of four skyscrapers in Manhattan. They were charged with defrauding three lending banks of more than $165 million in the purchase and financing of that real estate. The indictment claimed the Marcoses had amassed $103 million of those monies through embezzlement, theft, bribes, and kickbacks, and some of that dirty money was used to buy those buildings in New York.

Giuliani wasted no time putting into play the prosecutor's standard demonizing tactics, designed to convince the innocent public—the pool from which the jury would be chosen—that the Marcoses were the most abominable crooks ever residing on the planet. The prosecutors called their case against the Marcoses a "dead-bang" case of conspiracy and fraud.*

The FBI lost no opportunity to pile on. James Fox of the FBI's New York office proclaimed, "This case amounted to the Marcoses and their co-defendants using their position of trust to turn the Philippines' treasury into their own treasury."† If in defending the Marcoses I'd announced to the media that my clients were as innocent as lilies in the lily pond, but that the U.S. attorney was prosecuting them to get himself elected mayor of New York, I'd have been sanctioned by judges and hauled up in front of the bar association with my license to practice law at risk. But in New York City Giuliani was the mouth of Power. And Power plays by its own rules.

Few would assert that Ferdinand was an exemplary fellow. His opponents, his biographers, and, indeed, some reputable reporters contend that Marcos stole billions from the Philippines, and that during his twenty-one years at the helm of this troubled vessel he served not as its captain but as its private owner. His enemies, yes, and his claimed impartial biographers as well, have charged that he instigated and ordered the wholesale murder of his opponents, that he excelled in every form of theft, bribery, embezzlement, blackmail, and graft known to the creative criminal mind, and that he was an expert in all varieties of political corruption, including some that Marcos himself invented. Many volumes have been written that detail Marcos's greed and foul play, but most ignore that Marcos built more schools, hospitals, and infrastructure than all of his predecessors combined. And he had always been a loyal enough friend of the United States.

Our country had provided Marcos hundreds of millions of dollars in aid that had been crucial in buttressing his rule over the years. With the exception of Jimmy Carter, from the beginning of his twenty-one-year tenure Marcos had been "our guy." Four of our presidents waltzed across the international dance floor with him. Some of our darkest national disgraces have been our support of various tyrants. But the United States betrayed the Marcoses and created its own criminal conspiracy when it kidnapped them and brought them to the United States under false promises. If you or I commit the crime of kidnapping it could easily result in a sentence of life imprisonment.

---

* "Marcos: Safe Haven?" *Los Angeles Times,* July 19, 1988.
† John M. Doyle, "Marcos, Imelda, Six Others Indicted on Racketeering Charges," Associated Press, October 21, 1988.

Still, hand it to Ferdinand. He hadn't yet pulled his last dirty trick. On September 28, 1989, nearly a year after he and Imelda were indicted, and before Giuliani could get him to trial, he up and died. But Imelda, his widow, was alive and available for prosecution, and Mrs. Aquino, then the president of the Philippines, was heard to say in one of the many Philippine dialects, "I want that wicked widow in prison, and I am going to get what I want or the U.S. can kiss their bases good-bye."

To defend themselves the Marcoses had hired lawyers from both coasts, lawyers I'm told were paid fees totaling $8 million. With Ferdinand dead, and with a long, complicated trial looming, these lawyers recommended that Imelda plead guilty, not to mention that Marcos's death left her without access to the Marcos monies. In short, she had no funds to pay additional attorneys' fees. Beyond that, her lawyers were advising her that if convicted she could get up to thirty years in an American prison. But they gave her the good news: They'd worked long and hard for her and had been successful in bargaining with the prosecutor for a prison term of a "few years." They had even investigated the various federal prisons in the United States, they said, part of the plea deal they made for her was that she'd be sent to the best federal pen in the country.

But the lady wasn't cooperative. She wasn't even grateful. "Why would I plead guilty when I'm not?" she asked. Imelda then launched a search for a champion. She asked her trusted friend, Doris Duke, the tobacco heiress, for help. Ms. Duke knew Ben Cassidy, a young lawyer in Honolulu (whom I had never met), and he recommended that she hire me, "that country lawyer from Wyoming." So one day in late January of 1990, little more than six weeks before Imelda's trial was to begin, I received a call from Cassidy. Would I come to Honolulu to meet Mrs. Marcos? She needed someone to fight for her.

"You should go talk to her," my wife, Imaging, said. "If you were dead and somebody was prosecuting me, I'd want a lawyer like you to look into it." My wife has a proven insight into both the unknown and the unknowable, and I listen to her.

Mrs. Marcos met me at the Honolulu airport with her international smile and a fresh flower lei that she slipped over my head, after which she led me to a waiting limousine. "Mrs. Aquino won't let me return Ferdinand's body to his homeland," she said, "and he cannot defend himself from the lies and false charges of those evil people. I want you to defend him."

Defend her dead husband?

Yes.

She directed the driver to a cemetery that extended up a long hill covered with small grave markers. I followed her along a path to a prefabricated metal toolshed, the kind sold by Sears. Inside rested the coffin of Ferdinand Marcos.

She spoke to the closed casket as if the contents could hear her. "Mr. Spence is here," she said. "He will defend you." Then she said something in their native tongue, something that sounded loving and private. On the way down the hill she turned to me and in a quiet but determined voice she said again, "I want you to defend Ferdinand."

We were then driven to the seaside residence of Doris Duke and ushered into a large auditorium-sized living room with a twenty- or thirty-foot ceiling exposing a configuration of beams that added to its structural and decorative magnificence. Ms. Duke soon made her appearance, along with a large Newfoundland dog. In early old age she was thin, frail, and deliberate in her speech. She was obviously alert. As for me, I knew little of Ferdinand Marcos, and what I'd heard wasn't especially inspirational. I knew nothing of Imelda, not even about her two thousand pairs of shoes, and I knew nothing of the case I was being courted to defend. I didn't run in the same circles as Ms. Duke or the former first lady of the Philippines. I was used to the mountains of Wyoming with neighbors I knew, not the towering landscape of Manhattan filled with hard-eyed people all looking straight ahead who passed one another on the streets as if the world were populated with treacherous strangers.

Ms. Duke's butler served us those bite-sized white sandwiches without crusts but with a thin slice of cucumber inside, maybe a smear of mayonnaise. The butler had just set the tray down on the coffee table when the Newfoundland dog decimated the tray's total contents in one lap of its monstrous tongue. The butler froze. Ms. Duke smiled, patted the dog, and motioned the butler to bring in another tray of sandwiches.

I found myself drawn to this widow, Imelda Marcos, a woman trapped in a foreign land who'd been betrayed by the power base of the United States, including Ronald Reagan, a woman in exile who wasn't even permitted to return the body of her beloved husband to his homeland. She wore a queenlike grace and presence I'd rarely encountered. She asked for no sympathy. She seemed brave beyond understanding. Here was a woman driven not by fear for herself, but who only asked that the legacy of her dead husband be defended. Ms. Duke agreed to help Mrs. Marcos with my fee.

The next morning I awakened to the cold, hard realization that I'd agreed to represent the former first lady of the Philippines in an upcoming trial only a couple of weeks away, and I didn't have the first idea what the case was about, except that a politician I'd never heard of by the name of Rudy Giuliani was determined to put this likable woman in prison, where she'd probably die. He'd promised a conviction.

Imelda was not going to be judged by a jury of her peers, one composed of Philippine people, some of whom loved her, and most of whom would have an insight into the history and mores of their country. In New York she'd be judged by jurors who knew little or nothing about her or her country. I felt no urge to defend her dead husband, but I did want to defend a woman who wanted to defend her dead husband. I'd known more than a few who, for good reason or not, had wanted live husbands dead.

In the meantime the Aquino government had begun handpicking Giuliani's witnesses against Mrs. Marcos. And I was about to confront the top dogs in the FBI, and the CIA, not to mention Rudy Giuliani and two presidents, Ronald Reagan and George H. W. Bush, all of whom had entered into their own conspiracy to get that evil, money-hogging witch of a woman, Imelda Marcos. Their uniform message to all who would listen— and, of course, America's media listened—was that this greedy, grasping thief had betrayed the Philippine people's trust, and that she and her husband had hauled off untold billions from that piteously impoverished country. Whether or not any or all of those allegations were true was not at issue in the case, the only issue being whether Imelda Marcos *herself* was guilty of *any* crime. In short, had she, in concert with her husband, knowingly absconded with monies stolen from the Philippines or elsewhere and hidden the monies in those four New York skyscrapers?

I knew that in the Philippines the rich were rich beyond understanding and the poor were hungry and hanging on to the ragged edge of hopelessness. Corruption was a way of life. I'd seen the lost and homeless in our own country pushing stolen grocery carts down the street that contained their total possessions, the most valuable of which was often a dirty blanket. But when every proclaimed independent news source joined in portraying Imelda Marcos, the widow, as a depraved international criminal, a ravenous

rapist of the poor, one might find oneself beginning to believe their stories. Either such stories were cruel political fictions or Imelda herself was
a walking, breathing lie. I had to trust somebody's assessment of her, and
I ended up trusting my own.

Giuliani assigned the case for trial to one Charles LaBella, an imperi-
ous, humorless, middle-aged fellow, a career prosecutor, who, by reputation, was the best in the Southern District of New York. On the first day of
the trial we found ourselves in a federal courtroom as large as the audito-
rium in some of the cathedrals I've visited, one with high ceilings and a lot
of marble, carpeting, and gold leaf. I walked over to introduce myself to
LaBella. He refused to take my hand. He looked at Imelda like a man be-
holding something filthy and untouchable. I knew Imelda must be afraid,
but she'd become an expert at clothing fear with a pleasant smile. I thought
she needed to hear me say it: "Well," I said to her, as was my commitment
in every case, "we're in this together. Before they get you they'll have to
kill me with an ax."

American trials are widely advertised as fair to both parties. However,
the challenge of some trial lawyers is to discover ways to destroy fairness
and at the same time not violate the rules that protect it. Under federal
court rules the prosecutor, LaBella, was required to designate his exhibits
in advance of trial to eliminate any surprise. The same rule applied to us
on the defendant's side of the case. No secrets at trial was the simple rule.
But LaBella had it figured out. Before I entered the case, he'd designated
some three hundred thousand exhibits. I could read a thousand documents
a day for a year and still not have read them all, much less understand how
this whole untidy trainload of paper fit together to make a case for the
prosecution. Before we'd entered the case, the judge had ruled against
requiring LaBella to be more specific. One of Imelda's former attorneys,
John Bartko of San Francisco, seemed to know something about the documents because he'd stored them on his computer. I had to rehire him.

We'd caravanned to New York City, Imaging and I and my secretary,
Rosemary McIntosh. There we were joined by Bartko and Ben Cassidy,
who'd gotten me into this unholy war in the first place. Imaging and I
rented a small suite in the Dag Hammarskjold Building in Manhattan.
Imelda was also staying there with her entourage, which included her
personal doctor, one of her sisters, who was a nun, a tall silent man who
served as her bodyguard, and sometimes her son and daughter.

"I remember you, Mr. Spence," Judge John Keenan said when I sought admission to his court for the trial. He was peering down at me from his bench with a judicial smile appropriate for a happy lynching. "We taught at Harvard Law School together one summer. I'm glad to have you in my court." He was referring to Harvard's program of inviting lawyers and judges Harvard professors thought had something of value to offer their students. "I'll admit you in this case, Mr. Spence," Judge Keenan said, "but don't come asking me for a continuance. Will you be ready for trial?"

"Of course," I said with my best big Wyoming smile. In truth, I didn't know how I was going to get ready for such a trial in the couple of weeks remaining. And probably I'd have been no better off if I'd been given a year to prepare. Too much to absorb—not only the evidence I'd actually have to face, but an accurate history of the Marcoses, the way of Philippine politics, at least an introduction to the Philippine culture, and a knowledge of who the scores of witnesses from the Philippines were who'd be testifying against us. What was their story, their interests? How could I cross-examine and impeach them? I'd never been to the Philippines. To me the country was just a smattering of small dots on the globe over by China somewhere.

I could at least prepare an opening statement that was focused on Imelda, and the Power at hand that was attempting to destroy her. I spent many hours with the lady. Suddenly it was March 21, 1990, and there I was in Judge Keenan's courtroom at Foley Square facing our first day of trial.

Imelda, Judge Keenan, and I were all born in 1929. But it wasn't like a class reunion. Judge Keenan himself began picking the jury. Most federal judges question the prospective jurors, while in most state courts the lawyers do that work. From the moment he began questioning the prospective jurors, Judge Keenan left little doubt that the jurors chosen would be *his* jury in *his* case. And his case was a first—the first in U.S. history in which the wife of a former foreign head of state was prosecuted in this country. As the judge worked the prospective jurors in his chambers, we lawyers sat mute. If we had a question to ask a juror, it was first addressed to the judge, and he alone decided if he would ask it.

Many of the prospective jurors had heard something about the case—most often about Imelda's thousands of shoes. And Keenan would ask, "Will you hold this against her?" "No," each juror would dutifully answer. But in the depths of their secret hearts some jurors must have felt they'd be accomplishing great good by ridding society of this contemptible woman who had all those shoes while many of her countrymen went barefoot. After more than a week of the judge's one-man show in jury selection, and after we'd exhausted all the challenges the law would allow, we ended up with a jury—the judge's jury, to be sure. LaBella seemed happy. He still wouldn't speak to me, not a word, not even a yes-or-no nod of the head. It was as if I did not exist, and if I did it was too appalling an experience for him to endure. But I was beginning to appreciate that gift.

I believed Judge Keenan's nature was, by default, to be fair. But remember: He was a federal judge, and federal prosecutors were trying to convict a freshly branded enemy of the United States. Would he be insensitive to the needs of his country? It had already become clear that he didn't cater to the likes of me who sauntered into his courtroom in a cowboy hat, threw the same on counsel table, and by my simple presence took up far too much room in his courtroom.

To ensure Imelda's conviction, the Aquino administration sent its private spokesperson to further infect the media with more noxious stories against her. The Aquino spokesperson appeared in court every day. He said his mission was to "let people know what Mrs. Marcos was really like." The Aquino people also hired one of New York's savviest public relations people, John Scanlon, who'd previously worked for Ivana Trump, Donald Trump's former wife. During our trial the media's releases against Mrs. Marcos got so thick and mucky I complained to the reporters attending the trial that "propaganda from the Philippine government in your news reports has made it impossible for my client to receive a fair trial." That was, of course, foolishness on my part. My complaints only encouraged the reporters to pile on more. Still, every morning when Mrs. Marcos and I arrived at the courthouse we were greeted by large crowds of Filipino well-wishers. They adored her. Some spoke loving words to her in their native tongue. And she responded to them with the gentleness of a caring, nurturing mother.

On April 3, 1990, two weeks after jury selection had begun, the feds finally began their case. Debra Livingston got the nod from LaBella to make the government's opening address to the jury in a packed courtroom. She was short-haired, blond, slender, reasonably young, and as businesslike as an IBM computer in good working order. She'd graduated from Harvard with honors and was an editor on the *Law Review,* a powerful set of academic accomplishments. She reflected the humor of her lead, LaBella, which was as hilarious as a migraine at midnight. She wouldn't speak to me either.

"This is a case about theft, fraud, and deceit on an incredible scale. It is a case about stolen money and money grabbed by fraud, over $240 million that the defendant stole and then secretly brought to New York to buy four buildings in Manhattan."

Livingston's words were wounding, but Imelda sat quietly with a small sad smile on her face and with her hands folded on the lap of her black mourning dress. The vestiges of her early beauty were still worth noting. In her second breath Ms. Livingston accused Mrs. Marcos of obstruction of justice, that catchall crime that could convict a hen of hiding the fruits of her crime by sitting on her eggs.

Ms. Livingston exhorted, "She plundered the Philippines" and "exported the fruits of her fraud to this country. She misused our banks to cover their wealth and to operate a criminal enterprise. And don't be misled. She was a powerful personage in the Philippine government—a cabinet minister and mayor of Manila. She and her husband were 'partners in crime.' They earned a salary of about $20,000 a year but received millions and millions from bribes and kickbacks. She treated the Philippine National Bank in New York as her private piggy bank."

In the first four minutes of her hour-and-a-half opening Ms. Livingston called Mrs. Marcos "a thief" twice and "a fraud" ten times; she said she was guilty of "deceit" twice; that she "harbored stolen property" three times; that she "laundered money" twice; that she "grabbed money" and was "engaged in a criminal enterprise." She used the word "secret" fifty-seven times, as close as I could keep track—secret bank accounts, secret purchases, and the secret of all secrets, too secret to reveal even to the jurors. Ms. Livingston wanted the woman convicted of every count in the indictment. Every one. Each count carried a maximum of twenty years. Anger leaked out from around her flat-sounding words like venom dripping from the fangs of a stepped-on rattler.

I began my opening statement by telling the jury that what happened in the Philippines was like my hand. I showed my palm. "The United States attorney calls this side of my hand kickbacks and bribes. But there are two sides to the hand." I showed the jury the top of my hand. "It's my great responsibility to show you the other side of the hand. When this evidence is all in you'll discover that the 'web of fraud,' as Ms. Livingston calls it, was created by Ms. Livingston herself, and by those who have interests in the outcome of this case, governments who wish to see Mrs. Marcos convicted for secret reasons not being revealed in this courtroom.

"This is a woman who lived with her beloved husband for thirty-five years, saw him in sickness and in health and was there when he took his last breath. Her position is simple: 'I am going to defend my husband. His lips have been sealed by death. He can't defend himself. You can do what you wish with me, but you cannot do this to a man who has spent his entire life as a servant of the Philippine people and who laid his entire fortune and life down on their behalf.' Mrs. Marcos was born in Manila, the daughter of a good lawyer who was poor. When she was eight her mother died, leaving her father with eleven motherless children and the family in dire straits. They moved to Leyte, to the country, and life was hard. The area was poor. By 1941 the Japanese bombed Manila and they bombed Leyte—about the same day they bombed Pearl Harbor.

"Imelda was twelve years old. Her father was a tall man, six feet two, and lighter in complexion than most in the Philippines. He could be taken for an American and had to hide from the Japanese.

"She witnessed the Japanese brutally kill her countrymen. She saw beheaded Americans. Members of her own family were beheaded, the heads stacked up in trucks, truckloads of heads. There's a story that will help you understand her passion for jewelry. When she was a little child her family had only one asset—a necklace of jewels. It was the family's entire fortune. One necklace was all they had to live on during the war.

"As the youngest in the family she carried that necklace—the family entrusted it to her—and everywhere she went she had it hidden under her clothes. Once in a while they'd take a bead off of the necklace and trade it for something to eat. When the war was over nearly all of the beads were gone, but the family had survived.

"She was wounded in the war, and she was there when MacArthur returned, a girl, barefooted and singing. She sang a song called 'God Bless the Philippines.' It was 'God Bless America' except the words were changed to 'God Bless the Philippines.' MacArthur heard her singing, and he took her to the American troops and she sang to them as a child.

"Along the way she met a man by the name of Irving Berlin who was entertaining the troops, and he heard her sing 'God Bless the Philippines.' He stopped this girl and said, 'It isn't, "God Bless the Philippines," it's "God

Bless America.'" It was then that Irving Berlin decided to write a song that became a national favorite called 'Heaven Watch the Philippines.'

"Imelda went to college, but she never had enough money to buy a book, and never owned one. She worked in the cafeteria. At twenty-two she finished college and moved to Manila with five pesos in her pocket—less than a dollar. She lived with relatives. She worked in a music store. She was able to play the piano, and she sang and sold sheets of music in the music store by playing them for the customers and singing, and she worked during the war as a volunteer at the American hospital taking care of American soldiers.

"One day she met the minority floor leader in the House of Representatives in Manila. His name was Ferdinand Marcos. He fell in love with her, and eleven days later they were married. He bought her a seven-karat diamond ring worth a big chunk of change. Fifteen thousand people were invited, and most came to the wedding. She and Ferdinand took a world tour for an entire year as their honeymoon." I said to the jury, "I tell you this for one reason. You never heard in the prosecution's presentation of the case a simple but crucial fact—prior to the time that Mr. Marcos became the president of the Philippines, he was one of the most wealthy men in the country."

I told the jury that there came a time when Imelda got sick. Ferdinand took her to the Presbyterian Hospital, to Johns Hopkins and Walter Reed—the great hospitals in this country. What was wrong with her? She couldn't bear the pressure of being a public person, not this simple girl who had grown up in the country. She was suffering a nervous breakdown.

"By this time, Ferdinand was the head of the Senate with a sparkling political career ahead of him. He was brilliant, a great orator, an economist, a lawyer, a man who had visions for his country, and he wanted to become the president. But Imelda, this shy person, couldn't endure the hard gaze of the public eye. Then one day the doctor said to her husband, 'You know, Mr. Marcos, if you want to cure your wife I'll tell you what you have to do. Give up politics, give up the public life. That will cure her.'"

I took two steps closer to the jury and quietly said, "Here is what Ferdinand replied to the doctor: 'If that will cure my wife, I'll give up the presidency and I'll give up politics.' Imelda heard her husband, and she said, 'No. If I mean that much to this man, then I will become his first lady,' and she began forcing herself into her new role. She was often emotionally disarrayed and exhausted. But over time she was able, by sheer determination, to overcome. More and more she took part in his campaign. She traveled from province to province in the Philippines doing what she did best—singing. She and Ferdinand campaigned all over their country, and in 1965, Marcos won the election.

"From that time on he put Imelda in charge of important projects. She would go to businesses and ask for their support for good works. She built hospitals, she built the heart center, she built the kidney center, she built the school for boys, she built the school for girls, she built the school for orphans, and she built the Asian Center in the Philippines. She was the one in charge of putting out the markers that tracked the Bataan Death March along which our American boys suffered and died during the war.

"And the Philippines got the Nobel Prize for the refugee center which she helped build in twenty-nine days to take care of twenty thousand refugees, boat people who fled from Vietnam—the Nobel Prize for Peace—this evil woman. She built cultural centers, she built the Philippine International Convention Center, she built the folk art center, she built the national trade center, she built the Plaza Hotel, which is not Donald Trump's Plaza Hotel, I assure you."

I looked over at Ms. Livingston. She seemed on the edge of sleep. But Judge Keenan jumped up as if to alert her. He leaned over the bench and stared down at her. It was as if he were shouting to Ms. Livingston, "Couldn't you at least offer up an objection? If you object I will stop him." I pressed on. "At the National Arts Center, the first lady arranged to bring in gifted children from the provinces to Manila, where they were housed and fed and permitted to grow and create.

"Ladies and gentlemen of the jury, you will see that Mr. Marcos treated his wife as a queen. On behalf of the Philippine people she eventually met the great leaders across the world. She opened Russia to the Philippines. Ferdinand sent her ahead of him to China, and she helped open China to the Philippines. He sent her to meet with Khadafy. You'll see this woman was beloved by the people. They called her Mamma.

"In the meantime, Marcos was kicking up serious problems at home. For the Philippines to become a self-sustaining country the people needed to own land. He took lands that were owned by a few families and cut them up into seven-acre plots, which were turned into small rice-producing farms. Before that time the Philippine people couldn't support themselves with rice."

Judge Keenan finally exploded, and without an objection from Ms. Livingston he hollered, "The court sustains the objection under Rule 401 of the Federal Rules of Criminal Procedure. There's nothing relevant about that."

Mr. Spence: "What I mean to point out to Your Honor and to the ladies and gentlemen of the jury is that—"

Judge Keenan interrupted, jumping up again, and peering over the bench at me as if I were the bad boy in the class who'd just been caught cheating. "Don't point anything out to me, just make your opening to the jury, sir!"

That little repartee between the judge and me was his clear message to Ms. Livingston that he was inviting her to object. He'd do the rest. After that she did, and he did.

I pressed on. When I talked about the shoes I saw several jurors smile. I told them the Philippines had hundreds of mom-and-pop shoe manufacturers who'd send Imelda shoes hoping the first lady would be seen wearing them. Most didn't fit, but when the Marcoses appeared in this country the first thing we saw was newsmen zooming in on the shoes she was wearing.

"And so it was Mr. Marcos's great desire that his beloved wife become a symbol for his people, this poor girl who drank out of foxholes during the war—"

> MS. LIVINGSTON: "Objection, Your Honor."
>
> JUDGE KEENAN (Loud and belligerent with a slam of his hammer): "Sustained!"

I pressed on:

> "Ferdinand Marcos was born in 1917 of middle-class parents in the harsh north country, an area called Ilocos Norte. He was a man who excelled in everything—a boxer, a wrestler, a debater, and a lawyer. He is charged as one of the racketeers in this case—"
>
> JUDGE KEENAN (Without the faintest sound of sympathy in his voice): "Mr. Marcos, sadly, is not here; he is not on trial. His character is not before the jury, and will not be before the jury. Proceed and make a proper opening." At that moment the judge convicted me as a lawyer who was conducting himself *improperly* before the jury. How could such a lawyer be believed? I began anew:

"Thank you, Your Honor," I said quietly. Then I continued:

> "Mr. Marcos ran for the House, and he said, 'If you will elect me congressman now—'"
> MS. LIVINGSTON: "Objection, Your Honor."
> JUDGE KEENAN: "Sustained!" (Shouting) "We are not going to go back to Philippine election campaigns. We are going to try the case that is in this indictment before this jury and before this court!"

I began anew:

> "Mr. Marcos's wealth, prior to the time that he became the president, was known by the heads of state everywhere, including our own President Reagan, who told the American people publicly—"
> MS. LIVINGSTON: "Objection, Your Honor."
> JUDGE KEENAN (With naked disdain and impatience): "Whatever President Reagan might have told the American people is not before this jury and will not be before this jury concerning Mr. Marcos." (One might remember in passing that the judge had been appointed by Reagan in 1983 to the federal bench.)

I began anew:

> "What was the origin of Marcos's wealth? After the war, Manila was leveled to the ground. Not a building was left standing. This man, Marcos, believing in the Bahayon spirit, which means a spirit of togetherness, began to invest his monies in Philippine industries at the very time when they were in their infancy, and by 1985, he was extremely wealthy."

Over Ms. Livingston's objection the judge permitted me to put a large world map on the board to illustrate the location of three small islands off the coast of the Philippines and only five miles from Vietnam. "One of those islands belongs to the Philippines, one to China, and one to Vietnam, and so you could have actually stood on Philippine soil and watched the Vietnam War."

> JUDGE KEENAN: "Let's get to the facts of this case."
> MR. SPENCE: "Please, I ask the court's indulgence."

JUDGE KEENAN (Hollering again): "No, you will not have my indulgence, you will open properly. You have had a lot of indulgence, you have been going for quite a while. Let's get to the issues of this case, sir, please!"

The jury seemed shocked. If I had been Mrs. Marcos I could have seen the guards at the penitentiary opening those steel doors. I felt her helplessness and fear—my own feelings in tandem.

"There was a concern in the Philippines that the country was going to be taken over by the Communists. Such is our concern today, because the United States had its most important bases in the Philippines; its entire presence in the Asian area had been established on those bases."

I told the jury that not only did Marcos discuss the threat of a Communist takeover with his old friend President Reagan, he and George H. W. Bush, the former head of the CIA and Reagan's vice president, worried about it together. Bush said, "We know your need to move monies out of the country to establish a Communist takeover fund, so why not invest in American properties? The whole world, including the Japanese, is investing in American properties."

I told the jury, "So Marcos began to purchase New York real estate, eventually the four New York buildings that are the centerpiece of the prosecutor's case here."

In 1972, a typhoon devastated the Philippines. All utilities, including water, were destroyed. Crops were lost, factories smashed, and the Communists were set to take control. "Marcos declared martial law. It would take the army to get the lights on again and the farms and factories moving again. Marcos ruled by decree. We know something about martial law in this country. Abe Lincoln declared martial law. Today, six of our states in this country have provisions for martial law."

MS. LIVINGSTON: "Objection, Your Honor."
JUDGE KEENAN: "Sustained!"

"The prosecution's charges here begin when Marcos declared martial law in 1972. We've never experienced armed Communists about to take over our government, attempting to blow up our Congress, to kill our president, and stab our first lady. These threats exploded when, but a few miles off Philippine shores, Vietnam fell, and close by Communist China was staring in.

"Marcos couldn't protect Philippine monies against a Communist take-over by simply depositing them in a New York bank. Marcos took extreme measures to hide the funds, a matter undisputed here, because you don't have a security fund unless it's hidden. And we'll discover why the government was able to put this case together so quickly—what Marcos did was an open secret between Marcos and our CIA."

In 1974 the Laurel-Langley trade agreement between the United States and the Philippines was terminated. This agreement had served the interests of foreign businesses that could acquire 100 percent ownership in all areas of the Philippine economy. New requirements for foreign investment were put in place that caused multinational corporations to flee the Philippines in droves, and by 1983 the country found itself moneyless. Things were desperate.

"But suddenly money began to come into the Philippines. One witness will testify that the first week $25 million came into the country. It wasn't a loan. The next week in came $50 million more. One of the witnesses will testify that as much as $300 million, and another as much as $400 million, came back into the country to meet the crisis. That money was from the Marcos sock, from monies that had been planted outside the Philippines for just such an emergency.

"So when you hear evidence of Marcos putting monies in secret funds, it's true. He was not only the country's political leader, he was its economic source and the guru that kept the Philippines alive all of those years. The question you'll decide is whether he was engaged in a racket against his own people."

I told the jury that the ownership of the four New York buildings was a pending case in the Philippines. "Mrs. Marcos has never claimed the ownership of the New York property," I said.

"After the Aquino government took over, that government held an auction in New York of property they seized from the Marcoses. They seized her bedsheets and her pillows. They seized the picture of her with the pope and sold it for $450. They seized the president's private humidor in which he kept his cigars. They seized and sold her precious family memorabilia. They even seized her paper flowers.

"So as to the rest of the story—some of it is difficult to understand because we are a different culture, a different people with different customs. Certainly she is not being provided with a jury of her peers, any more than I suppose—"

MS. LIVINGSTON: "Objection."

JUDGE KEENAN: "Objection sustained!" (Now speaking to the jurors) "You are a jury of her peers! Under the laws of the United States and the Constitution of the United States you are properly sworn to judge this case and to decide and pass upon the guilt or innocence of Mrs. Marcos. That's why we took all those days to pick the jury and did it as carefully as we did."

The judge was eating me for lunch.

MR. SPENCE: "Ladies and gentlemen of the jury, I don't mean to suggest you are not a proper jury. I don't mean that at all. But it's like Mrs. Reagan being tried by a Philippine jury.

"When you go back to the jury room you must decide: Were they crooks, as Ms. Livingston said? Did they intend to cheat their people? If Mr. Marcos was engaged in a racket, so was the CIA. If this was illegal racketeering, then every president of this country who knew about it—"

MS. LIVINGSTON: "Objection, Your Honor."

JUDGE KEENAN: "That's argument. That's not proof of what you are going to prove. Sustained! Desist from that, sir!" He was red-faced and still hollering. It was always worse after lunch, and as I was to discover, it got still worse toward evening.

"Now, I want to talk to you a bit about Mrs. Marcos's knowledge of what was going on. Mrs. Marcos never wrote a check in her life. She never saw a bill or paid one. Ms. Livingston overstepped quite a bit in her statement to you. President Marcos made the decisions."

I tried to tell the jury how the Marcoses were kidnapped and brought to this country under the false promises of our government, but the judge threw another fit and sustained Ms. Livingston's objections. But suddenly he reversed himself when I told him President Reagan had made promises to Marcos.

JUDGE KEENAN: "This is something you are going to prove?"

MR. SPENCE: "Yes."

JUDGE KEENAN (Seeming surprised): "All right, go ahead."

I told the jury how Marcos had been promised that if he peacefully stepped down he and his family would be safely airlifted to Ilocos Norte, his homeland. "This coup took place on the twenty-fifth of February, 1986, but the United States knew as early as the eighteenth of February that the coup was going to occur, and the CIA provided support for that coup against this country's old, loyal friend, Ferdinand Marcos. He was a sick man and on dialysis. He'd survived two kidney transplants. That night the Marcoses were taken to Clark Air Force Base. Then about one in the morning they were awakened and told, for their own safety, they had to get out. They boarded an airplane believing that they were going to go to Ilocos Norte. They landed in Guam, a United States possession, and ended up in Hawaii."

I spoke quietly, sadly to the jury:

"I dreamed I could give an opening statement that everybody would be proud of, and I haven't been proud of the way this one has come off, the worst in my career, and I'm sorry, but I have done what I could do, and the best that I could."

I told the jury about the so-called Philippine Commission on Good Government that had the power to take the property of a Philippine citizen without a court hearing, and how that commission had made deals with witness after witness for their testimony against Mrs. Marcos in exchange for that government's agreement not to confiscate their holdings. And after those witnesses left this country they couldn't be prosecuted for perjury here for their lies, because no extradition treaty existed between the Philippines and the United States. Ms. Livingston objected, and Judge Keenan sustained her objection with full-blooming fury. I thought I had the right to tell the jury the facts they'd hear that would undermine the credibility of the government's imported witnesses from the Philippines. The judge disagreed.

By the time I was ready to conclude my opening statement I'd been held up by the court as a capital charlatan, one of those phony defense lawyers who habitually violated the rules. From a juror's standpoint, that had to be true, because Judge Keenan, a judge who often smiled at them and who was obviously bent on seeing that the jury got only proper evidence, had almost always come down on the side of the prosecution—clearly the right and just side of the case, especially if the juror was a loyal American. I ended my opening telling the jury out of deep respect that the case would be left in the hands of the greatest institution of justice remaining in this country and in the world—an American jury.

he next morning Bartko and I drove to the courthouse, and although we occupied the same car, we were worlds apart. I hadn't slept. I felt as if I were digging out from under the wreckage of a hurricane. In the event of a conviction and to protect Mrs. Marcos's rights on appeal I was required to move for a mistrial. Bartko was afraid of further enraging the judge, but despite his strong dissent, I made my motion in the judge's chambers, saying in part, "Your Honor's response to my statements as disbelief, disapproval, or incredulity impassioned the jury against Mrs. Marcos." I argued that considering his conduct as a whole he had ruined her right to a fair trial.

The judge bristled like a porcupine with a stick in its ribs. "Overruled! I have never heard an opening statement that departed from the rules further than your opening statement yesterday." He said more off the record with words that failed to reveal his acceptance of me as a member of the human species.

We faced even more serious problems in the media. One paper reported that "Spence clashed with the judge, suffered damaging surprises at the hands of a skilled prosecution team"—again affirming that this intruder from the West had no business in a real court of law—"and stumbled so badly once during his opening statements that he appeared to insult, of all people, the jury [referring to my comment that Mrs. Marcos was not being tried by a jury of her peers]. Spence is finding out just how far away he is from Jackson and the sanctuary of Wyoming cottonwoods. . . . Nor did his homespun, country style hold up well inside, in a courtroom with more pinstripe than buckskin."* And the reporters seemed consumed by a throbbing thrill over Imelda's shoes, my cowboy hat, and alleged buckskin jacket. (I never wore it in court.) Besides, as everybody knew, the Marcoses were crooks. So what was left to try?

aBella called his first witness to a packed courtroom. The prosecutors pitched hundreds of documents to the jury, one document at a time, and before the trial was over they'd interrogated ninety-five witnesses.

---

* William C. Rempel, "Champion of the Legal Lost Cause," *Los Angeles Times,* April 17, 1990.

Jurors fought off sleep. Judge Keenan sagged in tedium. One paper reported, "The judge slowly slid down in his chair until only the crown of his balding head remained in view, like the sun slipping below the horizon." Sometimes he got up and stretched like my old dog who'd lain too long on the living room floor with no squirrels to chase. Mrs. Marcos sat quietly with a small, pained smile on her face. I sat beside her trying to appear as quietly disinterested as she.

On cross-examination I often asked no questions, or at most I might ask, "You never had any contact with Mrs. Marcos, did you?" and the answer was almost uniformly "No." I tried not to attack these helplessly trapped Filipinos who, under pain of losing their property in the Philippines, were ordered to testify against Mrs. Marcos in America.

"You are not here because you want to be here, isn't that true?" I might ask.

"Yes, sir."

"You came here at the expense of the Philippine government?"

"Yes, sir."

"You own a business in the Philippines?"

"Yes."

"Are you worried that if you don't testify to suit the Aquino government you might lose your property?"

LaBella: "Objection!"

"Sustained."

One witness, Andres Genito, a businessman who'd been granted immunity from prosecution, described how Marcos collected kickbacks from a Japanese government program that paid reparations to the Philippines for World War II damages. But under my cross-examination he joined the other witnesses.

"You're not suggesting by your testimony that Mrs. Marcos did anything wrong, are you?" I asked.

Long silence. I pressed him. "Yes or no."

"No," Genito finally admitted.

By the end of the day I was often too tired to exercise or go out for dinner. Mrs. Marcos would sometimes come down from her upstairs apartment with something to eat. She was always accompanied by a tall, silent bodyguard who stood in the shadows of the entry hall and who carried down the dinner that she had prepared for me, and that I chewed at as we reviewed the day.

"What do you feel about what happened today?" I'd ask. I trusted her instincts. She'd spent a lifetime in political battles, and her assessments of people were valuable to me.

"We're doing fine," she said. "The jury, all but the man on the front row on the far left, likes you. He's a young buck in the pasture and wants to own it all. He will come around. But that judge, he doesn't like you too much. He likes himself a lot."

One Monday morning I asked Imelda how her weekend had been. She said, "I had a nice time. I took a ferry ride past the Statue of Liberty."

"Why?" I asked.

"I wanted to look up at the lady. I was thinking what I would do if I were convicted."

"What would you do?"

"Why, I'd run for president of the Philippines from an American prison," she said, as if her answer should have surprised no one.

Imaging, who was with me much of the trial, had grown to love Imelda and appreciated her attraction to beautiful architecture, furnishings, and art. And they had something else in common: They knew how to stand behind their men and to nurture them through dangerous wars. And I missed my longtime partner Ed Moriarity, who was holding down the fort in Jackson in our other cases.

I found out after the trial that Ms. Livingston was daily provided briefings from a panel of experts who sat in the courtroom and assessed the progress of the feds' case. I also found out after the trial that the prosecutors expected me to call a celebrity witness. They decided to beat me to the punch. They called George Hamilton, the handsome, always marvelously tanned actor, who was a friend of Mrs. Marcos and had received a large loan from Mrs. Gliceria Tantoco, also a friend of Mrs. Marcos. LaBella had charged Hamilton as an "unindicted co-conspirator." LaBella's offered excuse for this abuse of a decent, innocent man was LaBella's naked claim that Hamilton was a conduit by which the Marcoses funneled money out of the Philippines. I thought Hamilton was being called to embarrass Mrs. Marcos by suggesting she had some sort of intimate relationship with him that would contradict her heretofore unquestioned devotion to Ferdinand.

LaBella proved the loan by Mrs. Tantoco to Hamilton (which he had paid back in full) and at last found himself with nothing more to prove by his witness. On my cross-examination Hamilton said he'd never borrowed money from Mrs. Marcos. Then I threw the door wide open. "You felt close to Mrs. Marcos?" I asked him.

"Yes. I met her in Manila when I was promoting a movie entitled *Love at First Bite*. My brother was ill. He suffered from the same disease as Mr. Marcos—a liver and kidney malfunction."

"Why did that bring you close to Mrs. Marcos?"

"I believe she saved my mother's life. When my brother died, my mother wanted to commit suicide." Hamilton's head was bowed, and he was staring into his fidgeting hands. Then his voice broke. "Mrs. Marcos brought my mother to the Philippines. I think the only reason my mother is alive today is because of Mrs. Marcos." He began to choke. The judge ordered that I go to another subject. A pall of silence invaded the courtroom. But LaBella and Livingston acted as if nothing untoward had taken place.

If any testimony touched Mrs. Marcos, it was usually soon dispelled. An example—my short cross-examination of an aging domestic servant:

"You knew Mrs. Marcos quite well?" I asked.

"Yes."

"How did you feel about her?"

"She was always kind to me. I loved her."

The prosecutors knew their case to this jury was falling apart, and La-Bella began dropping stacks of exhibits in front of his witnesses. Standard court procedure required him to first bring the exhibits to my table and show them to me, but LaBella followed no such rule.

> LABELLA (Without showing me the exhibits he'd put in front of the witness): "We offer into evidence Exhibits 593 through 642."
>
> MR. SPENCE: "I haven't seen the exhibits, Your Honor."
>
> JUDGE KEENAN: "Don't you dare misrepresent to the jury that you haven't seen those exhibits. They were presented to you last night," and the judge forthwith allowed the prosecutor's exhibits into evidence.

LaBella dumped another couple of dozen exhibits in front of his witness and offered them. Since LaBella hadn't shown me which exhibits he had just put in front of the witness, I had no idea whether those he'd shown me the night before were contained in the pile.

MR. SPENCE: "Your Honor, I simply haven't seen these exhibits—"

JUDGE KEENAN: "I've had enough of this. I told you to desist in your misrepresentations to the jury. One more time and I will take action, and you know what action I am referring to!"

He continued denouncing me as the jury looked on.

I was shocked. I have never been held in contempt by any court in my entire career. I saw his attack as uncalled for and as his further attempt to discredit me permanently with the jury.

"I have a motion to make," I said.

"The jury will be excused!" the judge said, still at the top of his lungs. The jury was led out by the bailiff. "I suppose you want to move for a mistrial?" the judge said, his anger in full flame.

"I'm not sure what motion I want to make," I said, "but since you suggest it, yes, that will be just fine. I move for a mistrial. This jury cannot possibly give Mrs. Marcos a fair trial in view of what you've done here. You've painted me as a fake who will misrepresent the facts to the jury. You know I couldn't possibly know what documents the prosecutor was offering in evidence when he hasn't shown the documents to me that he's offering. I've been in a lot of courts in my day, but I've never had a judge accuse me of misrepresentation. I was not misrepresenting. I was telling the truth."

"So what do you want me to do about it?" Keenan asked.

"That's up to you. You caused it. You figure it out," I said. I felt beaten and incompetent.

Judge Keenan called the jurors back and proceeded to tell them what a fine lawyer I was, how I was only representing my client to the fullest, and that the jury should not consider in any way what he had said about me. He went on for a considerable time trying to erase what was obviously his error, which he never once admitted. He was, of course, the judge.

"That should do it, Mr. Spence," the judge finally said. "Proceed." But the judge's explosion created the opening Bartko had been waiting for.

On Wednesday evening, May 31, 1990, the day the judge emasculated me in the presence of the jury, Bartko called a meeting. At the meeting were Imelda and I, Imelda's doctor, her son Bongbong, her sister the nun, Bartko, and Cassidy. You better get rid of Spence, was Bartko's advice to Imelda: "Spence's trouble with the judge is poisoning the jury, and you're going to be convicted."

Her doctor took her blood pressure. It was high. I said, "I think you should take mine, too, Doctor," and he did. Mine was even higher. Imelda listened carefully to their arguments and asked each of those present for their advice. Her son joined with Bartko and Cassidy, as did her sister. After she'd listened thoughtfully to each she made her decision: "Mr. Spence will stay on as my lawyer. He never wanted me to plead guilty." She was saying another thing—*this man, Spence, cares about me,* which proved once more that caring is contagious. Loyalty is also contagious. She told the press, "It is comforting to have someone like Mr. Spence fighting for me." Bartko had prepared a letter of resignation for me to sign. My fingers refused to hold the pen.

The next morning Mrs. Marcos suddenly fell facedown on the counsel table where she was sitting. She was throwing up blood that covered much of the tabletop. She was soon lifted to a stretcher, administered oxygen, and hauled to the hospital by ambulance. Later a reporter from the *New York Times* sauntered up to me. "Where did you get the blood capsule, Spence?"—a question that underlined the blind cynicism of the attending media.

The following morning the court clerk approached me: "Please don't tell the judge, but tell Mrs. Marcos that I lit a candle for her at church." And the tough old marshals who guarded the courtroom against every species of crook and criminal, and who must have grown calluses around their hearts as thick as bull leather, sent flowers to her in the hospital.

Along the way I'd felt solace from a wonderfully kind-faced black juror, a woman who sat near the middle of the jury box in the first row. When the judicial pot got boiling and I was about to be dumped in like a squirming squid, I sometimes looked over at her. I could read sympathy on her sad face. We never exchanged a word, not then nor since, but I thought she knew what was happening and understood. I needed help, and, of course, Imaging called Eddie Moriarity, my faithful partner, and told him to come. He got on a plane and was there the next morning. His job was to guard my backside while I finished the case.

I knew that LaBella, like all prosecutors, was hoping we'd call Mrs. Marcos to testify. But why would I turn this precious woman over to them to relentlessly attack and abuse, not for an hour or two but for days? I thought I'd proved our case on the cross-examination of the government's train-load of witnesses—that if there was any unlawfulness, none was ever connected to Mrs. Marcos. Moreover, I thought that if we had gotten through to those tough old marshals, we'd probably also earned the jurors' support. I rested our case without calling a single witness in defense.

Suddenly the *Los Angeles Times* seemed to awaken. That paper reported, "Not one of 95 prosecution witnesses testified unequivocally that former Philippine first lady Imelda Marcos engaged in the coercion, bribery and kickback schemes that marked her late husband's graft-tainted regime."

The judge called a recess. He'd be gone for several days, he said. We learned he'd taken a trip to Washington, D.C. I hoped it had nothing to do with the case. On his return his attitude had miraculously and marvelously changed. He'd become more circumspect, even slightly thoughtful. He stopped his hollering and his pacing up on the bench. Either he'd walked into the blazing light of truth, or he was suffering the onset of a serious judicial heart ailment (from which most federal judges are immune), namely, compassion for the accused.

But with the jury out of the courtroom he suddenly erupted again. This time he was pointing at the prosecutors. He said he wasn't convinced they'd proven their case. "What am I doing here at 40 Foley Square trying a case involving the theft of monies from Philippine banks?" I'd been arguing that from the beginning. Why was he just seeing it now? What had happened during his brief trip to Washington? Perhaps nothing.

LaBella rested the government's case. We of the defense made our standard motion to dismiss the case based on the failure of the government to make its required proof. I let Bartko make the argument, and I thought he did a good job. But the judge did as judges most often do—he let the jury decide.

*I*t was June 25, 1990, and LaBella was still steaming when he began his final argument. Was the man born angry? He argued for five hours, often at the peak of his passion. "Imelda Marcos was not in a glass tomb. She was in the thick of things." I saw jurors pull back in their seats as if to dodge his onslaught. Then he'd fall off into eye-closing tedium that dragged us through endless exhibits and testimony that promised to cast the most caffeine-hyped listener into webs of involuntary slumber.

Did Imelda know about these ill-gotten monies? LaBella asked. "Of course! Of course!" LaBella hammered those two words with his fists against the podium like a drummer gone wild. "Of course, of course," she knew. She had to know. She'd been the mayor of Manila. She lived with a billionaire. She was the closest human being in the world to Ferdinand Marcos, and of course she knew everything he was doing, consulted with him, and advised him. "Of course."

It had become an "Of course" case.

Still, I thought I must be missing something. How could LaBella be so angry if the lady were innocent? Maybe Bartko was right. Maybe I was no longer fit to represent Imelda—all those witnesses and exhibits I didn't fully understand, and there crouched LaBella snarling and tooth-baring like a mad mastiff over the body of a case that to me seemed barren of bones. When LaBella finally sat down I could feel fear welling up along my rib cage. In the jungle it would have been the moment to fight or flee. I'm not a good runner.

In the morning it would be my time, and my only time, to address the jurors. I argued all night in feverlike dreams with visions of Imelda running for president from behind the cold steel bars of an American prison. What if I failed her? Maybe I should have listened to Bartko. Eddie Moriarity gave me his reassuring Irish smile. One had to trust. And the one one had to trust was oneself.

I approached the jury box. The jurors were fixed on me. I began:

"Remember the little lady in the TV advertisement who opens up the hamburger and asks, 'Where's the beef?' I'm going to quote what Mr. La-Bella said yesterday about the purchase of those four buildings. 'These were no doubt funded by stolen money.' What witness testified to that? What document shows that? Where's the beef? And do we want to get a simple lock on this case? LOK stands for lack of knowledge—knowledge that they've tried over and over to dump on Mrs. Marcos.

"The Secret Service and the FBI knew where she was at every moment. There isn't a shred of evidence she ever hid anything. To four presidents of this United States of America, these were decent, honest people. The four presidents of the United States of America knew what they were doing—"

> MR. LABELLA: "Objection, Your Honor."
>
> JUDGE KEENAN: "Sustained."
>
> MR. SPENCE: "If the United States of America through the FBI and the Secret Service knew what she was doing—"
>
> MR. LABELLA: "Objection, Your Honor."
>
> JUDGE KEENAN: "Sustained."

MR. SPENCE: "If the United States government believed these people were all right, then why couldn't she believe her husband?

"I am reading from the transcript of Mr. Gadup's testimony: 'You told us that Mr. Marcos told you from time to time not to tell Mrs. Marcos about certain matters. Do you remember that?'

"HIS ANSWER: 'Yes.'

"'You followed President Marcos's instructions in that regard, did you not?'

"HIS ANSWER: 'Yes.'

"Now, those are facts, ladies and gentlemen. Those aren't Mr. LaBella's 'she-must-have-knowns.'

"Even Genito—remember Mr. Genito? [I read from his testimony.] 'So you're not suggesting to anybody she did anything wrong, are you?' This is my cross-examination of Genito.

"HIS ANSWER: 'No.'

"'Did you ever in your life go to Mrs. Marcos and ask her to do anything improper?'

"HIS ANSWER: 'No.'"

I walked over to Mrs. Marcos and put my hands on her shoulders. "I will say this much: If she were charged with being a champion spender we don't need a trial. But spending lots of money isn't a crime. I mean, if that were a crime the Queen of England wouldn't be safe and the wives of the sultans wouldn't be safe, nor the late Grace Kelly, nor the Empress of Japan. She was a world-class shopper, but she was and is a world-class decent human being as well.

"The great danger in this case is the 'big S.' It's called suspicion. Suspicion isn't proof."

My argument consumed most of the day. "And so, ladies and gentlemen, who wins this case? If you set her free the government wins. Do you know why the government wins? Because the system worked. Because justice has been done. And do you know who the government really is? The government is we. We are the government. And so everybody wins."

I ended by saying to the jury that I wanted to tell them a story.

LABELLA: "Objection, Your Honor."

JUDGE KEENAN: "The objection is overruled. You know you've heard the story, and I've heard the story. Tell the story, Mr. Spence."

MR. SPENCE: "It must be a very good story if you both have heard it before."

JUDGE KEENAN: "That's for the jury to decide."

This was the judge's last chance to undermine me, telling the jury that my final words to them were a shopworn story with no sincerity attached.

I turned to the jury. "Ladies and gentlemen, this is the story of a wise old man and a smart-aleck boy. The smart-aleck boy wanted to show up the old man as a fool. The boy had captured a small bird in the forest. His plan was to go to the old man with the little bird cupped inside his hands so that only the small tail of the bird protruded. Then he'd say with a sneer, 'Old man, what do I have in my hand?'

"And the wise old man would say, 'You have a bird, my son.'

"Then the boy would say with confronting disdain, 'Old man, is the bird alive or is it dead?'

"And if the old man said the bird was dead, the boy would open up his hand and the bird would fly away free into the forest.

"But if the old man said the bird was alive, then the boy would begin to crush the bird in his cupped hands, and to *crush it* and *crush it* until the little bird was dead, and then he'd open his hands and say, 'See, old man, the bird is dead!'

"So the smart-aleck boy, as planned, came to the old man with the bird hidden in his cupped hands, and he said, 'Old man, what do I have in my hands?'

"The old man said, 'You have a bird, my son.'

"Then the boy said, 'Is the bird alive or is it dead?'

"And the wise old man softly said, 'The bird is in *your hands*, my son.'

"And ladies and gentlemen of the jury, Imelda Marcos is in yours."

I walked back and sat down slowly next to Mrs. Marcos. Her hand was trembling.

*I*t was LaBella's right to deliver the last argument, and he delivered what the press termed "a scathing rebuttal" that left Mrs. Marcos in tears and one juror wiping her own eyes. He stacked packs of freshly minted Philippine pesos on the rail of the jury box. "Can't you see the money? Wouldn't we know where this money came from? Wouldn't we know that Ferdinand Marcos was enriching himself by stealing millions from his country's treasury? And they"—pointing at me—"say she knew nothing!"

LaBella finally closed by predicting his victory. "When you look at all the evidence you will be convinced beyond a reasonable doubt that Imelda Marcos is guilty as charged."

In his instructions to the jury, Judge Keenan told them that she could be found guilty even if she "closed her eyes" to whether stolen money was used for investments in the United States.

If she "closed her eyes"? *Suspicion?*

After the jury was sent off to deliberate, one of her many supporters asked her what she would do while awaiting the verdict.

"I'll just pray," she said. "Life is fragile. I'll handle it with my prayers."

The jury was out five days, during which Mrs. Marcos spent much of her time at the nearby St. Andrew's Church. I suffered every nightmare that a creative mind could concoct. I reargued the case a hundred times. Mrs. Marcos should have hired a real lawyer. The country lawyer should go back where he came from and talk to those simple, honest people, not to sophisticated New York jurors.

Despite my screaming doubts, the rational part of me continued to seep up. That part said we'd won the case, the judge's last stab notwithstanding. I told Mrs. Marcos there'd never be twelve good citizens who'd find her guilty. This was a case of caring versus anger, love versus hate. Mrs. Marcos stood for the former, LaBella and his crew the latter. I believe that love trumps hate. On Monday, July 2, 1990, the jurors marched into the courtroom with their verdict.

The foreperson held the verdict tightly to his chest as if he dare not let it go. I looked into the faces of each of the twelve. They wouldn't look at me. My God, had I misjudged these people? Jurors who find against you usually look away as if to say, "We've rejected not only your case, but you as a human being." I looked at the dear black woman with the soft eyes. She would not look at me.

The foreperson released the verdict to the clerk, who handed it to the judge. He read it to himself, and without a hint of expression handed it back to the clerk.

"Ladies and gentlemen of the jury," the judge began, "harken to your verdict."

The clerk began to read. "We, the jury, duly impaneled and sworn, do find the defendant Imelda Marcos not guilty on count one.

"Not guilty on count two.

"Not guilty on count three."

Oh, Lord, I thought, did they compromise and find her guilty on the one remaining count?

"Not guilty on count four."

The courtroom was packed with Marcos friends and loyalists who erupted in cheers and tears as this three-month nightmare finally ended. Mrs. Marcos stood softly weeping.

It was Imelda's sixty-first birthday.

Mrs. Marcos invited me and the jury to a celebration, but I was desperate to get home and attend to affairs that had suffered in my absence those many months. Most of the jurors joined her. The kindly black woman was there. I wish I could have told her how much I appreciated her during the trial. Later Mrs. Marcos shared with me a conversation she had with the woman.

"Do you know why I knew you were innocent?" she asked Mrs. Marcos. "Why?"

"Because," she said, "Mr. Spence cared so much for you."

The media still delighted in referring to Mrs. Marcos as "the Steel Butterfly." But Imaging, who'd grown to love Mrs. Marcos, summed her up more accurately: "Imelda was extravagant in many ways—in spending money, in her love of beauty, in her generosity and her caring for people." Imelda said she was allergic to ugliness. In ways, I thought, she and Imaging were sisters under the skin.

After the verdict Imelda left immediately for St. Patrick's Cathedral, where she crawled on her knees down the full length of the center aisle to the altar. She bowed her head to the floor and gave her thanks to the Lord.

I dropped by Judge Keenan's chambers to pay my respects. One can make room for a judge who conducts himself in ways that hurt you and your case so long as you recognize he is, in fact, a decent person who, like all of us, is the victim of his own personality. Too many judges come to the conclusion that they have been gifted from above with some sort of supernatural wisdom. Judge Keenan had a keen sense of justice, but I thought it was skewed in favor of the government. I thought perhaps he couldn't help himself, considering that he was dealing with the likes of me.

In any event, I wished to pay my respects and stopped by his chambers to say good-bye and to wish him well. He couldn't have been more cordial.

I immediately understood why lawyers liked him. I found myself liking him. Along the way he said, "I want to congratulate you, Mr. Spence. You are the best criminal defense attorney who has appeared before me. I want you to know something: This is only the third time in my tenure that a jury has returned a verdict of acquittal in my court." His statement didn't surprise me. Many federal courts enjoy conviction rates of well above 90 percent.

I thanked him for the compliment, but I thought he was being overly generous. And I thought that if I ever tried another case before him he'd be as tough and unrelenting and impatient with me as before. At the same time, one must wonder if his explosive reactions to me didn't have something to do with me and the way I behave. I'll admit: We never see ourselves as well as others see us.

*I*n 1991 Imelda Marcos was permitted to return to the Philippines. She faced a reported nine hundred civil and criminal cases that had crowded the Philippine courts for years. She won all but one or two of the cases, and those she lost were overturned by the court of appeals.

She served in the Philippine Congress from 1995 through 1998, representing her birthplace, the Leyte province in the central islands. She returned to politics in April of 2010 at the age of eighty and was reelected to Congress, where she still serves.

"In politics, you don't only use your heart or head," she said. "You also use the soul of a mother, the selfless giving of a mother." As for our case, she said, "I won on my birthday. I was alone, widowed, helpless, penniless, and country-less. But even the Bible says there is a special place in hell for those who oppress widows and orphans." Then with gentle eyes she offered that small, kindly smile I'd seen so often. Somehow I felt she'd forgiven her tormentors long ago.

This case stands for something more than just another story about how Power, one step at a time, has led us to the brink of a police state. Here we have seen how Power, through its voice, the corporate media, captured the minds of an entire nation. The hatred of the Marcoses by those who'd never met them, never knew them, and many who'd never heard of them descended on the nation like the plague. An irreversible loathing of the Marcos name was as solidly implanted in the minds of intelligent, discerning citizens as any religion in the minds of the faithful. No truth existed except that the Marcoses were agents of the devil, and that Mrs. Marcos was infected with her husband's villainy.

What is the danger of a force so prevailing that the composite mind of a nation can be captured? Ask those who have experienced life in a police state. Ask those who once saluted Hitler as his goose-stepping troops marched by.

THE NEW AMERICAN GESTAPO

Although he and I had been on the same stage at programs for the American Association for Justice, I'd never met Geoffrey Fieger. Tall, long-haired, dynamic, often outspoken, even at times outrageous, he was one of the country's great lawyers and had an enviable record of winning for the people. Now he was in trouble and asking for my help. He'd been charged with violating election law by funneling money to the tune of $127,000 to John Edwards's 2004 presidential campaign. According to the indictment, Fieger had reimbursed his employees for their contributions to Edwards. This was a common practice across the land, and when the issue came up it was never dealt with criminally. At most, fines were imposed. Imaging thought the case was surely some kind of political vendetta, and I agreed. But I don't like political cases, because I don't like most politicians. Usually they represented only themselves. And it seemed to me that if Fieger had done what he was accused of, he had, in fact, broken the law. "I looked at the statute," I said to Imaging. "It prohibits giving money to a candidate in the name of another—against using straw men, like Fieger's employees."

She was unconvinced. "All your cases don't have to have blood and gore. Maybe you should take a case like this to show the people what's really going on in this country's political wars." The people only know what the politicians tell them. "Isn't there a difference between using a *fictional* name to make a contribution, and reimbursing someone who uses his *own* name to make the contribution and who simply gets reimbursed?" I'd always thought Imaging would have been a great lawyer.

I'd heard how George W. Bush's Republican "Pioneers," his largest fund-raisers, routinely solicited bundles of contributions from employees of banks, brokerage firms, and corporations. Some of these employees later received bonuses that more than made up for their contributions. There was never any suggestion that anything illegal was taking place when Bush did it. Still, I didn't like political cases.

Imaging kept at me. "Fieger is one of us. He's a people's lawyer. And the country needs good lawyers to fight for the people. If he gets anyone but you to defend him he's likely a goner—he loses everything, and his kids and his wife will be out on the street. They'll keep him in prison for the next twenty years just to prove to lawyers like you that their fight for citizens' rights is over. You have to defend him."

Fieger had seemed unbowed on the phone. "My crime wasn't the bonuses given to our employees. My crime was butting heads with George W. Bush." I liked the part about butting heads with Bush. And it was true that in Michigan from the governor on down, the state was controlled by a political party that Fieger characterized as "the new brand of Republicans—political reactionaries, throwbacks to the witch-hunting days of Salem." I listened while Fieger made his case. He said, "I threw myself into a political holocaust during the nearly ten years I represented Dr. Jack Kevorkian." Kevorkian—Dr. Death, as he'd become known—was the unremitting champion providing assisted death for fellow human beings who were in terminal, incurable suffering and were begging to die. Fieger had successfully defended Kevorkian in half a dozen murder cases that resulted in the big political guns being turned on Kevorkian's lawyer.

"I took on their Republican governor, [John] Engler, who was Catholic. I took on their legislature that was Republican. I took on their Supreme Court of Michigan that was both Catholic and Republican. I took on their Oakland County prosecutor, Richard Thompson, who was Republican. I took on the police. Looking back, I must have been out of my mind to think I could survive." Was Fieger courageous or just unwise? The line between is narrow. He said, "The words of my former law partner Michael Alan Schwartz still ring in my ears: 'Never be a victim.' I was determined not to be a victim."

Fieger told me that one day while he was driving home listening to a radio talk show, Michigan governor John Engler was on, and a listener called in and asked how they could stop Dr. Kevorkian—the said Dr. Death. Engler's answer came without hesitation: "Disbar Fieger, that's about the only way." Fieger said, "Soon after that, grievances were filed against me by the boatload, and they all bore the fingerprints of Engler and the radical Republican religious right."

Describing his attitude in those days, he alluded to Arthur Miller's *The Crucible,* in which an eighty-three-year-old man is put to death as a witch. The method of his execution is slowly crushing him under a mounting load of boulders. "The old man's last, defiant words were 'More weight!' I was young then," Fieger said. "And I was rebellious. And I could take more weight than those bastards ever imagined. I was at war with everyone, including the Attorney Grievance Commission."

As if he hadn't already poked the hornet's nest enough, in 1998, Fieger declared his candidacy for the Democratic nomination for governor, and to everyone's surprise but his own he beat the preordained candidate of the Democratic power brokers. The Democratic power brokers wanted no part of this controversial lawyer and promptly walked away from Fieger, leaving him to battle the incumbent Governor Engler on his own. Fieger launched a frontal attack on Engler, who he believed was unfairly claiming personal credit for the national prosperity created by Bill Clinton. That war would earn him the further enmity of Michigan's powerful Republicans.

Fieger lampooned Engler in his campaign ads. He portrayed the man as a corpulent political animal and a hypocrite who claimed to be antigovernment but who had only held government jobs himself. Fieger said Engler was gifted with the vindictiveness of Richard Nixon. He kept an enemies list. And Jack Kevorkian and Geoffrey Fieger were at its top. Fieger lost.

In the 2000 presidential primary, Governor Engler volunteered to head the George W. Bush campaign in Michigan against the then-maverick senator from Arizona, John McCain, who was posing a threat to the anointed Bush as the Republican presidential nominee. Engler publicly guaranteed he'd deliver Michigan to Bush. Fieger said, "That promise by Engler was like dropping chum into a tank of sharks. I took the bait." Fieger ran a series of radio commercials taunting Bush and tying him to Engler. In a parody of the then-hit movie *Dumb and Dumber,* he created and narrated ads entitled "Dumb, Dumber, and Dumbest," referring to Bush, Spencer Abraham (the Michigan Republican senator running for reelection, who later lost), and Engler. His ads gained the attention of the national press, and NPR did a half-hour special on how Fieger, a Democrat, was sticking his nose into the Michigan Republican presidential primary. Fieger even urged Democrats to vote in the Republican primary for McCain, and when McCain won big in Michigan, Bush and his hatchet man, Karl Rove, were furious. And Engler was humiliated.

Predictably things got dirty. How dirty? Rove even began suggesting that McCain had fathered a black child, when, in fact, McCain and his wife had adopted a dark child from Bangladesh who had been given to them by Mother Teresa. In Bush's Michigan concession speech he railed against Fieger, stating at least three times that good Republicans couldn't let "that Kevorkian lawyer" mess in their politics. "Now I had some new and even more powerful enemies," Fieger said. And when Bush was reelected in 2004, he chose as attorney general Alberto Gonzales, whom Fieger had previously dismissed as an "intellectual peewee."

Fieger's prosecution began with a complaint by a disgruntled former employee named Eric Humphrey who appeared in the Detroit FBI office and claimed that Fieger had reimbursed employees for political donations to presidential candidate John Edwards. According to Fieger, within hours Humphrey's story was run up the political flagpole to the highest levels in Washington, D.C. And within a few days, on May 18, 2005, and unknown to Fieger, the feds called a grand jury to investigate him.

This brand of secret investigation can go on for months, even years. First, the FBI *secretly* serves a warrant on your bank, and up pop all of your personal bank records. You thought your bank would protect you—at least give you notice. But *no*. The FBI gained access not only to Fieger's bank records and canceled checks but also to those of every employee, friend, or family member who'd given to Edwards and who had later been reimbursed by Fieger.

The grand jury had already been in secret session for about six months investigating Fieger when, on November 30, 2005, roughly eighty FBI agents were flown in from all over the country for a coordinated raid on Fieger's office and the homes of his employees. One agent even flew in from Iraq. The sheer size of this operation was unprecedented. This is more bodies than the government threw against Osama bin Laden at Tora Bora. The cost was astronomical.

At seven o'clock sharp on the evening of November 30, this army of government agents attacked Fieger and his employees. Some agents came stomping into his law office, where employees were still at work, and pairs of FBI agents pounded on the doors of other scared employees, some of whom were home alone. It was dinnertime for most. Some had children at home, and parents and children alike were in shock. Surprise and intimidation are the agents' stock-in-trade, and as they marched into citizens' homes they inspired utter, unremitting fear.

"Why are cops at my door?" the Fieger employee wondered. "This must be a mistake." But the message would soon be clear from the G-men: "Listen, chump, you're as guilty as Fieger. You got reimbursed, didn't you? This was Fieger's money to Edwards, not yours, right? Admit it. Do not lie to the FBI! That's a federal crime." They were told that unless they cooperated they'd be accused of joining a conspiracy to violate federal law, and the FBI expected the said "subjects" to flip and become witnesses for the government against Fieger to save themselves—standard government procedure in this land of the free and the home of the brave.

On August 24, 2007, almost *two years after the FBI's original raid,* the foreman of the grand jury signed an indictment against Fieger. The indictment was drafted under the direction of an assistant U.S. attorney by the name of Lynn Helland. Fieger would face ten criminal counts along with "obstruction of justice," the charge that's almost always thrown in when the government wants to make sure it hits the target with something. The thirty-page indictment charged conspiracies to violate federal election campaign laws, each of which carried a maximum of five years in prison and a quarter-million-dollar fine. "Obstruction of justice" carried another ten years and another quarter-million-dollar fine. If you ever got out of that hole you'd be old, broke, and broken. In spite of my initial resistance, the facts of the case and Fieger himself grabbed me. Dirty politics is like a deadly virus. It keeps changing forms. It can't be eradicated. But individuals can be saved. I told him I'd take his case.

No trial date had yet been set, but the media circus began immediately, and Fieger was cast as "that Kevorkian lawyer." Every photo caught him with his mouth wide open—a raging big mouth. When I took on the defense, the media provided detailed accounts of some of my controversial cases and noted that "the famed lawyer" had never lost a criminal case, implying, of course, that the guilty Fieger had brought in a hired gun, namely me. The government of the United States of America was being portrayed by the media as the underdog, like a crippled Boy Scout out there just trying to earn his merit badges.

The *Detroit Free Press* published a readers' comments section. Two came forth with these dandies: "Fieger's arrogance finally caught up with him. Using low paid employees as straw donors? That's just stupid."

The second commenter reflected, "OK, this is just smarmy. I always thought Fieger was just this side of the law, but I think he crossed the big old line this time that is going to bite him in the butt."

In an interview with the *Detroit Free Press* Fieger said, "I picked Spence because he's the greatest trial lawyer who ever lived, except Darrow. [Why did he ruin the fantasy with that exception?] I couldn't pass up the honor of being represented by him." The truth: I was seventy-eight years old, and I wanted peace, and I needed my afternoon nap, and I felt about as able to take on the U.S. government as to fight Muhammad Ali in his prime. A smidgen of good sense would have probably kept me from taking the case in the first place.

The case would be tried in Detroit, but it would be months before the trial date was set. In the meantime, we argued that the case should be dismissed. We had a library full of decisive motions against the case we wanted to file. And in the meantime, what about the others who had endured this two-year living nightmare—not only Geoffrey, but his wife, Keenie, and all of his employees and friends who'd contributed to Edwards and had been reimbursed by Geoffrey? What about his mother? He even reimbursed his mother. I was often to argue, "I suppose Mr. Fieger, a brilliant lawyer, understood that when his mother gave money, and he reimbursed her, that he knowingly and intentionally transformed her into a criminal, a member of a conspiracy to violate federal law?"

In one pretrial argument I told Federal District Judge Paul D. Borman that this two-year investigation could have been completed in two weeks. But week after week the prosecutors often subpoenaed only one Fieger employee to the grand jury. Who would be called next? Such is one of Power's favorite tortures. Even Geoffrey's employees couldn't talk with him lest the feds would claim they were involved in a conspiracy to obstruct justice. Employees were afraid to talk to one another for fear they'd be indicted along with Geoffrey.

These were folks who needed their jobs, and jobs in the law business are hard to come by. They had families to support. And the feds were stretching them on a rack of conflict. They could probably earn freedom from any threatened prosecution if they turned on Fieger and helped the feds convict him, but they were loyal employees, and they'd never intended to commit a crime. Several of his employees hired lawyers they couldn't afford to pay. Geoffrey offered to pay their lawyers, but even that might be used by the feds against him as evidence supporting a charge of a conspiracy.

After a couple of Fieger's lawyers stood up to the feds, the FBI began its usual intimidation. The feds threatened to prosecute the children of one of the lawyers who worked for Geoffrey. The kids had given to Edwards and had been reimbursed by their father. That lawyer told the feds, "Bring it on!" Surprisingly, the feds backed off.

Geoffrey's fees, of course, were contingent on his winning his client's cases. If he didn't win he couldn't pay his employees and keep his law office afloat. No doubt the feds believed Fieger, awaiting trial, would fold under the pressure and go broke. Who'd hire a lawyer who'd been indicted by a grand jury for violations of federal crimes? Hire him today—he'd probably be in the pen tomorrow.

I learned to admire Geoffrey Fieger even more as I saw him fight on without the first willingness to give an inch. "More weight" seemed to be his answer. How his wife, Keenie, was able to survive with her young family was also inspiring. While her husband continued to fight and win his cases, she continued to be a quiet, loving mother. What must a woman do whose nest filled with children is in serious jeopardy, and whose husband is being attacked from every side by the prosecutors and the media? Her husband needed help. But who was there to help her? I saw a calm, powerful woman with a quiet smile. I saw kids living a normal life. I saw Keenie absorb her husband's frustration and anger and not take it on. It made me proud to be their lawyer.

In the meantime the Bush gang, with Rove jerking the reins on Attorney General Gonzales, was using its power to play its usual politics across the land. With a vindictive fire, the likes of which I'd never seen, this bunch expelled eight U.S. attorneys who refused to buckle under their demands to bring certain political prosecutions. "Do what we say or get out" was their message. Attorney General Gonzales had been absorbing the heat from the national press for his abuse of the system and was about to resign. He stayed on just long enough for the grand jury to return an indictment against Fieger, after which, the next day, Gonzales slipped back into the fog of anonymity, from which he has never reappeared.

I, too, needed help. I called on my old friend David Nevin, whom we remember from the Weaver case. We knew how to work together. He made quiet, kind space for my sometimes troublesome ego and filled in where I got frustrated with the technical stuff of the law. Besides, he was a great trial lawyer in his own right, with a genius for organizing and telling an effective story.

My impression was that we could have done worse than Judge Borman. He was a man who offered a pleasant demeanor accompanied by a ready smile, and he was one of those rare judges who had been a criminal defense attorney. Our first motion was to have the case dismissed because it was clearly a "selective and vindictive prosecution." What do those words mean in the law?

Suppose, for example, there are a hundred citizens out there who from time to time park in a certain spot marked BUS STOP, and they've been doing so for years. Then one day Billy Jones insults a prosecutor at the town picnic—called him "a sold-out mother-maker," or something. When Billy is subsequently charged by the prosecutor for parking in that same spot, it's clear that it's payback. The law says, "No. No. That is a selective and vindictive prosecution." We began our own prosecution—one against the feds for their "selective and vindictive prosecution." Indeed, it had become common practice in politics for interested parties with money to reimburse those without funds for their campaign contributions.

We had support for our claim from unlikely political allies. Jack Beam, a former Republican assistant U.S. attorney appointed by President Gerald Ford, commented on the Fieger case: "This kind of politicization is a shame. I'm embarrassed that this is my old Justice Department. It is reminiscent, and I don't think I exaggerate, of Nazi Germany." And Michigan's Republican Party chairman, Saul Anuzis, inadvertently admitted to the underlying politics. He expressed hope that Fieger's indictment would "give pause to members of the trial bar about the nature of their apparently too cozy of a relationship with liberal Democrat candidates." In plain words he was saying, "If you trial lawyers are hanging out with those liberal Democrats, your goose will get cooked."

In our pretrial brief we argued that the Justice Department had been "hijacked" by Republican political operatives and "turned into a weapon to silence political dissidents like Mr. Fieger and others threatening the Republican stronghold in this country." We cited a recent study by two academicians, Donald Shields and John Cragan, who examined the number of public corruption investigations and prosecutions brought by the Bush Justice Department under its Public Integrity Section chief. Shields and Cragan concluded that under Noel Hillman's leadership between January 2001 and December 2006, U.S. attorneys nationwide investigated seven times as many Democratic officials as they did Republican officials, "a number that exceeds even the racial profiling of African Americans in traffic stops." If this wasn't selective prosecution, I don't know what was. By the time of our case, Hillman had been rewarded for his work with a federal judgeship in New Jersey. We also noted the disproportionate resources that had been dedicated to Fieger's case. Ninety-nine percent of campaign finance disputes had been resolved civilly by the Federal Election Commission. On what grounds had the Justice Department selected Mr. Fieger and his firm as the target of the largest campaign finance investigation in the history of America?

In one of our pretrial motions we pointed to the fact that the U.S. attorney's *Manual for Election Crimes* held that campaign finance violations "are either not crimes or do not warrant criminal prosecution" and proposed that the vast majority of statutory violations should be "handled non-criminally by the Federal Election Commission under the statute's civil enforcement provision." In other words, don't use the election laws to put people in jail. If there are violations, treat them with fines. We listed twenty-one cases with facts similar to Fieger's that had been resolved without a criminal prosecution.

Judge Borman held us all at bay while he asked Assistant U.S. Attorney Lynn Helland why it had taken so many federal agents to conduct their investigation. Smiling, the judge said, "I'm just trying to figure out how it went down." He said he couldn't recall that many agents involved in any other raid during his thirteen years on the federal bench. Still smiling, and to our complete bewilderment, he ruled against us on our motion to dismiss the indictment. We hadn't established sufficient cause to dismiss this sham? Perhaps we shouldn't have been bewildered. Judges are human, and they have an incentive to pass the buck to juries.

Now we faced the upcoming trial and a jury panel composed of citizens who'd been barraged with the feds' propaganda against Fieger. The top dogs in the Department of Justice in Washington, D.C., must have believed that Assistant U.S. Attorney Helland needed some help. If Helland needed help, the government had hundreds of experienced, highly skilled prosecutors from whom to select his co-counsel. So why would that office tap a nice, innocent-appearing young man who ought to provide little competition for any run-of-the-mill criminal defense attorney? The young trial lawyer's name was Kendall Day. But behind Day's youthful innocence lurked an experienced prosecutor who had been involved in some major criminal cases, including the prosecution of the notorious Washington lobbyist Jack Abramoff. I thought his choice was a smart tactical move by the powers that be in Washington, D.C., who saw Day as a rising star. Juries liked him. Besides, throwing an apparent kid in to fight Spence would shore up the illusion that the government was, indeed, the underdog.

Day didn't disappoint. On his first day before the trial, Day, in open court, complained to Judge Borman that Fieger was airing TV ads attacking the government's investigation. He asked Borman to put a gag order on Geoffrey to stop him from taking his case public. Our David Nevin replied: The government had been using the media for months telling the potential jury pool what a vile, conniving criminal Geoffrey was, and in turn Geoffrey shouldn't be allowed to speak back? Nevin argued that the Department of Justice's own handbook said prosecutors should consult with the department's Public Integrity Section at headquarters *before* opening a criminal campaign in a finance case, to which Helland confessed, "I screwed up." But the mistake was inconsequential, Helland argued, because the Public Integrity Section in Washington, D.C., itself had independently opened an investigation of Fieger at almost the same time.

We called Judge Borman's attention to the Third Reich tactics of Helland himself, who actually had asked grand jury witnesses whom they had voted for in certain elections. *Whom a witness voted for?* "Is this a political case or not?" I asked the judge. Helland claimed such questions were relevant because "they could identify inconsistencies between financial and voting support," whatever that was supposed to mean. "Was it invasive?" Helland asked. "Yes. Was it improper? I don't think so." Judge Borman just kept on smiling.

Then Helland's boss, the local U.S. attorney Stephen Murphy, and two of his assistants stepped up and asked to speak to the judge. The judge smiled back and said, "Of course." For the first time these three lawyers were suddenly claiming they were disqualified from overseeing the Fieger case. Why? I asked. All three of these prosecutors had apparently been involved in this case for the last seven months. Why did it take them seven months to conclude that on some unspecified grounds it would now be wrong for them to try to put Fieger away? "None of this really passes the smell test," I argued to Judge Borman. But we were being stonewalled by the prosecutors.

Then Helland advised us that he had been talking to the judge in one of those forbidden, secret ex parte conferences we'd encountered in the Singer case. The feds, because they deal in matters of national security, have the right, in rare cases, for such clandestine conferences, but this wasn't such a case. The question seemed to come down to exactly who was running this case—the judge or the prosecutors? We would soon find out.

Harper's Magazine took a look at what it unabashedly called "a political prosecution," pointing out that "using the office of U.S. attorney to wage a political vendetta is a crime under sections 1505 and 1512 of the Criminal Code. In fact, it's a far more serious crime than the allegations brought for campaign finance violations."*

Judge Borman took more than three months to write his thirty-page opinion. He acknowledged what appeared to be the political motivations behind the case, noting that Helland, the lead prosecutor, admitted this was the first prosecution involving reimbursement of campaign contributions that he knew of in the twenty-some years he'd been working in the department. In the past, purported violations of election laws had been left to the Federal Election Commission for appropriate sanctions, if any.

Judge Borman also questioned why Murphy and his assistants had disqualified themselves after seven months. He also noted he'd been essentially stonewalled. The judge gave the prosecutors a few more days to come clean. In response, the prosecutors filed their response claiming the judge had made substantial errors in his opinion without specifying the same, and at last revealed that their recusals were because Murphy and the other two had contributed small sums of money to Stephen Markman's campaign for the Michigan Supreme Court. It took them seven months to remember that?

The judge backed off. He overruled our pretrial motions, including our claim that the feds' prosecution of Fieger had been "selective and vindictive." Why did the judge overrule our motions? I make no claim to know.

The pretrial publicity fight in the media accelerated. Yes, both sides wanted to influence any citizen who might later be called as a juror in the case. Geoffrey, who could never be silenced, not with a gun at his head,

* Scott Horton, *Harper's* Browsings blog, January 25, 2008.

claimed in an ad that the George W. Bush administration had declared war on lawyers and compared that to the Nazi campaign to rid Germany of Jews, Gypsies, Catholics, unionists, and lawyers. The ad featured unpretty photos of Bush, Vice President Dick Cheney, and former attorney general Alberto Gonzales.

Day and Helland complained that this publicity could set potential jurors against them. They asked Judge Borman to order Fieger to pull the ad. Judge Borman, referring to Fieger's ad, said, "This one is just totally off the wall and outright blatant given that we have a jury trial coming up." He ordered Fieger to pull the ad. And finally he ordered our trial to begin on April 14, 2008.

We filed a motion for a change of venue because many potential jurors might hold deep animus against Geoffrey because of his defense of Kevorkian. In support we handed over a bulging scrapbook of newspaper clippings of virulent comments made in readers' columns against Fieger, stories and photos that showed him to be someone we'd lock the front door against, and affidavits demonstrating that Geoffrey's reputation in the community had been sullied by the media and that a fair trial in Detroit would be impossible. Our motion was promptly denied. We next contested the jury panel. It didn't contain a proportionate share of black jurors. In addition to the fact that Geoffrey and Keenie had adopted two black children, Geoffrey was something of a folk hero to the black community for his work on behalf of African Americans. Judge Borman said no—but kept on smiling.

he trial began as scheduled, and as his first judicial act Judge Borman dealt Fieger a death blow. He ruled we couldn't even intimate to the jurors that Geoffrey had been the victim of a political witch-hunt instigated by the Bush people. Then the judge ordered a media blackout for both sides. The prosecutors immediately used a tactic to subvert his order. They filed a forty-one-page document they styled as "a trial brief" that was brimming with hate-Fieger material, a diatribe that had been designed for the media's eyes. The media took to the prosecutors' "brief" like starving street waifs invited to a feast at McDonald's. That "brief," which was supposed to be under seal for the judge's and our eyes only, was filed as an ordinary paper in the court documents and had been left naked for the media to read and report.

The "brief" included the names of the government's witnesses and what they were likely to say. It claimed Fieger had been warned by one of his own lawyers, Todd Weglarz, that the practice of reimbursement was illegal. Weglarz had made a contribution to Edwards and had been reimbursed by Fieger. And it quoted Weglarz: "Should there ever be any type of investigation into those contributions, I am greatly concerned about the effect it would have on my ability to maintain a license to practice law." According to the "brief," Wensdy White, a consultant for Fieger's newsletter, would testify that Fieger also called her to warn her not to talk to the FBI. Fieger was quoted as saying, "Just tell them you donated to the John Edwards campaign and that you support him."

Quotes from the brief immediately appeared in local papers. According to Day, he had made a mistake in failing to file the brief under seal. I argued for a dismissal of the case. I told the judge, "If we filed a forty-page press release with a gag order in effect, you'd have me down there in the crossbars hotel. There's no end to their dirty tricks."

"Overruled," said Judge Borman with his kindly smile.

I asked for at least an apology from the prosecution.

No, Judge Borman said. He thought his mere admonishment of the government would do. I thought their misconduct had the potential to permanently poison the case.

As is usual in federal courts, the judge questioned the jurors as to their qualifications to sit on the case. No, the judge ruled, I couldn't ask a single question to any juror. Many federal court judges allow counsel to question jurors, since the lawyers know their case better than the judge, and the right to question jurors is nearly always allowed in most state courts.

Jury selection and the opening statement are the two most important phases of any jury trial. It's during these times that the attorney is able to create a tribe with the jurors and to create trust and establish credibility. I have often said, "Give me a fair and honest voir dire [jury selection] and a well-delivered and truthful opening statement, and the case is over so long as I never betray the jurors' trust." That first opportunity is lost when, as in this case, only the judge can question jurors. Although Borman had once been a public defender, it didn't mean he knew how to select a jury or that he'd ever been an effective trial lawyer. He asked the same questions one most often hears from judges in the federal courts.

The *Detroit Free Press* ran a story that would further emphasize the government's underdog status, quoting Wayne State law professor Peter Henning, a former lawyer in the U.S. Department of Justice, who said, "Gerry Spence is one of the most celebrated lawyers in recent times. He is legendary, and it will be interesting to see how he handles himself." The article laid out my well-known cases and noted that I'd hired David Nevin, who "played by the rules, but who also won by the rules," implying, of course, that Spence won by the use of unspecified tricks and improprieties.

The paper published another series of op-ed letters that revealed, in part, why we'd asked for a change of venue. One reader wrote that "a lying, cheating son-of-a-b#*ch is finally getting his due." Another wrote, "Fieger is a self-serving blowhard. He got caught with his hand in the cookie jar and I hope he gets what he deserves. Disbarment. A little jail time would be nice too. It would be cool to see Fieger and Kilpatrick [the former mayor] in the same perp walk." The paper ran only one letter that opposed an immediate hanging: "Give Spence a chance to get a fair trial for his client. He represents what is right about good lawyers, and let's see if he can teach his client and D-town about the abuse of power that seems so pervasive in this case on both sides."

After the judge had finished his jury selection, both sides had six peremptory challenges, meaning that each side could dismiss a total of six prospective jurors from the case without stating a reason. I'm not a big fan of jury consultants, but Fieger wanted me to use Lou Genovic, who'd often helped him in civil cases. He and Genovic chose the jurors we'd excuse. The case would be heard by sixteen citizens—the standard twelve plus four alternates—eleven male and five female jurors. Two were African American.

Next, Judge Borman delivered a list of persons we were forbidden to mention by name to the jury. "Do not mention George W. Bush, Governor Engler, Karl Rove, or Attorney General Gonzales." Moreover, we were ordered not to argue to the jury that the law does not prohibit reimbursement. The judge gave us one defense, and only one: I could try to persuade the jury that Geoffrey Fieger didn't *know* he'd violated the law when he made his reimbursements. I could try to convince a jury of intelligent citizens that a great lawyer, one of the brightest persons I have ever known, didn't understand that reimbursing one's employees was a crime when, to the contrary, Judge Borman would be telling the jurors that reimbursement *was* a crime? I saw the marshals slapping the cuffs and chains on Geoffrey Fieger and hauling him off to some concrete hole.

In his opening statement Helland, in a floor-flat monotone, said the case was about deception and illegal fund-raising. Helland was as jovial and appealing as a reawakened mummy. He didn't need to be charismatic and a Mr. Nice Guy. He was doing the public a service, prosecuting a known crafty criminal, this Fieger individual, who thought he could violate the law and get away with it.

When it came my turn to make my opening statement to the jury, I asked Fieger's wife, Keenie, to stand up with the Fieger children. She held their new baby in her arms. I introduced them to the jurors. With a sneer Helland asked if they were going to give testimony. I said I wanted the jury to see the real people behind our case. "This is no place for babies and mammas to be," I said. "I'm going to ask that they be excused at this time."

Then I told the jury that Mr. Day, that nice young man, was under the direction of a Mr. Welch from Washington, D.C. And I motioned to Assistant District Attorney Lynn Helland, and I told the jury that he, too, was under the direction of Mr. Welch of Washington, D.C. I thought that might tell the jury who the real parties were on both sides of the case: Mom and the kids on our side; Mr. Welch, a head honcho in the Department of Justice from Washington, D.C., on theirs. The judge stepped in. No, Helland was *not* under the direction of Washington, D.C. But the judge was wrong. Helland took his orders from Welch in Washington, D.C., the same as Day. But who was the jury to believe, the judge or that crafty, slick lawyer from Wyoming?

I told the jury that they'd seen Geoffrey on television, and some might not like him, but he fought for the little guy. "He fights big government and corporations that stomp ordinary people under." Then I held up an enlargement of what became known as section 441f of the law.

"Let's read this together," I invited the jury as I held up the cardboard in front of the jurors: It read: "No person shall make a contribution *in the name of another person* or knowingly permit his name to be used to effect such a contribution."

I said, "The contributions in this case were made *in the name of the persons who gave the money,* and they were reimbursed by Mr. Fieger." I told the jury the people's contributions were totally voluntary. Only half in his firm contributed. He decided to reimburse those who wanted to give but couldn't afford to. In the end he treated everyone alike and reimbursed even those who could afford it. It was that simple.

I took my argument to the edge by contradicting the judge's position: There was nothing on the books, I told the jury, that said that *reimbursement* was illegal. "We don't have secret laws in this country," I said. "The word 'reimbursement' doesn't appear anywhere in these statutes."

I told the jury that Geoffrey had reviewed the law, and that in forty years there had never been a case that said reimbursement was a crime. Nor was there a U.S. Supreme Court case that said so. I said, "The prosecutors see Mr. Fieger with only one eye, and that's an evil eye, and it's *their* eye."

I pointed out that if reimbursement were a crime, then the government could make criminals of all of us. A husband reimburses his wife. A parent reimburses the child. Mr. Fieger reimbursed his mother. Were all of these people—wife, child, and mother—part of some evil conspiracy? And if the law is as clear and clean as it's written there, and as Mr. Fieger saw it, I asked them, who would expect that you would be dragged into a court of law and charged with ten counts as a criminal? There are no secret crimes in this country, *no secret crimes.* I likened it to driving up to an intersection where there was a blank sign. Then a cop pulls you over and claims you violated the law. Should you have known what was written on that blank sign?

"Every contribution here was made in the name of the person who made it, *not in the name of another* as the law prohibits. Their contributions were made by their personal checks, not some phony check, and those checks were delivered to the Edwards campaign.

"So Mr. Fieger didn't believe it was a crime, and sixteen lawyers in his firm gave, intelligent men and women, and none of them saw reimbursement as a crime. If you read the law as we have read it together, you can see that there is no crime stated on the face of the law. So there can't be a crime."

I waited for that truth to take hold.

Finally I said, "On November 30, 2005, came shock and awe. At least eighty FBI and IRS people descended upon Mr. Fieger at night. You would have thought he was Osama bin Laden at Tora Bora, or that they were trying to get the head of the Mafia family. It was seven o'clock at night. Some of the lawyers were working late. Can you imagine how it would be—innocent people sitting there working at night and in storms the FBI? The people were frightened. The FBI went into Mr. Fieger's private files and took away eighty-seven thousand—that's how bad they wanted to get him—eighty-seven thousand documents from his office, most of which had nothing to do with this case whatsoever.

"At the same time, other agents of the FBI, along with the IRS, went to the homes of those who had given to Edwards and knocked on their doors. Can you understand how that would be—at night, and you're a single mother at home with your baby, and here come two government men knocking on your door wanting to ask you questions. These agents had no right there except to serve the person with a subpoena to appear before the grand jury. But the people didn't know that. The people opened their doors and the agents burst in. And they began to interrogate these folks about something that had happened two years before.

"Some of the folks couldn't remember anything. Even the lawyers, most of whom are civil, not criminal, lawyers, were frightened. The people were told they were felons; they were told they had violated the law. One agent asked a lone mother, 'Is this a picture of your son?' 'Yes.' 'Well,' the FBI agent said, 'he needs a mother.' What was the implication? Then he asked, 'Did you let Mr. Fieger use your name?'

"They questioned a man named Lloyd Johnson: 'Well, Mr. Johnson, you have two boys?' 'Yes.' 'Your boys gave money to Mr. Edwards?' 'Yes.' 'And you reimbursed them?' 'Yes.' The FBI went to see the boys, and one of them had just started a job as a high school wrestling coach. The FBI came to the school where he was working with his team and they said, 'We want to talk to you.' The boy said, 'Please, please. I'm in a meet. What do you want to talk to me about?' Finally, he was able to get them to go to his little apartment later."

At this point, Judge Borman interjected, "You have ten more minutes."

"Thank you. I didn't know I used so much time," I said. "They were threatening to charge Mr. Johnson. They even went to his girlfriend, who's now his wife.

"And who are the *real* conspirators here? There are eight charges here, but within those charges there are many other charges. *Obstruction of justice.* Mr. Rees, the head FBI man sitting right here [I pointed at him], called Mr. Fieger on the phone the night of the raid. 'What are you doing?' Mr. Fieger asked. Rees was babbling, excited and in charge of this huge invasion with all of those agents. Finally he asked Mr. Fieger, 'Did you give any money?'

"Mr. Fieger said, 'I didn't give any money to anybody. I gave money to my employees.'

"'Well, what about Mr. Kenney?' Rees asked, referring to a former partner.

"'You'll have to talk to Mr. Kenney,' Mr. Fieger said. Of course, Mr. Kenney had died some time before. And the FBI knew he'd died and Mr. Fieger knew he'd died. Everybody knew. But Geoffrey Fieger was thereafter charged with obstruction of justice because he told the FBI to talk to a dead man.

"I want you to know that these people [referring to Fieger and Ven Johnson, his partner who was charged with him] are not criminals, they're good, bright men. Mr. Rees knows that, but they're charged as common criminals, charges that will take away their freedom for long periods of time."

Helland: "I do object to that."

Judge Borman: "I'll sustain the objection to that."

I pressed on. "They [I pointed to Helland] say Geoffrey was deceptive. They showed you the books. When you take out the employee's tax and all the rest, the employee was reimbursed a sum *exactly* equal to what they gave to Edwards. And he [pointing to Helland] didn't show you the document in which all of this was revealed. The books were open. The books showed exactly what happened. There was no attempt to cover it like you might see with GM or Ford, who would have hundreds of employees give and at the end of the year they'd get covering bonuses. The accountants and the IRS found there was nothing wrong with what Mr. Fieger did from a tax standpoint. But they also had these IRS agents out there that night scaring these people.

"Well, who are the *real* conspirators here? Who is really out to get Mr. Fieger in any way they can get him? We don't need the *powers that be in Washington, D.C.,* telling us what we should do here in Michigan; not those people. [I pointed to Helland and to Rees sitting next to him.] These are not the people we answer to.

"Thank God we've got juries like you. And we don't have to answer to anybody, *not to anybody.*

"I'm about to leave you, but I'll be with you for the next weeks. I hope you'll see that what was done here was done innocently and honestly. Mr. Fieger and the others may have disagreed with *the powers that be in Washington, D.C.* But that isn't the test. The test is did they *knowingly, willfully* violate the law?

"I think you'll find, when all of the evidence is in, that Mr. Fieger, Mr. Johnson, and none of the lawyers and none of the people who are all good citizens, who all live here, who fight for ordinary people like you, that none violated the law in any way. And I just have to say again, thank God for juries. Thank you for being here.

"We can say *good-bye* to the FBI.

"We can say *good-bye* to *the powers that be in Washington, D.C.*"

I sat down.

*I*t was the first thing in the morning following my opening statement. The jury was still in the jury room. Helland stood in front of Judge Borman shouting objections to my opening statement. It violated the judge's order about mentioning politics. He wanted the judge to tell the jury, in effect, what a bad person I was—to make it a case between the judge and Helland on one side and this misbehaving, untrustworthy Wyoming lawyer on the other, and, further, to tell the jury to disregard what I said in my opening about *the powers that be in Washington, D.C.,* and further still to tell the jury that what Geoffrey did was a crime.

Judge Borman responded, leaning down over the bench and shaking his finger at me. He admonished me thoroughly for having disregarded his earlier rulings. I wasn't even to whisper to the jury about Washington politics. I told His Honor that I intended only to convey to the jury what Geoffrey Fieger believed to be the law. His beliefs were germane to whether he willfully and knowingly violated the law, right? Besides, Helland hadn't objected then and waited until now, the morning after, to complain. You learn in the first year of law school that if you don't object at the time of the supposed offense you can't come whimpering to the judge afterward.

The judge ordered the jurors in. After they were seated, the first thing the judge did was to smile over to the jurors and say, "Mr. Helland works for the U.S. Attorney's Office in *Detroit*, not the Justice Department in Washington." That made me a judicially decreed liar, right? But who, in fact, was giving the ultimate orders in the case? Was his name Karl Rove?

Now Steve Fishman, the lawyer for Fieger's partner, Ven Johnson, followed with his opening statement and made substantially the same arguments to the jury. "It makes no sense to think Johnson knowingly broke the law," he said. "Among those Johnson reimbursed was his own daughter. Why would a successful lawyer, with nothing to gain, intentionally put his own daughter in legal jeopardy?" Fishman also claimed his client had no responsibility anyway because of a phenomenon that became known as "the Johnson pencil defense": Although Ven Johnson was a partner, Fieger ran the firm, and Johnson "couldn't buy a pencil without Fieger's approval."

*T*he time had come for the prosecution to make its case. A talented young clerk, a lawyer-to-be whom I liked a lot, a kid named Jim Harrington, was called by Kendall Day as the prosecution's first witness. Jim admitted that his $2000 check would have bounced but for his reimbursement by Fieger. I cross-examined the young man. Had he been forced to give the money? No. He said he had looked into John Edwards and found he was a trial lawyer. "I thought this was a great guy," Harrington said of Edwards. "I was excited." He told the jury he'd been asked to contribute by Ven Johnson, and he knew that Johnson wouldn't "put him in harm's way" if Johnson had believed reimbursement was illegal. He was stunned when the FBI came to his door. We were off to a good start.

But Kendall Day seemed undaunted. He called a former police officer named Paul Broschay, by then a lawyer in Fieger's firm, who admitted that not only did he give to Edwards in his own name, he had his wife and two daughters give in their names. Fieger had reimbursed them all, and all had been pursued by the FBI. Going after Broschay himself hadn't been enough. The feds sent its agents after his daughters. Yes, that's one way the FBI gets a witness to flip to the government's side of the case—go after his kids. Broschay said that when one of his daughters called home to Daddy, hysterical, he'd had enough. He told the FBI to get out of his house.

Tania Rock, Fieger's former personal secretary, was a potentially dangerous witness. I'd tried to interview her before the trial, but she wouldn't talk to me (as she'd no doubt been instructed by the prosecutors). This case could blow up in our faces; Lord knew what she might say. I'd made a lot of Geoffrey's home life and displayed his wife and children in court to the jurors. What if Tania now admitted to some clandestine affair? After such a betrayal of both Keenie and the kids and the jurors as well, the jurors would stampede to the jury room to convict Geoffrey.

The prosecutors served Tania with what is known as a "Kastigar letter." It provided her "use immunity," which meant the government couldn't prosecute her based on the facts she testified to. However, in terms that would make a polar bear shiver, it also required that if she didn't cooperate with the government her immunity agreement would be no protection. Although she sought to be sophisticated and professional in her demeanor, I saw how frightened the poor woman was—there in a public courtroom testifying against her former boss.

Under leading questions from Helland, Tania told the jury that she'd warned Fieger that his reimbursements were illegal and that he'd shrugged off her advice. I demanded that the prosecutors produce the infamous Kastigar letter. I projected it up on the screen for the jury to see and asked Tania to read the letter, word for word, out loud to the jury. I was gentle with her. I said that the letter must have frightened her. Was she afraid? Yes. I liked the young woman and felt sorry for her, and I suspected the jury felt the same way. I didn't think the jury appreciated the chief prosecutor dragging a scared woman into the courtroom to testify against her former boss, for whom she must have still retained certain feelings of loyalty.

On cross-examination I asked her in a friendly manner if Geoffrey had ever turned to her for any legal advice in other matters. No, she said, and she admitted she hadn't wanted to testify against her boss. I'd learned from other sources that the FBI had gone so far as to ask her if she and Geoffrey had ever engaged in an extramarital affair. I asked her if the FBI had questioned her on that subject.

Helland objected—supposed affairs had nothing to do with making contributions to Edwards, he argued. Precisely, I agreed. We were demonstrating that the government was so bent on getting Geoffrey Fieger that they'd grab at anything to get him, to sully his name, to embarrass him, to put his marriage in jeopardy, anything to put more pressure on him, even to harass and embarrass this witness. I thought the jury got the point. The judge permitted her to answer. She denied ever having had any such relationship with Geoffrey and that ended her testimony.

Helland next called Eric Humphrey, the former employee who'd started the whole mess. He testified that Fieger fired him because he wouldn't contribute to the Edwards campaign. He said he'd warned Fieger that reimbursement was against the law and even showed him a newspaper article that reported how some other lawyer had been charged by the feds with these same crimes and had been put under house arrest.

Humphrey had been warned by Fieger about dragging into work late. He'd been let go by Fieger in 2004 for other reasons. There'd been threats by Humphrey of a suit against Fieger. By the time I'd finished my cross, I thought the man seemed belligerent and defensive. Ordinarily we do not relate well to contentious people. We are less swayed by what people say than by how they say it. An unfriendly demeanor turns us off. Why had Humphrey waited two years to complain about Geoffrey to the FBI? I thought the jury might wonder as well.

Changing pace, the government then called SueEllen Sandner, one of Fieger's paralegals, who had been reimbursed by him. Why they called the lady remains a mystery. Under my cross-examination Ms. Sandner ended up saying she was so disgusted with the way FBI Agent Jeffrey Rees treated her that she had refused to meet with the federal prosecutor in advance of her testimony if Rees were there. Rees had called her shortly after his agents raided Fieger's law firm, and at one point the prosecutors asked her to sign a statement, but the statement didn't include what she'd said—that "Mr. Fieger never asked me to lie or hide what I'd done." And, as she stepped down from the witness stand she said, "I don't think Mr. Fieger would ask me to do anything wrong."

We learned from Geoffrey's partner, Ven Johnson, that along the way the FBI had actually tried to use him to set Fieger up. They'd enlisted the help of a lawyer, another former employee. As planned in advance, the former employee had called Ven Johnson while the FBI was secretly recording the conversation. This lawyer told Johnson that he was concerned that Fieger's reimbursement had been illegal. Repeatedly during the recorded conversation he tried to get Johnson to admit there was something wrong with reimbursing, and Johnson as often asked, "What's the problem?" Finally Johnson got weary of the conversation and told him to talk to Fieger if he thought there was something wrong. That ended the intended trap.

Back again in the courtroom, Jeffrey Rees finally took the stand for the prosecution. He testified as to the planning and execution of their raid on Fieger's office and his employees, and about the law and the reason for the law—to keep big money out of politics. He came off professional, like the stereotyped FBI agent who was interested only in the facts. His testimony was truncated and curt. I had Rees on cross-examination for parts of four days.

I asked him why, on the night of the raid, he hadn't recorded his conversation with Fieger. Rees said it was against FBI policy to do so. I made the point that because the FBI doesn't record its conversations, its agents are free to edit their memories and their reports, without fear of contradiction.

I had Rees tell the jury about the mass preraid meeting of the FBI and IRS agents when Rees and the FBI actually gave a PowerPoint presentation preparing the agents for their invasion of Fieger and his employees. There had been a room full of FBI and IRS agents being taught together like schoolchildren in a government class how to conduct the raid, what questions to ask, and how to behave themselves. I was shocked. I asked Rees, "Have you ever been at a meeting with eighty to a hundred agents discussing a campaign contribution case?"

"Not before this one, no," Rees admitted. After Rees's testimony the prosecution rested its case.

We wanted Judge Borman to dismiss the case. The feds had failed to prove that any crime had been committed by anyone. I wanted David Nevin, our legal guru and ace trial lawyer, to argue our motion. His presentation to Judge Borman asking for dismissal was solid and powerful. He pointed out that the prosecutors had called only eleven of the sixty-four witnesses the government had listed. Not a single witness claimed that Fieger or Johnson believed he was committing a crime. If they knew they were breaking the law, Nevin argued, would Fieger have asked his late mother to contribute, and would Johnson have asked his daughter to give? Under the government's theory of the law, that would have converted both mother and daughter into criminals. But, as usual and as expected, the judge denied the motion, smiled at us, and ordered us to continue.

I wanted to rest our case without calling a witness. I argued that the jury was with us, that Geoffrey's testifying was dangerous. I pressed him with the obvious: He would be cross-examined by Helland, and he'd get angry and fight back and come off testy and belligerent, and we'd lose the goodwill we'd earned with the jury. I argued he should not testify.

But one can imagine how revved up Geoffrey was after those years of torture, and now these weeks in trial—the negative publicity, all the sleepless nights, and the senseless war the government had dragged him through. Geoffrey wanted to be heard, to be vindicated, to fight back. He was a warrior, and it is hard to disengage warriors from battle. He insisted on testifying.

I spent many long hours going over his testimony with him. I was not concerned about the facts of the case but about how he presented the facts. He would surely argue with Helland. Lawyers argue like ordinary folks breathe. Arguments between lawyers are often not pretty, and such a confrontation would not endear Geoffrey to the jurors.

I warned him that he had to treat Helland with kindness. But how can you be kind to someone who's been trying to destroy you? And how does one such as Geoffrey avoid appearing arrogant, even demeaning, when confronting one who has displayed lesser talents? I was asking him to conduct himself beyond his embedded personality. In short, he had to show his vulnerable human side, failing which the jury would reject him, and the doors to the pen would swing wide open without a squeak in the hinges. Over and over I reminded him, "Every time you raise your voice in anger, or wrestle with Helland, you're losing. And we know what losing means, don't we?"

He took the stand. He looked ready, eager. I began by asking him why he was testifying, given the fact that he knew he didn't have to. He gave the jurors a friendly Fieger smile. "I think it's important that the jury hear from me about what happened in this case. I know I have a target on my back."

I had him describe the raids on his office and against his employees and friends. He said it had been his worst nightmare. "I didn't know what was going on. I knew I had always been a target, but I never thought they'd actually do something like this."

He told how he'd grown up with a father who was a civil rights lawyer and a mother who was a teacher and an organizer for the teachers' union. She'd led the first teachers' strike in Michigan. He said his life was dedicated to fighting the powerful on behalf of underdogs. And, yes, in the process of his thirty-year career he'd gained powerful enemies.

"Would you knowingly do anything illegal?"

"I wouldn't start at the age of fifty-five to become a criminal," he answered, "and certainly not after the birth of my three children." Then he said it. "No court in history had ever said that reimbursement is a crime." Helland jumped up screaming his objection, his hands striking out at the innocent air. The judge could stop me from mentioning Bush or Cheney or Rove or the rest of the Republican gang, but he couldn't gag Fieger without opening a new door to a lot of trouble with the jury. Fieger was the defendant. The jury wanted to hear from him. His livelihood and family were at stake. Yes, his life was at stake. He had a right to be heard.

Geoffrey launched into his interpretation of the federal campaign finance law. Helland objected again in a loud, petulant voice arguing that the judge had already ruled on the issue. But even Judge Borman now saw that Geoffrey was entitled to tell the jury how *he* read the law. It was *his* interpretation. Before Geoffrey could be held criminally liable, the government had to prove that he knew his conduct was illegal.

"Does the word 'reimbursement' or any word like it appear in the statutes?" I asked.

"No, the word 'reimbursement' doesn't appear anywhere. And no court ever ruled that reimbursement was a crime," he said once more.

Judge Borman was glaring down at Fieger. His smile had vanished. He'd told the jury at the start of the trial that reimbursement was *illegal*. And here was this defendant in his court telling the jury about his view of the law to the contrary. Geoffrey might as well have donned the judge's robe when he said, "If Congress is going to make something illegal, they have to give us notice of it. We have to be able to know that what we're doing is wrong; otherwise we're all living in a fun house."

As we finished the second day of his testimony I thought he was doing fine—he had been respectful and warm and resisted the impulse to vent his anger and frustration. But what would happen when Helland began to wrestle with him? I told him that when he was cross-examined by Helland he'd be walking a tightrope across the River Styx. One misstep and he'd fall off, and that would be the end.

Helland began his cross of Geoffrey during his third day on the stand. He asked whether Fieger had written a memo setting out his legal theories on reimbursement. "I'm not in the habit of writing memos to myself," Fieger replied. "If I'd known what you were going to do I would have— and plastered it all over the wall." I saw a juror suppress a smile.

Helland asked Geoffrey why his employees might want to "voluntarily" write checks to support political candidates. That was a mistake. Fieger's quiet, sincere response: "You mean other than just being good Americans?" Helland was struggling. I didn't want him to struggle too much, though. Sympathies in a jury trial can flip in a hurry.

But Helland was no match for Fieger. When he asked a question, Fieger answered with little gems like this: "Your agents terrorized my staff, and to make sure that the public knew all the details, you alerted local television stations so their cameras could follow you around." Fieger called the FBI "politically motivated thugs" and went on to comment: "If somebody robbed a bank, you couldn't get more than three FBI agents on the case, much less the eighty or more who came down on us." Then he pulled up George Bush's infamous words: "It's called *shock and awe*." As Helland wrapped up, I wondered whether Geoffrey had gone too far. Did the jurors revert to some original distaste for him that might be lingering? It was too late to worry.

Fishman questioned Geoffrey on behalf of Ven Johnson. In response to his soft questions, Geoffrey described Johnson as meticulous and careful and cited those traits as reasons he hired him. Johnson wouldn't do anything to put himself, his co-workers, or his family at risk, Fieger said. "I couldn't get Ven Johnson to cross the street in the middle of the block if he thought it was jaywalking."

One must occasionally let levity lighten the morbid shadows of a criminal trial. The *Free Press* reported, "Despite the serious nature of the criminal trial for big-name lawyer Geoffrey Fieger, there have been plenty of funny moments—many of them caused by Fieger's famous, and mischievous, 79-year-old lawyer, Gerry Spence of Jackson, Wyo. As the jury was about to be called into the courtroom after a break in testimony today, U.S. District Judge Paul Borman asked lawyers if he should turn on the ceiling blowers to circulate air.

"'Mr. Fieger's already here,' Spence retorted, prompting laughter from spectators."

The *Free Press* went on to report, "Fieger, who has his own ideas about how his case should be tried, told Spence from the witness stand today that Spence hadn't asked him questions about a particular topic.

"'Wait!' Judge Borman interrupted. 'Who's the lawyer and who's the witness?' Spence simply shrugged his shoulders, sparking more laughter from the gallery and jurors." One must be careful with humor. If it pops up naturally, if it's appropriate and not mean-spirited or cute, it can be a welcome relief in such a heavy, often dreary expedition as a criminal jury trial.

The *Free Press* itself was looking for something more interesting to write about than the one-sided contest that was going on between Fieger and Helland. The paper reported, "A herd of lawyers, many of them alumni of Gerry Spence's trial lawyers' college, piled into the federal courtroom Wednesday, starry-eyed admirers of the defense lawyer who at least one of them called 'the greatest lawyer in history.'" I say, if a "great lawyer" was one who weary to the bone, operating on worn-out cylinders, couldn't remember names, too often misspoke, and was never certain how the case was coming down, then, yes, I fully qualified.

I thought the judge might retain his own sentiments concerning Fieger. The last I heard there is no brain switch that turns off the judge from himself. How might any judge feel about Fieger? In the past, if Fieger felt justified, he'd been willing to take on a judge in a full frontal assault, even a high court judge. Why, I wondered, would a judge, down in his deepest folds of feelings, retain anything but animus against this man? It is hard to be a good judge. It is much easier to criticize a good judge.

On May 22, 2008, we rested our case. I'd ended up taking Geoffrey's case because a free people require the likes of a Geoffrey Fieger to fearlessly take on Power. Many who wanted to watch the final arguments were turned away. Attorney Will Burke, who flew from North Carolina to watch my final argument, said he arrived at the federal courthouse at 4:30 A.M. to make sure he got a seat.

Now it was time for closing arguments. Kendall Day gave the government's opening argument against us. As usual in a criminal case, the prosecution gets two shots at the jury, the defense but one. After I made my argument, Helland would have the last word with the jurors.

"This isn't entertainment," Day told the jury. "This isn't *Law & Order.*" Day told the jurors that Fieger was a liar who believed he was above the law. "Fieger thinks he's smarter than you," Day said. "However, no one is above the law, especially a lawyer whose profession is to serve the law."

The advantage of Day's youthful appearance seemed to melt away in the heat of his disdain. "Fieger," he cried, "showed that he knew he was illegally funneling money to Democrat John Edwards's 2004 presidential bid. Fieger testified that he'd done extensive research into campaign finance law." Such research, Day claimed, amounted to "guilty conscience evidence" that went to the heart of the government's case. In substance Day's argument was: If you're careful and research the law you are obviously a criminal.

When Day finally sat down, my turn came to speak to the jurors. I laid out a simple formula for fair play. "You noticed that I did not object once to Mr. Day's opening statement. Why didn't I object to objectionable things? I wanted you to hear what he had to say. I didn't want to interrupt his train of thought. I didn't want the judge interjecting in response to my objections. And I hope that he will give me the same—"

MR. DAY (Jumping to his feet and waving in the direction of the bench): "Objection, Your Honor!" Day said on the edge of a shout. (There was laughter from both jurors and the audience.) "We have a duty to object!"

JUDGE BORMAN: "I'll sustain the objection. . . . Please proceed, Mr. Spence."

His Honor had sustained an objection to my *mere hope* that the prosecutor would give me the same fair treatment that I gave him?

Day followed what I thought had been the judge's clear invitation to continue making objections. He interrupted my final argument twenty-four times by actual count. That the judge occasionally overruled one of Day's objections made little difference, for the flow of the story and the drama the jurors had been waiting for after long weeks of dreary testimony were stopped cold.

Sometimes during an especially indecorous objection I would gaze off into space like a patient father enduring the carryings-on of a misbehaving child. At other times I would smile at the young prosecutor with forgiveness. At still other times, when I knew an objection was about to burst from the prosecutor's lips, I'd stop my argument, turn to him, and with a gesture offer my silence until he rose to make his objection. Sometimes I toyed with the judge in tired but good-natured exchanges, and although all of this tended to rip apart the structure of good argument, nevertheless, in the end I gave the government room to do itself in.

Day had used PowerPoint to gather up and present snippets of facts on a large screen, facts I thought that were out of context. So I asked, "How do you prove a case by snippets? That's an important word, *snippets*. Every time Mr. Day punched a button, we got another snippet on the screen. Snippet after snippet. If you took each small piece of the evidence that you heard, and pasted them together, don't you think you could make anyone look pretty bad?

"This is a case, ladies and gentlemen, about the intimidation of witnesses. They've even charged Mr. Johnson, who's done nothing, who ought to be home with his family and his daughter. They charged him hoping that he would flip against Mr. Fieger.

"It took courage for Mr. Fieger to take the stand. And the answer to his courage from Mr. Day is, 'You are a liar, Mr. Fieger. The jury should convict you because you are a liar.'

"They said Mr. Fieger was a savvy politician because he once ran for governor. Yes, he was a savvy politician. What does that mean? Does that mean that he violated laws knowingly and willfully because he ran for governor? Isn't that what you call profiling? Isn't that what you say about a kid walking down the street with his hat on backwards and his pants hanging and the shirt that comes down past his knees, and you say he must be a gang leader? It's called *profiling*. And they profiled Mr. Fieger without proof.

How is it in America we try to put people away based on profiling?" I looked at the two black jurors. And waited.

> MR. DAY: "Objection, Your Honor. The whole suggestion we profile—"
>
> JUDGE BORMAN: "I'll sustain the objection."

I decided to put it all on the table and see what Day and the judge would do with this truth. "So let me ask you a question," I said to the jurors. "Where did they get the power, the permission, to bring at least eighty federal agents down on Mr. Fieger? Where did that power come from? The authority to raid a lawyer's office has to be approved by the attorney general."

> MR. DAY: "Objection, Your Honor."
>
> JUDGE BORMAN: "I'll sustain that objection."
>
> MR. SPENCE: "Well, I guess you won't sustain this one, Your Honor. This inexperienced young man was sent here by the *powers that be.*"

I pointed at Day.

> "And he suggests there's nothing to be taken from that? I can remember when I was a young man, very young. I used to tell people how young I was, how inexperienced I was. And in hopes that that would gain me some advantage. Now at this time, I'm old. I tell everybody how old I am, hoping that I'll get a little advantage from that as well. But the people in Washington, D.C., aren't dullards. I mean, it was a brilliant move. This is a brilliant young lawyer. He's personable in a hateful case."
>
> MR. DAY: "Objection, Your Honor."
>
> JUDGE BORMAN: "I'll sustain the objection as to the term 'hateful.' The rules of civility apply."
>
> MR. SPENCE: "Let me see if this is all right. He's a nice young man in a political extravaganza."
>
> MR. DAY: "Your Honor?"
>
> JUDGE BORMAN: "Overruled. This is argument, so let's go ahead."
>
> MR. SPENCE: "What better, smarter decision was there than they send him here. Let's get this straight one last time. It's all right for them to examine every hidden, every single thing that Mr. Fieger did or said or parts of testimony and snippets along the way. Snippet here, snippet there, snippet someplace else. It is all right to test Mr. Fieger's

honesty and his integrity, but it is not all right for us to test theirs? I listened to Mr. Day's argument and I thought to myself, 'If it's a snippet, let's nip it.'"

I looked up at the judge.

"Now, having caused all this trouble, Your Honor, I find that this is a case about silencing a citizen. And I find it is a case about freedom of speech. What would it be like if we don't have freedom of speech? If we don't have freedom of speech, we don't have freedom."

MR. DAY: "Freedom of speech and those kinds of things—"

JUDGE BORMAN TO MR. DAY: "Counsel, this is argument in a political campaign contribution case. Overruled." (Was the storm passing, the sky clearing, the sun peeking through?)

MR. SPENCE: "So I'd like to talk with you a little bit about the facts of the case. I'm thinking about my friend Geoffrey Fieger, and who he is, where he came from. He's a man who has risen to some height in our community. Why?"

I said he was a man who wanted to carry on the work of his parents, to fight for ordinary people, a man who cared about them. The prosecutors asked what credit he expected to receive for his contribution to Edwards. Here's how Geoffrey answered that question. He said, "I will tell you what credit I got. I got an indictment with ten counts of felonies. That's the credit that I got."

I pressed on. "And of the eleven witnesses that they brought in here, not one of them ever said that he asked them to do anything that was dishonest. *Not one witness in this case.*"

I read from the courts instructions. "'The requirement that Mr. Fieger and Mr. Johnson acted knowingly and willfully means that the government must prove beyond a reasonable doubt that they were aware of what the law required and that they violated the law.' Not snippets," I added.

"'How could reimbursement be illegal?' Fieger asked. 'My wife works at home. If she wants to contribute and I reimburse her, she's suddenly a criminal, and so am I?' Mr. Johnson has a grown daughter in college. I think she's sitting in the courtroom. I can see her. When she contributes and he reimburses her, she is a criminal? Mr. Fieger's mother, your mom,

Geoffrey, wanted to contribute. And she did. She's on Social Security. She didn't have enough and you reimbursed her.

"Geoffrey looked at the statutes. 'How do you interpret that?' he said to himself. 'It must mean that you can't contribute in the name of people you take out of the phone book—go down, buy checks, and say this is from them.' That's what that statute said to him. Very frankly, it also said it to me.

"I was lying awake last night thinking about this case. Hope you were sleeping," I said to the jurors. "I thought about when I was a kid and we'd go down to the riverbank in the mountains of Wyoming. And we'd lie down on the bank with a snare. It was just a wire with a loop on it. There's the trout nice and innocent swimming against the current a little bit. I'm flat on the ground so the trout can't see me. I let the snare down real easy over the trout's head. And when I get it over the head, just behind the gills, I jerk it up hard, and out comes the trout. That political contribution law is a snare, a law to get unsuspecting people like Mr. Fieger.

"One day a fellow named Humphrey visited the office of the FBI to tell them that Fieger fired him because he wouldn't make a contribution to Edwards. The people from the government were so eager to get Geoffrey that they forgot to ask any questions about Humphrey's past or why he had waited *two years* to lodge his complaint with the FBI.

"Now the government agencies rushed in to open their case files against Geoffrey. Not only the United States Attorney's Office in Michigan, but at the same time, the Public Integrity Section in Washington, D.C., opened their files. In one day, Mr. Rees got *both* to open files, they were so excited. They had their star witness, Mr. Humphrey, and finally they were going to be able to prosecute Mr. Fieger.

"Mr. Fieger didn't know that they were investigating him. This was all *secret*. Wouldn't a fair person pick up the phone and say, 'Mr. Fieger, we've got a man in here by the name of Eric Humphrey. Do you know anything about him?' What do you think Mr. Fieger would have said? They didn't talk to Mr. Fieger. They didn't talk to anybody that knew Humphrey, didn't talk to his wife, didn't talk to his police chief. They didn't talk to anybody. They just got this investigation going that became the largest investigation of its kind in the history of campaign contribution law."

MR. DAY: "Object."

MR. SPENCE: "That's the law."

JUDGE BORMAN: "I'll sustain the objection to the historical fact. Let's go ahead."

"Now after Humphrey comes in, Mr. Fieger is still going along his merry way, kind of like the trout lying peacefully in the clear water in the rapids—just there doing his thing. But while he's doing that, Rees is sending out secret subpoenas to the banks and to everyone who contributed. Mr. Fieger doesn't know that they're subpoenaing records from all over the country—getting those checks from everywhere. And this goes on for seven full months."

I turned to the judge.

"I can tell, Your Honor, that this jury is getting awful tired. Could we have a recess?"

JUDGE BORMAN: "Go on for twenty more minutes."

MR. SPENCE: "They are probably getting sweaty bottoms."

JUDGE BORMAN: "Let's not go there."

Smiles from the jurors.

MR. SPENCE: "So what did I end up saying before the sweaty bottoms?" Whereupon the reporter then read back my last statement.

"Now, Mr. Rees testified there was no pressure put on the witnesses. Reading the FBI's reports, we never saw a single reference to any kind of intimidation, including the FBI telling witnesses they could be charged with felonies. You heard witnesses *say* they were told by the FBI that they were felons. That they could go to the penitentiary for what they did. *No pressure?*

"Now comes a raid with eighty or more government agents. Counsel doesn't want me to call it a raid. How about we call it a nightly visit? We're going to make a nightly visit with two FBI guys in trench coats and their guns and their badges and their files—make a nightly visit on these folks and tell these folks that they are felons. That they violated the law. That they could go to the penitentiary.

"And that grand jury was in session for a matter that could have been resolved in two weeks, or at least two months, not two years. Why did it take that long? Why do you think they did this? 'If we can't convict him, we can destroy him.'

"The people in their own offices in the Fieger firm were afraid to talk to each other. These are teams that work together trying to help people. Now they couldn't talk to each other. 'If we talk to each other, we might get charged with obstruction of justice.'

"There is a word called *betrayal*. We all know what betrayal is. All of us have one time or another been betrayed by somebody. But our government can betray us as well."

> MR. DAY: "Objection, Your Honor."
> JUDGE BORMAN: "This is argument. Overruled."

I continued, "When the government, with all of its power, misuses its power, it's called *betrayal*. Every one of those poor people who came into this courtroom under those compulsion agreements believed they were potential felons, and that they could be put in prison. None were told by the prosecution that they, nor Mr. Fieger, nor anybody else involved in the case, could not be guilty of a felony unless they *knew* what they were doing was illegal and did it anyway; 'willfully' is the word. That these government agents did not so advise the people seems like blatant betrayal to me.

"Mr. Fieger has been charged in this case with doing things *secretly*. Who is *the mother of all secrets here*? The mother of all secrets is the government. The grand jury was *secret*. The papers that were served on the various banks were all *secret*. The Paychex records, you saw them, those were all *secret*. They descended upon these people with those agents at night, *secretly*. The rights of the people were held *secret* from them. They were never told they didn't have to talk to the FBI. They got the IRS in as well to make sure that there wasn't any escape."

Over Day's objection I read to the jury the closing statement in the files of the IRS. That agency concluded, "This investigation should be discontinued."

I read to the jury the court's standard instruction: " 'The defendant has no obligation to present any evidence at all.' None. 'Or to prove to the jury in any way that he is innocent.' The instruction goes on to say: 'The government must prove *every element* of the crime charged beyond a reasonable doubt.' "

I read further: " 'The indictment is not any evidence at all of guilt.' I had

Mr. Fieger bring me some of his children's play blocks. I'm going to play with them because there's part of me that's still a child."

I told the jury that the indictment was a document that stacked charge on charge, the basic charge being *giving in the name of another*. "The first two charges in the indictment were based on that. Sixty-four different people made up these first two charges. And out of sixty-four different persons supposedly involved, only eleven came to court?" I stacked up the first two blocks. "Then the next two blocks are for causing a corporation to give, and I'm going to challenge Mr. Helland here."

> JUDGE BORMAN: "Counsel, that's inappropriate to challenge other counsel. Just argue to the jury. Don't make it personal."

I continued, "Section 441b of the law says it is unlawful for a corporation to make a contribution in connection with any federal election. I challenge the *record* in this case to produce a single check that was written by the Fieger corporation to John Edwards. The checks were from Mr. Fieger personally to his employees that he reimbursed. So the next two blocks [I put two more on the stack] are the two charges that the prosecution brought for his corporation giving to Mr. Edwards. So now we have four blocks, one for each charge.

"These next four charges are for causing Edwards to file false reports. Mr. Fieger never saw a single report that was ever filed by Mr. Edwards, and never talked to anybody. Mr. Baldick from the Edwards campaign was on the stand and never said a word about it. How could Mr. Fieger be guilty of causing Edwards to file false reports when Mr. Fieger didn't even know they were made? Four reports, one for each quarter?" I pointed out that if there had been sixteen quarters there would have been sixteen charges, each one a felony. With the last four, there were now eight blocks stacked up.

"But of course, that's not all. There's a charge of conspiracy. Now, a conspiracy, the judge tells us in his instructions, is an *agreement* to do something *unlawful*. In the beginning one must ask whether it was an *illegal* act. You can't have a conspiracy to *not* commit a crime. So there's your conspiracy. It sounds like they're dealing with the Mafia and there are bodies in the bottom of the river.

"There's one more charge to make the ten. You know what I'm going to do here, don't you? [I am reaching for the bottom blocks.] When you take those two bottom blocks out—that he violated the law by giving in the name of another, and you find that he is innocent because he had no knowledge that that was wrong, this is where the indictment goes." I pulled the two bottom ones out and the whole stack came tumbling down. Several jurors nodded in amusement.

"Now I want to talk about the last charge, which is obstruction of justice. There's an old adage among trial lawyers that if the prosecution doesn't have a case you'll hear lots about obstruction of justice. This is a charge that the prosecution can manufacture themselves. Let's see what has been manufactured here."

JUDGE BORMAN: "Wait. Sorry, Mr. Spence, just wanted to make sure." I couldn't guess what the judge was worrying about. I continued.

MR. SPENCE: "Let's start with Mr. Rees." (Day interrupted, likely thinking that the court had been giving him a sign.)

MR. DAY: "Your Honor, that's not how charges are brought."

JUDGE BORMAN: "Overruled. This is argument. You can respond."

MR. SPENCE: "Mr. Rees sure taught Mr. Fieger something. You better not tell an FBI man to take a hike or you'll be charged with the worst crime—the one with the heaviest penalty—obstruction of justice. Mr. Fieger obstructed justice with Wensdy White when he talked with her?" (I read from Wensdy's testimony.) "She said, 'He reiterated to me that he thinks that the charge isn't valid.' That was obstruction of justice?

"You remember . . . innocently, she didn't know she could even talk to Mr. Fieger, because she thought if she talked to Mr. Fieger she would then have to call up Mr. Rees and tell him what he said."

JUDGE BORMAN: "Sustained." The judge was now taking on the role of both prosecutor and judge by sustaining objections that Day hadn't even been made.

MR. SPENCE: "So the question comes to me, who's guilty of obstruction of justice? Who threatened the witnesses? Who told—"

MR. DAY: "Objection, Your Honor."

JUDGE BORMAN: "This is argument. Overruled."

MR. SPENCE: "Who told witnesses they were guilty of felonies? Who told witnesses that they should admit to crimes that they didn't commit? Who held secret from the witnesses that they couldn't be guilty of anything unless they knowingly, willfully violated the law? Who's really guilty of a conspiracy here? Are these two here [I point to Day and Helland] guilty of a conspiracy? Or do we have a joining of hands between the *powers that be in Washington, D.C.*, and the United States Attorney's Office in Michigan?"

No objection.

I went on to say, "You know this law may be imperfect. It's been on the books for forty years and was written by a bunch of politicians in Washington. But they didn't want a law to be used for improper purposes. And so they put in words that say you have to *knowingly and willfully violate this law*. And that's the protective device.

"Most of us learn that ignorance of the law is no excuse, but that's for laws like robbery and murder—laws where we all know what the law is. But this is a law that's hard to understand. And the politicians who wrote it surely must have known that. Yet, during all of this testimony, I don't think I ever heard the words 'knowingly and willfully' ever leave the lips of Mr. Day or Mr. Helland. Of all of the things they put up on the board, I never saw them put those words up there. Of all of the witnesses that testified, none of them were ever advised about that absolute heart of the law. They kept it secret from everybody.

"The bottom-line question is this: Have they, with their snippets, proved that this man is a criminal? If you find that there was *no knowing and willful* conduct on his part, the answer to this is very simple and very quick.

"I have a vision here, folks. I came a long way to defend a good man. And I have a vision here that we can all walk out of this courtroom together free, all of us. That Mr. Fieger can go home free to his Keenie and to his family. That Mr. Johnson can go home to his family and his daughter. We can all walk out of this courtroom feeling proud. Because, folks, seldom do citizens have an opportunity to do something that's great.

"This case stands for American citizens fighting against corrupt power. It stands for courage. It will be taught in the law schools of this country, a guide to justice as envisioned by our founders. It stands for the proposition that juries like *you* are the last wall against an invading tyranny. And that the people, juries, ordinary people in a democracy, are the ones who keep us free.

"I am about to leave you. This is my last case. I will be eighty in January, and it's time for me to put down the sword. But I am humbled and I'm proud that it's been with you in this case for this good man."

*H*ere is a trial lawyer's definition of helplessness: the moment when I'm forced to sit as silent as a tomb and listen to the prosecutor's attack with no chance to reply. It's like a fighter forced against the ropes with his hands tied behind him while his opponent pummels him mercilessly. But still we assert with pride that in America the accused gets a fair trial.

Clearly, Lynn Helland and Kendall Day had devised a plan going into the final arguments. Day would disrupt my argument with continuous objections so an effective closing argument would be impossible, and whatever points I might make Helland would obliterate in his final argument without fear of any response from me. Get ready for the marshals to drag Geoffrey Fieger off to the nearest federal pen.

Helland began with a frontal attack. He stared at Geoffrey sitting next to me. "On every important point in this case Geoffrey Fieger isn't worthy of your belief," Helland hollered, his tone hard and filled with contempt. "But the most offensive thing that happened in this case was when Geoffrey Fieger testified and lied." His arguments sounded reasonable, but they came off like pancakes without the butter and syrup. He was speaking into his notes when he said to the jury, "Fieger knew that reimbursing other people's contributions is wrong."

Helland referred to the night of the raid, of "shock and awe" as we called it, when Rees of the FBI had Fieger on the phone. Rees asked, "Did you reimburse your employees, Mr. Fieger?" Then Helland quoted Fieger, who supposedly answered, "Nobody got reimbursed. It's absurd to say I funneled money."

Helland had no choice but to embrace Humphrey. "Eric Humphrey—we're all uncomfortable with him. But Eric Humphrey is human. Eric Humphrey tried to warn Mr. Fieger about the illegality of what he was doing . . . as did at least seven witnesses, all of whom put him on notice that he was violating the law."

Helland turned to metaphor. He said, "Suppose Mr. Fieger asks you to take a potential client out for a nice dinner in order to get the person to hire his law firm. He tells you to go to this really fancy restaurant. But you say, 'I can't even afford the appetizers at that place.' Mr. Fieger says, 'Don't worry about it, I'll take care of it.' So you go to dinner. You put it on your credit card. You give Mr. Fieger the bill for it. A week later, three hundred and fifty bucks, the cost of the dinner, shows up in your bank account. The question is, who paid for that dinner—was it you or was it Mr. Fieger?

"Mr. Spence and Mr. Fieger have said that the word 'reimbursement' does not appear in any of the statutes we've been looking at. Well, let me suggest that's another attempt at lawyer trickery. You need to know a reimbursement of a political contribution is a crime. Judge Borman said it earlier in the trial. The law says you can't make a contribution in the name of another." Helland shrugged off my stacking of the blocks as misleading since each crime charged was independent of all the other charges. That said, he argued on.

"Ask yourselves, if Mr. Fieger thought he was doing the right thing, why did he lie to Jeff Rees? Why did he tell Wensdy White and Shant Gharibian [who owned the gym where Fieger worked out] to just say you supported Edwards? Why did he tell those folks not to talk to the FBI? Why did he pay an extra $35,000 to make these reimbursements look like bonuses? [He was talking about paying withholding and Social Security on the reimbursements.] The reality is Mr. Fieger knew all along that he was doing the wrong thing.

"The defense would like us to apologize for bringing this case. But we don't apologize. Our job is to enforce the laws, and we do it fairly, we try to do it effectively. We didn't bring this case for political reasons or because anybody was out to get Geoffrey Fieger. If he was a Republican or an unknown and sitting there, we'd be bringing exactly the same case. Lawyers shouldn't be able to deliberately break the law and get away with it.

"But after you deliberate, after you've had a chance to look at the evidence, we do ask you to return verdicts of guilty as to both defendants and on all the counts they face. Thank you."

Judge Borman: "Thank you, Mr. Helland."

I hadn't objected once.

*I*t was the twenty-eighth day of May. The judge had instructed the jury about all the ramifications of the law, especially the law of conspiracy and obstruction of justice. He again told the jury that Geoffrey had violated the law with his reimbursements. The only question remaining for the jury's determination, after twenty days of trial and pages and pages of the judge's instructions, was whether Geoffrey *knew* he had violated the law.

After the judge had completed his instructions, the jury trudged out. I thought they were exhausted physically, mentally, and emotionally. Taking his instructions as a whole, I wanted to shake like an old dog covered with fleas. I wanted to roll in the dirt and get rid of all of the language, the charges and exceptions, and exceptions to the exceptions, all of which, in the end, made the charges more biting. It had been many hours since my last words were spoken to the jurors.

But I thought there was too much for the prosecutors to overcome. The toxic trail of politics had been revealed. As in nearly every jury case, the unspoken question from the standpoint of the jurors is, which side is more credible? And that meant, which lawyer would the jury follow? That question was reduced even more: Which lawyer cared the most? And was his caring genuine? And even further, was his caring justified? In the end, each juror's own feelings would dictate his or her vote. Would a conviction of Geoffrey Fieger protect them, or would it simply forward the interests of Power, which looms as an ever-waiting leviathan that can attack and destroy a citizen at will?

After two days of deliberations the jurors went home for the weekend, without a verdict. Geoffrey knew and I knew that quick verdicts are not the rule for an acquittal. But Geoffrey was shaken. "What's going on?" he asked. "Will we win? What's taking them so long?" Over and over these same questions came tumbling out of troubled lips. This is one of the most fearless lawyers I have ever known. But he was human, and the case was beyond his control. He was a man who had always been in control. He was helpless, and his life was in the hands of twelve strangers he'd never met outside the courtroom, and a judge looking down with that smile.

I told him this jury would never convict him. If I had any doubt it was smothered by the weight of the case on our side—and the jurors had to embrace Helland and Day at a deep emotional level to convict. I thought that both Helland and Day had failed to move the case out from under the shadows of partisan politics. I also thought that both Helland and Day had failed to gain the trust that jurors require before they are willing to destroy another human being. A conviction here was not screaming out as *the right thing to do*.

But during nearly every hour of each day it was the same: "What's taking them so long? Will we win?" My answer to Geoffrey was always the same. "We will win. Trust the jury."

The media wasn't so confident. One commentator raised an alarming possibility: "In a mesmerizing performance [Spence] commanded the room as can few others. . . . Spence is charisma personified. But Spence made one mistake in his argument that could cost Fieger his freedom. 'If this prosecution can happen to Fieger, it can happen to any of us,' he said. It is a powerful argument in the right case. But . . . who was Spence talking about? The fact is most Americans cannot conceive of giving more than $100,000 to a political candidate by using employees as straw-men. This is not a case of the Government versus Everyman. Much though it pains me to admit this, there was power in the Government's assertion that 'Fieger thinks he is smarter than you.' With wealth comes, alas, arrogance."*

Geoffrey wanted to know if the journalist's comments would influence the jurors. I said no. The fellow writing the news story was selling newspa-pers. The jurors were real people with their own personal lives at the fore-front of their judgment-making.

On their fourth day of deliberations the jury finally announced they had reached a verdict. They looked solemn and exhausted as they entered the courtroom. The judge read the verdict to himself as we held our breaths and I grew light in the head. His smile had vanished. Then he returned the verdict form to the foreman. We had to hear "not guilty" ten times in or-der for Geoffrey to walk out a free man. Guilty on even one charge would take him away to a hard, dark place for a long, long time. We heard the jury foreman in a monotone announcing, "Not guilty. Not guilty." We needed to hear it eight more times. I felt a growing weakness in my body as the foreman continued to read down to the tenth and final charge, "Ob-struction of justice."

As he came to the tenth charge, the foreman stopped and looked over at us. For a moment, I feared he was preparing us for the worst. But then: "Not guilty."

Had I heard him right? There was pandemonium in the courtroom, cheers and clapping and people rushing to hug and congratulate them. Ven Johnson was acquitted of all ten counts as well.

The press descended on Fieger. "I'm very pleased with the American sys-tem and the jury," Geoffrey said. "I thank the jury for listening. I hope this puts an end to political prosecutions in the age of Mr. Bush."

The media recounted that Fieger was facing a maximum penalty of ten years in prison had he been convicted of obstruction of justice, along with a sure loss of his law license. Both Fieger and Johnson, the media reported, would have faced a maximum of five years for each of the other charges.

---

* Norm Pattis, quoted by Walter Olson, *Overlawyered.com*, May 30, 2008.

Lynn Helland said, "We're obviously disappointed, but grateful to the jury for the hard work they put in." The press reported that he again denied the case was politically motivated. Helland was asked but wouldn't put a price tag on the cost of the case to the government. "We never, ever figure out how much an investigation is going to cost, and we're not going to start here," Helland said.

Geoffrey and we, his lawyers, left the building together and found the jurors, all but one, waiting for us on the street corner. They chatted happily with Geoffrey and offered him their congratulations. One juror, a college student from Clinton Township, said she'd finally been swayed by the fact that there was no logical explanation for why Fieger and Johnson would commit career suicide over political contributions. "I can't imagine you would intentionally destroy your lives and the lives of the people around you," she said. That was our case. The jurors had heard us.

I now took the opportunity to talk to the media. I told the media I believed Mr. Bush attacked Geoffrey Fieger for his support of John McCain in the 2000 Michigan primary. "When a political party uses government resources as a weapon against its political enemy, such is a prelude to a totalitarian government. What frightens me more than anything is that unless you have the assets that are necessary to support a thorough preparation of your defense over a long period of time, and are able to secure the right support team, there isn't a chance in the world you can prevail against the U.S. government that has you as its target."

Geoffrey threw a party for the jurors. I left early. I was most grateful to my friend David Nevin, who day after day covered my back and made some of the best legal arguments I've heard in a court of law.

If the jury had convicted Geoffrey Fieger, he would still be in prison, where he would have read the unabashed, unashamed pronouncement from the Supreme Court of the United States in the case of *Citizens United v. Federal Election Commission*, a five-to-four decision that took the last great leap to convert America into a corporate oligarchy, a land finally, utterly owned by Power and Money. That case allowed the massive wealth of corporations to be invested in political campaigns with little or no restriction. We are owned in one way or another by this corporate oligarchy.

Fieger had been dragged before a federal criminal court to answer the government's claim that he violated campaign laws by reimbursing his family, friends, and employees. In the year 2010 in the said case of *Citizens United*, the Supreme Court decreed that corporations are free to make open, unhidden, and *unlimited contributions* in elections, holding that the law prohibiting the same violated the First Amendment of the Constitution—the right to free speech.

Remember, corporations are *not people*. But they've been granted the rights of people. I've never heard a corporation speak, not one word. I've never seen a corporation languishing in prison, not one minute. I thought the irony was so sweet. Geoffrey was charged with giving in the name of another, but that is what corporations have done from the beginning. Their money comes from persons, but the person's contribution is made in the *name of the corporation*.

Then, on April 2, 2014, the United States Supreme Court handed down its decision in *McCutcheon v. FEC*. That case wiped out the overall limit on what a wealthy donor can give to political parties during an election cycle. Justice Stephen Breyer, in a biting dissent, wrote, "Where enough money calls the tune, the general public will not be heard." What if Geoffrey Fieger had been convicted? Would the prosecutors petition the courts for his release, along with an apology from the government for having destroyed an innocent man, or would he still be rotting away behind bars?

Today a tiny handful of super-rich in a nation of 317 million souls can purchase the government. The eternal promise of a democracy has become little more than a cruel myth. So dear Americans, let us loosen up our back muscles, heretofore not accustomed to bowing, and get ready to bow, very long and very low, to our new God. Its name, of course, is Big Money.

CASE 7

HELL'S UNSPEAKABLE CONTEST

Dennis Williams called me as soon as he walked through the prison gates to freedom. His voice was gruff and raspy like a fighter who'd taken too many blows over the larynx. He was excited and trying to tell me his story as if this were his only chance to convince me I should take his case. He was saying something about DNA, and that the real killer had confessed.

"I was just twenty when the cops hauled me in," he said, "and I'd never even heard of them white kids before."

I was having trouble putting the man's story together, but he said he and three others had been pardoned by the governor of Illinois.

Pardoned?

Governors don't usually pardon poor black men unless some power-laden understory is at play. I told Dennis I was going to have a lawyer by the name of Peter King, a good friend of mine, talk to him, and maybe after that we could get together.

I called Peter. He was soon to report that on October 24, 1978, Dennis Williams had been tried by an all-white jury for the murder of a young woman and her boyfriend, both white. Dennis and three other black kids, later referred to as the "Ford Heights Four," were charged with raping the girl numerous times. Then both the girl and her boyfriend were shot in cold blood.* Dennis had been summarily tried and convicted.

---

* In addition to my personal representation of Dennis Williams, many of the background facts surrounding the cases of the Ford Heights Four were gleaned from *A Promise of Justice,* by David Protess and Rob Warden (New York: Hyperion, 1988), a work that has proved to be an eminent guide not only to passionate journalism but to its reward, an exposure of truth and justice. This book, better than any other I know, tells us the story of a broken justice system that, for once, was patched together by people who cared enough to make it work.

Now, after seventeen years in hell on death row in the Menard Correctional Center, where Illinois caged its most notorious killers (including John Wayne Gacy, who'd been sentenced to death for the rape and murder of thirty-three boys and young men), Dennis Williams had finally been freed, and he wanted justice.

"You need to meet Dennis," Peter King said. "This is a good man, with a good case, and I'm bringing him to Wyoming to meet you." And in December of 1996, there they were: Peter King, Dennis Williams, and the case they wanted me to take.

Dennis was thirty-eight years old, but he looked a couple of decades older. He was of medium build and rough on the exterior, a man with deep lines in his face and a quick, straight way of speaking. He looked at me as he spoke as if to determine whether I exhibited the faintest signs of trustworthiness, and he walked with an uncertain gait.

I'd lit a fire in my study fireplace, and we pulled up comfortable chairs. I wanted him to describe his life in prison, how he'd been treated at Menard—facts about his damages. I wanted him to tell me how it was for an innocent human being to be penned up like an animal waiting to be slaughtered—for a crime he didn't commit.

"You get so you can get along pretty good," Dennis said. "They learn who they can push around and who they can't. I could take 'em on pretty good."

"What do you mean?" I asked.

"I had me a few incidents," he said. "But they had me in my cell all the time down there on the row. They treated us like tomorrow we was gonna be dead anyway." He said he lived those seventeen years on death row in a six-by-ten cell and sleeping, when he could sleep, with his head up against the toilet, as such cells had been designed by some thoughtful prison architects. He didn't want to talk about his life on death row.

"I got rights," he said. "They stole seventeen years of my life from me. How come them cops can take my life when they knew I was innocent, and they don't get punished the same as any other criminal?"

"That's a good question," I said. "But cops and prosecutors don't like to convict themselves."

"Yeah," he said. "I know."

"We have no power over Chicago cops, or the prosecutors either," I said. "They do what they do. But they can't stop us from suing them for your damages." Then I asked, "If you had the money, how much would you pay to get back those seventeen years you spent on death row?"

He just looked at me for a long time. In the silence I saw his fragile inner self leak out through invading tears. He turned away and finally began to talk again, and he talked on endlessly, as if he would never be heard again. His anger was the progeny of unimaginable years of injury inflicted by those he should have been able to trust—cops, lawyers, judges, and the law itself. All had betrayed him.

Dennis's story began when searchers found the body of Carol Schmal, a young white woman, in a falling-in, abandoned town house. She was nude from the waist down; her pants and panties had been torn from her. She was lying in a pool of blood, and a sheet of plywood had been thrown over her. Later the body of Larry Lionberg, her boyfriend, was found along a creek bed close by.

Dennis told me that a few nights after the murder, a car full of cops came to his house, woke everybody up, laughed at his mother who was vainly protesting, and without an arrest warrant took Dennis for a midnight ride to that old caved-in house.

"They cuffed my hands behind me," Dennis said, "and then a cop pulled out his gun and stuck it to my head and said, 'Nigger, if you don't tell me in three seconds what happened I'm gonna splatter your damn brains on the wall like you did that girl's.'"

I saw fear creep onto Dennis's face as he recounted the story. "I didn't know nothing. I'd never been anywhere near that place. Then the fat cop said to the cop with the gun, 'What ya waiting for? Here, give me the god-damned gun. I'll kill that son of a bitch.' He grabbed the gun, stuck it to my head, and pulled the trigger."

Dennis said he heard a click from the pistol. "You put in the wrong clip," the fat cop said. "Give me the one with the bullets in it."

Dennis said he heard the cop reloading the pistol, and once again the cop pressed the pistol against his skull. "Nigger, I'm gonna kill you," the cop said.

"You're gonna have to," Dennis said. Then the first cop wrestled the gun from the fat cop, saying, "Don't do it. No use riskin' your career over this fuckin' nigger."

Charles McCraney, an unemployed black man with a spotty reputation, had his eye on the reward of a couple of thousand dollars that had been offered by the owner of the filling station where the Lionberg lad had worked, and where both he and his girlfriend had been kidnapped— and then murdered. McCraney called the cops. The filed police reports stated that on the night of the murders McCraney saw four black kids run into the abandoned town house at about three in the morning. The next day McCraney saw Dennis in the crowd that had gathered in the field around the body of Larry Lionberg. McCraney said Williams was asking people, jokingly, whether they had shot "those people." McCraney said he overheard Dennis say, jokingly, "I saw them jump when they shot them."

McCraney said he'd been watching a certain show on TV, *Kojak,* when he saw four black kids run into the old house where Carol Schmal's body was found. But we discovered that that show ended at ten minutes before one in the morning—hours before the time of the murder.

Among other gifts to the police was McCraney's statement he'd seen Paula Gray with the boys that night. Paula was a reportedly slow black girl from another poor family. She turned out to be the girlfriend of Kenny Adams, a member of the Ford Heights Four.

Half a dozen white male cops without a warrant took Paula Gray from her home in the middle of the night and treated her to one of their infamous midnight rides. They dragged her into the scene of this brutal murder. Carol Schmal's blood was still drying on the floor. The cops took turns questioning Paula. Without getting the answers they sought, they took her into "protective custody," without a parent present, without a court order or warrant, without a lawyer to protect this girl, little more than a child, who'd never spent a night away from home. They locked her in a motel for two nights, where their questioning continued until she was exhausted.

Then the cops and prosecutors dragged Paula in front of a grand jury. She ended up telling the grand jury that she witnessed the rapes and murders—she saw it all by the flame of her Bic cigarette lighter, the only light available that night in that dark, deserted house. She said the girl was raped seven times, and Dennis shot the girl twice in the head.

Under oath, and the leading questions of the prosecutor, Paula told the grand jury that the Ford Heights Four marched Larry Lionberg to the creek, where Dennis Williams shot him twice in the head and Willie Raines shot him once in the back.* Dennis threw the gun in the creek.

---

* Willie Raines was known as Willie Rainge at the time. For the story of the change in spelling, see Bill Lueders, "Justice Defiled," *The Isthmus* 23, no. 48 (1998), www.truthinjustice.org/raines .htm.

I thought it wouldn't take much of a lawyer to destroy Paula Gray's testimony with even a halfhearted cross. One couldn't hold a Bic cigarette lighter for even five minutes without severely burning one's hand. And the only way Paula could have known the exact location of five different shots into the bodies on two people at two different sites was for that information to have been planted into the girl's mind by the cops and thereafter rehearsed over and over until she knew her answers by heart. Even Howard Vanick, in charge of the investigation, didn't believe she'd seen the boys throw the gun in the creek. "A nigger never gets rid of a gun," he said.

Perhaps Paula wasn't as slow as people thought. Before the case came to trial she said the cops forced her to lie, and at a pretrial hearing she insisted, "I didn't hear nothin.' I don't know nothin'. I ain't sayin' nothin'."

But the prosecutors knew how to fix that. They charged Paula with perjury. Remember: She testified under oath to the grand jury. So remember: If you lie because you're forced to lie, and you later gather the strength to confess that you lied, and you try to correct it, well, you will now go to prison because you refused to continue to lie. Gotcha!

Without Paula's testimony, the prosecutors found a jailhouse snitch who was willing to make a deal. He would testify that he heard Dennis Williams and Willie Raines admit to the crimes. The snitch later admitted he concocted the story with the assistance of the prosecutor, in exchange for leniency.

The state, of course, was required to provide these four kids with a lawyer before they hauled them off to death row. The lawyer provided, Archie Weston, also black, ended up representing three of the Ford Heights Four along with Paula Gray. Verneal Jimerson, one of the four, couldn't be tried because Paula was the only witness who tied him to the murders, and she'd recanted her prior statements that had implicated him.

A serious and obvious conflict of interest exists when one lawyer represents more than one defendant charged with crimes arising out of the same incident. Their defenses may differ, and the mitigating circumstances offered to shield each against a death verdict are always keyed to the individual's history. Moreover, a bad lawyer for one ought not be a bad lawyer for all. Fundamental law demanded that these kids be provided separate, competent defense attorneys. But why spend a lot of the state's money on lawyers when everybody knew these "niggers" were all guilty, and they killed two innocent white kids?

Archie Weston failed to object to his representation of multiple defendants. Later the appeals court judges frowned slightly but held that the kids had no right to complain. Weston had waived the error by failing to raise it at the first opportunity. What did they expect of Weston, a poor man himself? He needed the money.

Then the judge, without prior notice to Archie Weston, set the trial of Dennis Williams, Willie Raines, and Kenny Adams almost immediately. Weston was shocked. He thought he'd come to court that morning for a routine pretrial hearing. Instead, the judge had called a jury to hear the case and ordered the trial to commence forthwith.

Weston complained, he cried, he even screamed that he wasn't ready for trial. He begged that he be given sufficient time to prepare his case for four black kids, three of whom were facing the death penalty. (Paula was charged with perjury.) But the judge knew what to do with black killers. Get them to trial; get them to the pen; get them out of the pen by strapping them to the gurney; and give them the needle. What's so difficult about that?

At trial Charles McCraney told his story to an all-white jury, the prosecution having kicked off all the prospective black jurors with their peremptory challenges, again something no competent judge would allow. And again Weston failed to object, so that error was also waived.

During his testimony McCraney let it slip that the cops had him sign a statement—standard operating procedure. But when the cops took the stand they testified they didn't take a statement from McCraney. He was merely mistaken. Why would they bother taking a statement from a witness so pure and precise, with a memory as permanent and pristine as McCraney's? By the time of trial, whatever statement McCraney had signed had disappeared. Nothing in writing remained that could be used by the defense to contradict his testimony, assuming Weston could have figured out how. McCraney not only grabbed the offered reward, he got himself relocated at taxpayers' expense to a rural community about seventy-five miles southeast of Chicago, a town that provided a better living environment than the decadent slum where he'd been rotting.

By this time it had become stock knowledge in Chicago that the cops were keeping two sets of books—the official file and what they called their "street file." The street file was secret and held the facts, especially those that might suggest any misconduct on their part. The official file that supported the case of the cops was as fictional as it needed to be.

Proving the rest of their cases against Dennis Williams, Willie Raines, and Kenny Adams was an easy job for the prosecutors. They brought to court the standard employee of the police department to give his supposed scientific opinions. Prosecutors like to give such witnesses a professional-sounding title. They're often called "criminalists" and claim to know all about blood and hair and other physical evidence.

This "criminalist" testified that he analyzed a couple of Caucasian hairs that had been recovered from the back seat of Dennis's car. He said they matched the hair of Carol Schmal. This alleged scientist, referring to non-existent statistics, claimed that the chances were only 1 in 4,500 that the hair sample from Williams's car did not match that of the victim. Hair typing is what is known as "class evidence," and therefore an expert can only say that a given hair came from a class, not from a certain individual. Microscopic hair-comparison analysis to link a defendant to a crime has been ruled unreliable by the National Academy of Science. Then the said criminalist went on to testify that at least one of the rapists had been a "type A secretor," a blood type that is shared by a quarter of our population. He said that both Dennis and Kenny were type A.

Now all the prosecution needed in order to shove innocent kids into the death house was for the jurors to hear, through the anguished tears of the victims' parents, a description of their dead children, and to see photos of their once happy, living kids followed by up-close police photos that revealed a nauseating tangle of flesh, blood, and death. Why should the jurors do more than order their morning coffee, return guilty verdicts, and get on with their busy lives?

What about Paula? Less than a week after Paula had appeared before the grand jury with the story that had been grafted into her terrorized brain, she was hospitalized with an "acute schizophrenic reaction." But that had no impact on the judge's sentence. He knew all he needed to know to render justice against the child. He said that Paula was "street-wise" and that her "violence and cruelty" had drawn her willingly into the crime. Was she mentally disadvantaged? "In her own environment she is aware and intelligent." He gave her fifty years for perjury.

Before the case was submitted to the jurors, the prosecutors withdrew their request for death against Kenny Adams because he hadn't been a shooter. In fact, they offered Kenny a way out: All he had to do was testify against his friends. Kenny Adams refused. Something magical, even holy, is witnessed when such unshakable honor is revealed in the human species.

But the judge was on Kenny Adams with blinded vengeance. Here are the words that fell so easily from the judicial mouth: "He was there when violence was being contemplated. As a high school graduate he was knowledgeable that serious harm was a probability. By his inaction, he committed murder. By his silence he participated." He gave Kenny seventy-five years.

The verdict of death that the prosecutor sought required a hearing for Dennis Williams and Willie Raines before another jury—all white, of course. Those jurors wasted no time in rendering the death penalty against Dennis. They couldn't agree on Willie. He ended up with a life sentence without the possibility of parole.

"Do you have anything to say before I pronounce sentence?" the judge asked Dennis.

"It's all a prefabricated lie," Dennis replied. "They had those witnesses lie."

"Are you ready to be sentenced?"

"I really have no choice," Dennis replied.

"I now sentence you then, Mr. Dennis Williams, to death," the judge said without wasting any more words.

What the judge meant by a sentence of death was death by lethal injection. Under his order Dennis would be securely strapped to a gurney—five straps, the first beginning just below the neck and the last ending at the ankles. Then needles would be inserted into both arms. In one arm, three different deadly drugs would be intravenously delivered into his helpless body.

First, on the signal of the warden, a large dose of sodium thiopental would be delivered—it's intended to cause unconsciousness. This would be followed by pancuronium bromide, a muscle relaxer that paralyzes the lungs and diaphragm. Dennis's respiration would slow. Finally, potassium chloride would be introduced into the IV. That would cause his heart to stop. Death usually occurs approximately seven minutes after the injection process begins. According to the Texas Department of Criminal Justice, the cost for the drugs used in lethal injection is $86.08. But I suspect that in Texas they buy those drugs wholesale.

Not contained in the judge's sentence of death was that Dennis's last vision on earth would be looking up into the faces of those who hated him. They would hate him because they believed him to be a murderer—

yes, like them. They would hate him because he is black. And those who hated him would be the ones to whom he would say good-bye.

Dennis Williams's court-appointed appellate lawyers dutifully pointed out Archie Weston's woeful failure as a cross-examiner, his failure to object to the introduction of the hair evidence obtained in a warrantless search, and his failure to make even routine motions, including a motion for a new trial.

Poor Archie had other things on his mind. He'd been accused of mishandling the estate of an elderly woman. Later, a $23,000 judgment was entered against him that he was unable to pay, so his home was seized and sold at a sheriff's sale. And the Illinois disciplinary officials of the bar were investigating him for unspecified misconduct and had subpoenaed his records. When he failed to comply with the subpoena, they began disbarment proceedings. Weston confessed that during Dennis's trial he was so hard up and stressed that he couldn't think straight.

Before the state could kill Dennis, the appellate judges were required to review the trial record. This takes years, during which Dennis would rot away in prison hoping with faint hope that one day a just system would give him a just trial. Only Justice Seymour Simon was shocked. He wrote, "The way this case was railroaded to trial embarrassed the defendant in his defense and prejudiced his rights. To force a triple capital case as complex as this one to trial under such circumstances was an abuse of judicial discretion." But the majority on the appeals court found that the trial had been good enough and scheduled Dennis's execution for the following November.

How must it be to sit as an appellate judge, judging not another human being but a name on the front page of a bulging, boring brief of dead legalese authored by court-appointed lawyers who themselves have never met the accused?

"They must be using form briefs these days," one appellate judge might say to another. "Read one, you've read 'em all. They all holler for a new trial."

"Right. I feel like a garbage disposal unit for the judicial system." He laughs. Little merriment in the laughter. "How'd your golf game go yesterday afternoon, George?"

In the appeals court you might hear the defendant's court-appointed lawyer, scared, pale, with a voice like a one-stringed banjo, arguing on behalf of his client who's been sentenced to die. Death fills the air with its foul breath. But a couple of judges have already been lulled to the edge of sleep by the lawyer's voice that touches nothing human in them.

Like morticians, judges get used to Death.

Important cases are waiting to be heard—corporations with multibillion-dollar issues, contract violations, patents, stockholder suits. The courts cannot clog commerce. In the real world people cheat, steal, and lie. They claim they've been damaged, they whine, moan, and threaten, and, yes, they kill each other. Judges hear it all. And some black killers want a new trial after they raped an innocent white girl and killed both the girl and her white fiancé?

We are told to *presume* the defendant's innocence, and although such approaches the divine and is an ideal we Americans embrace with pride, it cannot displace the knowledge we've gained from our own experience in life. That knowledge forms our attitudes in every case, and rarely does it presume innocence.

Here's what all but one judge held in Dennis's case: "Although the evidence is in large part circumstantial, it does *tend* toward a *satisfactory* conclusion and produces a reasonable and *moral certainty* that the defendant committed the murders and rape" (my emphasis). One might wonder what that judge would say if the doctor who operated on the judge's child reported that the operation *tended* to be satisfactory even though the doctor had been guilty of gross malpractice? And, of course, the *moral certainty* referred to in the decision depends on whose morals we're examining.

Once in a while, when the stars are in proper alignment, a majority of the judges on an appeals court will grant a new trial—perhaps to send a message to the lower-court judges to be circumspect. Why should we have appellate judges if they don't order a new trial once in a while? Job security.

In 1982, after four years in prison, Dennis Williams was ordered a new trial by the Illinois Supreme Court. The grounds: ineffective assistance of counsel—yes, the said Archie Weston. Here, in major part, were the grounds for the court granting a new trial: "We have concluded that his [Archie Weston's] financial and bar problems may well have had an effect on counsel's ability to represent his client in the trial of this capital case, and we can no longer say, with any degree of assurance, that Williams received the effective assistance of counsel guaranteed by the Constitution. We accordingly conclude that he must be given a new trial."

Although this was Kenny Adams's lawyer's *first* jury trial, his work met the expectations of the Illinois court, and Adams's sentence of seventy-five years was upheld.

Paula had also been decaying behind prison walls those same years. Human endurance is like shoe leather. It can walk over only so much pain and terror before the souls are worn through. Sensitive prison authorities had housed this small, defenseless girl in the women's sex-offender wing, something like throwing a baby chick in with a pack of crazy cats. She wasn't large enough or strong enough to physically protect herself. But her nascent need to survive taught her that if she acted out against authority, even in small ways, she'd be sent to solitary confinement, where she'd be safe, at least from the cats. Then one day the prosecutors came to her and offered her a way out of hell: Lie again, Paula. All you have to do is change your story back to your original lie, and you can go free.

At last Paula agreed to retell the original story she'd been taught by the cops. When she was asked if she'd been promised anything for her testimony, which, indeed, was perjured testimony, she quickly denied any promises, which was yet another perjury. In 1987, and based on Paula's testimony, both Dennis and Willie were sent back to prison, Dennis still awaiting the needle. Verneal Jimerson was recharged and tried and sent to death row. But Paula finally got home.

What did these innocent victims of Paula's testimony think of her? Unmitigated hate would be an understandable emotion. But Willie Raines felt compassion for her. "Anybody with any common sense would know they put a lot of fear into her. She did what they told her to do."

We need to step back in time to understand the rest of our story. But for the tireless work of Professor David Protess and award-winning journalist Rob Warden, and a team of eager kids in a journalism class, the executioner's needle would have found its mark.* The backstory begins with Girvies Davis, known to his fellow inmates as "Preacher Man." He was awaiting execution on death row. Those who knew Preacher Man said

---

* The following story about Preacher Man, and the tireless work of Professor Protess and Rob Warden along with Protess's journalism students, can be found in better detail and in the voices of those who lived it in *A Promise of Justice* by David Protess and Rob Warden (New York: Hyperion, 1998).

he was a kindly, quiet man, a "gentle soul," some called him. He'd made an unfortunate draw of parents from the big draw box in the sky. His mother was a black prostitute in an East St. Louis slum. He never knew his father. He was a fourth-grade dropout. He learned to read and write on death row under the tutelage of Dennis Williams. Awaiting his execution, he earned a high school equivalency degree.

Students under the leadership of Professor Protess, at Northwestern University's Medill School of Journalism, began to look into Preacher Man's case. These students were stunned to discover that when he signed his confession he was unable to read or write, a seemingly irrelevant fact that his lawyer never bothered to mention to the judge who sentenced Preacher to death.

Preacher Man said his confession had been forced from him at gunpoint on a deserted road in the middle of the night. And the police logs confirmed that the officers had favored him with what they called a "drive-around for evidence" and that he signed the confession at four thirty in the morning. Professor Protess called it "a case of poor man's justice."

Rob Warden, then employed by the Cook County State's Attorney's Office as an ambassador to the city's public interest community, was an advocate against capital punishment and had been working on Dennis Williams's case. But as the time for Preacher Man's execution loomed, Dennis convinced Warden to drop his efforts for Williams and try to save the Preacher Man.

Warden organized the Girvies Davis Clemency Committee in a massive effort to save Preacher Man. It consisted of sixty lawyers, academics, religious leaders, and former law enforcement officials. They distributed a hundred thousand copies of a brochure that summarized the findings of the students. They made press releases, held press conferences, and even tried to convince the governor that clemency for Preacher would not be unpopular with his supporters.

The law firm of Jenner & Block had for more than a decade provided a pro bono team of lawyers to fight for Preacher Man's life. Their efforts went all the way to the U.S. Supreme Court, where those lofty judges passed the buck back down to the Illinois courts and refused to take the case.

Preacher was executed at Stateville Correctional Center at Joliet, Illinois. Some mammal, claiming to be a member of the human species, stuck a needle in Preacher's arm, and another unidentified bipedal turned on the poison, and Preacher Man died with love, along with those deadly chemicals, in his heart. He said the helicopter ride to the death house at Joliet was "fun."

"Try not to mourn for me," Preacher said. "I'm at peace. Move on with your lives. Just try to help people like me who get caught up in the system." His final request was for Protess and his journalism students to fight for Dennis Williams. "I know he's innocent," Preacher Man said.

The first real break in Dennis Williams's case came when Willie Raines received a call from Rene Brown, the investigator the Williams family had once hired. He'd finally been unable to continue in the case when the Williams family could no longer dig up or borrow the monies to keep him on. But he'd found a police report that intrigued him, a hospital interview of a man named Marvin Simpson. He read it to Willie Raines over the phone. Raines called Professor Protess, and Protess sent three of his journalism students to excavate for a new set of facts buried somewhere in thousands of pages of old police files.

At the bottom of the eighth box of documents, the students found three handwritten pages of a 1978 interview that had been conducted five days after Carol Schmal and Larry Lionberg had been murdered. The police had interviewed a man injured in a car accident, one Marvin Simpson, who'd told them he knew the identities of the murderers because he was with them on the night before the killings occurred. One of the officers had written by hand:

> On Wednesday night, 10 May 78, at approx. 2030 hrs, Marvin, Dennis Johnson, Ira, Arthur (Red) and Johnnie were sitting around by Marvin's mother's crib. . . . Dennis Johnson started talking about doing a score.*

Simpson told the officers that Red admitted to him that they'd raped "the white broad." Simpson mentioned a Buick Electra 225 that had been involved in the murders of Carol Schmal and Larry Lionberg, and he identified merchandise that had been taken from the filling station where Schmal and Lionberg were abducted, all facts that had been buried those many years in the cops' secret "street files."

---

* Again I credit Professor David Protess and Rob Warden for their account of this epic case in their book, *A Promise of Justice.* And thanks to Laura Sullivan, one of Protess's bright and determined journalism students, for her story published in the *Baltimore Sun* on June 27, 1999, on how these kids came to solve the murders. I have referred to her work as well.

A Ford Heights police officer who'd been present when Simpson was interviewed said he'd taken notes. These notes had disappeared. The police had actually seized the Buick Electra 225 shortly after their interview with Simpson. That car, too, had disappeared.

Thankfully, once again, Professor Protess and three of his journalism students, Laura Sullivan, Stacey Delo, and Stephanie Goldstein, took to the case with a frenzy. Williams's execution date was looming. He'd probably be executed in less than a year.

Despite the students' zeal they couldn't find Dennis Johnson, who'd been implicated by Simpson. Turned out Dennis Johnson had died of an overdose in 1993. Eventually, with the help of Professor Protess and Rene Brown, the investigator, the students found Ira Johnson, who was serving a life term for a murder he'd committed *after* the murder of Carol Schmal and Larry Lionberg. Ira was Dennis Johnson's brother. Arthur "Red" Robinson and Juan "Johnnie" Rodriguez were the other two men.

Laura Sullivan reported her first visit to Ira Johnson. She said it had been a cold day in late February 1996 when she and her student partner, Stacey Delo, found Ira Johnson in the Menard Correctional Center—the same complex in which Dennis Williams was waiting on death row. She described Ira Johnson as one who "could look right through you and dismiss you, even as you sat in front of him. He was a strange mix of danger and aloofness. . . . Something about him was evil."

Laura and Stacey made repeated visits to Ira Johnson at Menard Prison. Johnson was often vile and offensive, Laura said. He played his circular games that went nowhere, and they were about to give up on him. But as they were leaving Stacey said to Johnson, "We're giving you a chance here to do one thing right in your life. Your brother would have wanted you to take it."

A couple of days later they received a letter from Johnson in which he admitted that "them boys didn't do that shit" and that it was going to take some time for him "to think that shit over." The letters between them continued, as did their visits. Finally, near the end, they learned that Johnson and his brother sold drugs to Ford Heights police officers, and he told the girls that his brother, Dennis Johnson, was one of the killers.

In the meantime Rene Brown had been working on Red Robinson. Brown told Laura and Stephanie he thought Robinson was ready to talk, and talk he did. The girls met with him and started their tape recorder. He said he was there that night when they kidnapped the people from the gas station, but that he'd run out of the town house before the two were killed. He claimed that Ira Johnson and his brother raped and shot the woman.

When the girls went back to see Ira, they told him what Red Robinson had said. At first, Ira said Red lied. He ended up confessing that the four had intended only to rob the gas station, but that Ira's brother wanted the girl. "They couldn't take her and leave the guy behind," Ira said.

Laura recounted the rest of Ira's story: The four finally drove Carol and Larry to the abandoned house, forced Carol and Larry inside, and forced Larry to watch while Dennis Johnson and Red Robinson raped her. Dennis Johnson then shot her while she was on her knees and told Robinson to shoot her, too.

Dennis Johnson was worried that one of the four would tell, so he made sure that they all took part. He told Ira and Johnnie Rodriguez to take Larry outside. Ira said, "Larry got up and started walking. He kept on walking, through the yard, through the field outside, until he reached the creek's edge. Then he stopped."

Continuing in her report, Laura Sullivan quoted Ira as saying, "'Larry never said a word to Ira. He never tried to run. He never fought back. He never even turned around.' Ira said he held up his gun and shot Larry in the back of the head. Sitting at the table, Ira was barely whispering." She said he began to cry.

After that, Laura said, Professor Protess presented to the district attorney the confessions and "a slew of other information" that he, Brown, and the attorneys had collected. Protess had originally found courageous, caring, and competent lawyers to fight for Preacher Man, and *without fee*. Now they continued in their work for the Ford Heights Four: Mark Ter Molen of Mayer, Brown & Platt; lawyers from Jenner & Block; Lawrence Marshall, a Northwestern University law professor; Matthew Kennelly (soon to become a federal district court judge); and a well-known civil rights lawyer, Flint Taylor. The district attorney agreed to DNA tests, then a new science. Swabs taken from Carol Schmal exonerated the Ford Heights Four and showed that Robinson and Dennis Johnson had raped her. And the lawyers won pardons for the four from Governor George H. Ryan of Illinois.

On June 16, 1997, Ira Johnson and Red Robinson were charged with kidnapping and murder. Facing the death penalty, both pled guilty and received life in prison without parole.

We recall that Ira Johnson was serving time in Menard for another murder he'd committed before the journalism students found him there. Had Simpson's leads not been buried, had the cops done honest work rather than cook the evidence that convicted the Ford Heights Four, Ira Johnson's murder victim would have been saved. And the lives of innocent citizens, the Ford Heights Four, would not have been scarred and wasted.

*W*e sued Cook County and its cops. Why didn't we sue Scott Arthur and the other prosecutors? The law protects prosecutors from most civil suits even when they intentionally offer tainted evidence to the jury. And, as we often see, prosecutors use the police as a shield. Scott Arthur was quick to retreat to that position, asserting that prosecutors can only present the evidence the police present to them.

As for the cops: Given that the DNA evidence proved the innocence of these four kids, and Paula Gray as well, wouldn't the police come forward and at least admit they made a mistake? After others had confessed to the crimes and after the governor had issued his pardons, the cops still took the position that they had prosecuted the guilty parties.

We took the cops' depositions. They admitted nothing. We were finally able to corner McCraney, who suddenly had a near-total loss of memory. The only officer who was willing to freely talk to us was George Nance, the chief of police in Ford Heights. He had always thought the boys were innocent. "Not the type to commit these crimes," he argued. None had criminal records except for Dennis, who, as a kid, took an uninvited ride on somebody's motorcycle and got himself arrested for it.

Preparing for trial, we traveled to Menard Prison, where Dennis had been housed all those years on death row. By the time of our visit, death row had been shut down. We took a model maker with us to create a replica of the cell where Dennis had lived. Dennis came with us. When we walked past Preacher Man's cell he stopped and teared up.

"Preacher Man was innocent, you know," Dennis said. "They killed an innocent man, and they had to know it. All Preacher Man ever did to them was pray for them."

I tried to move on, but Dennis lingered. "If it hadn't been for Preacher Man I wouldn't be here. He got Protess and his kids after the cops."

We hired investigators and experts and tore into the records. We labored months at preparing for trial. I spent many days with Dennis. In his fifteen years on death row he'd never touched or been touched by another caring human. He felt only the hostile, hard hands that shackled him, and he spent twenty-three hours a day in that concrete cage. He ate all his meals with a metal tray on his lap. He was provided no knife with which to eat, not even a plastic one. He had to pick up the meat and tear it with his teeth.

We were to discover that some of the abuses we saw in the Ford Heights Four cases had an ignoble history in the Cook County Prosecutors' Office, where previous prosecutors had played a game referred to as "Niggers by the Pound." That evil sport was at last reported by the *Chicago Tribune* on January 11, 1999.

Over the decades, racial prejudice had obscured the first flicker of justice from the eyes of those then charged with its delivery to the citizens of Chicago.

On his first day as a prosecutor assigned to a trial courtroom at the Criminal Courts Building, Michael Goggin slid into the chair next to the judge's chambers and his shoes struck a most unusual object—a bathroom scale.

"What's this?" Goggin recalls asking another prosecutor.

"That's for the Two-Ton contest," came the response. . . .

There was an ongoing competition among prosecutors to be the first to convict defendants whose weight totaled 4,000 pounds. Men and women, upon conviction, were marched into the room and weighed.

Because most of the defendants were African-American, Goggin recalls now, with no small degree of discomfort, the competition was described in less sensitive terms behind closed doors— "Niggers by the Pound."

With little delay the judge set our case for trial, and the Cook County lawyers found themselves facing what they had so ardently attempted to avoid. Now the truth would come out big-time, and the public would get the story in the media, one rotten morsel at a time. The Cook County lawyers had a sudden change of heart. They wanted to settle.

The amount of the settlement was the only issue. But how could the lives of these boys, now men headed into middle age, represent nothing more than money? No one would go to jail. No one would even say, "I'm sorry." Again we faced the recurring problem: If we settled, the people would never know of the underlying corruption in the system because we had allowed the system to buy its way out. Dennis felt the same except in deeper reaches.

Doubt, delay, and devilish uncertainty are always the order of the day in every such case. Experiencing a trial sometimes feels like finding oneself dropped into a room filled with noisy, gibbering psychos—lawyers and even the judges—all of whom are trying to act as if they are sane. And what sane result, if any, finally emerges years later is anyone's guess. Moreover, a delay of years is meaningless to the justice system since the system enjoys a perpetual life, while the accused, guilty or not, can die without having tasted the first morsel of justice.

Dennis had waited long enough, and he didn't trust the system. He wanted simple things. He wanted to sleep at night in a good bed, to have decent, healthy meals, to eat his meals with a knife, fork, and spoon, and to own a home and a car. After days of negotiations we arrived at a settlement figure that we could recommend to our clients, $36 million to be divided among the Ford Heights Four. All had agreed that Dennis, who'd been on death row those many years, had suffered the most and was entitled to the largest share—$12 million. The other three divided the remaining $24 million equally. Dennis said he would gladly give every penny back if he could recapture the seventeen years of his lost life. Was justice served by this settlement? Money in a money system buys everything, even justice. Suffering, degradation, and the loss of life are measured by the only measurement available—in dollars.

Tom Decker, a dauntless, devoted trial lawyer with a loyalty to his client that would survive to his last breath, represented Paula Gray. Cook County refused to give Decker the time of day. He sued to have Paula's record cleared, and for a court's determination that this poor girl had been abused and tormented to the point that she became little more than a talking puppet for the prosecutors. In a three-hundred-page decision, Circuit Court Judge William D. O'Neal agreed. Paula's good name and rights were totally restored.

Of course the Cook County State's Attorney's Office appealed Judge O'Neal's ruling, but the appeal was rendered moot in November of 2002 when Governor Ryan granted her a pardon based on innocence. Then and only then did the county rush in, and after more than two decades it paid Paula's trustees $4 million for her seven years in prison, and for the loss of her life. These are the rare breed of lawyers and judges who keep our hopes alive in this notorious game of justice.

How does someone such as Dennis Williams, an innocent kid whose life was stolen with perjured testimony—how can he regain any semblance of normalcy after surviving seventeen years in hell?

Money couldn't buy his fundamental needs. He needed a family, and friends. He needed the experiences we all encounter in a normal life. Even though he'd been innocent, the system could not return him to his original innocent self.

Peter King became Dennis's counselor and friend and found trustworthy people to manage his money. Dennis was a warm person and had an enduring personality. He and Peter's oldest son became like brothers. Peter and Dennis often saw each other daily. Dennis would trust few others and lived constantly under a cloud of paranoia. He was especially suspicious of women, who flocked to him after his newly acquired wealth. He was never completely free. He refused to leave home without calling someone to assure himself of an alibi if he were again wrongfully charged. He even kept his driver's license on the car seat so if he were stopped by the police they wouldn't shoot him as he reached for his wallet.

Dennis looked for pleasure and excitement after the bloom of youth had wilted inside prison walls. A couple of times he visited Imaging and me in Jackson. Perhaps we offered something approaching a place where he could see trusting people who cared about each other and who were trying to live meaningful lives.

He took trips on riverboats, where he liked to gamble. He told Peter he got a rush from throwing the dice. I thought that might be because his life had been like stepping up to the big craps table of fate. The bad rolls of loaded dice put him on death row—lying cops, lying witnesses, and an incompetent lawyer. But he also won the big one when good lawyers and DNA evidence proved his innocence.

How could one be deprived of one's life and not be hardened into chronic anger? "I don't think I could give a description to my anger," Dennis said. "But it exists. I don't think that anger is the answer. It's going to hold me back. I can't think clearly if I'm angry. Instead, I try to focus my energy on creating." The one thing that kept him sane was immersing himself in his painting. "When I'm painting I achieve something approaching a meditative state." He was self-taught and over the years had become a painter of some accomplishment. He was a bright man with unexplored talent.

Dennis said, "If I'd depended on the system to correct itself, I'd have been dead a long time ago. Living next to the execution chamber all those years gave me strength. I realized I didn't have to take but a few steps and I'd be behind that door."

After his release, Dennis worked as a counselor in a youth program on the west side of Chicago. He was a part-time student at Governors State University, and he campaigned for justice reform.

At three in the morning on March 20, 2003, the phone rang at Peter King's home. Dennis's fiancée was screaming over the phone. She'd found Dennis slumped over dead in his home. He'd suffered a seizure disorder and died of a brain aneurysm. He was forty-six years old. He'd been free from death row for five years and nine months.

Today, a national organization whose mission is contained in its name, Campaign to End the Death Penalty, reports these staggering statistics: "African Americans are 12 percent of the U.S. population, but 42 percent of prisoners on death row. . . . Of the over 18,000 executions that have taken place in this country's history, only 42 involved a white person being punished for killing a Black person."*

The cases against the Ford Heights Four were born of and nurtured on blatant racism. Still, one asks, what is the relevance of those tragedies today? Many claim that racism is America's infamy of the past, that African Americans have the same and equal rights as their white neighbors.

Every night in prime time we are presented television dramas starring black performers. Many of our celebrated athletes are black. Rarely is a commercial shown that fails to include at least one black person up front, and even ads offering the most expensive automobiles and the finest apparel are populated by handsome black men and women. We see drama after drama that either supports interracial marriage or presents it as the norm. Miscegenation laws—laws criminalizing interracial marriage—that as late as 1963 were still in force in twenty-four states have been held unconstitutional by our Supreme Court. The "n-word" has become so abhorrent that blatant racists dare not use it, not even among themselves. (With exceptions: Richard Pryor, the black comedian, became famous and earned millions by shocking his audiences with constant barrages of that prohibited word.) We have a black president and a black first lady, and their family resides in the White House. How, then, Mr. Spence, can you claim we are still a racist nation?

Racism has gone underground.

---

* Campaign to End the Death Penalty, www.nodeathpenalty.org/get-the-facts/six-reasons-oppose -death-penalty.

Duke University sociologist Eduardo Bonilla-Silva calls it "racism without racists" (and has written a book by that same title). He argues we are seeing a new way of maintaining white domination in places like Ferguson, Missouri. "The main problem nowadays is not the folks with the hoods, but the folks dressed in suits," he told CNN. Bonilla-Silva says that "the more we assume that the problem of racism is limited to the Klan, the birthers, the Tea Party, or to the Republican Party, the less we understand that racial dominance is a collective process and we are all in this game."*

We need new words to expose what racism has become—I call it "the hidden racism of the innocent," another way of saying that we are racists without knowing it. Bonilla-Silva says, "Color-blind racism is the new racial music most people dance to. The 'new racism' is subtle, institutionalized and seemingly nonracial."

I know that racism is alive and throbbing beneath the surface throughout America. I know it is because none of us want to talk about it, and none of us will admit to it. Speaking the "n-word" approaches the same level of contempt as defecating at the dinner table. Our personal racism is never acknowledged, not even to our closest friends, not to our spouses, not even to ourselves. Its shame is on the same level as incest.

Racism in America still stands naked except when it is hurriedly covered by white prosecutors using their ever-ready tool, the grand jury. I am thinking of the white cop who killed a black unarmed teenager in Ferguson. No charges by the grand jury. I am thinking of a Staten Island grand jury that, under the direction of the prosecutor, cleared a white NYPD cop in the chokehold death of Eric Garner during his arrest for peddling loose cigarettes. I grieve the death of Tamir Rice, a twelve-year-old African American boy in Cleveland who was carrying a toy gun and was shot by a white officer within two seconds of the officer's arrival at the scene. He died the next day.

Examining FBI data between 2010 and 2012, *ProPublica* concludes, "Young black males in recent years were at a far greater risk of being shot dead by police than their white counterparts—*21 times greater*" (my emphasis). *ProPublica* says its risk analysis "seems to support what has been an article of faith in the African American community for decades: Blacks

---

* John Blake, "The New Threat: 'Racism Without Racists,'" CNN.com, November 27, 2014.

are being killed at disturbing rates when set against the rest of the American population."*

Throughout this book we have been examining America's police state as it has existed in seedling form to the present. From our standpoint as ordinary citizens, are we still free, or is our freedom but a sly and cruel myth fed to us by Power?

Are we capable of distinguishing between our fantasy, our hope, yes, our faith that we are free on the one hand, from the alarming approach of a police state on the other? And if we discover the truth, can we bear it? Will we confront it?

None of the cops and none of the prosecutors who had stolen the lives of the Ford Heights Four and who cast innocent kids into the hell of those vile prisons were ever charged with a single crime, nor did any miss a day's pay as discipline for the years of human suffering they imposed on these innocent citizens and their families. The irony here is that the police and prosecutors with all their power will fade away into the impenetrable shadows of history while Dennis Williams and his friends, once poor, helpless black kids, will continue to brighten our memories.

---

* Ryan Gabrielson, Ryann Grochowski Jones, and Eric Sagara, "Deadly Force, in Black and White," *ProPublica*, October 10, 2014, http://www.propublica.org/article/deadly-force-in-black-and-white.

CASE 8

GIVE THE SPARROW TO THE HAWK

They stood stiff as old stumps, he in a clean pair of starched bibs holding a sweat-stained cowboy hat against his chest, and she standing close, but not touching her husband. She was wearing a flowered Sunday dress and low-heeled, round-toed black shoes. Her lips quivered when she tried to hold a smile. Please, would I defend their son, Albert?

Their boy was charged with the murder of a young woman named Beverly Bright, a fellow worker, a pretty young thing with swishing red hair, a perky nose, and eyes that hinted at a bridled passion on the verge of escape. She'd been stabbed five times, once clean and clear through the heart. Albert had signed a confession to the murder. Why would a confessed murderer suddenly want to go to trial?

"We ain't got much, Mr. Spence," Jeff Hancock, the boy's father, said in a voice that sounded like hard static. His forehead was white from the steady shelter of his old Stetson. "All we got is our ranch. We'll sign it over to ya for yer fee if you'll take Albert's case."

I'd seen it all before—parents who'd sacrifice whatever they had to save their young. Win or lose, they'd be homeless if I took their offer.

My partner Eddie Moriarity offered Hancock a quick smile. "Albert ever in trouble?"

"No, sir. Never. They forced him to sign that confession."

"Ever lose his temper and hurt anybody?"

"No, sir. Why, Albert wouldn't argue with a pup," Mr. Hancock said. "I was maybe too hard on him. Taught him to respec' authority. I was in the service, and I learned if ya cause no trouble ya get no trouble. That's what I always said."

"Did he have girlfriends?" I asked.

"Albert never had himself a date. He was a homeboy. Why, when Albert goes huntin' with me he won't even take a gun." The Hancocks were honest, hardworking, longtime citizens in the county. The state had released Albert on bail secured by their small ranch.

The next day, Mr. Hancock brought Albert to the office. He was barely twenty-one, weighed less than 110 pounds, and looked fifteen. He was blond and pale as a featherless bird. He wore thick glasses that made him look like a blinking sparrow.

I took Albert in with a long stare. "If you didn't kill anybody, why did you confess?" I asked.

Albert just shook his head, his eyes examining both sides of his hands. He struggled as if his words were jammed up in tight places. "I didn't kill anybody."

I leaned over my desk toward the kid and spoke to him in a quiet voice. "You were there when she was murdered. If you didn't kill her, who did?"

He looked down again and mumbled his words in his high small voice that sounded like an off-key flute from the other side of the mountain. In staggered spurts he told the same story he'd been telling all along. He and Beverly were janitors at the State Training School for mentally disadvantaged children, and they were working that night, and a big man with a knife made him haul the woman's body down the stairs and threatened that if Albert called the police he'd kill Albert's family. It was the way he spoke, in flat, unemotional words. He spoke as if he weren't present to hear them.

Surely Albert had been suffering in some frenetic landscape. His screws loosened, his controls failed, and he exploded into murder. We hear of cases like that all the time—someone who's your quiet, law-abiding neighbor and one day ends up on the rooftop trying to shoot everyone in sight. I thought there could be an insanity defense for the boy.

Beverly Bright, thirty, five foot two, and filled out in convivial places, had that walk and a trigger smile. She must have been approaching terminal boredom living with her husband in Hudson, Wyoming, a wide spot in the road that offered a couple of restaurants, one with a closed-down whorehouse upstairs. She made dates on her CB radio with truckers as they came driving into the area at night, tired, alone, and lonely.

When Beverly didn't come home that night, Terry, her husband, drove the twelve miles from their home to the State Training School on the outskirts of Lander. He couldn't find Beverly, so he called the cops, who eventually found her bloody body stuffed under the staircase. When a wife is murdered, the cops look first at the husband. Did he have a motive? Did he have the opportunity? Answer both in the affirmative and you've got yourself a bona fide suspect, one a jury will convict with a little creativity from the cops and prosecutors. But Sheriff C. A. "Peewee" McDougall wasn't interested in Terry Bright. He had an easier target—that strange-looking, strange-acting kid I'd begun to call "the sparrow," Albert Hancock.

When Sheriff McDougall asked Albert to come to his office and talk to him about the murder, Mr. Hancock told Albert, "Sure, son, go on in and tell the sheriff what ya know. They gotta find the killer, and maybe you can help 'em." Then, Mr. Hancock said, the cops hauled Albert off to Casper, Wyoming's major city 150 miles down the road, "to take one of them lie detector tests." Hancock shook his head. "Albert said they forced him to say he done it."

But what if you were a small, timid ranch kid, alone, facing the sheriff and the chief of police pushed together in a tight office, and after they worked you over for hours they hauled you to the polygraph expert in a town 150 miles away? There another cop trained to use the polygraph to gain confessions took over, and you're swimming around in confusion, scared and exhausted after hours of heavy interrogation, and they promised that all you had to do was sign the paper and things would go better for you.

On the other hand, what if you killed the woman and were fighting back guilt and remorse and fear, and you remembered the nightmare of her screaming, of her crumpled body on the floor soaked in blood, and the smell of death, and finally you couldn't fight it anymore, and when the lie-detector guy said you should get it off your chest you heard yourself hollering, "Yes, I did it. I did it!" What then?

Sheriff Peewee McDougall and I had previously endured an arid eight-year relationship. He'd been the sheriff during both of my four-year terms as Fremont County prosecutor. People just seemed to tell Peewee what happened. If they were guilty, they confessed. But when Beverly Bright was murdered I'd been out of the prosecutor's office fifteen years.

I launched into Albert's case with a sound strategy: I'd send the boy to Dr. Robert Fairbairn, a competent, careful psychiatrist I knew who'd doubtlessly find Albert "not triable by reason of insanity." That road was not only just and humane, it would avoid a long, expensive trial, something a poor rancher like Jeff Hancock couldn't afford, and the court would send Albert to the state hospital in far off Evanston. There Albert would receive the treatment he needed—or at least that was the official promise. And justice would prevail.

"But Albert ain't insane, Mr. Spence," his father insisted. "He's as sane as you and me. He just got pushed around by them cops."

I said, "Mr. Hancock, if Dr. Fairbairn doesn't find Albert needs treatment in the state hospital I'll defend Albert for free."

So the Hancocks drove Albert the long miles to Denver to see Dr. Fairbairn. Dr. Fairbairn had Albert admitted to a psychiatric hospital where he observed the boy for two weeks. He even administered truth serum to Albert—not once, but twice. Dr. Fairbairn reported that not only was Albert legally sane, but he was as innocent as the sparrow. The good doctor insisted Albert's story was true.

True!

My partner Eddie said, "The jury's going to see Fairbairn as another paid witness testifying for a lotta bucks for a couple of crooked defense lawyers who're tryin' to get a murderer off." I knew he was right. Even if Albert's story were true it would be a hard sell to any jury.

Finally I said, "Well, Eddie, I was talking again when I should have been listening. I promised Mr. Hancock that we'd defend Albert for free if Dr. Fairbairn found that he was sane and innocent. Here we go again—big case, no fee."

Eddie laughed. As a kid he'd been the Montana state wrestling champion at about 120 pounds, and he was still nourished by a good fight. "We've been broke before," he said.

We'd be pitted against a dedicated, intransigent, competent prosecutor, one I'd helped train. Arnold Tschirgi was tall, dark, and trim and looked like a tight end for the Pittsburgh Steelers. When I was the prosecutor I hired him as my deputy. Tschirgi grew up on a ranch and had the values of a rancher—endless hard work and a desire to do the right thing. I also thought he was driven by a dominating desire to beat his former boss, namely me. He often flashed an embarrassed but misleading smile, as if he weren't too sure he should be in your presence. But I saw him as the hawk, fully capable of chewing up a sparrow like Albert.

So I woke up one morning realizing we'd taken a case against two men who knew me as well as I knew them. After eight years of our working together and circumventing each other, McDougall, in his own pragmatic way, thought he had me pegged. And Tschirgi thought he could predict me like the cows coming down to water in the morning. And, yes, I thought I knew them as well.

*T*he case was set for trial in Lander, Wyoming, where the murder oc-curred. The local paper carried every bloody detail of the killing, and most of the stories referred to Albert as "the confessed killer." The local judge granted us a change of venue, and he chose Judge Paul Liamos, from Newcastle, to officiate in the murder trial of "Black Sundance," Beverly Bright's CB handle. As if by the joking of Mother Fate, the case was trans-ferred to *Sundance,* Wyoming. When the judicial dust settled, Eddie and I found ourselves in that small lost town up north near the South Dakota border, population a little over a thousand souls. As if prophetic, Sundance was in *Crook* County.

Sundance offered a couple of filling stations, a couple of cheap motels and a couple of bad cafés, a grocery store, a hardware store, a funeral home, and a locally owned bank, together with half a dozen churches. To get there you drove those long, weary, desolate backcountry roads of Wyoming. On the way you'd see herds of antelope or, at night, deer crossing the highway or a jackrabbit that would run in front of your headlights.

It was early summer and already hot, but Albert appeared to be on the verge of shivering. I got the impression that if I asked him his name he might look up at me with those large, blinking eyes and not know how to answer. I'd tried to talk to the boy, to get a sense of who he was. He was bright enough. Got through high school with good grades. But he seemed as afraid of me as he'd been of the cops.

What if Dr. Fairbairn was right? What if Albert was innocent and we failed him and his poor parents, who were sick to the bone with worry over an innocent child? Could Terry Bright, Beverly's husband, have been the murderer? He had the opportunity and the motive. But I wasn't ready to reach that dark conclusion. Before we'd entered the case an investigator whose actual name was Buck Rogers had worked for the public defender's office and spent a year or more running down leads like a bird dog in a chicken house.

"What about the Kenyon guy in Buck Rogers's report?" I asked Eddie. "More than one witness will say Beverly was always going in and out of the guy's construction trailer parked at the school. He was her old flame. And she broke it off just before she was murdered."

"Yeah," Eddie said. "And, remember, her father, Billy Kane, says that if you're going to go talk to Kenyon you better go armed and be ready for trouble, because that man is dangerous."

Albert had described the killer to Rogers. "He was about six feet tall, weighed 175 pounds, or more. He had dark hair, parted a little on the left. He had the tips of two fingers partly gone. This was on the left hand, I think. Anyhow, the one finger [indicating the middle finger] was gone all the way to the nail, no nail at all. He didn't have a watch on, and on his forearm he had what looked like a spot of blood, brown, a mole, birthmark or something like that. He had hairy arms and short sideburns. He had a deep voice, seemed calm. Something strange, he laughed once in a while, while I was doing what he said to do."

"Why did you do what he told you?" Rogers had asked Albert.

"He said he'd kill me if I didn't. He said if I ran that sooner or later he'd find me and kill me."

"How did you manage to get away from him?"

"When I had the mop in the sink, after mopping up some of the blood, I saw he didn't have the knife in either hand, so I ran. He ran after me, and I slammed the outside door on his hand I think, because he yelled then. I ran to the Administration Building and got inside. I didn't tell any-body, I guess, because I was so scared I didn't know what to do."

I said to Eddie, "How does a kid who is being forced at knifepoint to drag a body down the stairs remember those minute details?"

"Some minds take detailed photographs," Eddie said. "Some minds make photographs that are out of focus. And some turn out the lights."

Rogers found a man who called himself "Alligator." A couple of wit-nesses said Beverly had a fight with Alligator the night before the murder, which Alligator denied. He said to Rogers, "By God, if they've got anything on me, let 'em get a warrant!"

Later Rogers had a highway patrolman check out Kenyon's fingers. His report: "They look as good as yours and mine."

Several witnesses claimed Beverly liked to tease the residents at the Wyoming State Training School, boys grown to men who were still housed there living sparse, loveless lives. One of the residents she teased had been in love with her, and after he'd seen Kenyon take her into his trailer house the resident grabbed Beverly, threw her down, and tried to beat her up. But Bright said that for her size his wife was very strong and agile. Perhaps she teased because she thought her attention might be all they'd ever get from an attractive woman.

An inmate resident at the training school told Rogers that on the night of the murder "I saw a red car, red Chevy. Time, about good dark. Man went inside of building. The lights on all over. Man short. Didn't look like Terry."

A cook at a local café told Rogers that about a month before the murder a man came in one night and was sticking a knife in the table. The knife had a black handle. The man said, "Would you like me to show you what I can do with a knife like this? I'm pretty good with it." The cook told him to get out. The knife wasn't a hunting knife but "a big one that folded."

The cook said the man had fingers that had been injured or amputated; he didn't know if he was with Beverly, but he was in the group. Later our investigator, Mike Johnson, interviewed Fingers, as we referred to this individual. He said he and Beverly had gone to school together. Fingers remembered she was a redhead, but he claimed he didn't remember who she was until someone showed him her picture. Two injured fingers on a tall, dark man? Yes. And he'd driven a red car that belonged to his mother.

Our investigator asked some questions of Jane Judson, the young woman who'd been with Beverly and Alligator the night before her murder. Beverly and Jane had been talking about marriage. Beverly said, "Don't knock it, because marriage is a wonderful thing." She said her husband was a really good person. She told Jane that she told her husband about her dates, and that she told Alligator she told her husband she was having a drink with him. Jane said she didn't think that Beverly was trying to pick him up, but "she seemed pretty friendly."

Our files contained a statement by one of Beverly's friends who said Beverly complained she had to pry her husband out of a chair to get him into bed. On the other hand, another witness said she was saving up her sick leave and vacation time to have another baby, that she'd decided to call off her carryings-on and stay married and faithful to her man at home.

On a Monday morning, May 22, 1978, the trial of Albert Hancock finally got under way. We walked into that old one-story, square, yellow brick courthouse that supplied a courtroom of light oak paneling large enough to hold seventy-two people plus the jury, the clerk, the court reporter, a judge at his bench, and the lawyers sitting like cardboard cutouts at opposite tables. The courtroom provided a feeling that nothing changes, because things there were too tired to change.

Sheriff Peewee McDougall sat at the counsel table next to Tschirgi as if to guard the prosecutor from all anticipated danger. Albert wore new denim pants and a four-button denim jacket—all the buttons buttoned over a white dress shirt that was also buttoned at the collar, his black Sunday tie neatly in place. His worn black Sunday shoes were newly shined. He looked as if he were about to hear the preacher. But what he'd hear would be the prosecution bent on one objective: to haul Albert off to the state penitentiary. Albert gazed blankly out into the crowded courtroom.

The prospective jurors were a fair sample of folks from that rural Wyoming county—rancher types with fresh green cow manure on their boots, their wives, alongside their husbands, with rough hands and sunburned faces from harsh exposure to the elements. The jury panel included miners, laborers, a teacher, a plumber, and a couple of government workers. Among the prospective jurors were two who could readily be pegged as either an undertaker or a life insurance salesman, the only men in town who wore suits on weekdays.

Tschirgi wanted to keep jurors who said they might be prejudiced. "Thank you for being so forthright, Mr. Rafferty," Tschirgi said to the prospective juror. "But as a fair man you can surely put aside your prejudice, listen to the evidence, and give this defendant a fair trial, isn't that true?"

Juror: "Yeah, I s'pose."

I wanted the juror off. I asked, "Mr. Rafferty, what magic eraser are you going to use to erase the prejudice from your brain so you can enter this case with a blank mind?" The juror just stared at me. I continued, "I don't like pork chops. Perfectly good food, but nobody can change me on that."

Juror: "Nothin' wrong with a good pork chop."

Judge Paul Liamos: "This is a trial, not a culinary school, Mr. Spence. I'll excuse Mr. Rafferty. Thank you for your service, sir." Judge Liamos was a patient man in his fifties, graying, balding, and with a not-to-be-messed-with frown molded on his face. He wore the traditional judicial black robe—black for death?

It was spring, and laboring men hadn't worked all winter. The ranchers had springtime irrigating and calves to brand, and the judge excused them for "hardship." A couple of jurors said they didn't want to pass judgment on anybody, especially someone charged with murder. Those were the jurors we wanted, but they, too, were excused by the judge. After five days of jury selection I felt we'd created a sort of tribe that consisted of the jurors, Eddie, and me. Maybe we had a shot at an acquittal. But Tschirgi seemed happy with the jurors, too.

"What am I missing?" I asked Eddie.

"Don't worry," he said. "Let's try our case."

Judge Liamos struck his gavel and turned to the lawyers. "None of the witnesses will remain in the courtroom while this trial is taking place. Further, I order the witnesses not to talk with each other concerning their testimony, and the lawyers for each side will convey my order to their witnesses."

I watched Arnold Tschirgi take long, confident steps to the lectern, his arms loose and swinging as if he were ready for hand-to-hand combat. I always start a trial with the uninvited visitation of "belly butterflies." Tschirgi smiled his quick, boyish smile at the jurors and began describing Beverly Bright, an attractive Wyoming girl raised on a ranch, a friendly sort who would run up and kiss you hello, man or woman, a young woman brimming with a zest for life, a generous heart, a wife loved by her loving husband and a mother by her five-year-old daughter.

"And Albert Hancock, over there," Tschirgi said, pointing, his voice suddenly escalating to an angry, nasal crescendo, "*that* man stabbed her to death. Then he dragged her mortally wounded body, soaked in her own blood, down seventeen stairs and tried to hide her underneath the staircase in the basement."

White silence filled the courtroom. Jurors stared in horror at the alleged killer sitting between his parents, a strange-looker who stared back at the jurors through those thick glasses.

And the motive for murder? I knew Tschirgi couldn't prove a motive. He said maybe Beverly Bright insulted Albert when she asked him if he was still in high school. "Albert didn't take to that very well. Maybe he was in love with her. Maybe she betrayed him."

Tschirgi kept hard hawk eyes on Albert as he described to the jurors each knife wound—five deep, deadly stabs. I could see the knife sinking in to its hilt, again and again, to the blaring beat of the radio she always kept at high volume as she worked.

Tschirgi claimed there was a small unidentified bloodstain on Albert's pants. Whose blood? All mammals from mice to moose, all birds and beasts and jumping frogs, have blood in their veins.

Tschirgi told the jury that Albert was repeatedly assured that he didn't have to tell the police anything, that he could have a lawyer, and when Albert was in Casper for his polygraph, the operator, Dave Dovala, once more reviewed Albert's rights with him. It was all so clean and clear and kind, and Albert thereupon voluntarily confessed the murder. Case closed.

More than that, according to Tschirgi, Albert said right there in the presence of his parents, "I'm not a very good liar. I killed her."

Tschirgi said, "During the trip home Albert Hancock confessed *yet again*. He shouted, 'I *blasted* her in the stomach with the knife.'" I felt my own stomach cramp. I looked over at Albert. His eyes were wide and wild, like a small, trapped bird.

"Well, Eddie," I said at the recess, "what do you think?"

"I think Tschirgi's got the jury pretty well horrified and hating Albert," he said. "Especially that woman on the far right in the back row. If looks could kill, Albert would be one dead little sparrow."

Yet, after torching the jurors with his raging fire for hours, I thought Tschirgi had failed to provide a convincing answer to a couple of questions that wouldn't go away: Why did the sparrow kill Black Sundance? And if he didn't, who did?

*T*he next morning shortly after 9:00 A.M., I began my opening statement to the jury. The operational word in every competent defense is *attack*. If you're explaining and defending, you're losing. The prosecutor, the cops, their pathologist, their criminalist, and their trainload of experts all work as a team. They, too, know how to win: *Attack*.

I told the jury that the evidence in the case pointed to a murder Mr. Tschirgi and the cops didn't investigate. Why was the prosecutor presenting an incomplete case after more than two years? Instead the cops picked on a poor, scared kid and bullied him until he signed a pathetic piece of paper the prosecution wanted to pawn off as a voluntary confession.

Tschirgi objected. As intended, his objections were interrupting the flow of my opening.

I asked the jury to remain patient. Truth does not come galloping up on a white horse. It plods into the courtroom one witness at a time, one day at a time. Tschirgi had used a favorite metaphor of mine when he told the jury that we lawyers were guides through the forest of facts. I said yes, but if we follow the wrong guide we'll be lost. "We were deeply sorry about Beverly Bright's death and sad for her grieving family. But this human tragedy, so wretched, so unjustified—"

Tschirgi objected and was sustained by the judge.

I turned to the knife that Tschirgi told the jury was the murder weapon. I spoke to the knife: "Hello, *Knife*. Who are you? There are endless thousands like you, and none have anything to do with this case. You just happened to be a knife the sheriff found in some drawer. How does it feel to be held up as a weapon that killed an innocent young woman?"

Tschirgi claimed that Dr. Thorpen, the pathologist, said the square indented wound on Beverly's forehead, the size and shape of the setting in a man's ring, might have resulted from her being dragged down the stairs. I spoke to the stairs. "Hello, *Stairs.* You had no square protrusions on your surface. And her face and head were battered, revealing a beating not by you, Stairs, but by the ring on a man's fist. How does it feel to be blamed for something you didn't cause? Besides, Albert never owned a ring.

"And the medical facts established a violent attack consistent with a powerful man with a motive to first injure and then to kill. She was smashed in the face with her glasses on. You will see the marks." I reminded the jury how Mr. Tschirgi suggested that anemic motive for murder—that Albert had been insulted months before by Beverly Bright when she asked if Albert was still in high school. That was the motive for a brutal killing? I slowly took in each of the jurors. Their faces began to soften.

I told the jury that several witnesses had seen Albert in the time frame of the killing, and none had seen any blood on him. His pants had been washed? His folks didn't own a washing machine. His mother went to town once a week to the Laundromat. By the time the officer picked up Albert's clothes and boots, she hadn't gone to town with the week's wash.

The cops fingerprinted Albert, but his prints were never recovered anywhere at the bloody scene. At the same time, there were other suspects—a husband and a jilted lover, to name just a couple, and not a single suspect was ever printed.

"What else hasn't Mr. Tschirgi told you, and why?" I asked. "The officers had taken scrapings from under Beverly Bright's fingernails. They contained human skin and blood. But there wasn't the first scratch on Albert, and now, interestingly, those scrapings have disappeared.

"And by the way," I said, "why wouldn't the officers talk to me? They'd talked for hours to a frightened kid who was all alone, but not to me?"

Tschirgi objected, and Judge Liamos sustained.

The jurors kept peering at Albert. I interrupted my argument and said in a quiet way, "I see you watching Albert for his reactions as I talk to you. Remember: He is young and he is frightened. How might we look to others when we're being accused of a horrible killing? We are not *how* we *look*, but how we *are.*"

Tschirgi objected. The judge said for me to move on.

I told the jury that in school Albert was always the little bird in the corner. "On their small ranch he didn't want to hurt or kill—not even a chicken for dinner. He has never received so much as a parking ticket. People laughed at this strange, quiet boy with the thick glasses, but he is respectful of everyone, even those who push him around. He knows bullies because Albert's kind are their favorite victims." I turned and looked at the sheriff and let the thought take hold in the minds of the jurors.

"The more Albert tried to tell the cops what happened, the more they called him a liar and terrified him. Well, here in this courtroom we're going to finally tell his story to twelve good citizens who have no desire to convict an innocent boy.

"That night at the training school, Albert and Beverly were in the teachers' lounge. She seemed disturbed. We discovered later she was in love with a high school sweetheart who lived in Shoshoni, and she'd been having an affair with him, but for her family's sake she'd broken it off the day before. The night before, she'd made a date with a trucker whom she'd met on her citizens band radio. She had a drink with the trucker at a bar. Her girlfriend was with her. The man had propositioned her."

Tschirgi objected. I stopped my opening and turned to Judge Liamos.

"Your Honor, as I address the jury and present the facts of our defense, Mr. Tschirgi keeps looking over at the jurors shaking his head. I don't believe this conduct is proper or fair." The judge called us to the bench. At the bench Tschirgi denied my complaint. But the judge said that if this were true he should desist.

I continued, "The night of the murder Beverly Bright said to Albert, 'Wait a minute, I want to show you something.' She went downstairs from the teachers' lounge, where they were having a chocolate drink. The loudspeakers were on. She didn't come back, and at last Albert went down to see why. He found her standing in the doorway bleeding. She said, 'Call the police.' Albert said there was a big man standing there."

I told the jury how the cops wouldn't believe him and said he was lying, and how Sheriff McDougall finally said, "Well, if you're telling the truth, you'd be willing to go to Casper and take a lie detector test, wouldn't you?" Albert thought he should ask his father. And that evening his father said, "Yes, son, you have nothing to hide."

Albert's so-called confession to the polygraph operator seemed incoherent and filled with blanks. I said I thought it a prime example of the disintegration of a boy's fragile psyche on the one side and the betrayal of his rights on the other.

"He signed the paper, and he asked the polygraph operator if what he signed would keep him from becoming a police officer.

"What? Yes, he wanted to know if by signing the paper it would keep him from becoming a police officer," I said again.

I told the jury that we sent Albert to Dr. Fairbairn and that the doctor found Albert was not insane. He was timid, pathetically so, and easily led to agree with authority, but the story he told was the truth.

Tschirgi objected. The judge said I should move on.

I told the jury that even Beverly Bright's father, Billy Kane, thought Albert was innocent. Mr. Kane knew of another suspect he believed killed his daughter, and he wanted him investigated. But McDougall had his man—no, his boy—and neither he nor Chief Robert Campbell made any further investigation. To do so would be an admission they held doubts about the guilt of Albert Hancock and had rushed to judgment—to a wrongful judgment.

I took in each juror. I waited. Then I said, "That decision by those officers caused another murder—the merciless murder of *Truth.*"

Prosecutor Arnold Tschirgi's first witness was Terry Bright. The right decision, I thought—to call the grieving husband. He was a nice-enough-looking fellow, understandably sad and nervous. He said he received a call from his wife about six thirty or seven o'clock on the evening of the murder. He was at home, their CB base station blaring away in the living room.

I wondered how it might be to lie on the couch and listen on your CB radio as your wife made dates with other men. What he heard we'd never know. He said he'd been awakened around 10:00 P.M. by a call from Barbara Rieman, who had a date to meet Beverly for a drink after work, but she'd never shown up.

He testified that he awakened again about 4:00 A.M. to find his wife still not home. Worried, he drove to Lander from their home in Hudson, taking their child with him and leaving her with his mother-in-law, Pauline Kane, and drove on to the training school nearby. Her car was there. By this time it was around four thirty in the morning. The lights were on in the building where his wife usually worked, in Emerson Hall. He honked his horn, and Mrs. McCullock, an employee at the school, looked out her upstairs apartment window.

He didn't go into Emerson Hall. Instead he drove back to his mother-in-law's and phoned Mrs. McCullock. She said she knew nothing about his wife's whereabouts. He stayed at his mother-in-law's until about six and drove to the Husky Café for coffee. About six thirty he returned to the school, found a door partially opened, and entered Emerson Hall to loud, pounding music from two radios. He hollered for his wife. No answer. He shut off the radio on the stage and hollered for his wife twice more.

In the south end of the building he saw his wife's coat hanging on a door-knob across the hall from the janitor's closet. He started back toward the gym and saw a cup of what he thought was spilled coffee on the floor, went up on the stage and hollered for his wife a couple more times, and then, as he left the stage, saw his wife's glasses on the floor near the spilled coffee. He ran up to the McCullock apartment, called the switchboard operator for a supervisor, and then called the police. It was about seven in the morning when Officer Watan found Beverly Bright's body at the base of the stairs.

On my cross-examination Bright admitted that Tschirgi provided him a copy of his prior statement, one he'd given the officers a full week *after* Albert had *already* been charged with her murder. It was as if McDougall knew his investigation was incomplete and needed Bright's statement in case anyone asked why he hadn't at least asked a few questions of the murdered woman's husband. Bright admitted he'd read his statement five or six times.

My questioning of the husband went like this:

> Q: She [his wife, Beverly] told you that a man who called himself "Alligator" propositioned her the night *before* the murder?
> A: Yes. She said he made a pass at her that night.
> Q: You deny that you were angry?
> A: I trusted her.
> Q: You knew she met him through a CB radio date?
> A: Yes, she told me.

He denied ever striking his wife or threatening to hurt her. He admitted knowing that John Kenyon, his wife's high school flame, had a trailer on the school premises, where Kenyon was working. She'd told Bright about him as well. But he insisted he wasn't a jealous person.

Q: Mr. Bright, did you tell the sheriff about her CB dates?

A: I don't remember.

Q: Did you tell anyone?

A: I don't remember.

Q: You listened to her conversation with Alligator on your CB radio the night before the murder?

A: No.

Q: You're sure?

A: Yes.

Q: You heard her talk to other men on the CB?

A: Yes.

Q: That must have been painful for you.

He looked down.

Q: You must have loved her a lot.

A: Yes.

Q: Did you object to her meeting others via the CB?

A: No, sir.

Q: No?

Q: Surely that wasn't your choice.

A: No, sir.

I thought he seemed smothered in pain.

He said his wife had called him about six thirty in the evening on the night of the murder. He didn't remember why she called him, and he didn't remember if she mentioned Alligator that night. He insisted there were no marital troubles between them.

Q: It must have tormented you that she was meeting with other men.

A: No, sir.

Q: No?

He didn't answer.

Q: Didn't you imagine what they were saying to each other? What they were doing together?

A: No, sir. I trusted her.

He owned a Buck skinning knife. No cop had ever asked him for his knife or his clothes.

He'd been in the service—spent time in Okinawa and the Philippines.

Q: Were you ever trained in the use of the bayonet as a knife?
A: Yes.

I had Bright demonstrate with a knife how he'd been trained to hold one, the thrust made with the palm up, but he said, "You wouldn't use an upward thrust if you were taking out a sentry from behind."

That evening after court I lingered with Albert. "I need your help," I said. "Why did you confess to something you didn't do?"
I waited. I could hear the rain on the windows.
Finally he said, "I didn't want to cause any trouble."
And that's all he would say. Perhaps it was all he could say.

Tschirgi's next witness was a man I'd known many years, Larry Lee, the Fremont County coroner. Lee unwittingly mentioned a witness meeting in Tschirgi's motel room that seemed in violation of the judge's order not to talk among themselves about the evidence. We remember that he ordered the witnesses separated from the courtroom in an effort to keep the prosecutor from presenting a rehearsed set of facts.

I charged to the bench arguing that the case should be dismissed for this intentional violation of the court's order. "I want Mr. Tschirgi sworn, along with the others who were in attendance at that meeting in Mr. Tschirgi's motel room."

Tschirgi resisted. He was the state's attorney and was immune from giving testimony. "This is a search for the truth," I argued. "This is not choir practice where all the members are taught to sing the same tune."

Tschirgi finally had had enough. He charged that my arguments had been derogatory and demeaning, and he now demanded the right to testify. In chambers he was sworn by the judge. He admitted that he had not conveyed the judge's order to his witnesses as a group. He had mentioned it to some at different times, but he couldn't remember which witnesses and at what times. Tschirgi argued that there was no more said than what everyone read in the Casper paper each morning. We had suffered no injury.

"So it all comes down to this," I argued back. "The judge says don't talk about your testimony. And Mr. Tschirgi's excuse for the violation of your order is that they could read it in the morning paper anyway?"

In the end I couldn't prove what was or wasn't said, nor who said it, nor in the presence of whom. I knew Judge Liamos had no choice but to overrule my motion to dismiss the case. But I hoped my motion had been a warning to Tschirgi. On the contrary, the war was only escalating.

On my cross-examination of Coroner Lee I asked:

> Q: The bloody handprint on the wall was important evidence?
> A: Yes.
> Q: You'd expect the officers to preserve it?
> A: Yes.
> Q: Did you or they preserve it?
> A: No.
> Q: If the victim had been stabbed in the heart while she was standing, you would expect to see blood on the walls?
> A: Yes.
> Q: There was blood on the walls, but only at thirty-four inches above the floor.
> A: Yes.
> Q: The cup on the floor wasn't fingerprinted?
> A: No.

Lee said there were no defense marks or cuts on the dead woman's hands or arms, that is, cuts from the knife suffered when she might have attempted to protect herself. He thought that was unusual. "I assumed she was hit pretty hard the first time," he said.

Every morning for certain, and some days at multiple times, we found some grounds to move for a mistrial. It got so tense in the courtroom that Chief Campbell took a position leaning up against the beverage machine in the lobby rather than sitting near any witnesses, and he refused to talk to anyone so he could never be accused of violating the court's order.

When Tschirgi called Chief Campbell to the stand, I braced for the attack. He was potentially the most dangerous witness yet. He looked very official and imposing as he walked to the witness chair dressed in his uniform. He smiled at the jurors, took his seat, made himself comfortable, and waited for Tschirgi's first question. His mission was to convince the jurors that Albert Hancock wasn't a sparrow but a confessed vicious murderer sitting there among the citizens, something like a snake coiled up in the living room.

Tschirgi began by taking Campbell through yet another endless recitation of the measurements of buildings, their rooms, and their hallways. Then, as if there hadn't been enough blood testimony already, Tschirgi had Campbell tell again in detail where all the blood was and the quantity of blood at each and every location. I began to believe the jury might convict Albert for no better reason than that Tschirgi had them crazy with all the blood. Someone had to pay for it. Why not that weird-looking kid sitting over there between his parents?

"Surely," I said to the judge, "we all have an inkling by now that there was a lot of blood at the scene. But it's as if blood has become the state's entire case. We will stipulate that the scene was drenched in blood. Perhaps, now, we can move on."

"Objection," from Tschirgi.

"Sustained," from the bench.

My feeling of compassion for Terry Bright returned when Campbell testified that Bright was standing near the corpse of his wife when Campbell came in. Campbell said to Bright, nodding to the body, "Who is she?"

"It's my wife," Bright said.

Finally Campbell began to testify about the bloody print on the wall. "How many fingers did you see on the handprint?" Tschirgi asked.

"I could see the thumb and three fingers—just a portion of maybe the little finger."

A finger missing on the print!

Tschirgi had Campbell show the jury a picture of Beverly Bright's face taken at the funeral home after she'd been embalmed. One could still see distinct "bruising" on her forehead, Campbell called it. That was about the extent of this important witness's testimony. I wondered what trap, if any, had been set for me?

On cross I discovered that neither McDougall nor Campbell nor any of their officers prepared any reports of their investigation. We know it's standard police procedure to make detailed reports in all felony investigations, especially in a murder case.

> Q: Chief Campbell, you were aware that if you made reports the defense attorneys could get them.

TSCHIRGI: Objection.

THE JUDGE: Overruled.

A: Yes.

Q: That's the reason no reports were made by the officers in this case, isn't that true?

A: No.

I turned again to the bloody print on the wall.

Q: I believe you told us you thought that print was insignificant?

A: I believe I said it had no value.

But the handprint on the wall had been destroyed.

The cops had not saved Beverly Bright's coat. "No significance," the chief said, but he couldn't remember how many pockets were in her coat or what was in her pockets.

The chief said the victim's purse was returned to her husband. He couldn't recall what she had in her purse. The purse's contents were also insignificant, he said. He did, however, remember there was about $150 in the purse.

Q: Do you remember seeing an address book in her purse?

A: No.

Q: But you made no report, so you're testifying to the contents of her purse from memory these years later?

A: Yes.

Q: Could an address book have had some value in a murder case?

A: Yes.

I suddenly changed the subject.

Q: Do you leave room for the possibility that there was a love triangle involved here?

A: I have no reason to believe that in this case.

Q: Would a love triangle be a possible motive for murder?

A: Anything could have been possible.

Q: Did you ever discover if Beverly Bright had been involved in any indiscretions?

A: No specific ones that I can remember.

Q: Would you want to find out if such indiscretions were more than a possibility?

No answer.

Q: Are you aware of the relationship she had with John Kenyon?

A: Yes.

Q: Did you learn that during the week of the murder she'd broken off a relationship with her former lover John Kenyon?

A: No.

Q: Were you waiting for a carrier pigeon to bring you that information?

No answer. Tschirgi hadn't objected.

Q: Did you ever talk to Jane Judson?

A: Yes. In the conference room of the school.

Q: Did she tell you about Beverly Bright making a date through her CB radio with a man they called Alligator?

A: Yes.

Q: Did you record that interview?

A: No.

Q: You didn't learn whether Alligator made a pass at her or not, isn't that true?

A: Yes.

Q: Did you inquire of anyone whether Terry Bright was upset with his wife over her conduct?

A: No.

Q: Or if he threatened her?

A: No.

Q: Do you know if anyone made such an inquiry?

A: No.

Q: Did you know about Terry Bright's training with a bayonet?

A: Yes. I heard Dr. Thorpen and Terry Bright talking about it in the motel room. [I gave the judge another knowing look.]

Q: Did you try to determine by Mr. Bright's past conduct if he was the jealous type?

A: No.

Q: You knew that one of the first persons suspected in the murder of a wife is her husband?

A: Yes.

Q: Sometimes fights between husband and wife get out of control and someone gets killed.

A: Yes.

Q: This is more likely to happen to wives who are promiscuous.

A: Yes.

Q: You learned that she went into bars?

A: Only on one occasion. It was not uncommon for her to make such dates.

Q: The only one you know about was with Alligator when she made a date with him on her CB.

A: Yes.

The chief never tried to discover who called Beverly Bright on the night she was murdered. He'd learned she'd been upset from the call.

Q: Did you ask Terry Bright if he made the call?

A: No.

Q: Did you even ask him the last time he talked to her?

A: No.

Q: Did you ask him the last contact he had with her?

A: He said before she went to work on the afternoon of the fifth.

Q: Would it have interested you if you had learned he made a call to her about 6:00 P.M.?

A: At the time, no. I would like to look into it now.

Q: Once Albert signed that confession your investigation stopped, until we got into the case, isn't that true?

A: Yes.

I showed the jury photographs of Beverly Bright's face both before and after the embalming. One photo showed the square indent on the woman's forehead that we thought came from a square setting in a man's ring. The number six juror would not look at the exhibit. But the number one juror was staring at Chief Campbell with obvious contempt.

Q: Did you see any evidence there [referring to the photographs] that Beverly Bright was beaten?

A: I saw evidence of a woman who was dragged down seventeen stairs.

Q: If that injury came from being dragged down the stairs, then why did you find her glasses at the *top* of the stairs, not the bottom?

No answer.

I asked that her glasses be produced. The clerk handed me a sack that contained the glasses.

Q: Were her glasses bent?

A: No.

I asked Campbell to remove the glasses from the sack.

Q: Look down on the nosepiece. Are the glasses bent?

A: Yes.

Q: You are noticing that now for the first time?

A: I never noticed this before.

I handed the glasses to the jurors to inspect. Jurors three, four, and five were clearly upset with Campbell. Juror three was glaring at him. Juror nine covered her face with her hands.

Q: Is it your present opinion that Beverly Bright wore her glasses in that bent condition prior to her death?

A: No.

I had Campbell circle on the photo the bruise on the deceased's nose. When the photo was passed to juror number six, she again refused to look at it and shoved the photo to the number five juror to her left. Number Six, as we came to call her, threw me a look that suggested I'd be better off meeting Dracula with a toothache in a dark alley than her.

Q: Did you look for anyone who wore a ring with a square mounting?

A: No.

Q: Did Terry Bright wear such a ring?

A: I don't know.

fter court Eddie and I changed from our court garb for our evening run at the Sundance high school track—to run out the pent-up poisons that chew at you all day in the courtroom, the anger and frustration stuffed into the gut and the emotional lid slammed shut.

Then the next morning I continued my cross of the chief.

Q: Were there any prints on the paper cup that was found lying on the floor?

A: I don't know.

I asked that the cup be produced.

Q: Do you see three prints here?

I was pointing to prints that had been dusted and clearly appeared on the cup.

A: Yes, there appears to be a partial, one in the center that is a partial, and, yes, a third.

Q: Do you know whose prints these are?

A: Yes. I think they're Mr. Smith's.

Q: Smith was a member of the Lander police force?

A: Yes.

Q: Did you take Mr. Smith's prints?

A: No.

Q: If someone claimed this cup was retrieved out of the garbage [we'd been told this was the case], would you agree with that?

A: No.

Q: When you talked to the resident named Victor, he told you he saw a *white* car behind the school.

A: Yes.

Q: What color was Mr. Bright's car?

A: It was a white Universal Jeep.

Q: What time did Victor say it was there?

A: Late at night.

Q: Would it surprise you if Victor told our investigator, Mike Johnson, that he saw a man run out and get into the car?

A: Nothing he'd say would surprise me. If you suggested something to him he would probably say anything.

Q: Where did you talk to Victor?

A: In the sheriff's private office.

Q: Did you record him?

A: No.

Q: Did you even take any notes?

A: No. I didn't think he was confused when he saw a white car there.

Q: Did you, or anyone you know, fingerprint Victor?

A: No.

Campbell must have forgotten his earlier testimony in one of the pretrial motion hearings when he admitted they *did* fingerprint Victor.

Campbell said he couldn't produce the skin scrapings from under Beverly Bright's nails because the crime lab used up the entire sample in testing. But the crime lab reported it had returned the scrapings. Campbell also admitted that no one saw any blood on Albert's clothes on the day of and after the murder.

I asked him about the suspect we called Fingers. They'd made no inquiry about this man. None.

Then I skipped to Judy Peabody, an employee at the school, and her knife, which McDougall alleged was the murder weapon. They'd taken no prints off Mrs. Peabody's desk. He said he went through Beverly Bright's car, which was parked at the school. He couldn't remember what was in it or in its glove box.

Q: Well, Chief, was there anywhere in Albert's confession where he actually said that he had killed Beverly Bright?

A: He didn't say he did and he didn't say he didn't.

I looked over at Tschirgi. He seemed unconcerned.

Q: You and Mr. McDougall had Albert in the police car all the way back from Casper, and you were interrogating him the whole two hours on that trip back. Why didn't you have that conversation reduced to writing and signed by Albert?

A: We were anxious to get home and file the charges against him.

Q: Let me read from the transcript of an earlier hearing in which you were telling what you said to Albert concerning a "waiver" of his constitutional rights: I quote from your sworn testimony. You said you told Albert, "If you waive your rights you can have an attorney—you can have an attorney with you, but if you waive your rights you don't necessarily want an attorney." Didn't you think that was a wee bit confusing?

A: No.

Q: Are you saying you can waive your rights to an attorney and still have an attorney?

A: Yes. A person can disregard a waiver at any time.

Q: You, of course, explained that in detail to Albert before you began your interrogation?

A: No.

Judge Liamos had recessed the trial for the day. I waited for the courtroom to clear, let Albert's parents spend a little time with him, and then, in the quiet of the courtroom, talked with Albert again. He seemed slightly more comfortable with me.

"So, Albert, how did you think our day went today?"

"It was OK," he said.

"Aren't you angry at Chief Campbell?"

"It doesn't do you any good to be angry," he said.

"Well, no, but aren't you a little upset with the investigation that Campbell made?"

"Well, I was disappointed." Then he looked off across the courtroom with his eyes focused on something I couldn't identify.

Dr. James Thorpen, the pathologist, was next on the stand. During his career he'd completed between 3,000 and 3,500 autopsies. He was a friendly sort, a balding man with a round, happy face. I wondered how anyone could be happy after having cut up thousands of human bodies in various stages of decay. I liked him. I thought he told it as he saw it and had no hound in the hunt.

He testified he inventoried the contents of Beverly's pants pockets: thirty-two cents (two dimes, two nickels, two pennies), along with three keys. In the left pocket of her blouse were five packages of Great Western sugar. In her right pocket was some cellophane with a paper clip through it, the cellophane appearing to be a label off of a vanilla bottle. I recite these apparent irrelevancies because we can tell something about a person by what the person has or fails to have in his or her pockets. She had no medicine in her pockets, not even an aspirin. No comb, no lipstick, no perfume—she was there to work. And the keys? What door did they unlock? No one knew or had tried to find out.

Dr. Thorpen testified Beverly had been stabbed five times with a blade at least four inches long and at least an inch wide. The first wound was in the upper left shoulder; the second through the ribs and into the left lung; the third through the front of the third rib and completely through the heart; the fourth extending into the liver and showed some twisting of the knife blade; the fifth into the right abdominal wall, cutting the many loops of the small and large intestines. It was a gaping wound through which a portion of the large bowel was protruding.

All the wounds, except the wound through the heart, were inflicted with the cutting edge of the knife *down*. The wound through the heart was the opposite—the cutting edge of the knife *up*. Respecting the first four wounds, the knife was held like a sword, the cutting edge down. But when the killer struck her from the back, resulting in the wound through the heart, the knife traveled in a downward arc until the cutting edge ended up. The doctor could not say in what order the wounds were inflicted.

Beverly Bright had been beaten, the doctor said. There were horizontal streaks of blood on her glasses and blood on her nose. Might we not agree that someone was at least marginally upset with the woman? But nobody had ever heard Albert raise his voice to anyone.

My cross-examination of Thorpen was of an honest witness who readily admitted that he'd heard other witnesses discuss the facts of their testimony at meals and in Tschirgi's motel room. Thorpen said the blood splatters on the wall, waist high, were from "many different directions." And he said the assault against her occurred at more than one location.

As for the knife: the top, noncutting edge was flat or rounded. Hilt marks were left by the knife on several of the wounds; the hilt was likely longer at the knife's bottom than its top.

Thorpen thought the wounds were consistent with Beverly having been first beaten and then stabbed to death. He said that the injury to the back of her head was consistent with a larger man pounding the woman's head into the wall. Perhaps, he speculated, at some point the assailant was on top of the victim on the floor just inside the gym at the doorway, where the doctor observed that the blood on the floor was smeared.

Thorpen had come to the scene before the body was taken to the mortuary. He'd found her body lying facedown in a heap. He thought the body had been moved before he got there. He thought that the urine pattern on her clothes from involuntary voiding after death was consistent with the corpse lying on its back.

The marks and splatters of blood told him there was "an element of pursuit and assault." The bloody handprint on the wall was six or seven inches long, about the same size as Thorpen's hand, not the more diminutive hand of Albert.

I asked the doctor:

Q: Did Mr. Tschirgi ever sit down with you along with all the exhibits and facts and ask you to give him a blow-by-blow reconstruction?

A: No, sir. Not as such.

Q: Considering the frenzied, furious, violent, willful stabbing and beating, the assailant must have been filled with hate and anger?

A: Yes.

Q: Something had to motivate such a killer?

A: Yes.

Q: You have told us that the food in Beverly Bright's stomach was not completely digested?

A: Yes.

Q: She ate at about 5:00 P.M. but was alive yet at 8:00 P.M., probably later. That would be at least three hours during which her food had not digested?

A: Yes.

Q: An emotional upset can stop food from digesting?

A: Yes.

Q: The facts here are consistent with the deceased suffering an emotional upset?

A: Yes.

Q: Were you ever told that Beverly Bright had a telephone call at six thirty that evening?

A: No.

Q: Would you have wanted to know what the call was about?

A: Yes, sir. That would be significant.

*J*udy Peabody, Tschirgi's next witness, testified about the knife. She'd purchased it with state funds and kept it hidden in the back of the center drawer in her desk. She got worried that it might have been the murder weapon, especially since Albert cleaned her room. She went to her desk with her husband and another witness, opened the drawer, and, praise all saints, there was her knife, and it was along the side of the drawer, not the back. (She forgot that she told Mike Johnson, our investigator, "When I would open and shut the drawer, the knife would come forward, and I would each time shove it back.")

She told the jury that the last time she used the knife was in October of 1975—used it to cut up potatoes on a camping trip, washed it, and returned it to the drawer. When she and her husband and the witness retrieved the knife, it had moisture on the blade, along with lint, she said. She called Peewee, who immediately sent the knife to the state lab. The report that came back claimed the knife had human blood on it, but in such a minute amount that it couldn't be typed. No fingerprints. My cross-examination was fitted to a lady who I believed was terrified that the knife she'd bought with state funds and that sat in her desk all these years had become a murder weapon.

> Q: You and I have never discussed your testimony, isn't that true?
> A: Yes.
> Q: You've discussed it with Mr. Tschirgi?
> A: Yes.
> Q: When was the first time?
> A: In Mr. Tschirgi's office in March of '76.

She admitted discussing her testimony with Mr. Tschirgi four more times, most recently that morning.

> Q: Before today, did they [pointing to the prosecutor's table] also give you your statement to read to refresh your memory?
> A: Yes.
> Q: It is merely a one-page statement which you gave in March of '76 to Mr. Tschirgi?
> A: Yes.
> Q: You have reread it at least five times, isn't that true?
> A: Yes.
> Q: Since you've been to Sundance, have you been shown the knife by Mr. Tschirgi?
> A: No.

Inked initials appeared on the knife. I asked:

> Q: You saw no person initial the knife, did you?
> A: No.
> Q: Did the sheriff tell you these were his initials?
> A: No.
> Q: Do you know whose initials these are?
> A: No.
> Q: How can you tell us that this is the knife that came from your drawer?

The witness wouldn't answer the question. Finally she said:

> A: I have no reason to doubt the officers of Fremont County about the knife they initialed.
> Q: Please look at the knife.

She took the knife gingerly into her hands as if it might turn on her suddenly.

> Q: Were these initials on the handle the last time you saw it and before you came here?
> A: No.
> Q: Where did you last see the knife?
> A: In the basement here in the courthouse.
> Q: Is the knife in the same condition as it was on March 8, 1976?
> A: No.
> Q: Then you saw streaks?
> A: Yes.
> Q: Now it is polished and shined?
> A: Yes.
> Q: Did you polish and shine it?
> A: No.
> Q: Who else did you see in the basement here besides Sheriff McDougall?
> A: Chief Campbell.
> Q: That knife was used for camping?
> A: Yes.

Q: It was not under your exclusive control?

A: No. Paul Scott used it. But I know Paul well enough to know he would never let anyone else use the knife. He is so responsible, I know he wouldn't.

Q: But do you know if anyone else used it?

A: No.

Q: How about Mary Morehouse?

A: She used it in 1975 on a camping trip.

Q: Residents from the school were on that camping trip?

A: Yes.

Q: Would you know if a resident cut himself on the knife?

No answer.

She said that when McDougall came for the knife he "just reached in and took it out. And then he removed the knife and looked at the blade and put it in a plastic bag." I wondered: Could anyone take an oath that this was the murder weapon?

*T*hen Tschirgi called the state lab technician, one Richard Dixon, who was trying to explain how the items sent to the state lab were returned to the Lander police—twenty-two items by his records. On cross I had him count the items in the box. There were only eleven. So I was later to refer to his box as "Pandora's box." What evidence was missing, and where had it gone?

*E*ddie and I were running after court again on the high school track. "This track is a metaphor for what goes on in court each day," I said. "We go around and around and cover the same ground over and over and the landscape remains the same."

"Their case is starting to fall apart," Eddie said. "I been watchin' the jurors. They seem like they're with us, Gerry. I been wrong before, but I think they're comin' around."

"How about Number Six?"

"Six and nix," Eddie said, and laughed.

*A*t last Peewee McDougall, sitting next to Tschirgi at the counsel table, took the stand. McDougall was born in Scotland in 1914 and claimed he was born within sight of Edinburgh Castle. After you sorted him out, what you found was a practical man who wanted to get along, then go do some roping with one of his good roping horses. He had that dour countenance—reminded me of Alfred Hitchcock in a cowboy hat and boots. He had a quick smile that put you off guard. But now, when he looked back at me from the witness stand, the smile had retreated.

Peewee was a man driven by a well-concealed intelligence. He had no formal education, but he'd become a champion of common sense. You can see him standing there with his hands hanging by their thumbs from his belt, a big silver cowboy buckle in front, a man in his early sixties who stood about five-seven, broad through the shoulders, little pot belly, but nothing to be ashamed of for a man his age. McDougall, who had a believable way about him, would be Tschirgi's bridge to victory. If Peewee said it, well, it was the by-God truth.

McDougall testified that before he questioned Albert he said to the boy, "I understand you want to talk to me. But I know you want to go to Beverly's funeral first. After that you can come back and talk." Albert went to the funeral and returned to the sheriff's office at about 3:00 P.M. "He came into my office with Chief Campbell. There were questions I wanted to ask him," the sheriff said, "but first I had to advise him of his rights."

Of course.

Then that troublesome word "waiver" came up. McDougall said that Albert didn't know what that meant, and McDougall told him it meant "that he could talk to them now, and that at any time he wanted an attorney he could have one." All nice and clean and innocent as a Girl Scout selling her cookies door to door.

Then McDougall began asking Albert his tricky "What if?" questions:

"What if your prints were on the desk?" He claimed Albert said they must have gotten there when he was cleaning the desk.

"What if we found your prints on her wristwatch?" Albert supposedly said he needed to see what time it was. "Well, didn't you have a watch?" Another of Albert's feeble answers: "I was havin' a hard time gettin' to my watch because the sleeve on my shirt was too tight."

McDougall's next: "What if your prints are on the knife?"

Albert's supposed answer: "I took it out to see how sharp it was." (That answer put us in deep trouble.) I looked at Albert. He was shaking his head no as if a palsy had struck him, his face pale, his hands folded on his lap holding tightly onto each other.

McDougall insisted he had no idea what kind of knife to look for—that is, until Mrs. Peabody came to him and ushered him to her desk, where he reached in and retrieved a knife from her middle desk drawer. Prints on the knife? Not even Peewee's were on the knife, although he'd taken the knife out of the scabbard with a thumb and forefinger at the base of the knife's handle, which was leather, not wood as Mrs. Peabody testified.

The sheriff testified that he asked Albert if they could take his finger-prints. Albert said OK.

Could the sheriff have the clothes he wore that night? Albert said OK.

Could the sheriff search his car? Albert said OK.

Peewee testified that he'd made arrangements for Albert to be "interviewed"—the benign word he used—by a man in Casper, a polygraph operator. And this "interview" was totally up to Albert. "Voluntary" was the next word McDougall used. Albert thought that he should ask his father.

In short, everything the cops did with Albert was copacetic, lawful, and voluntary. He simply up and confessed to killing Beverly Bright—that simple.

I began my cross-examination of Tschirgi's star witness by having Mc-Dougall admit that Albert was shy, looked birdlike, had a soft voice and was sometimes difficult to hear, looked nervous, and smiled a lot when he talked. Although he himself looked hard and tough, McDougall claimed he was open and sensitive to people's fears. He came off like a bull sniffing a rosebud. He admitted people might be frightened of him—especially backward, timid, shy farm boys. He agreed that the murder of Beverly might have been extraordinarily shocking to Albert. It even shocked McDougall. And folks were afraid, he said. They wondered if they were suspects.

Although he'd asked a lot of questions in this murder case, he'd made no notes. Yet he told us word for exact word what Albert said to him. He claimed he was patient with Albert. Yes, he admitted he had a bad left ear. He didn't know how long it had been bad, but he didn't miss a thing when Albert talked to him on March 6, 1976. I asked:

Q: If your left ear was bad you wouldn't know if you missed some-thing, isn't that true?

A: Right.

Q: And sometimes your memory is affected by what others say they recall?

A: Yes.

Q: You especially wanted to solve this murder because you're facing some other unsolved murders in your county, isn't that true?

A: Yes.

He admitted to three as I named them.

Q: You'd better solve this one vicious killing.

A: Yes.

Q: Now, on the ninth of March, five days after the murder, Albert didn't just toddle down to your office on his own accord. *You called* the school to send him down.

A: Yes.

McDougall wasn't happy with where we were headed. His mouth grew sour. The eyes narrowed. He said Albert's story that he was ordered to drag a body down some stairs and mop up the blood and that Albert then escaped from the killer seemed odd. He admitted that Albert, a backward farm boy, was likely afraid when he came to the sheriff's office. Chief of Police Campbell was also there, a man six-one or six-two who weighed two hundred pounds or more. Albert was seated between the two. From where Albert sat he could see the jail and hear the officers on their police radio. Then McDougall shut the door.

Q: Would you say that to be shut in a small room with the door closed surrounded by two big officers might be frightening?

A: Yes, I'd say he'd be frightened. Might depend on your conscience.

Q: Some people get so frightened they get the facts confused.

A: Yes, could have happened.

Q: And when people get confused they come off as guilty?

A: Yes. I've seen that many times.

Q: Don't you know as an officer who has interrogated many people that one of the principal tools of interrogation is *fear*?

A: No, sir.

I waited a long moment, looking from juror to juror.

Q: You tell the suspect what a "tight fix" he's in, isn't that true?

A: Yes.

Q: That makes them afraid?

A: Yes.

Q: You put the knife down on the table in front of him, didn't you? [My guess.]

A: Yes.

Q: You think if you put such a weapon down in front of an innocent farm boy, a suspect in a bloody murder, that that would further frighten him?

A: Yes, sir, it would frighten any farm boy. But not if he was innocent.

Q: You think only the guilty would be frightened?

A: Yes.

Q: Then you showed him a bloody photo of the dead girl. [Another guess.]

A: Yes.

Q: Have you ever had a good friend, and then had someone show you a photo of that person dead and in a pile of blood?

A: No.

Q: As a sensitive person, it would shock you, wouldn't it?

A: Yes.

Q: Some people can take quite a bit of horror, and some can't stand to see a photo of blood, isn't that true?

A: Yes, but Albert wasn't shocked at all.

Q: How do you know that?

A: He never said anything.

Q: And you questioned Albert for more than four hours?

The next morning McDougall was still on the stand. The sheriff admitted they found no motive for Albert to kill Beverly Bright; Albert had no history of violence; he'd never been in any trouble, not even a parking ticket. There was no physical evidence to tie him to the murder. McDougall admitted he'd obtained many confessions through the years. He said he had a recorder and could have recorded everything he said to Albert before they took him to Casper to meet the polygraph operator, but they recorded nothing. He wouldn't admit that statements had been made by the officers to Albert that he wouldn't want a jury to hear.

I asked McDougall:

Q: There were a good number of residents at the school who could have committed this killing.

A: Yes.

Q: And you learned Beverly Bright had a lot of men in her life?

A: Yes.

Q: And there was only one suspect who said anything to you, and that was Albert.

A: Yes.

Q: You wouldn't have put him through all of this if he hadn't come forward, isn't that true?

A: It helped.

Q: Here was a boy who was raised right, and who did what good citizens are taught to do—to come forward and help law enforcement.

A: Yes.

Q: Don't you make room for the possibility that the killer thought that Albert was a resident at the training school: "You drag her down there. You mop the floor. You don't tell anyone or I will kill you." And all the rest.

No answer.

Q: Your mind is made up, isn't it?

A: Yes.

Tschirgi hauled me up to the bench. I was abusing Sheriff McDougall, he said. The judge didn't agree, but Tschirgi's complaint told me I was cutting an unwelcome swath through his case.

Q: Albert told you the man was of medium height and weight with dark hair?

A: Yes.

Q: Did you ever ask the supervisor that night what Albert told him?

A: No.

As for Terry Bright, McDougall did not check out his alibi, didn't search his car, didn't check his clothes, didn't take his prints nor show him the supposed murder weapon, the knife. He admitted that in the killing of a married woman the first person to consider as a likely suspect is the husband. He also admitted that sometimes innocent people confess crimes when they've suffered coercion either physically or psychologically. Then after all of those hours of intense questioning under Sheriff McDougall and Chief Campbell, they sent the boy to the polygraph operator in Casper.

Q: You asked Albert if he didn't want to go to her funeral—it's shocking to go to the funeral of a friend, especially if you're accused of killing her?

A: Yes.

Q: You sent Albert to the funeral before you began your interrogation of him?

A: Yes.

Q: And going to her graveside would be extremely moving?

A: Yes.

Q: You knew her parents were there, weeping, and her little daughter as well.

A: Yes.

Q: That would add a lot of shock and emotion.

A: Yes.

Q: Even if Albert were innocent he'd be in trauma.

A: No he wouldn't.

Q: When he came back you showed him those bloody photos, didn't you?

A: Yes.

Q: And you gave all of the crime scene photos to the Casper polygraph operator, Dovala, isn't that true?

A: We gave him all that we thought would be helpful.

As for his search of Albert's car, McDougall said he glanced at the seats. He was looking for blood. He found no blood, and saw nothing that would lead him to believe the car had been washed. The sheriff didn't look closely in the trunk. He didn't recall if he looked under the seats. He couldn't remember what kind of a car it was, the kind of seats or their color.

Q: But you remember the details of four hours of interrogation of Albert?

A: I don't know what all I talked to him about.

Q: Practically speaking, you were exercising control over Albert.

A: Yes.

Q: One of you in your office said, "You *zapped her* or you *blasted her*," isn't that true?

A: That was said, yes.

Q: So a good deal of what you say Albert said was what you told Albert in the course of your four-hour interrogation of him, isn't that true?

A: Yes.

Q: And what Albert didn't know, he later learned from the Casper guy.

A: Yes.

Q: Have you ever gotten a confession after having lied to an accused about a fact?

A: No.

Q: But what you asked Albert was: "What if your prints are on the knife—what do you say about that?"

A: Yes, I said that. And if I was innocent I would have said, "That's a damn lie."

Q: Your question wasn't exactly a lie, but it implied to Albert that his prints were on the knife. It was a trick question to this boy, wasn't it?

A: No.

McDougall had earlier admitted that there were no fingerprints on Beverly's watch.

Q: It was 7:00 P.M. and you had Albert go with Campbell to be printed, isn't that true?

A: No. It was a little after five thirty.

I read to him from a transcript of his testimony at a motion hearing in which McDougall had earlier said it was 7:00 P.M. when Albert was printed, and that the printing took fifteen minutes.

A: Well, that's the way it reads.

Q: That's the way it *was*.

A: Well, I'm wrong on that.

Q: You knew Albert was not experienced in the law.

A: Yes.

Q: And the best way for him to protect his rights was for him to have a lawyer.

A: Yes.

The scowling old devil. A part of myself kept prodding me to remember that I liked him. Couldn't help it. He was tough, but not in-your-face tough. He was honest according to his own code and abided by it, the niceties of the law notwithstanding. I never thought Peewee was overly burdened with compassion. He called the drunks "pukes," and the Indians "warwhoops." His understanding of those whose experiences were different than his was nearly nonexistent. I thought Albert was one of those.

He admitted that if Albert had been his son he probably would have gotten him an attorney. The public defender had his office in the same building in which McDougall and Campbell were interrogating Albert. McDougall insisted he told Albert he'd be *questioned* by another police officer in Casper. But I called his attention to his earlier words at one of the motion hearings. Then he testified that he told Albert he would be *interviewed*. The power of words.

I drew McDougall's attention to Campbell's statement that he thought Albert looked confused. McDougall argued back, "I didn't think he was confused, but I wouldn't deny that Campbell said that." He said that he knew Albert desperately wanted to prove his innocence, so since they hadn't gotten a confession they took him to someone who was good at getting confessions. McDougall told Albert he could prove his innocence there. *Prove* his innocence? In America? My best memory is that in America the state must prove your guilt. And beyond a reasonable doubt.

Q: Didn't Albert's father ask you, "Shouldn't I get an attorney for Albert?"

A: Yes.

Q: You knew that Mr. Hancock was a poor rancher?

A: Yes.

Q: And that their son was the most important thing in the world to them?

A: Probably.

Q: You wanted the Hancocks to trust you?

A: Yes.

Q: You suggested to the Hancocks that Albert talk to Mr. Tschirgi?

A: Yes.

Q: But you also knew that the prosecutor wouldn't help them.

No answer.

Q: You never told them about the availability of a public defender in the same building?

A: No.

Q: And all the way home from Casper, a two-hour trip, Chief Campbell and you had that secret tape recorder that was sometimes turned on and sometimes turned off, isn't that true?

A: I was driving. I don't know what Campbell was doing. He was in the back seat. Albert was in the front seat next to me.

Q: You didn't tell Albert or his parents that the man who was going to "interview" Albert in Casper, this Dovala person, had special psychological training, did you?

A: I didn't tell them that.

Q: As for the word "interview": One is interviewed for a job, isn't that true?

A: Yes.

Q: And later Albert asked you if what he told the poly operator in Casper would keep him from being hired as a police officer?

A: Yes.

Q: Do you think Albert's question showed Albert had a clear understanding of what was happening?

A: Well . . .

Q: Wouldn't a straight answer from you be "That *was* strange. You bet, I thought he was confused"?

A: No, sir.

Q: Don't you think that the Casper poly operator, Dovala, was a hundred percent effective in breaking the boy down with his psychological expertise?

A: No.

Q: But you sent him there to get a confession, not to be interviewed, isn't that true?

He didn't answer. I didn't push him. The jury knew the answer. McDougall admitted he saw Beverly Bright's purse. But he didn't see the money in it. Didn't go through her billfold. Didn't see her coat. As a matter of fact, he saw nothing in her little office. Whatever evidence was there that might point to the killer was lost.

The sheriff hadn't gathered Albert's school records. They were exemplary. He was in the National Guard and had security clearance, but Mc-Dougall hadn't checked his records. Nor did he check with any of Albert's teachers, his 4-H leaders—no one.

Q: You never checked Terry Bright's fingerprints.
A: No, I didn't.
Q: Billy Kane, Beverly Bright's father, came to you and told you he didn't believe that Albert did it.
A: Yes.
Q: Mr. Kane even told you he went to the state cops and asked them to do something?
A: Yes.
Q: Don't you think that in all fairness you should go back to Fremont County and complete your investigation?
A: I figger it is complete.
Q: You thought so when you got Albert's confession, isn't that true?
A: Yes.
Q: What would you do for him if you found he was innocent?
A: I would do what I could for him.

Again I stayed with Albert after court adjourned. I wanted to reassure him.
"Are you afraid, Albert?"
He didn't answer.
"You know, Albert, before they get you they have to kill me with an ax."
Suddenly he stiffened in panic.
"That's just an expression, Albert. Nobody is going to kill anyone. Not you and not me."
"I didn't do it, Mr. Spence. Sheriff said I did." He looked at me as if I should understand.

It was no surprise when Arnold Tschirgi called to the stand the Casper polygraph operator, David Dovala. In Casper, and alone, Albert had been ushered into Dovala's small office. Dovala assured the jury that he had advised the boy of his rights. That terrible machine men have manufactured to catch liars when they know the machine itself lies, the infamous polygraph, sat on a stand in front of Albert, waiting for its next victim.

Dovala was a tall man, six-three, and weighed a couple of hundred pounds or more. He claimed that after he administered Albert his rights he asked, "Do you wish to talk to me now?" and Albert said he did. Why not? This was the man to whom McDougall had sent Albert so that the boy could prove his innocence.

> Q: (Tschirgi) What happened after the two of you sat down in your office?
>
> A: (Dovala) I asked him questions and he answered them. The tape was given to my secretary, and she typed up the confession.
>
> Q: Then what happened?
>
> A: I had him read it, he signed it, and it was witnessed by both Sheriff McDougall and Chief of Police Campbell.
>
> Q: Were his parents there *after* he signed it?
>
> A: Yes. His father said the only reason he signed it was because he was pressured. I said to Albert, "Albert, you are twenty years old now. You might as well be a man." Then Albert said, "I did it."

Dovala testified he didn't threaten Albert and offered no inducements or promises. He treated him kindly and sympathized with him. He saw no evidence of fear, no emotion, although he was emotionally withdrawn; he saw no remorse. Albert was alert and understood, Dovala said.

> Q: (TSCHIRGI) What was your method of interrogation?
>
> A: I sat in a quiet room and just talked casually, treating him with respect. I said he should get it off his chest and tell the whole truth.
>
> Q: Did you ask him to write out his confession?
>
> A: He said he didn't know what to write. He seemed to freeze. He clammed up.
>
> Q: So you recorded what he had to say?
>
> A: Yes, but he didn't speak as freely after the recorder started as he did before.

Tschirgi offered the so-called confession into evidence over my objections. It was allowed by Judge Liamos.

Dovala read it to the jury.

The jury was enraptured. Some looked sternly at Dovala. Some glanced from time to time to see how Albert reacted. Albert sat there and blinked.

And blinked.

Dovala, reading from the confession:

"Where did you get the knife from that you used?"

"I don't know, really."

"Was it your knife, or what?"

"No."

"What kind of knife was it?"

"A hunting knife, I guess."

"A hunting knife. Does it—was it a folding knife or one that, uh . . ."

"It was in a scabbard."

"Did you take it to work with you or what?"

"No."

"Do you have it home now?"

"No."

"Do you know what happened to the knife?"

"I musta dropped it someplace."

"I just want you to tell me what happened."

Albert started speaking, but the recording device supposedly failed for a while. Blank spaces in the transcription . . . What was omitted no one will ever know. It picked up again with Albert saying, *"And I helped her."* Then more blanks. Finally Albert said, *"It didn't make any sense, it just felt like a Dr. Jekyll and Mr. Hyde."*

Albert said in the supposed confession that he and Beverly Bright had not been arguing. He didn't know if he stabbed her more than once. He didn't know, but he must have dragged her downstairs. He guessed he took the mop and mopped up the blood. He did not sexually assault her.

He denied trying to cover things up by saying he saw someone running. He did see someone. Dovala told him that that person didn't have anything to do with the killing, and Albert said, "I don't think so."

When he was shown a picture of a bloody handprint and asked if it could be his, his answer again was not recorded—*"unintelligible."* Albert said he didn't touch her. Didn't get his hands bloody. He saw the mop in a photo and said it was the mop he used to clean up. He didn't know if she was alive when he left her.

Dovala read where she ran into the gym and she asked, "What's the matter with you?" He didn't know where he stabbed her. Dovala suggested she then fell down, and Albert agreed.

Next Dovala asked Albert, "And then you dragged her down the stairs where they found her? Is that where [more *inaudibles*] initially true?" Who knows what that question was about? But Albert's answer was also inaudible.

"Have you ever done anything like this before?"

"No," Albert answered.

And that was a confession to a murder? A killer who had stabbed a woman five times with a large hunting knife and doesn't know if he stabbed her more than once, and doesn't know what happened to the knife or where it came from; a killer who dragged her body down the stairs leaving a massive, bloody trail and can't confirm the basic facts of the murder, except what he was told.

I began my cross-examination. Dovala admitted he had some psychological training and put it to use employing his own techniques. He said McDougall and Campbell provided him a set of facts. I found myself wondering: Wouldn't Dovala have to give both McDougall and Campbell a lie detector test as well if Dovala was to rely on the facts they fed him? Where does truth telling begin?

Q: If the sheriff told you incorrect information, then you may have proceeded incorrectly, too.

A: Yes.

Q: How many times prior to today have you talked with Mr. McDougall about this case?

A: Don't know. [I let that answer go.]

Q: How many times to Chief Campbell?

A: Don't know. [I let that answer go.]

Q: How many times to Mr. Tschirgi?

A: Don't know. [I let that answer go.]

His cumulative insistence that he didn't know how many times he'd spoken to McDougall and Campbell or even Tschirgi about the case was met with my I-can't-believe-it raising of my eyebrows. What was he hiding?

Q: Did you talk to Mr. Tschirgi today?

A: Yes.

Dovala had identified eight photos that he showed Albert. Death, blood, horror.

Q: So did you induce Albert to give this confession?

A: No.

Q: What does "induce" mean?

He threw his head back and looked up at the ceiling.

A: It means, "To get someone to do something."

Q: Would this be a better definition: "To offer something to someone to do something"?

He nodded yes.

Q: We are not all motivated by the same inducements, isn't that true?

A: Yes.

Q: You are not afraid of me?

A: No.

Q: Some people are afraid of police officers?

A: Yes.

Q: And such fear varies from person to person?

A: Yes.

Q: You have heard of people being brainwashed?

A: Yes.

Q: Have you heard of persons who have given false confessions?

A: Yes.

Q: Albert was under stress when you interviewed him, and you knew it?

A: Yes.

Q: No way to measure accurately the amount of stress he was under?

A: No.

Q: You are under stress right now?

A: Yes.

Q: And tolerance to stress varies from person to person?

A: Yes.

Q: You work with streetwise criminals?

A: Yes.

Q: Albert wasn't a streetwise criminal, was he?

A: No.

Q: You saw Albert as timid and shy?

A: No.

Q: Would it take more stress to break a streetwise criminal than Albert?

A: Yes.

Q: You needed Albert's trust and tried to get it?

A: Yes.

Q: You talked down or minimized the crime of murder, isn't that true?

A: Yes.

Q: Part of your procedure is to minimize the crime and to get the subject to trust you, isn't that true?

A: Yes.

Q: Did you know that officers McDougall and Campbell talked with Albert about his wanting to be a police officer?

A: Yes.

Q: Would it be an inducement to ask Albert to clear this up in order to get a job in law enforcement?

A: Yes, it could be. But I didn't offer that inducement.

Q: He told you about a man running outside by the building?

A: No. He told me several different stories during the interview.

Q: He did tell you he didn't kill Beverly Bright, didn't he?

A: Yes.

Q: His parents weren't present when he signed the confession?

A: No.

Q: Only you, Albert, and the machine were present?

A: Yes.

Q: And he was scared?

A: Yes.

Dovala admitted he might have used double questions on Albert—trick questions. Here's one such question from Dovala to Albert: "Did she run into the gym *after you stabbed her*?" His answer either yes or no to this question agrees that he stabbed her. Another of Dovala's trick questions: "Is this an accurate picture of *how she was left*?" Either yes or no assumes he knew how she was left.

Q: You tried to ask him fair questions?

A: Yes.

Q: But you asked him, "Where were you standing when you stabbed her?"

He didn't answer.

Q: And when you asked him to write out his confession he said, "I wouldn't know what to write," isn't that true?

A: Yes.

Q: Have you ever seen persons so frightened that they cried, lost control, so frightened that they even wet their pants?

He nodded yes.

Q: Did you hold out to him that you might be one to help him?

A: It might appear that way.

Q: You didn't tell him you were questioning him as a favor for McDougall?

A: No.

Q: Did Albert know your purpose was to get a confession?

A: I don't know.

Q: Didn't you tell him he could go home if he answered your questions?

A: No.

Q: Did you tell him you were a disinterested person?

A: Could be, but I was.

Q: Did you tell him you were a police officer?

A: I introduced myself as a police officer.

I looked at the words on the so-called confession again. Did the author lower his voice, smile, raise an eyebrow, look threatening? Dead words on a page cannot tell how the words were said.

Albert was in that little room with Dovala for three hours. I could maybe read the Book of Genesis in three hours. Probably be a better person if I had. Thinking of Albert, one can grow old in three hours.

I asked Dovala:

Q: Did Albert ever get out of that room until he signed the confession?

A: No.

Q: Did the sheriff tell you they found a print on her watch?

A: Yes.

Yes?

Q: You believed him?

A: Yes.

Yes?

Q: You called this to the defendant's attention?

A: May have.

I'd prepared many hours for this cross-examination. The last question about the print on the watch had never crossed my mind. Sometimes when the mind is open, truth sneaks in.

Had the sheriff lied to Dovala when he told him they found a print on the watch? I took a quick glance over at Eddie. He looked sad. Tschirgi was strangely silent and immobile. A lie at the heart of a case often destroys the case. The jury knew that McDougall had already testified there were no prints on Beverly Bright's watch. I looked over at the jury and let silence underline Dovala's crucial admission. Then I continued:

Q: You told Albert he'd be better off if he confessed?

A: No. I told him he would feel better if he told the truth.

Q: Did you tell him that no one would believe his story?

A: I don't know.

My cross-examination was beginning to cause the borders of Dovala's voice to vibrate in approaching anger. One wondered how Albert would have reacted to that sound, alone in Dovala's office for three hours and bundled in his own blanket of fear. I looked over at Albert. He was staring at the floor, and his mother was holding his hand.

Dovala admitted that despite his best effort he was unable to find a motive for the murder.

I turned back to the confession.

Q: In several places you talk about "the stabbing." Did Albert ever once say, "I stabbed her" or "I killed her"?

A: No, sir.

Q: These were *your* words.

He nodded.

Q: You say, Officer Dovala, that everything that Albert said to you was in that confession.

A: Yes.

Q: And you said that Albert told you he got the knife from a desk drawer in the Administration Building?

A: Yes.

Q: Show me where that's in his confession.

A: It doesn't appear in the confession.

*T*he next morning, Dave Dovala was still on the stand. I said, "There wasn't any way for Albert to prove what was or wasn't said." This veteran police officer turned to the jury and said, "*You can put him on the stand.*"

I immediately moved for a mistrial.

We bounded into the judge's chambers. The sound level of the arguments there could have punctured a sturdy ceiling. I told the judge in low English that this was an experienced police officer who knew full well that Albert was not required to take the stand, that Dovala had, in open court, in front of this jury, violated Albert's constitutional rights and made a mockery of His Honor's attempt to preserve his right to a fair trial. I am told I threw my pen. It was not aimed at the judge, but it went flying across the judge's desk.

Tschirgi offered to talk to his witness and get it straightened out. The judge said, "Well, let's see if you can."

I thought it better to have Dovala confess to the jury that he'd made a grave mistake rather than have the judge give one of his perfunctory instructions. Once an important witness for the state admits error, the foundation of the state's case begins to expose more ominous cracks. During the recess Tschirgi talked to Dovala, after which I began my cross-examination anew.

Q: Do you remember what you said to the jury about how Albert could *prove* what he actually said to you?

A: Yes. I am sorry I said that. It was an error on my part. What I said was a mistake.

Q: You know that Albert has no duty to *prove* anything in this case?

A: Yes.

Q: It is your duty to fairly and accurately record what was said during your interview, not his.

A: Yes.

Q: And you only recorded what you wanted to record, isn't that true?

A: Yes.

Q: And when you talked to Albert he didn't have an attorney there, did he?

A: No.

Q: No attorney to bring out his side or to ask his questions.

A: No.

Q: But he told you he was scared and someone else had killed her?

A: Yes.

Q: And you told him that wasn't true.

A: Yes.

Q: You knew or have heard how afraid Albert was that he'd be killed by this man, the murderer?

A: I read that in the newspaper.

Q: Don't you think you should have better information than newspaper information before you pass judgment on the guilt of another?

No answer.

Q: Did you ever interview Terry Bright?

A: No.

Q: Would you have interviewed him if you'd been asked to by Sheriff McDougall or Chief Campbell?

A: Yes.

Dovala was excused. He walked from the witness stand without looking at the jury, or any of us. The bailiff opened the door for him. I looked over at Tschirgi. Had the sparrow somehow escaped the hawk?

Tschirgi rested his case.

I made the standard motion for a dismissal of the charges—insufficient evidence to sustain the prosecutor's case. My motion was denied in the standard way with the standard comment by the judge: The jury should decide. I called Sheriff McDougall back to the stand. Good place to start—a quick, frontal attack on the enemy.

I asked McDougall if after having heard all of the testimony in the case he had reopened his investigation. McDougall gave me a someday-I-will-catch-you-behind-the-barn look. His answer was no. "I have no further questions of the sheriff," I said, and dismissed him.

I called Dan Brown of Hudson, who said he lived about a quarter of a mile from the Brights on the same dead-end street. On the night of the murder he saw a car leave the Brights' residence at about ten or eleven. He couldn't see who was driving. I asked if the sheriff had ever talked to him. No, he said.

In my opinion John Kenyon could be considered a viable suspect—his explosive temper and their recent affair. I called Henrietta June West, Beverly Bright's best friend.

Q: Did you know about her affair with Mr. Kenyon?

A: Yes, she said she had always loved him, and she believed that a woman could only have one true love during her life, and he had been her one true love. She said they had drifted apart after high school, but when he came to Lander on a construction job at the school they found each other again. She broke off her affair just before her murder. She had a good husband and loved her child and was going to stay home.

She said that the night of the murder Beverly had wanted to talk to her alone. Beverly was nervous and fidgety, but before they could talk they had to go back to work.

But Kenyon had all his fingers!

As Henrietta June West was testifying, some of the jurors kept watching McDougall for his reaction. Why had this testimony been kept from them? Tschirgi didn't cross-examine the woman.

*T*he time had come for us to call Dr. Robert Fairbairn, our psychiatric expert. He was a tall, middle-aged man with a full head of gray hair, slender and elegant in his appearance. He looked from one juror to another as he answered my questions in a quiet voice and with the style and poise of an expert.

He told how he had interviewed Albert under sodium amytal, not once but twice, during the two weeks that he studied him in a Denver psychiatric hospital. That drug, when given by an intravenous drip, is reputed to act as a sort of truth serum, which is to say that one under the drug will often relate information that he or she would have otherwise blocked.

Dr. Fairbairn told the jury the story Albert related to him under the influence of the drug. It was the same story Albert told Buck Rogers two years before we got into the case—about the large dark man with a knife who commanded Albert to drag the body down the stairs, hide it, and mop up the blood. Dr. Fairbairn believed that Albert had been intimidated into making a confession, that the confession was not given voluntarily, and that Albert failed to understand its gravity.

I asked the doctor:

> Q: How do you explain that Albert agreed to this so-called confession?
>
> A: Albert is the kind of person who says things to placate those in authority.

He described Albert as childlike, immature, frightened, unable to cope, and socially inept. The doctor said, "I wasn't surprised that the murderer didn't kill Albert as well." He said he had administered sodium amytal to Albert because I, his attorney, had been doubtful of Albert's story. The doctor said he believed Albert, and to settle the matter he wanted to see how he would react under the drug. As a result of his interview of Albert while he was under the influence of sodium amytal, he was convinced that Albert was telling the truth.

Tschirgi cross-examined and began by wrestling with the doctor on what was opinion versus fact. "Do you leave room for the possibility that your opinion is wrong?"

Dr. Fairbairn replied, "Yes. The problem chronically exists. I use the words 'I think,' or 'I believe,' or 'Usually.'"

I had never heard an expert say it as honestly. Most often they say their opinion is the all-be-damned truth, and if you don't like it you are an ignorant jack handle.

I watched Dr. Fairbairn walk from the courtroom. Had he saved Albert, or was he seen by the jurors as one of those quack doctors who think they can fool a person with their fancy talk?

It was decision time again. We dared not put Albert on the stand. In his state he'd be unable to understand the implication of the questions put to him, and helpless to convince twelve people of anything except that he was incompetent as a witness. Dr. Fairbairn's testimony put Albert's story clearly before the jury without Albert having to utter a word. Through his testimony the doctor had become Albert.

It had been hard for me to get close to Albert. It was easier for me to care about his parents, especially his mother. I've always preached you have to love your client. Sometimes that's a very big order. But if you don't have genuine feelings for your client, you can't ask the jury to do what you can't do—to care for your client.

Dr. Fairbairn had revealed Albert Hancock to me in a way that permitted me to better understand him. Here was a frightened, naïve farm boy who had single-handedly fought off big, tough cops for hours on end, and who at last said words that taken together fell short of an understandable confession of murder.

"Is it time?" I asked Eddie.

He nodded yes. I announced, "The defense rests." There would be no more witnesses, no going back.

But Tschirgi wasn't done. As we've learned here, the state has the right to the last word. Tschirgi called a witness who swore that Kenyon had been at a Masonic Lodge meeting in Shoshone between 7:10 P.M. and 9:15 P.M. on the night of the murder. Kenyon couldn't have traveled the forty-five miles to Lander in time for the murder, which was committed between 6:45 P.M. and 8:00 P.M. But why hadn't Tschirgi called Kenyon himself to testify to his whereabouts? Was he afraid that under my cross-examination Kenyon might explode, and if he did I could argue to the jury that they'd witnessed the same untamed rage that Beverly Bright had faced the night of her murder?

After that, Tschirgi rested his case.

Arguments on the judge's instructions to the jury took all day. Eddie took the lead. The judge ended up giving his standard instructions in a murder case: The state would be required to prove Albert Hancock's guilt beyond a reasonable doubt. The accused had no duty to prove his innocence. Albert Hancock was presumed innocent. The jury would decide what witnesses were or weren't credible—and the confession must be voluntary.

The following day was the Fourth of July. How was it that Madam Fate, still laughing at her own little jokes, arranged things so that the final arguments in this case, in Sundance, Wyoming, for the murder of Black Sundance, and in Crook County, should take place on the Fourth of July?

Arnold Tschirgi came marching into court decked out in a white suit, a red and white polka-dot shirt, and a blue tie. I objected to his costume in chambers. Tschirgi said, "Isn't it patriotic to convict murderers on the Fourth of July?"

I saw the judge parcel out one of his rare distant chuckles. He pretended to thumb through his rule book. "I know of no rules that dictate the color of the prosecutor's garb. The only requirement here is that the lawyers dress appropriately, which includes a coat and tie. This is the Fourth of July. I hold that red, white, and blue are appropriate."

Tschirgi had Terry Bright seated in the courtroom with his little seven-year-old daughter. I asked the court to exclude the man and his child, who were "hate props." The judge agreed that the child should be removed. "I don't want her, at her tender age, hearing statements about her mother," Judge Liamos said.

Then Tschirgi walked up to the podium with a pretty box, about the size of two shoe boxes. It was wrapped in bright paper with a big ribbon around it. I knew what was coming. I'd used the prop years before when Tschirgi was my deputy. As is said, "What goes around comes around."

"This is more of Mr. Tschirgi's theatrics and another improper prop," I argued at the bench.

"What do you intend to do with the exhibit, Mr. Tschirgi?" the judge asked. The jury was still waiting in the jury room.

"I'm going to show that this box is the defense in the case. When you take the pretty wrapping and ribbon off of the box and open the box, there's nothing inside."

"No," the judge said. "*You* have the burden of proof. The defense isn't required to put anything inside the box. You're not going to use that. Let's see if we can keep to the law."

Arnold Tschirgi began his final argument by gifting the jurors with that bashful, faint smile of his and quietly acknowledged that the jurors had been delayed in their haying and housework because of this trial. He thanked them for sticking it out—doing their duty—in this, the longest criminal trial in Wyoming's history: seven weeks.

Then, like any good storyteller, Tschirgi set about to cast the characters in this drama. There were decent citizens who were mercilessly attacked by me, the defense attorney, as well as competent law enforcement men who, despite my shameful assaults against them, did not stray from their duty. He was the underdog, thrown into this fight against "that world-famous lawyer, Gerry Spence. He is a man who can say anything and make people believe anything. He is a master at ripping honest witnesses apart, in turning their innocent efforts to tell the truth into something ugly. We have listened to seven weeks of it, and we have had quite enough!"

He caught his breath. "But let us not forget the most important survivors of this tragedy—the victims in this case." In an ever-rising voice he asked, "Doesn't the victim's family have any rights? Ask Albert Hancock over there if they had rights." The prosecutor's accusatory finger was shaking in a palsy of anger at Albert, who huddled between his father and mother as frozen as a corpse. "He gave no warning to his friend Beverly Bright, and suddenly turned on her and *blasted* her." Tschirgi's voice elevated into an exploding nasal scream. I felt myself jump.

"Here the victim was put on trial. Her lips were sealed by his bloody knife. She could not speak out in her own defense. And her mourning family have also been put on trial. *And he blasted her!*" he shouted again.

"Have you ever met Beverly Bright?" Tschirgi pulled an empty chair up in front of the jury and began talking to it as if Beverly Bright were seated in it. "Terry says you two have been married eight years. You are attractive, outdoorish, you laugh and talk to people. You like people and are flirtatious. You were last seen alive at 6:30 P.M. on March 5, 1976. The world-renowned defense attorney in his inimitable style tried to break down your husband, Terry Bright, and failed. He couldn't crack Terry. But

Albert Hancock, sitting over there, confessed to your murder. He made his confession to a mild-mannered police officer, Dave Dovala. Justice for your cruel, untimely death will finally come to you and your family."

Tschirgi set a roll of wrapping paper on the lectern, paper about a foot wide and perhaps forty or fifty feet long. He'd written his argument on that scroll in two-inch letters with an ink marker so that as he made his arguments he pushed the paper forward, and it piled up on the floor in front of his lectern creating a physical reminder of the immense factual basis for his case—an argument fifty feet in length. Maybe more. If he'd made the letters even larger, his argument could have encompassed a hundred feet. But I ought not be critical, because Tschirgi had seen me use that device more than a decade before when I was a young prosecutor experimenting with various techniques I'd been inventing for final argument. I tried to look calm.

Then Tschirgi jumped up to the witness stand, sat down, and took on the role of Dr. Fairbairn. He stared out at the jury with a glass of water clutched in his hand and, with elegant exaggeration, began taking rapid sips from the glass. "He was the driest man I've ever seen in a courtroom," Tschirgi said. "He drank more water than all the other witnesses combined. We see that in people under tension, or who lie. The dry-mouthed head-doctor, Dr. F." Tschirgi was beginning to shout again. "He failed, flopped, flunked, fizzled, and he's full of it." No one smiled. Several of the women in the front row watched the prosecutor with growing signs of alarm.

"That is the killer of an innocent woman," Tschirgi cried. He turned to Albert. "He sits in this court begging that you not believe him. 'Do not believe me when I say I just turned on her and *blasted* her. I am a liar. Believe me now, but not then.' What more is there to say? Do we set this liar free? I am asking you to do your duty, to keep us safe, to convict Albert Hancock of the murder he committed on an innocent woman and to thereby set us all free."

I felt the power of the prosecutor's words. Had it been that clear from the beginning? His words came through mightily, and their volume could have caused the courtroom structure itself to shudder.

How would I be able to convince a jury of twelve intelligent citizens that this strange story of Albert's was true? Was Dr. Fairbairn's testimony enough?

I fought the ever-returning, overpowering, chronic fear—that one day I'd watch some cop with a wooden heart slap the shackles on my client and haul him off to the penitentiary, in Albert's case, an innocent kid, as helpless as a side of beef in the butcher shop. I had kids of my own, and whenever I saw a kid having fun, or accomplishing things that made his parents proud, I would think of Albert, helpless, in that concrete hole, and I would know that had I worked harder and been smarter he might be free.

I had to convince nine women and three men that they were being asked by a good man, the prosecutor, to do something wrong—to convict an innocent boy. Two of the women came into the courtroom wearing sunglasses. Had they already decided to convict Albert and needed their sunglasses to cover their tears? Number Six had gazed at Tschirgi like a doting mother watching her son play his first solo on his trumpet.

It was my time to argue. Attack. But the attack had to be effective and lasting. I had often said that if a criminal defense attorney hadn't won his case by the time of his final argument it was too late. I pushed back ominous words that kept creeping in:

You're due to lose.

If one is prone to give advice, as I confess I am, it was time to give advice to myself. "You're a criminal defense attorney. A true warrior supposedly has no fear. He inspires fear in his opponent." As always, and thankfully, ancient genes began creeping in to convert fear into the mind-set of the warrior. I was afraid, but in my mind's ear I heard the echo of my promise to Albert: "Before they get you they'll have to kill me with an ax."

I began slowly in a quiet expression of genuine sorrow. "Yes, victims have rights," I said. "What kind of satisfaction would the Brights enjoy by convicting Albert? What kindness do we show a grieving family by adding to their grief—that in their names, Albert has also been sacrificed? Is there no end to this nightmare?" I waited for the jurors' silent answer.

"Mr. Prosecutor asks you to convict on passion and hate. Is it right for a prosecutor to *use you* as an instrument of hate for the benefit of the sheriff, who needs a conviction but refuses to do the work of competent cops to capture the killer? Worse, the killer will still be at large. Hate is the stuff of lynching. God help us that we are past those shameful, bloody times in this country.

"I want to talk with you about our case without any gimmicks. We don't need empty chairs. We don't need a fifty-foot scroll with our argument printed on it in two-inch letters. We need to just talk plainly and honestly about this tragic human drama we've witnessed together these seven weeks. One thing we must remember: This case is not about either Mr. Tschirgi or me. It is about truth. Where is the truth hiding, and why?

"When a prosecutor doesn't have a case, then all that's left for him is to create fear and hate. And if you hate Albert, Mr. Tschirgi doesn't have to prove his case against Albert. Hate becomes his only case. Mr. Tschirgi is capable of making a fair argument. I've known him to be a fair man. And you are entitled to hear a fair argument.

"His problem is, of course, that the only fact he has is what the cops call a 'confession,' a pathetic piece of paper riddled with blank spaces, a paper that turns out to be nothing more than a scared kid saying what the officers wanted him to say, and even then, as Campbell admitted, Albert never once said he killed Beverly Bright.

"That paper, on its face, shows that Albert didn't know the facts of the case. Where did the knife come from? He didn't know. What did he do with the knife? He didn't know. What kind of a knife was it? He didn't know. 'A hunting knife, I guess.' What did he do after he stabbed her—a beautiful trick question. 'Then you dragged her down the stairs?' His answer is recorded as 'inaudible.' This, with the other blank spaces, is the best that Officer Dovala could get from this boy after three hours alone with him in another one of those small rooms? That pathetic piece of paper along with all of its blanks proved one thing: Albert didn't know what happened except what he learned as he was accused over and over with this murder—first by McDougall and then Campbell for four hours and then Dovala for three. He learned the facts from them.

"If there was a murder with blood everywhere as if it were spread from a lawn sprinkler, shouldn't there be blood on Albert's hands, his clothes, his boots? Shouldn't the police find his fingerprints somewhere at the murder scene?

"But compare the testimony of Sheriff McDougall to that of Dr. Fairbairn. The cops were after a confession—to get it any way they could. Sheriff McDougall sent the boy to the funeral, where he saw grieving parents and family. Probably the only funeral he'd ever been to. What effect does that have on an immature mind such as Albert's? Ask Sheriff McDougall. He knows.

"In Casper he was totally under the control of another cop, Dave Dovala, for those three hours, and interestingly, Dovala neglected to record what he said to Albert and what Albert said to him. Can you imagine a farm boy who never sat still for five minutes in his life being cooped up for three hours in a small room with a cop who never once let him out, not once, who continued to question him without mercy, for three hours, and who failed to record what was said until he thought Albert was ready to talk? Even then the so-called confession is a confession only because the prosecutor calls it one. I will tell you what it is: It is the obliterated track of something that went on in that room, something we will never know, and that Dovala took pains to make sure that we would never know.

"And after that Albert was with McDougall and Campbell for two more hours on his way back to the Lander jail. No lawyer. No parents. No one to protect him. Surrounded by cops. Even his rights were intentionally misrepresented to him. He had as much chance to survive that onslaught as a crippled rabbit thrown into a pack of coyotes. But once he signed that paper, *then* they let him have a lawyer.

"Were they fair to Albert? Have they been fair with you and given you a clean, professional, credible case that you can rely on, a case you can feel comfortable with, one you can accept as true beyond a reasonable doubt so you don't have to stare up at the ceiling at night wondering if you sent an innocent kid off to a life of torture?

"Facts are like a coloring book. The picture that comes out depends on who chooses the crayons. The suspect, Fingers, is at large and uninvestigated? Why didn't the prosecutor bring Kenyon *himself* to tell you where he was that night? Why isn't he here?"

I stopped for a moment to let my argument settle and to begin anew. "Compare Albert's treatment by the police to the treatment he got from Dr. Fairbairn. Albert's stay with Dr. Fairbairn was in a secure, safe hospital. He was treated with respect and kindness. He told Dr. Fairbairn what happened. The doctor put him under truth serum, not once but twice. The same story emerged. The doctor says it is his opinion that Albert was coerced into giving that so-called confession. Can we understand why?" I'd been standing in front of the jury box taking in each juror, one at a time, speaking to each for a sentence or two, being careful to bring each juror into my conversation.

"In this country we're not permitted to do what these officers did to Albert. We are not permitted to tell him falsehoods—that if he waives his rights he can have an attorney. We are not permitted to work him over for hours and then say to a jury that his statement was voluntary. This is America. And this will always be America so long as jurors preserve the rights of the least of us, the rights of the weak and the poor—as long as even the lowly sparrow is counted."

Some lawyers claim they can read jurors. Sometimes I think I can, but

I've been wrong. Perhaps when I saw kindness on their faces they were only being polite. Three jurors had their arms crossed. Bad sign. Were they crossing me out? A couple of jurors kept watching Tschirgi as I argued. When I looked at Number Six she turned her head in obvious disgust.

"His Honor has told you that you are the judge of the credibility of the witnesses. Were Chief Campbell and Sheriff McDougall fair? Did they do their job competently? Or did they take the easy route against a helpless kid? Did they get the truth from Albert, or did they get empty words from a terrorized boy?" I turned again and looked at Albert sitting between his parents. They all looked beaten.

"When I sit down, I will never be permitted to speak to you as a jury again. But as you deliberate you will do a better job in answering Mr. Tschirgi than I could were I permitted to do so. You have twelve good minds and twenty-four good ears. You have heard and understood better than I. And we have a right to trust you and we do.

"I must say something more about Albert. He is a sparrow. And as we know, out in the universe, behind the sun, every sparrow is counted." I turned and pointed to Tschirgi. "The hawk wants the sparrow. He demands the sparrow. Yes." I waited. Then suddenly I said, *"Give the sparrow to the hawk!"* One of the women in the front row, the one wearing sunglasses, shook her head no. No!

I quietly thanked the jury and sat down.

*T*schirgi jumped to his feet for his rebuttal argument. He seemed near the point of explosion, ripping with energy to stomp down, once and for all, the unconscionable sophistry of "that world-famous defense attorney."

"What you heard here was 90 percent lawyer talk from the defense attorney," Tschirgi said in his high, lilting tones. "What you heard was garbage. The murderer was someone else? There's a whole world out there of possible murderers, but only one in the whole world who confessed this killing. Lawyer talk!" He ripped off a sheet from his notebook, crumpled it, and threw it in the wastebasket.

"This was not the right knife?" He held up the knife in evidence and waved it at the jury. "There is a world of knives out there, but only one with human blood on it that came from the desk drawer where Albert cleaned. All the rest is lawyer talk," and he ripped off another sheet from his notepad, crumpled it, and dumped it in the court's wastebasket.

"Blood all over! Splatters everywhere! But none on Albert!" He crumpled page after page representing my argument and threw each with a vengeance in the wastebasket—"lawyer talk." I thought that if ever there was a piece of paper that should be wadded up and thrown in the garbage it was the so-called confession of Albert. But my time to speak to this jury was over. Forever.

Number Six was smiling at me as Tschirgi laid it on. She couldn't keep her eyes off of me. She might hang this jury, and we'd have to struggle through another endless trip into the snake pit. There is no place on the face of this earth more dreadful and helpless than sitting in a chair in a courtroom listening to the prosecutor tear your argument into shreds and being powerless to speak another word in defense. Tschirgi returned once again to his theme. "We don't need to prove anything more. *He blasted her!*"

Finally Tschirgi brought his argument to a close with a thunderous climax. "Do not let this case be decided on the fancy words of a world-famous defense attorney." I should have objected, but I didn't want to emphasize either his argument or my fear of it. "I ask you, each of you, to test your knowledge of the truth here, and once that test has been made, to return your verdict of 'Guilty as charged.' Thank you."

I thanked him to myself, grateful that his argument was over. He'd been a powerful adversary. The jurors marched out quietly to decide their verdict. They'd been dragged through the meat grinder of a jury trial. Did they have the energy to argue a single word for Albert Hancock? The Hancocks walked out of the courtroom with their son. They looked as if they'd just walked a hundred miles carrying their son on their backs. I wanted to rush up to them and say, "I wish I'd done a better job for you."

I turned to Eddie. He looked down and silently busied himself clearing up our table of notes and notebooks. We were finished. It was over. Then he patted me on the back and smiled as if to say, "It'll all be all right."

Tschirgi walked up. "I didn't like the way you treated Peewee," he said, and walked on by.

*I*n the days that followed I never saw a happier, more secure, more confident lawyer with a jury out deliberating his case than Arnold Tschirgi. He was jovial and joking. He even smiled at me and said good morning. I hadn't slept. It's at times like this I remember how to pray. The prayer goes like this:

"Dear Lord, please just let me win this one, and I promise I will never try another case. Never."

In ways, my waiting for a jury's verdict is worse than waiting for the birth of one of my children. There, everything was predicted to come out all right. But not so, waiting for the birth of justice.

Eddie and I went out to the track to run. Run off the pain that feels like a broken cement mixer churning in the belly. We ran harder than usual and were panting.

"You did good," Eddie said.

He was just trying to ease my worry like the loyal friend he'd always been.

"I shoulda—"

"I don't wanna hear any shouldas," Eddie said. "Too late for shouldas."

"Tschirgi is pretty happy," I said. "He must think he won."

"He isn't going to let you know what he really thinks."

The next morning we were all at breakfast, the whole trial contingent, the judge and the reporter at one table, Tschirgi and McDougall at another, Albert and his parents at still another, and Eddie and I sitting in the far back. "Well, Tschirgi and McDougall are sure having a great old time at breakfast this morning," I remarked.

Albert, I thought, actually looked a little happy.

I suffered those same fever dreams I'd suffered as a child when I was sick with the flu. I was fighting echoes and dissolving faces, and arguing about an ocean of insane things I couldn't identify, and I couldn't hear my own voice. I suffer these recurring nightmares for weeks following every trial.

Eddie said he slept all right. But he looked tired. I thought his was the harder role. He had to be a friend to a man who was in chronic anxiety over the case, and, at the same time, he bore his own worries for the case. His insights were often startlingly accurate, and he had more wisdom than his younger age should have provided. He was like a buddy in war who would live or die with you in the same foxhole.

At lunch we met Tschirgi and McDougall coming out the door of the café as we entered. I said, "Arnold, you want to drop the murder charge and take a plea to manslaughter?" I was testing how solid he might be on his case.

He gave me his smile like a kindly father to an errant child. "We came this far. We'd just as well go all the way."

"Well, what if they're hung?"

"We'll do it again." He gave me that smile again.

"Do we want to spend the rest of our lives together?" I asked. I smiled back.

"Can't think of a better way to spend the rest of my life," Tschirgi said. And he laughed.

"Maybe he thinks these rancher types will go for Peewee," I later said to Eddie.

"Maybe they will," Eddie said back. "But you're kinda their type, too. I think most of the mothers liked you, all but Number Six."

I endured a second night of agony and more fever dreams. I can't imagine the hell the Hancocks were suffering. No verdict. Was the jury hung? We were sitting on the steps of the courthouse waiting, waiting. We watched the jurors approaching after their lunch. Eleven were walking together. Number Six was walking behind the group, alone. She looked long in the face.

"Well," Eddie said. "Looks like we might have a hung jury, all right." And the next day after lunch it was the same. Number Six was walking still farther behind, and all alone. The message was clear to me. We had a hung jury.

I'd kept worrying about Albert's parents. If we lost, his mother would surely die. Mothers cannot bear the pain of witnessing the endless torture of their children. And I thought his father would probably die soon thereafter. And Albert would end up as a member of the living dead in that concrete rectum called a prison. If only I could have stood tall and composed and handsome like Gregory Peck in *To Kill a Mockingbird*. "The majority of the jurors are for us," I said to Eddie. "Surely I'm right on that. But sometimes I get fooled."

"We're not wrong," Eddie said. "Number Six has always been against us. And Number Six is against the other eleven. So that means that eleven are for us and one against."

I trusted Eddie. "I wonder how Tschirgi sees it?"

"He and all the rest think they won the case."

"Maybe they're just posturing," I said.

Eddie shrugged his shoulders.

"Let's have a talk with Tschirgi," I said.

We found Tschirgi sitting in the courtroom reading. "I suppose you think you've won the case," I said for starters.

He didn't answer. Just gave me that far-off smile.

"We got ourselves a hung jury. I don't want to try it again," I said. "Maybe we should take a majority verdict and go home. I hear this case has about bankrupted Fremont County, and if we try it again it will for sure. I know it would break us."

He surprised me. "A majority verdict? Well, I'll give it some thought."

"We couldn't do it without Albert's consent," I said.

"Would Albert agree to it?" he asked.

"I don't know," I said. "It would be pretty much up to his parents." A majority verdict in a criminal case when the law requires a unanimous verdict—can the parties agree to change the law? It had never been done in the history of the criminal law so far as I knew.

"His parents will agree if you tell them to," Tschirgi said.

"The judge would have to agree to it. He's probably as tired of this case as we are," I said.

"You want to go talk to the judge?" he asked.

We found the judge sitting in chambers staring out the window. Wearily he asked what pleasure we were about to bestow on him. He tried for a smile. He was a good-natured sort, but I thought he'd seen enough of us. He, too, knew the jury must be hung. He had a card that he kept looking at from time to time when one of the lawyers came charging into his chambers with another motion. The judge held the card up.

"Do you know what this card says?" the judge asked.

Like children we shook our heads no.

He handed it to us. "Here's how I feel about this trial," he said. The card was a drawing of a couple of vultures up in a tree looking down on a living being. One vulture was saying to the other, "Retain your patience." We laughed, as was our duty. Civility is hard to come by waiting for a jury's verdict.

We told him we were thinking about being bound by a majority verdict. "You'll have to get everyone's agreement on the record," he said.

I explained it to Albert and his parents. Albert had a right to a unanimous verdict. If the jury couldn't unanimously agree, the judge would declare a mistrial, and we'd have to try the case all over again with a new jury. We might not be as fortunate the next time as I thought we were now. I told the Hancocks I believed we had a majority with us—how Number Six, who was always against us, hung back from the rest, and how that surely meant that the rest of the jurors were for us.

"We came this far with you, Mr. Spence. We're going all the way. Whatever you say," Mr. Hancock said. I looked at Eddie. He nodded. "Let's do it," I said.

We called in the court reporter. Albert, his parents, Eddie, and I were all present. I explained it to the Hancocks on the court reporter's record: If the majority was for us Albert would go free. If the majority was against us Albert would be sentenced to murder by the judge. We were also giving up our right to an appeal. Albert's parents both agreed on the record. In his small, distant voice Albert agreed as well.

Judge Liamos called us all into chambers—Albert and his folks, Tschirgi, Eddie, and me. We read into the record what I had explained to Albert, but the judge wanted to hear it himself. We were again on the record. The judge was speaking to Albert and his parents.

"Do you understand that if the majority of jurors have voted to convict you, you will be found guilty and I will sentence you the same as if all twelve had found against you?"

Albert nodded.

"You have to say 'yes' or 'no' out loud for the record," the judge said.

"Yes," Albert said.

"Do you understand that you are giving up your right to a unanimous verdict and your right to appeal?"

"Yes."

"And if I find that this jury is hung, we would have to select a new jury and try this entire case over again. Do you understand?"

"Yes."

"And if the case were tried again, you could be found innocent. Do you understand you are giving up all those rights?"

"Yes."

"Mr. Spence and Mr. Tschirgi, you have agreed to this?"

We both said yes.

The judge, as if the gates to his freedom had suddenly been opened said, "Well, folks, I want to congratulate you. This has been a hard-fought case. That you should resolve this case in this manner speaks highly of all concerned." He called for the bailiff. "Bring in the jury," he ordered.

We watched the jury march in. They were tired. They looked over at our table, at me. None smiled. Faces of doom. I thought, "Oh, my God, have we made a mistake?" Then the lady in the front row with the sunglasses gave me a smile. Like a kiss from an angel. And the old rancher at the end of the front row gave me a friendly nod. Number Six turned her head away. *I knew.*

We were waiting for the judge to take the bench. I saw the desperate face of Mrs. Hancock, a mother whose child was in mortal jeopardy and who would live or die in the next few minutes. And she was helpless to save him. I leaned over to the Hancocks and said, "It's all right. It's going to be eleven to one for us."

Then Judge Liamos took the bench. The relief I'd seen on the judge's face just minutes before had vanished. Had he changed his mind? Could he change his mind in the face of our agreement? "Gentlemen," he began, addressing both Tschirgi and me, "I have given this matter further thought." Oh, no! He *had* changed his mind. "I want both of you to know that if either side wishes not to be bound by the agreement you have made, I will set it aside."

He turned to Tschirgi first. "Mr. Tschirgi?"

"I'm all right with it," Tschirgi said in a confident voice.

"Mr. Spence?"

"Yes, Your Honor, we'll be bound by it."

The judge addressed the jurors. "Do you have a foreperson?"

"I'm the foreman," the man in the front row said, the one who had given me a friendly nod.

The judge addressed the foreman. "Mr. Foreman, the parties have agreed to be bound in this case by your majority verdict, whatever it is. Where does this jury stand on the question of the defendant's guilt or innocence?"

"Eleven to one for *not* guilty," the foreman said.

"Do the parties want the jury polled?" the judge asked.

"No," Tschirgi said.

"No," I said.

Mrs. Hancock was hugging first me and then Eddie. Jeff Hancock stood looking dumbstruck. Then he came up to me and said a simple "thank you." He was quiet even in the pandemonium of the courtroom. His eyes said words his lips were frozen against. He shook Eddie's hand. "You were the best," he said to both of us.

"Does this mean I can go?" Albert asked.

I have told the story of this case because it stands for a fundamental proposition: that despite all the safeguards of the criminal law, good men with honorable intentions, men such as McDougall and Campbell and Tschirgi, may be in error, and the system, like a ship tumbled in the tumult of a hurricane, is capable of righting itself.

The case also provides answers as to why the innocent confess to crimes they didn't commit. From the time we were bouncing babes we were taught where to bounce and how. We do as we're told by authority. Through our formative years our parents were authority figures, as were our teachers. Endless government officials from the dogcatcher to the parking-meter lady daily exercise authority over us. The police have unmitigated power. They direct traffic. We follow. They blow their sirens. We pull over. Whatever they demand, we are in the habit of obeying. At work, for all of our lives, our employers tell us what to do, where and when. Our government taxes us, and we pay without a street fight. In retirement we strictly follow the rules we must in order to obtain the benefits of our retirement that we've earned. And even at death our bodies are disposed of according to the law.

We do not revolt against authority. We do not scream in the streets when the rights of others are wrested from them. We make no undue disturbance in public places. We stand in line waiting our turn, even if it is painful to do so. We allow people we have never seen and will never see again, under color of authority, to search us at airports. Rarely do we exercise independent judgment, and when we do, our judgments are subject to the scrutiny of authority.

Cattle walk quietly down the killing chute to be butchered because they are domesticated and respect our authority. Our minds are polluted with propaganda from the power structure, and we accept their statements even when they lie to us, including their pronouncement that we are free.

Is a case such as Albert's so unusual, a case based on a false confession? False confessions may be the single leading cause of wrongful convictions in homicide cases,* and according to records compiled by Professor Brandon L. Garrett at the University of Virginia School of Law, and reported in the *New York Times* on September 13, 2010, more than forty people charged with serious crimes have given confessions since 1976 that DNA evidence later showed were false. Unfortunately DNA evidence wasn't available to Albert, nor is it in most criminal cases today. Indeed, thousands may be in prison based on false confessions. The lengthy questioning of the accused is most often not recorded, so the actual method by which the confessions have been obtained is rarely revealed.

As in Albert's case, the lie detector is used to extract confessions, the operator pointing to the machine and claiming it proves he's lying. The young and those mentally unable to defend against authority, even the av-

---

* FalseConfessions.org, www.falseconfessions.org/fact-a-figures.

erage citizen, may succumb after hours of intense questioning, often in endless, ruthless relays by the police to the point where exhaustion is the torture from which the victim, hopeless to longer resist, at last succumbs.

By the time we finished with the testimony of the police, it became clear that their lack of notes and any recording of what was said erased all history of their interrogation methods. In retrospect Dr. Fairbairn's opinion was right. Albert's confession was not voluntary. Albert was as vulnerable as the sparrow to the hawk.

The ordeal of a murder trial slashes permanent scars across the lives and psyches of even the most innocent. Albert Hancock has lived a worthy life these more than thirty years since he walked out of the Sundance courtroom, a citizen freed by a jury of his peers. He lives in a large city with his wife of many years. He has contributed to the rearing of four children. They are successful, law-abiding citizens. He has been steadily employed as a confidential messenger for a delivery company. He once made a delivery to Scotland. I wondered if he'd passed by Edinburgh Castle near where Peewee McDougall was born. Madam Fate was still probably laughing at her tricks!

Patricia Hancock, Albert's mother, still lives in Wyoming. Jeff Hancock died on December 21, 2003. He was a rancher to the end.

Peewee McDougall made no further investigation following the case, nor did Chief Campbell. McDougall died July 22, 1994. Campbell is retired. Arnold Tschirgi lives in Lander. He is a worthy and respected member of the bar and still practices law.

I asked Albert, "How did you ever survive that trial? Weren't you afraid? How did you make it day after day?"

"I wasn't afraid," Albert said.

That surprised me. "Why weren't you afraid?"

"Because I knew I wasn't guilty."

EPILOGUE: WHERE DO WE GO FROM HERE?

P*lease* hear me clearly:
   We need the police.

We need prosecutors and judges as well. And I make room for the proposition that we are well served by our fear of their power. Indeed, we have
been taught to fear power from our earliest times—fear of parents, of teachers, of our bosses, fear of rejection by our peers. In short, fear plays a controlling role in the lives of all of us. And fear causes us to make lawful
choices in our lives. Fear helps provide an orderly society. We want to be
safe. We fear chaos and crime, and we're willing to overlook occasional
police misconduct as the price we must pay for a predictable, safe society
in which to pursue our lives.

At the outset we believe most police and prosecutors are working to
achieve a peaceful, crime-free community. We believe that they have our
best interests at heart. Some may occasionally cross the line, but they are
only human. We are all prone to err. Sometimes the police themselves are
faced with circumstances in which fear takes over, and to protect themselves they may overreact. I would be doing the police as well as society a
gross disservice to argue that all police are villainous crooks wearing a
badge, and that the words "cop" and "killer" are synonymous. Such is not
my belief. But what, then, am I saying?

The police tell us their truth: They say we, the people, have no understanding of a cop's everyday encounters with drunks, muggers and thugs,
the marginally and utterly insane, the wife beaters and drug peddlers, to
mention only a few of the dirty, dangerous discards of society the police
daily face. Do we question their truth? How many times have you embraced that argument when you read in the morning paper about a current

spate of police brutality? And have you ever asked yourself, how have I come to accept the cop's argument as the whole truth without questioning how I came to believe it?

But who tells the people's truth? The large majority of law-abiding citizens know little about "what goes on out there." What we think we know we've been taught by decades of fictional TV cop shows sponsored by Power—the insurance companies, the mammoth oil corporations, international banks, car manufacturers, national loan sharks, pill pushers, and the various other offspring of Power. We've been provided entertainment, not the whole truth, by the voice of Power—the media. We've come to believe Power's propaganda in much the same way that we believe our religions—that our police and prosecutors will not prosecute and convict the innocent. Such would be un-American. But blind beliefs, cultural brainwashings, can hasten the end of a free people.

At the same time, the justice system lumbers along at the speed of a crippled worm while the prosecution chalks up conviction rates in our venerable federal courts as high as 97 percent, mostly attributable to the bargains made with guilty pleas.* That statistic, on its face, boldly belies the proposition that America provides its citizens with fair trials. Until *we* become "the subject" of a serious, life-threatening encounter with the police, we try to just get along, to raise our kids, love our grandkids, watch our favorite TV programs in the evening, take our deserved two weeks' vacation, and hope for a comfortable retirement and a merciful death.

Then one day one of our own, even one of us, becomes *the subject*. We are arrested. We are thrown in jail, and if we cannot be bonded out we will be imprisoned for months, even years, awaiting trial. We will lose our identity as a member of society. We are provided a number underneath our mug shot, and our history will be forever besmirched by a criminal charge blaring out at the world from our police record. Innocent or not, we will most likely become another number in a penitentiary or a convicted murderer on death row. Such a transforming process puts me in mind of the hawk sitting in a treetop waiting for the sparrow to fly by. At the precise moment of the hawk's strike, the sparrow loses its identity as a fellow bird and becomes the prey. To the police, when we become "the

---

* Gary Fields and John R. Emshwiller, "Federal Guilty Pleas Soar as Bargains Trump Trials," *Wall Street Journal*, September 23, 2012.

subject," we are no longer persons, and we'll be de-feathered, ripped apart, and disposed of in one way or another.

Members of the *police culture*—the police, the prosecutors, and too often, the judges themselves, are hatched from the same political womb. And politics has diseased the womb. The poor, along with our revered middle class, do not hire or fire our police. Police, prosecutors, and sometimes judges—even those on our highest court—too often are indebted to Power and become the servants of Power. I argue that political debtors are disqualified from delivering justice. One thing soon becomes clear: The quantum of justice available to most Americans is in direct proportion to that individual's social and economic status, which is to announce the controlling rule of law in America: *Little money, little status—little justice.*

The problem is simple to define. Power does not serve the people. *Power serves itself.* The personal needs of those who make up Power—from the police officer to the banker and corporate executive—all are in service of the self. Too many police have chosen their work in response to a personality that craves to dominate other human beings. Bankers who throw a widow out on the streets in winter are bullies diseased by a love of money. The corporate executives who will cut their employees to starvation wages in their psychotic quest for profit are bullies. Or the same executives will, at the expense of the health and lives of customers, ignore standard safety practices hoping to acquire yet more profit. The cases I've written about here each illustrate a different story, but are essentially the same story: a story about the same perverse incentive of Power—the uncontrolled, psychotic urge to dominate and intimidate the helpless in response to Power's compulsion to serve itself.

We remember that Sheriff McDougall charged Albert Hancock, a poor ranch kid, with a murder he didn't commit, all the while ignoring the husband and various lovers of the deceased as suspects. Albert was the easy mark for the sheriff, who admitted his need for a conviction. Power attempted to imprison this boy in concrete behind steel bars for life, where he would be raped and where he would die of torment and degradation. And what about the resulting end of life that would have been visited on Albert's decent, naïve parents?

The Weavers were poor and powerless. They were seen as religious fanatics isolated from the rest of the community. Power's malevolent incentive was to exercise itself for its own sake—to push around the defenseless because it could. To entertain themselves in that remote corner of Idaho, the feds didn't hesitate to trespass with armed operatives on the Weaver property and, without a warrant, to thereafter engage in an all-out war against the survivors of that besieged family who had dared live outside the religious boundaries of the mainstream. The charge had been sawing off a shotgun at the inducement of the feds themselves. The punishment was the killing of a boy's dog, then the murder of the boy, then shooting and seriously wounding the males in the household, and finally blowing the mother's head away while she held her baby in her arms. Justice never had a chance to raise its tromped-on head. Not a single cop spent a day in jail.

What reprehensible incentive moved Power in the John Singer case? Power always demands victims. Without victims, power is useless. Once again religious outcasts, those with little community support, became the easy target for Power's bullying. The crime was the Singers' refusal to send their children to what they believed to be a decadent public school. Their punishment was the death of a loving father and husband. With impunity the police shot him in the back while he ran for shelter. To this day no officer has answered for the killing of John Singer. Nor has his killer even been identified! Moreover, when his widow and children sought justice for his wrongful death, a respected federal judge bowed to Power and dismissed their cases, requiring the judge to write the longest decision of a federal trial judge in Utah's history.

Our celebrated FBI—Power personified—can charge an innocent, naïve, law-abiding lawyer, Brandon Mayfield, once a Kansas farm boy, with the mass train murders in Spain, the government's evidence being a phony match of his fingerprint and the fact, in flashing neon lights, that he was a converted Muslim. What an invitation to the blind compulsion of Power! The infallible FBI could nab an Islamic "raghead," as that slur is flaunted in the society of hate, and solve the crime of the century—and in Spain! But power blinded the FBI to its own fallibility. Had its false charges against Brandon not been exposed by the Spanish police, he would have surely faced the death penalty. Still, not one of the federal agents involved has even been reprimanded, nor will one lose a nickel from his pension.

Whenever I think of Fouad Kaady I see the barbarous incentive of Power in full, tragic, exalted force. The police, because they had power and the accompanying bullying needed to exercise it, could repeatedly unload their Tasers into Fouad's seriously wounded, naked body with as much concern as if torturing a crippled rat. Worse, they sought to further wound the already wounded before they killed him. When he couldn't escape and could no longer respond to their commands, these fully armed cops claimed they were afraid and emptied their pistols into the dying Fouad—to save themselves? His killing was passed over by the prosecutor's grand jury as if it exemplified proper police routine.

Our government can charge an innocent woman with multiple crimes in order to forward the international agenda of the United States, as in the groundless prosecution of Imelda Marcos. Power that included the president and other high government officials was willing to prosecute a once beloved friend of America, in exchange for our military needs. All we've ever heard of Imelda's trial is how many pairs of shoes she owned. Despite her continued popularity at home in the Philippines, where, with love and respect, she is called "Mamma," and where she still serves her country as a legislator, the media, the genuflecting voice of Power, has convinced nearly every American that Imelda Marcos is a greedy thief who escaped punishment because she had a smart mouthpiece.

The cops can frame a poor, innocent black kid, as they did in the Dennis Williams case, convict him of crimes he did not commit, and sentence him to death, after which he languished on death row for eighteen years, and, in the meantime, the prosecutors can laugh at their obscene game called "Niggers by the Pound." To this day neither the police, the prosecutors, nor the politicians have suffered the first consequence, perhaps not even a twinge of guilt at bedtime. Power for power's sake becomes the law, so that in the end, Power runs rampant and is answerable to no one.

The president of the United States, Mr. Power himself, can call upon the federal cops and the courts to forward his vindictive goals—to see that his political enemies are charged with crimes, as in the Geoffrey Fieger sham, an arrogant overt expression of unbridled power launched on a mission of revenge. And although after years of torment and torture a jury acquitted Fieger, not a single conspirator in that power play has offered the first apology for the resulting misery and damage to Fieger's life and to the lives of his family and co-workers. Even the law under which he was prosecuted has no meaning today since corporations and individuals are now substantially free to make unlimited contributions to political causes—a devastating wound to the rights of most Americans to take any meaningful part in the election process.

Power has one purpose: to satisfy itself. In doing so Power kills, wrongfully persecutes, and criminally imposes itself on the innocent. Yet the work of Power can be justified, even blessed, when it is exercised by a fully informed, intelligent people in pursuit of their rights as a free people. But the cry "Power to the people" is no longer heard. In its stead we too often hear the muffled, wretched response of the new American slave—"I got nothing to hide."

Finally staid old Harvard stuck its toe into the water to admit the obvious. In his scholarly work *In Doubt*, Harvard professor Dan Simon writes:

> The truth-seeking objective is most likely to be overridden in high-profile cases, where the pressures to solve the crimes are the strongest. In some instances, the adversarial pull results in deliberate police malfeasance, and even entails lying outright in court, a practice known as *testilying*.*

What the good professor might have added is this: Over the years these killings and wrongful prosecutions have taken place in nearly every city and hamlet across the country, mostly outside the glare of the media that too often sits blandly by blinking its sightless eyes unless called upon by Power to speak. Who cares about what happened to Mr. Nobody? "He must have had it coming," we say. "And, if not, it was he, not I. What do you expect me to do about it? I'm just an ordinary citizen. I have no power to take on the system. Besides, we need tough cops to protect us against the hordes of criminals who are roaming freely out there and daily threaten our lives and safety."

The police, prosecutors, and defense attorneys all want to win. *Winning* is the operative word. But winning is not geared to preserving the rights of the accused nor delivering justice. Winning has little to do with discovering the truth. We hear it like a worn-out mantra: He or she *won* a conviction, or she or he *won* an acquittal. *Winning*. But at what cost to justice? Winning and injustice are often unfriendly occupants in the same bed.

What happens when the police, in the name of winning and by whatever means, frame the innocent for murder? These helpless, often nameless wretches are themselves eventually murdered by the state after they've been tortured for years awaiting their fate on death row. We strap them to a gurney and insert the needles and usually no one cares. We may be ad-

---

* Dan Simon, *In Doubt* (Cambridge: Harvard University Press, 2012), p. 33.

vised of the state's killing with little more than a half-minute report on the evening news, after which we switch to the next cop show.

And the innocent die a slower, more torturous death. To know that one is innocent, but day after day, year after year, decade after decade one is penned up like a dangerous beast in the zoo—such is the ultimate torture. There the innocent will live out their remaining years in a cramped, concrete closet as the hated, and in the company of the hated. There they will die at the hands of other inmates, or by the clubs of sadistic guards, or from inadequate medical care, or, at last, from the accursed needle itself.

In the meantime the police officer's moral justification for his own criminal conduct that led to the conviction of the innocent citizen varies little from case to case. I've heard police argue, "Well, if he wasn't guilty of this crime he was guilty of one we never caught him at." I've heard others say, "Whatever we did was peanuts compared to what he did or would have done had he still been running loose on the streets. It's war out there. And we're going to win the war." Still others contend, "The laws we have to deal with tie our hands and let the guilty escape." I've heard others complain, "We do what we have to do to get those scumbags off the street. Read them their rights? Get them a mouthpiece? Right! The law forces us to use other means." And many of our citizens applaud such rationalizations, and quietly murmur, "It may happen to *them* out there, but it won't happen to me." And as a chorus to such universal rationalizations we hear the same dangerous words, "I don't worry about the cops. *I have nothing to hide.*" If one has been spawned in a fishbowl, how does one know the dangers of the river?

After the widely published accounts of the people's protests over the deaths of black citizens at the hands of the police—the choking death of the unarmed Eric Garner, the shooting death of the unarmed Michael Brown in Ferguson, Missouri, and the shooting death of the twelve-year-old Tamir Rice on a Cleveland playground as he held a toy gun—Americans seemed to have at last awakened. New York City mayor Bill de Blasio was seen by the police as having joined the people's protest, and at the funeral of one of their officers thousands of police in full dress uniform stood and in unison turned their backs against the mayor, their boss, in a shocking display of power and insubordination. When the police can, in open rebellion, display such power without fear of reprisal, is this not the conduct of the police in a police state?

SO WHAT CAN WE DO? If we can prevent the long-standing practice of wrongful killings and their cover-ups by our police and prosecutors, the entire justice system will tend to right itself, like a ship that is otherwise sinking. Let's take the easy ones first.

1. No more forced confessions. How can we stop our police who by exhaustion, false promises and fear attempt to extort confessions from those who are frequently the least able to protect themselves—like Albert Hancock, and most of whom are also impoverished? The answer is simple. All police interrogations from the first "hello" must be videotaped, *every word*, absent which any evidence of any admissions or confessions will be inadmissible at trial against the accused. No more hauling out the tape recorder only after the accused has suffered endless interrogations by teams of police and is on the margins of collapse. A defense attorney should be present at *all* stages of *every* interrogation, even when the accused waives that protection. So the cops wouldn't get their usual spate of confessions? For once, let the police and prosecutors prove their cases beyond a reasonable doubt as is required by the Constitution. The 97 percent conviction rate in federal jurisdictions would begin its descent toward justifiable statistics. And those charged with crimes, guilty or not, would receive the constitutional protection that a free nation demands.

2. All police must wear video cameras that fully reveal their conduct. In one California town officers began wearing cameras, and within a year complaints against police fell 88 percent—an astounding statistic—and specific grievances concerning the use of excessive force by police fell 59 percent.* Of course, these devices can be turned off or not worn at all. But a thoughtful legislature can and should pass laws that provide that in the course of any questioning between an officer and a citizen, if the cop's camera is ever turned off a jury is entitled to presume the cop's misconduct.

3. Better psychological testing for police candidates. Perhaps experts in the field can develop more effective tests to identify candidates who are not psychologically suited for police work. I know of no study that suggests that current testing has improved the selection of our police. Still, when

---

* *The Week*, September 19, 2014, p. 18.

challenged, police departments, state and federal, including the FBI, wave their testing in our faces, shrug their shoulders, and defend by admitting that their testing procedures are not infallible. Their tests serve at least one purpose—to provide an argument that the department tried to eliminate the bad would-be cop. A nation brimming with psychiatrists, psychologists, mental health experts, and other students of the species can surely devise new and more effective paradigms to study the personality of the police candidate. If we can select those most qualified to travel to the moon armed only with the American flag, surely we can do a better job of selecting those who travel our streets armed with pistols and clubs.

If the power of the police can't be properly monitored and controlled, if our ability to change the police culture is stuck in the dead goo of precedent, the result will produce a police state. That is my promise. Indeed, one may ask, have we become like a sleeping passenger on the bus, and when the bus arrives at its destination and comes to a jerking stop, will we awaken and ask, "Are we already here?"

4. A citizens' commission to oversee police conduct. As an adjunct of the state district courts, a commission should be created in each judicial district—let's call it the Police and Prosecutor's Control Commission (PPCC)—to receive complaints from citizens concerning police and prosecutor abuse. If you're mistreated or otherwise wronged by an officer, you would have the right to immediately file a complaint with the PPCC. If you're stopped by a highway patrolman who roughs you up, the PPCC would hear your complaint, and if it supports your complaint, it will present the same to the district attorney. If the complaint is against the district attorney or a member of his or her staff, the court would appoint an independent prosecutor to take over the case.

PPCC members would be selected in much the same way that we select grand jurors and would proceed under the general rules of a grand jury. Its finding of probable cause would be by a preponderance of the evidence and would require a supermajority of two-thirds. For obvious reasons former police officers and prosecutors and those close to them would be disqualified to serve on this commission. Similar commissions would be created by Congress to investigate complaints against federal officers. I suggest a commission membership of, say, twenty-four, to be drawn from the jury pool, a group large enough to fairly represent the community. Perhaps the first twelve, drawn at random, would serve one year, the second twelve two years, and from year to year thereafter half of the commission's membership would be replaced.

A special prosecutor—the PPCC attorney—would be appointed by the district judge. He or she would select such staff as might be required to properly investigate and present complaints made to the commission. The PPCC attorney would report annually to the district judge, who, with the consent of the commission, might reappoint the PPCC attorney for each succeeding year. Perhaps the people themselves would select their own special prosecutor in a public election held every four years.

Mrs. Kaady would have been able to file a complaint against the police for the murder of her son. And rather than the police investigating themselves, the PPCC would make its *independent* investigation and report the results and its recommendations to the district attorney, who must, by law, provide a timely, written, *public* report disclosing the action he or she took on the commission's complaint.

The details of the PPCC can vary. What is imperative here is that the citizen has a place to go with a complaint other than to the offending police themselves. That every abuse will be investigated from *outside* the police organization would serve as a powerful deterrent to police misconduct, especially if all proceedings before the commission against the officer would be open to the public. Finally the clear light of day would shine on the work of our own employees, the police. No longer would they be those feared killers out there who answer to no one; they would be disciplined officers who are careful to properly, legally, protect us all.

5. It's time we elevate our police to the status of professionals. Indeed, police work should become a profession on the same level as that of lawyers, engineers, and architects. If police are members of an acknowledged and respected profession, better applicants will be attracted, and the officer who sees himself or herself as a respected professional will tend to fulfill the expectations of the profession.

Today police are trained to confront violence with violence. We train soldiers to kill. We train our police the same. We train our police to disarm and subdue those who present a threat. Police become experts with weapons and learn standard tactics for survival in the wars out on the streets. Standing alone, the result of such training is to create a culture in which *they*, the police, are against *we*, the people. To the police, even the little old lady sitting quietly with her knitting may have a .32 caliber pistol lurking under her cloth. Police argue, you can't tell a killer by his or her looks. Too often you can only identify a killer after the killing. To the police, the potential enemy includes every being who walks, breathes, rides in a car, or attends a movie, every drunk in a bar, and every husband or wife in the bedroom. *Everyone.*

We must make radical improvements in the training of our police. We must begin creating a new and different people-friendly culture. In ways, a more paternalistic relationship is in order. If the police see the people in their community not as the enemy but as members of their family, as the young who need guidance, as the old and infirm who require help and protection, and as the tough and the wild (with certain character traits that the cop himself may possess) who need understanding and, from time to time, a caring and restrained sort of discipline—if we were to enjoy such a police culture, the danger of a police state would soon fade. Our police would be seen as respected participants in society, perhaps even as trusted friends.

To be sure, police must be trained to confront aggression. But their training must go further. The answer to a police call must be something other than an opportunity for an officer to kill. Police must become part of the community as persons; their service to the community must respect the community and, by their model, encourage the community's participation.

6. Additional suggestions for police training. We should provide officers better training on how to deescalate dangerous situations. Trainees would be enrolled in groups of less than twenty. At least a third of the group would be individuals from the community, including representatives of the poor from the ghettos and representatives of minorities. The group would be presented with the most frequent scenarios that the officer is called upon to solve—including the most dangerous ones. Members of the group will offer their suggestions. What would these people who are not police officers do facing the same situation? The answers from the civilians in the group will be different from the solutions offered by the police. Somewhere along the way ideas will blossom that are foreign in most police training—that caring and understanding are often the most important weapons an officer can bring to a crisis.

The discipline known as "psychodrama" is foundational to our training of trial lawyers at Trial Lawyers College.* The method is simply a

---

* Trial Lawyers College, www.triallawyerscollege.org.

role-reversal process in which the protagonist takes on the role of who-ever represents the person of power or influence in his or her life drama—for instance, one's father or mother. All of us are well adapted to this method of self-discovery. Don't we remember when, as children, we played different roles in make-believe? Psychodrama could work for police offi-cers as well as for lawyers.

The first question for every police officer is "Why did I want to become a police officer? What happened in my life that causes me to seek power over others? What has happened to me that gave birth to my need to dom-inate?" Our life-forming experiences usually came at an early age, and as adults we often find ourselves still acting them out. Any of us who have felt helpless in the presence of authority never want to feel such pain again. If I can understand why I'm prone to aggression, I will be better able to identify the underlying personal issues I'm trying to solve by becoming a police officer, and I'll become a better officer. Such group experiences can change how we see others and ourselves as well. Such group work among caring people changes lives. Every year, as part of his or her continuing education, the officer should return for further group work. Too often we forget what we've learned and slip back to old, dangerous ways that lie at the foundation of our personalities.

7. Reform the grand jury process. The grand jury is a favorite instrument of the prosecutor by which criminal proceedings against an accused are be-gun. Its abuse by prosecutors is legion. A grand jury is grand only because it typically has from sixteen to twenty-four members. Its function is not to try the accused for any crime, but to investigate and determine if there is probable cause to charge the accused with one or more crimes.

Prosecutors revel at the power grand juries provide against a so-called person of interest, that is, one who is being investigated for possible crimes. As we remember, in the Fieger fiasco the feds tormented Fieger for over two years with an ongoing grand jury, sometimes calling but a single witness a week. One of the primary purposes of that process had been to destroy with fear and financial ruin both Fieger and his partners and employees.

Under rules that are in existence today, like the unclean, "the subject's" lawyer must wait *outside* the grand jury room while his client is being in-terrogated by the prosecutor and the jurors. If "the subject" testifies, he or she does so without an attorney present to protect his or her rights. Wit-nesses are questioned endlessly by the prosecutors and are often dragged across impermissible lines with no judge to intercede. No judge is present. We remember in the Fieger case when the prosecutor had Fieger's former secretary under oath before a grand jury. With no one to stop the prosecutor or protect the witness, he questioned her about any possible sexual encounters she'd had with her boss, a matter totally irrelevant to any issue before the grand jury, and an obvious abuse of a helpless witness. Moreover, grand jury proceedings are secret, and a unanimous verdict is not required for an indictment. I ask a simple question that has been asked endless times over the centuries: How can any citizen prevent being wrongfully charged with a crime when the prosecutor, and the prosecutor alone, can decide what facts the grand jury will hear, and how and on what issues the witnesses will be questioned? In ways, the grand jury is the remnant of the inquisitions of old that included the persecution and the burning alive of thousands of innocent women as witches.

Reforms for the grand jury have often been proposed.* But as usual they've been defeated by Power's insurmountable fence of precedent, and few offered reforms have been adopted. The more important reforms should include the right of counsel for any witness called before a grand jury. And the failure of the prosecutor to present *known evidence* to the grand jury that substantially tends to exonerate the accused, whether such failure is intentional or by oversight, should bar the prosecution.

8. Outlaw the testimony of jailhouse snitches. What do we do about the predictable lies offered by nearly every jailhouse informant as a witness for the prosecution? We refer to them as "snitches," those fellow inmates of the accused who will testify that the accused admitted the crime to them. The U.S. Supreme Court held in a case known as *Giglio* that the prosecution's failure to reveal to the jury that a witness has been promised leniency or some other benefit in exchange for his testimony was a failure to present all material evidence to the jury, and constituted a violation of due process, requiring a new trial. That rule has been expanded in other cases as even our most conservative courts attempt to remedy wrongful convictions based on the known false testimony of jailhouse snitches.

Sadly, the high court's cases have had little effect in preventing the lies of snitches from contaminating a fair trial. If I paid a perjurer thousands

---

* See, for instance, "Federal Grand Jury Reform and Bill of Rights," May 2000, www.nacdl.org /grandjury.

of dollars to testify for my client, I'd be sent to prison and relieved of my license to practice law. I've never known a snitch who wouldn't gladly pay those same thousands, if he had them, to get out of prison. Instead, he purchases his freedom or a reduced sentence with his lies.

Despite the efforts of our courts to protect against snitch testimony, prosecutors have ways to circumvent the problem. Before the snitch takes the stand, the conversation between the snitch and the prosecutor will likely sound something like this:

> PROSECUTOR: Remember, Joe, when the lawyer on the other side asks you if I've made you any promises your answer is "No," right? And I haven't, right?
>
> JOE: Right.
>
> PROSECUTOR: You are doing this because you believe it is in the best interest of justice. That it's your duty to reveal these facts, right?
>
> JOE: Right.
>
> PROSECUTOR: I've told you to tell the truth and only the truth. Right?
>
> JOE: Right.
>
> At trial, on the cross-examination of Joe we hear the following:
>
> DEFENSE ATTORNEY: The prosecutor made promises to you, didn't he?
>
> JOE: No, he never promised me nothin'.
>
> DEFENSE ATTORNEY: You expect to receive some benefit from your testimony here, don't you?
>
> JOE: No, I'm just doin' what's right.

In fact, even if the prosecutor made no promises, he will likely provide some benefit to this cooperating witness down the line, and both he and the snitch know it. We tend to help those who help us. The star of *Giglio* shines down on us from on high, but rarely can it penetrate the thick cloud that covers the games some prosecutors play to obtain a conviction.

On the other hand, judges may attempt to dilute the effect of the snitch's testimony by advising the jury that they should receive it with suspicion. But the jury has heard the lie. And the prosecutor, to ameliorate the judge's instruction, will spread frosting over the snitch's cake of dung. The prosecutor will say to the jury things like "We have the duty to present to the jury *all* of the evidence. What would you think of us if we *knew* of Joe's testimony, but we didn't give it to you to consider? It's the defendant here [he points with scorn to the defendant sitting frozen next to his lawyer] who'd jump up with joy if you'd disregarded Joe's testimony. But we leave it to *you*. We *trust your ability* to judge the credibility of the witnesses, including Joe's." The games go on despite the best efforts of the high court to provide a fair trial. Too many innocents are sent to their deaths on the perjured testimony of snitches. A civilized society can no longer permit such testimony. The only way to stop these games is to simply, in the furtherance of justice, *outlaw all snitch testimony*, that is, testimony as to what another inmate supposedly confessed to the snitch while in custody.

9. Relief for the accused when, at trial, the prosecutor hides favorable evidence from the accused. As early as 1963 the United States Supreme Court handed down a landmark case now known simply as *Brady* in which the court ruled that prosecutors were required to reveal to defendants all exculpatory evidence, that is, evidence that tends to support the defendant's innocence. But too many prosecutors simply play with that high court's words, ignore their duty, claim they forgot, keep secret the evidence favorable to the defendant, and wait until they're caught (if ever) and then argue that the withheld evidence wouldn't have changed the result anyway and that no harm was done. A defendant simply relying on *Brady* or *Giglio* for a fair trial is already seeing the prison gates swinging open.

These enlightened Supreme Court decisions do little more than comfort the high court judges so they can sleep believing they've done all they can to make trials fair. Still, some judges like to play their own games. What judge on the court couldn't argue that the withheld evidence wouldn't have made a difference in the outcome of the trial? But a judge is not a juror, and if the withheld evidence was important enough for the prosecutor to hide it from the jurors, might we not conclude that it was important enough to change the outcome of the case? When there's been *any* intentional *Brady* violation, the case must be returned for a new trial or dismissed.

10. Dealing with the dangers of the "courthouse club." Over time local police, prosecutors, judges, and defense attorneys do their work together. They have to. The prosecutors know that when their opponents, the defense attorneys, need a little consideration in a case it will be reciprocated down the line. And defense attorneys find themselves pleading innocent clients guilty, believing they've provided the client with "the best deal possible," and prosecutors agree to more advantageous deals for those who are members of these informal but fully functional courthouse clubs. I know highly paid, private criminal defense attorneys who haven't tried a jury trial in years but whose reputations are "the lawyer to go to if you've been charged with a serious crime." Many judges look on, knowing how the game works. But such cooperation usually ends in guilty pleas, and the judge's caseload is thereby lightened. In the end, this "brotherhood" among opponents and the judge is a constant threat to justice. (It will be further considered in the following paragraphs.)

11. Curing the evils of overcharging. What can we do about the inherent evil of overcharging? I'm talking about charging a person with multiple crimes that arise out of a single incident. The prosecutor's motivation is to force the defendant, guilty or not, to plead guilty to one or more of the charges in exchange for a shorter sentence. We already know why *innocent* people plead guilty: They know they'll face jurors who believe they're guilty because jurors trust that the prosecutor wouldn't charge innocent persons. They know that jurors often compromise—acquit on some, even many, of the charges, but likely find the accused guilty of something. They know they will be appointed a public defender who convinces them, and rightly, that their conviction is foregone. They know that if they lose they will receive no mercy from the sentencing judge. Their lives will be truncated, their reputations lost, and the light of their future extinguished. Perhaps they will never see their spouse or children again, and their parents will die while they're in prison. Given the crowded dockets in most jurisdictions, in some cases innocent persons can plead guilty to a charge or two and get out of jail before their trial is even set.

Judges have the power to force the prosecutor to elect the one or two counts the prosecutor will present to the jury. But we remember that most judges were former prosecutors. Rarely do any judges insert themselves into the prosecutor's case. And, as we know, judges in the state courts are also politicians. Voters are enamored by those who have a record of being "tough on criminals," and judges are unwilling to take on the prosecutor lest one day the prosecutor-hawk sets its talons into the judicial bird. In the federal courts the judges are appointed for life by Power, and although theoretically they're not beholden to Power, they are, with rare exceptions, congenital members of the power structure.

Prosecutors often charge an accused with a felony carrying a prison sentence of years rather than a misdemeanor that arises from the same facts and is punishable by a few months or less in jail. For example, maybe a man has been charged with stealing an item from a local store. The prosecutor may charge the defendant with grand larceny, asserting that the stolen property was valued at an amount that lifted the offense to felony. In such a case the prosecutor doesn't need to display a startling array of talents to obtain a conviction. And any clear-thinking defendant, even if he's as clean and pristine as an early morning lily, will rush to make a deal that will free him in short order rather than run the risk of a felony conviction that will imprison him in some stinking hole for years.

Legislators must step up and chink these gaping holes in the judicial house that deprive thousands of American citizens each year of their constitutionally guaranteed right to due process. I offer little hope. When was the last time the people turned to the politicians for justice and justice was delivered?

A guilty plea to a criminal charge against a citizen must be examined with suspicion that the plea was obtained through force, intimidation, or other impermissible means. Is the plea the result of overcharging? Was it voluntarily given? Indeed, every guilty plea must be made to stand on its own after careful scrutiny by the judge. An immunized hearing before the judge (one in which the testimony of the accused is privileged and cannot be used against him) must be offered to the accused, a hearing in which the accused is represented, and encouraged to explain *why* he or she has agreed to the confession. Threats arising from an overcharged indictment, unconscionable delays in trials, incompetent counsel, and other motivations for a guilty plea must be discovered and, if they exist, dealt with appropriately. Justice requires no less. Due process demands it. And a guilty plea that was not voluntary to its hair roots must be set aside.

Yes, there are great judges out there. Great judges are like great painters or great chefs, or great fiddle players. The great ones cannot be great unless there are masses who never reach that airy status. I have been privileged to work with some great judges who have made me proud of our system of justice. They are the rare gifts to an otherwise suffering judiciary. All judges, both trial and appellate judges, have power, and the great ones will use it in creative ways to bring fairness into the case. If they do not dismiss the redundant charges, they can discuss with the jurors why a prosecutor overcharges, why overcharging is fundamentally unfair, and how the jury, if it chooses, can consider such overcharging as evidence that the prosecution has a weak case. Indeed, it's not that judges themselves have no power to bring about a better sort of justice. Instead, prosecutors and judges are more likely to form their own informal accords, the unwritten but fully understood covenant of which is to take care of one another.

The criminal defense bar is as much to blame for overcharging as any of the other members of this cozy congregation of judges and lawyers. I have known a few, but very few, criminal defense attorneys who have taken on the bad state court judge head-to-head when the judge ran for reelection. It takes courage to go to the voters with a story of the judge's inaction, abuse, or incompetence. But that's what elections are for. If defense lawyers have complaints, they cannot hang back and whimper like shivering children facing King Kong in a back alley and still pretend they are attorneys dedicated to the defense of the damned. It is their duty to the judicial system to take action, and if they muster the courage they can be successful. Even an unsuccessful attempt to unseat a state court judge will often have palpable affirmative results with that judge in the future.

12. We must get politics out of our judiciary. I acknowledge the power of the jury. However, judges are still sovereign in the courtroom. They determine what facts the jurors will hear, and what laws the jurors will apply, and how. Except for an acquittal, the judge can set aside a jury's verdict and grant new trials. As we've seen, a judge even has the power to dismiss a just case for civil damages. I am thinking of the Singer case. In court the judge is still the royal ruler, not a mere arbiter of fairness like a referee in a boxing match.

One may rightly ask, who are these judges, and why would any lawyer give up lawyering to become a judge? Some who found it difficult to make a living in the practice of law ascended to the bench. Some felt they lacked the talent or the emotional makeup to be successful as trial lawyers. Some bore a genuine desire to do good. And some, like some cops, had a yearning for power.

The judicial hide is tattooed with politics, along with the debts that politics produces. The way we select judges fails to create a judiciary in which a free people can enjoy their promised justice. Yes, there are numerous honest judges who strive to follow their own moral compasses. But even the best of our judges are riddled with conflict and often are compromised in resolving those conflicts. I am again put in mind of the admitted conflicts suffered by Judge Winder in the Singer case.

What to do? *I say judges should be drafted at random from the trial bar for a limited term.*

The drafted judge would serve for, say, three or four years and then return to private practice. The judge would be paid a reasonable salary and would also be rewarded by becoming a better lawyer, one who has experienced the workings of the judicial mind firsthand. He or she would spend no more time as a drafted judge than doctors spend acquiring their specialty. The names of all those who try court cases would be put in the canister and drawn as needed in the same manner that jurors are selected. (If by law we can demand that ordinary citizens give up parts of their lives to serve as jurors, can't we, with greater justification, require trial lawyers, who make their living in the courtroom, to contribute back to the very system that supports them?) The names of those who have served as trial judges would also be placed in the hopper from which, by random selection, our appeals court judges would be selected, but for a shorter term. And the political beast, Power, that once influenced—even owned—our judges will sit by the wayside whimpering and scolding, emasculated.

Some will argue that this method will open the door to individuals none of us would want on the bench. But we are suffering from a judiciary that includes tyrants and fops of every dimension, and we can't get rid of them because they've been appointed for life or they're better politicians than they are judges and are continuously reelected. Better that we have a bad judge for a short term than a bad judge for a life term.

If we need a couple more judges, a dozen or a hundred more, we'll draft them until their dockets are current. Those disgraceful delays that the accused or the injured must endure to finally get their chance at justice will no longer be part of our appalling judicial history. And bullying police and prosecutors will no longer find it possible to carry on their power games in courtrooms in which the judges are members of a cozy courthouse cabal. Moreover, we'll no longer be judged by men or women whose addiction to power led them to seek judgeships in the first place. Our new judges will be drafted.

Before I leave you I have one last plea: We must get Money out of politics just as we rid our bodies of killing cancers. We are diseased by Money. We are no longer a free nation if Money can buy our representatives while we stand in line to vote like the proverbial cattle at the killing chutes. Our elections on all levels must be publicly funded.

I love my country. I abhor those who use their power to defeat its prom-ises to the people. Over my lifetime I've seen the Power-owned media capture the American mind. The endless invasion of propaganda has eventually prevailed, and its message has become the accepted truth of a brainwashed nation that we are free, that the police and prosecutors are trustworthy and will protect us, and that in America there is liberty and justice for all. Such is a mythology that enslaves.

Instead, as we know, only the few, depending on their status and wealth, have even a far faint shot at justice. By adopting some of the solutions of-fered here we will begin our work toward a culture in which the criminal justice system is no longer a tool of Power to intimidate, control, and abuse the powerless. We remember the ominous prediction attributed to Sinclair Lewis: "If fascism comes to America it will be wrapped in the flag and carrying a cross."

We've come to the end of this trip together. I've discovered and learned much in this writing. And I'm grateful that you joined me in this journey. The victories of justice occur from small realizations that eventually seep into the collective mind. When I began my term on this earth, women were chiefly seen as the keepers of the home, the nurturers of children and their other child, the husband. Today women have joined us as partners in the blessed struggle for equality and freedom. In my lifetime I've seen minori-ties courageously fight their way up until they can breathe more comfort-ably in the company of their oppressors. These wars, won for a more just society, have come at the cost of much suffering and many lives. The com-mitment to that battle must remain at the forefront of our passion.

I hope that what we've shared together will be shared with others, and that we will find ways to speak to the many who have heretofore found themselves alone. None can predict where America will go from here. But the road we travel is ominous. One thing I know: An honestly informed nation can be trusted to eventually do right. Justice is the petulant child of truth.

And so, dear people, as the old man told the boy who clutched the help-less bird in his hands—I leave this precious bird of justice in yours.

ACKNOWLEDGMENTS

Let me start with Imaging, my wife, my life, my love, and my partner. Thank you, dear woman, for your hours of work and devoted attention here, your continued support, your sound insights, your faith in both me and my work, and your belief in its value. I could neither live nor write without you.

Thank you, John Sargent, for taking precious time out of a life overflowing with demands to find room for me, for never giving up on this old Wyoming man, and for putting me with Tim Bartlett. Your friendship, tolerance, and faith in me have been a treasured gift.

Thank you, Tim Bartlett, for seeing something of worth in me both as a writer and as a member of the species. Thank you for your dedicated work here, for your patience, your caring, and for making me, at this late date, a better writer. India Cooper was the copy editor here. She is magical. Her copy edits reflected a deep understanding of the stories, and the eye of a compassionate eagle. She revealed what old eyes could not see, and I am so grateful. And my thanks to Claire Lampen, editorial assistant, who reminds me of a Wyoming cowgirl keeping the herd together and the strays where they belong.

Thank you, Peter Lampack, my agent and friend, for always being there with sound advice and caring and your willingness to fight for what is right.

Thanks to my clients, both living and dead, who believed in me. I thank Randy Weaver and his family, Brandon and Mona Mayfield, the Kaady family, the Singer family, Geoffrey Fieger, and Imelda Marcos. Thank you, Peter King, for your friendship to both me and our mutual client, Dennis Williams. And thanks to Albert Hancock, who never lost faith.

I thank the loyal, supportive members of my law firm, one and all, who have always been there for me. I thank you, my partner, Ed Moriarity. When I went into battle your brilliance and loyalty, along with your willingness to lay it all down for me and our clients, made the difference for them and for me. You will always occupy your special place in my heart. Thank you, Bob Schuster, for your mammoth, unheralded work in the Singer case. And thank you for our years together and your friendship.

Thank you, Laury McGinnis, for your loyal support these more than twenty years as my assistant, and thank you, Rosemary McIntosh, for your help and friendship as my assistant for the decades before that.

I am grateful to my publisher, and to the fine crew of publicists and marketers without whose support the message of this book would remain in the shadows.

INDEX